365 Ultimate Cheese Recipes

(365 Ultimate Cheese Recipes - Volume 1)

Ebony Garcia

Copyright: Published in the United States by Ebony Garcia/ © EBONY GARCIA

Published on December, 07 2020

All rights reserved. No part of this publication may be reproduced, stored in retrieval system, copied in any form or by any means, electronic, mechanical, photocopying, recording or otherwise transmitted without written permission from the publisher. Please do not participate in or encourage piracy of this material in any way. You must not circulate this book in any format. EBONY GARCIA does not control or direct users' actions and is not responsible for the information or content shared, harm and/or actions of the book readers.

In accordance with the U.S. Copyright Act of 1976, the scanning, uploading and electronic sharing of any part of this book without the permission of the publisher constitute unlawful piracy and theft of the author's intellectual property. If you would like to use material from the book (other than just simply for reviewing the book), prior permission must be obtained by contacting the author at author@shellfishrecipes.com

Thank you for your support of the author's rights.

Content

365 AWESOME CHEESE RECIPES 9

1. "PAPARA? KVIETKA" Or Flower Fern Salad With Some Twists 9
2. Cinnamon Walnut Loaf 9
3. 'nduja Induced Amnesia 10
4. 1975 Dick Taeuber's Brandy Alexander Pie 11
5. 3 Ingredients Gnocchi Gratin 11
6. A Pear Of Apples Pie With Gruyere Crust 11
7. A Pistol For Paddy Garcia (with Apologies To The Pogues) 12
8. A Tuscan Inspired Savory Bread Pudding 13
9. A Very Short Cake 13
10. A Little Bit Different Lasagna 14
11. Almond Crunch Halva Ice Cream 15
12. Anchovy Cheese 16
13. Anchovy Onion Butter 16
14. Anytime Broccoli & Cheddar Fritters 17
15. Apostle's Fingers (lemon And Ricotta Filled Crepes) 17
16. Apple Küchl With Pistachios 18
17. Apple Ricotta Pie 18
18. Apple And Goat Cheese Pizza 18
19. Apple, Apple Butter And Cheese Crostata 19
20. Arugula And Spinach With Pears, Red Walnuts + Pear Dressing 20
21. Asparagus, Egg And Roasted Tomato Salad With Pine Nuts 20
22. Austrian Almond Strietzel 21
23. Avocado, Fried Egg And Gruyere On Country Bread 22
24. Baby Beet & Basil Spread 22
25. Baby Greens Greek Salad With Anchovy Crumbs 22
26. Bacon Cheddar Loaded Mashed Potatoes 23
27. Baked Bean And Cheese Burritos 23
28. Baked Feta Cheese With Sun Dried Tomato And Capers 24
29. Balsamic Goat Cheese Stuffed Chicken Breast 24
30. Banana Gingerbread & Sweet Lime Frosting 25
31. Banana Pudding 25
32. Banana Yogurt Brownies 26
33. Basil Corn Cream & Goat Cheese Bake 26
34. Basil, Mozzarella And Tomatoes 26
35. Bay (or Rosemary) Scented Ricotta Infornata 27
36. Bean Soup (zuppa Di Fagioli) Toscana, Primo (First Course) 27
37. Beet Crostata With A Pepper Parmesan Crust 28
38. Beet, Pesto & Goat Cheese Flatbread With Basil & Dill { Whole Grain} 29
39. Beetroot Orange Ice Cream 30
40. Best Chilaquiles With Roasted Tomatillo Salsa And Poblanos (and With Turkey Leftovers) 30
41. Best Stuffed Peppers 31
42. Big Green Wheatberry Salad 32
43. Black Pepper And Parmesan Panna Cotta 32
44. Black Sesame And White Chocolate Mousse Cake 33
45. Blueberry Zucchini Lemon Cake 34
46. Blueberry And Baked Ricotta Cheesecake 35
47. Boozy Beer Float (Peppered Honey Pear Ice Cream With Saison DuPont) 36
48. Boozy Dark Chocolate Cookies N' Cream Ice Cream 37
49. Breakfast Panini 37
50. Bresaola Surprise Rolls 38
51. Brie Fig Ice Cream 39
52. Broccoli, Blue Cheese And Leek Quiche .. 39
53. Bruschetta With Plums, Serrano Ham And Ricotta 40
54. Butternut Squash Ravioli With Caramelized Onions, Browned Pecans, Soaked Cranberries, And Apple Cider Reduction 40
55. Cacio E Pepe Biscuits 41
56. Cacio E Pepe Polenta 42
57. Caesar Salad Stuff And Dressing Recipe ... 42
58. Camembert And Bacon Sandwiches With Apple And Fennel Slaw 43
59. Caprese Panini 43
60. Caramelized Carrots With Herbed Goat Cheese "Snow" 44
61. Caramelized Fennel Pizza With Leeks, Ricotta And Orange 44

62. Caramelized Pear And Gruyère Torta 45
63. Caramelized Onion And Cheddar Palmiers 45
64. Caribbean Cream 46
65. Carrot Cupcakes With Cream Cheese Frosting 46
66. Cavatelli With Bacon, Corn, Mushrooms, And Parmesan, A La The Red Hen 47
67. Chard Wrapped Grilled Mozzarella With Kalamata Olives 48
68. Cheddar Corn Spoon Bread 49
69. Cheddar Cheese Biscuits With Bacon Jam 50
70. Cheese Latkes 50
71. Cheese Strata 51
72. Cheese And Lobster Bites 51
73. Cheesy Corn Y Scones 52
74. Cheesy Greek Style Baked Quinoa 52
75. Cherry Tomato & Homemade Chèvre Tart 53
76. Chicken Meatball Sub With Gobs Of Fresh Mozzarella 53
77. Chicken, Pepper, And Bean "Mexitalian" Casserole 54
78. Chili Verde Totchos 55
79. Chive, Herb Goat Cheese, And Tomato Frittata 56
80. Chocolate Chip Chocolate Cake With Raspberry Cream Filling And Orange Almond Drizzle 56
81. Chocolate Chip Chouquettes 57
82. Chorizo And Chard Pie 57
83. Cider Glazed Sweet Potatoes With Bacon, Pecans And Blue Cheese 58
84. Clambake Quesadillas 59
85. Cocktail Samosa 59
86. Cream Cheese Tart With Orange, Pistachios & Cardamom 60
87. Creamy Bucatini With Seared Brussels Sprouts 61
88. Creamy Chorizo Queso 61
89. Creamy Indian Noodles 62
90. Creamy Spinach Artichoke Dip 62
91. Creamy Spinach And Paneer 63
92. Cretan Tomato Salad 63
93. Croque Monsieur Cigars 64
94. Crostini Alla Romana 64
95. Crostini With Eggplant, Ricotta And Pears 65
96. Crostini With Ricotta, Truffle Honey And Smoked Salts 65
97. Crunchy Chicken And Brussel Sprouts In The Oven With A Melted Cheese And Wine Sa 65
98. Crustless Pizza 66
99. Crème Fraîche Cheesecake With Apple Cardamom Compote 66
100. Crème Fraîche 67
101. Cucumber And Radish Salad With Harissa Yogurt 67
102. Curds & Whey Biscuits With Infused Honey & Ricotta Spread 67
103. Curry Dip 69
104. Cyprus Easter Cheese Bread ("Flaounes") 69
105. Dark Meat Turkey Panini With Montasio Cheese Leftover Heaven 70
106. Devils On Hatchback 71
107. Double Toasted Honey Dijon And Strawberry Grilled Cheese 71
108. Dreamy Greek Eggs 72
109. Dungeness Crab And Fire Roasted Corn Chowder 72
110. Earl Grey Olive Oil Pound Cake 73
111. Easter Bunny Bread Bowl With Grana Padano Kale Artichoke Dip 73
112. Easy Broccoli Salad With Cheese Recipe .. 74
113. Easy Frittata Base Recipe 75
114. Easy Homemade Ranch Dip 75
115. Egg And Cheese Salad With Spicy Cilantro Pepitas Aioli 75
116. Endive With Bacon And Buttermilk Ranch Dressing 76
117. Farmer's Market Tomato And Ricotta Tart 76
118. Farro Casserole With Cranberries, Squash, Kale And A Sage Béchamel 77
119. Fettuccine Alfredo For One 78
120. Fig Jam Pizza 79
121. Fig, Ricotta And Pear Galette 79
122. Fonduta Con Tartufi (Truffle Fondue) 80
123. Fontina, Roasted Fennel & Spinach Seafood Tart 80
124. French Onion Soup In A Hurry 81
125. French Onion And Endive Soup 82
126. French Onion Rutabaga Baguette Au Gratin 82

127. French Baguette Sandwich 83
128. Fresh Fig And Goat Cheese Canapés 83
129. Fresh Figs For Breakfast 83
130. Fresh Ricotta And Peach Pizza With Honey Drizzle 84
131. Fresh Summer Salad With Raspberry Lambic Dressing 84
132. Fresh Tomato Tart 85
133. Fresh Mozzarella Stuffed With Cranberries, Pecans, And Maple Syrup 85
134. Freshies On Sticks 86
135. Frittata With Leeks, Sundried Tomatoes, And Fresh Parmigiano Reggiano 86
136. Garlic Bread Soup With Clams 87
137. Ginger Egg Cream 87
138. Glazed Shallot, Walnut, Sage, And Goat Cheese Pizza 88
139. Gluten Free Ritz Bits Style Crackers 89
140. Gorgonzola Grapes 90
141. Gorgonzola Potatoes Au Gratin 90
142. Gorgonzola Tart With White Truffle Honey, Pears & Radicchio 91
143. Green Eggs And Ham 91
144. Greenest Goddess Dressing And Dip 92
145. Grilled Apple Salad With Maple Mustard Vinaigrette 92
146. Grilled Flatbread With Peaches, Prosciutto, Mozzarella And Arugula 93
147. Grilled Foil Pack Chicken Nachos 93
148. Grilled Garden Sandwich 94
149. Grilled Lemon Tzatziki 95
150. Grilled Olathe Sweet Corn And Chicken Chowder With Goat Cheese 95
151. Grilled Peach And Mozzarella Summer Stack 96
152. Grilled Rye With Muenster, Avocado, And Sprout 96
153. Grilled Taleggio Cheese, Salami And Truffle Honey Crostone Di Taleggio, Salami Con Miele Tartufato 97
154. Grilled Watermelon With Tequila 98
155. Grilled Zucchini Orzo 98
156. Grilled Cheese And Bacon 99
157. Halloumi, Cranberry And Stuffing Bites ... 99
158. Ham, Gruyère, And Caramelized Onion Galette With A Fried Egg 99
159. Healthy Stuffed Manicotti Shells 100

160. Heavenly Kanafe.... A Syrian Dessert Made With Ricotta & Shredded Filo Dough 101
161. Herby Sweet And Savory Bread Pudding 101
162. Homemade Milk Kefir 102
163. Homemade Nutella Frozen Yogurt 102
164. Homemade Paneer 103
165. Homemade Gnocchi With Coriander And Roasted Almond Pesto 103
166. Hot And Spiced Butternut Squash, Goat's Cheese, Caramelized Onion And Pistachio Parcels 104
167. How To Make Ghee At Home, Pure And Simple 105
168. Incredibly Easy Jalapeno Pop 'Ems 105
169. Italian Rice Pie 106
170. Italian Sausage Strata 107
171. Italian Sweet Sausage Stuffed Shells With Four Cheese Cream Sauce 108
172. Jalapeño Cream Cheese Dip 108
173. Jasmine Scented Raspberry Breakfast Tiramisu' 109
174. Jersey Pizza With Roasted Garlic And Arugula 109
175. Joan Nathan's Chosen Cheese Blintzes .. 110
176. Juniper And Honey Pot De Créme 111
177. Kabocha Squash (Japanese Pumpkin) Braised In Milk 111
178. Kitty's Latin Tart 111
179. Kunafa With Mango Cream Filling 112
180. LAMB SOUVLAKI WITH ZUCCHINI TZATZIKI 113
181. Labneh Grilled Cheese 113
182. Lasagna Aperto 114
183. Lasagne Alla Bolognese 115
184. Layered Croissant Sandwich Casserole ... 115
185. Layered Grapes And Bread With Chèvre And Balsamic 116
186. Lazy Greek Pizza With Shrimp 117
187. Lebanese Maftoul Couscous With Roasted Butternut Squash, Mint And Feta 117
188. Lemon Goat Cheese Cheesecake 118
189. Lemon Souffle Pancakes With Raspberry Syrup 119
190. Lemon And Honey Cheesecakes 119
191. Lemon Mint Peas With Burrata And Breadcrumbs 120
192. Lemony Cheese Blintzes 120

193. Lentil Meatballs With No Meat And A Surprise Center 121
194. Lime Cado Bites 121
195. Loaded Cream Cheese Cookie Bars With Animal Cookie Crust 122
196. Mac And Cheese Pie 123
197. Mamma Linda's Cheesecake With Fresh Raspberries 124
198. Mango Coconut Burfi (fudge) 124
199. Maple Balsamic Kale And Egg Brunch Tart With Canadian Bacon And Sharp White Cheddar 125
200. Margherita Naan Pizza 125
201. Marinated Feta Cheese 126
202. Mascarpone Stuffed French Toast Fritters 127
203. Mayo Free Caesar Dressing 127
204. Mediterranean Pressed Sandwich ... 128
205. Melt In Your Mouth Stuffed Spinach Manicotti With Fresh Marinara Sauce 128
206. Middle Eastern Grilled Cheese 130
207. Mike Lepizerra's Polenta 130
208. Milk Soup 130
209. Minted Zucchini Soup 131
210. Mmmmascarpone Mashed Potatoes With Dill And Chives 131
211. Moussaka In Four Parts 131
212. Mozzarella 133
213. Mushroom And Sourdough Crusted Cremini Mini Quiches 133
214. Mushroom Stuffed Eggplant 134
215. Nathaniel's One Dish, An Easy Toast With Greens, Tomatoes And Cheese 135
216. Nectarine And Avocado Caprese 136
217. No Churn Ben & Jerry's Style Core Ice Cream 136
218. No Bread Savoyard Croque Monsieur 138
219. Not Budapest Mushroom Soubise ... 138
220. Old Fashioned "No Short Cuts" Strawberry Ice Cream 138
221. Olive CHA! Penade Goat Cheese Spread 140
222. Oma's Bavarian Cheesecake Bites ... 140
223. Parmesan And Truffle Popcorn With Chives 140
224. Parmesan Cheese "chips" 141
225. Parmesan, Oregano And Pine Nut Melts 141

226. Parmesan Panko Fried Summer Squash With Buttermilk Ranch 141
227. Pasta Ponza 142
228. Pastrami Rueben Mac & Cheese 142
229. Peach Basil Goat Cheese Galette 143
230. Peachy Buttermilk Sherbet 144
231. Persian Style Ice Cream (Bastani) ... 144
232. Persimmon Snap Cannoli 145
233. Philadelphia Style Peach Ice Cream 146
234. Pizza Appetizers 146
235. Pizza Piccante 146
236. Plum & Ricotta Crostini 147
237. Polenta, Parmesan, And Prosciutto Spoon Breads, ... 148
238. Pork And Pear Galette With Bleu Cheese And Brown Sugared Pecans 148
239. Potato Cheese Perogies 149
240. Princess Pasta 150
241. Prosciuto & Eggplant Rolatini 150
242. Prosciutto & Fig Stuffing 151
243. Prosciutto, Roasted Asparagus, Parmigiano Reggiano & Mozzarella On Ciabbata 151
244. Pumpkin Bread With Brie 152
245. Pumpkin Breakfast Parfait 152
246. Pumpkin Kale Mac And Cheese 153
247. Pumpkin Swirls 153
248. Quiche In Winter White And Blue 154
249. RUGELACH Cookies With Nutella & Chocolate Chips 155
250. Radish Goat Cheese Galette 156
251. Radish Salad With Curry Orange Dressing 156
252. Raisin, Pecan, And Banana Oatmeal With Flax Seeds 157
253. Rapturous Morel Marmalade 157
254. Raspberry Dark Chocolate Pavlova Ice Cream 158
255. Red Velvet Cheesecake 158
256. Red White & Blue Layered Buttermilk Cake 159
257. Refried Butternut Squash With Mozzarella And Gremolata 160
258. Ricotta Crostini With Confited Lemons, Thyme, And Walnuts 160
259. Ricotta Frittata 161
260. Roasted Acorn Squash And Goat Cheese Dip 161

261. Roasted Butternut Squash Cheesecake 162
262. Roasted Cauliflower And Barley Salad With Basil Croutons 162
263. Roasted Corn And Cojita Quesadillas 163
264. Roasted Eggplant And Sautéed Greens Lasagna 163
265. Roasted Squash Blossoms With Mozzarella And Walnut Oil 164
266. Roasted Sungold And Pear Tomatoes With Fontina And Thyme 164
267. Roasted Vegetable, Goat Cheese, And Spinach Quesadilla With Spicy Tomato Jam 165
268. Rosemary Cherries 165
269. Sage + Prosciutto Tartines 166
270. Salad ABC Apples, Bacon, Cumin Cheese 166
271. Salted Pumpkin Caramels 167
272. Savory Buckwheat Crepes 167
273. Savory Crêpes SuzetteLa 168
274. Savory Lokshen Kugel (Noodle Pudding) 169
275. Savory Mushroom Bread Pudding 169
276. Savory Baked Breakfast Stack 170
277. Savory Buttermilk Brioche With A Pear, Rosemary & Meat Filling 171
278. Savory Waffles With Goat Cheese And Lardons 172
279. Sexy Spinach Dip 172
280. Shavuot Ricotta Pastries And Potato Cheese Galette 172
281. Sheet Pan Broccoli Cheese Rice Casserole 173
282. Shiitake Mushroom Enchiladas 174
283. Shish Taouk With Toum (Chicken Kebabs With Garlic Sauce) 175
284. Shrimp Cocktail Dip 176
285. Simple Cheese Souffle 176
286. Slow Cooker Cardamom Rice Pudding ... 177
287. Smoked Mackerel Pâté With Horseradish And Dill 177
288. Smoked Salmon Red Onion And Feta Cheese Fritatta 177
289. Snickers Protein Smoothie 178
290. Soft Scrambled Eggs With Ricotta And Chives 178
291. Soufflé Omelet With Robiola And Sautéed Ramps 179

292. Southwest Cottage Cheese Muffins 179
293. Southwest Quinoa Salad With Sweet & Spicy Honey Lime Dressing 180
294. Special Cheesy Pasta 180
295. Spiced Lamb Salad 181
296. Spiced Plum Cheese Round 182
297. Spicy Cheddar Cheese Crackers 182
298. Spinach Arancini 183
299. Spinach Balls With Mustard Sauce 183
300. Spinach Gnocchi 184
301. Spinach And Ricotta Teacakes 184
302. Spread, Slice, Snip, And Go 185
303. Spring Onion Bread Soup 185
304. Spring Pea And Ricotta Crostini 185
305. Spätzle With Sage Butter, Parmesan, And Toasted Hazelnuts 186
306. Squash And Goat Cheese Lasagna 187
307. Squash N' Spice Milk 188
308. Stir Fry Pizza 188
309. Stovetop Mac & Cheese 189
310. Stuffed Veal Scallops With Chorizo And Manchego 189
311. Sublime Cheesy Potatoes 189
312. Sugar Free Tuti Froti Barfi 190
313. Sugar Snaps With Bacon, Maple, Feta And Mint 190
314. Summer Colour Mozzarella 191
315. Summer Corn Salad With Toasted Grains 191
316. Summer Salad With Fresh Mozzarella & Herbs 192
317. Summer Slab Pie 192
318. Summer Vegetable Galette 193
319. Sunday Sauce With Meatballs & Sausage (LC, GF) 195
320. Sweet Corn Arepa Pancakes 196
321. Sweet Potato Shrimp & "Grits" 196
322. Sweet Potato, Spinach & Goat Cheese Frittata 197
323. Sweet Savory Apricot Curry Cheesecake 197
324. Swiss Cheese And Chocolate Sandwich . 198
325. Tender Cherry Cheesecake 198
326. The Incredible Bacon Tamale 199
327. The Perfect Summer Salad (Watermelon, Feta, Avocado, And Mint Salad) 200
328. The Saints Grits N Eggs 200
329. The Zuppa 201

330. Tomato Soup (Ree Drummond) 201
331. Tomato Tarte Tatin Starring Triple Cheese 202
332. Traditional Fondue Fribourgeois Legendary And Original 202
333. Tri Colored Caprese Salad On Toast With Peach Balsamic Vinegar 203
334. Tropical Dessert Smoothie 203
335. Turkey Lasagna 203
336. Turkey Tetrazzini 204
337. Tuscan Roasted Chicken Stuffed Wtih Swiss Chard Couscous And Cheese 205
338. Twice Baked Potato Stuffed With Shrimp And Blue Cheese 206
339. Variation On Ronald Reagan's Mac And Cheese 207
340. Waiting For Bonaparte Muffaletta (The Remix Edition) 208
341. Warm Lentil Salad With Swiss Chard, Feta And Red Wine Black Pepper Vinaigrette 208
342. Waste Not Pasta 209
343. Welsh Rarebit Yorkshire Pudding For One 210
344. Whipped Feta Dip With Spiced Pita Chips 211
345. White Cheddar Fig Grilled Cheese 211
346. White Cheddar And Rosemary Mac And Cheese 212
347. White Chocolate & Poppy Seed Cake With Lemon Syrup 212
348. White Chocolate Cheesecake With Raspberry Sauce, Fresh Raspberries And White Chocolate Glaze 213
349. White Chocolate Whipped Cream 213
350. White Chocolate Cake With Dried Strawberries 214
351. Winter Panzanella 214
352. Yogurt With Marzipan, Poppy Seeds & Walnuts 215
353. Yogurt Tahini Sauce 215
354. Zucchini "Brake" 216
355. Zucchini Lasagna 216
356. Caprese Dog 217
357. Caramelised Onion, Goats Cheese & Cauliflower Quiche 217
358. Crisped Spanish Chorizo & Two Cheese Mashed Potatoes 217
359. Crustless Blender Cheesecake With Quick Raspberry Sauce 218
360. Green Chile And Cheese Pancakes 219
361. Harvest Cake 219
362. Loaded Baked Potato Quiche 220
363. Oreo Orange Cheesecake 220
364. Ravioli Di Fonduta With Truffle 221
365. The Best Mac & Cheese, Ever. 221

INDEX 223

CONCLUSION 229

365 Awesome Cheese Recipes

***

1. "PAPARA? KVIETKA" Or Flower Fern Salad With Some Twists

Serving: Serves 2 | Prep: | Cook: |Ready in:

Ingredients

- vinegar and water in a 1:3 ratio
- 1 small sweet onion, cut thinly into rings and halved
- 4 ounces excellent quality fatty ham, julienned
- 2 ounces proscuitto, julienned
- 4 small heirloom tomatoes, peeled and cut into long pieces (I added the excess juice in with the dressing)
- 1 ounce pickled fiddlehead ferns or asparagus, optional
- 1 ounce pickled green tomatoes, julienned, optional
- 6 ounces Brimskaya Brinza cheese, julienned
- 6 ounces fresh or freshly pickled refrigerator cucumbers, julienned
- 8 small dill gherkins, julienned
- 1 tablespoon capote capers
- 1 tablespoon chopped black olives, optional
- 2 tablespoons finely chopped dill, chives, and flat leaf parsley
- 1 hard boiled egg, chopped
- 2 seckel pears, julienned and spritzed with fresh lemon juice
- 2 tablespoons champagne or pear vinegar
- 4 tablespoons EVOO
- 1 teaspoon dijon mustard
- 1 teaspoon acacia or other similar honey
- 1 small bit of white anchovy, finely minced and mashed, optional, but recommended
- kosher or pink Himalayan salt to taste
- fresh milled pepper to taste
- 2-4 hearty artisan bread slices, buttered on the side
- serve on a bed of mixed seasonal greens, if desired

Direction

- Marinate the onion rings in the water and vinegar mix for 2-3 hours. Then drain and mince finely.
- Assemble all the salad ingredients together, add a dash of salt, and keep any greens you may want to use as a bed separate. Pack to travel. Keep salad chilled until serving.
- Combine the vinegar and EVOO, mustard, and honey with optional anchovy. Season with salt and pepper. Feel free to include any excess tomato juice in the dressing. Pack the dressing to travel, so it can be shaken well and poured later.
- When ready to eat, plate your salad, dress, and toss. Serve with hearty lightly buttered artisan bread.

2. Cinnamon Walnut Loaf

Serving: Serves 12 | Prep: | Cook: |Ready in:

Ingredients

- 1/2 cup walnuts
- 1 cup sugar, divided
- 1 2/3 cups cake flour
- 2 teaspoons baking powder
- 1 teaspoon kosher salt
- 1/2 cup whipping cream
- 1/2 cup sour cream
- 3/4 teaspoon vanilla
- 1 stick unsalted butter at room temperature

- 2 large eggs at room temperature
- 1-2 tablespoons demerara sugar, optional

Direction

- Preheat oven to 350 degrees.
- Cut a piece of parchment paper to fit the bottom of the pan. Spray a loaf pan (8 1/2" x 4 1/2" x 2 1/2") liberally with non-stick vegetable spray. Lay the parchment paper in the bottom of the pan and spray again. Set aside.
- In a mini-prep food processor add the walnuts and 1tablespoon of the sugar. Pulse until the walnuts are finely ground. Transfer the nuts to a medium bowl and add the flour, baking powder and salt. Whisk to combine and set aside.
- In a glass measuring cup add the whipping cream. Drop spoonfuls of the sour cream into the whipping cream until it measures 1 cup. Add the vanilla and whisk to combine. Set aside.
- In a large bowl add the butter and remaining sugar. Cream the butter and sugar together until light and fluffy, about 4-6 minutes, scraping the sides of a bowl with a rubber spatula occasionally. Add the eggs one at a time and beat into the butter mixture until fully incorporated before adding the second egg. Beat until blended.
- Add one third of the flour mixture and mix on low speed until just combined. Add 1/2 of the cream mixture and mix until just combined. Follow in the same manner with 1/3 flour, the rest of the cream and finally the last of the flour. Do not over mix.
- Use your spatula to scrape the bottom and sides of the bowl to make sure that everything has been evenly incorporated. Pour the batter into the prepared loaf pan and smooth the top. Sprinkle the top of the loaf evenly with demerara sugar, if desired for a slightly crunchy top.
- Bake for 50 minutes to an hour or until a cake tester comes out clean.
- Let the loaf rest in the pan for about 20-30 minutes before inverting onto a rack. Remove the parchment paper and flip the loaf right-side-up to continue cooling.
- Can be served warm or at room temperature.

3. 'nduja Induced Amnesia

Serving: Serves 4-6 | Prep: | Cook: |Ready in:

Ingredients

- 2 six ounce links, 'nduja
- 1 small burrata cheese
- 1 1 loaf, crusty oven baked bread with "eyes"
- 1 clove garlic
- Extra virgin olive oil (preferrably from California)
- mostarda di Cremona
- harissa
- alioli
- fennel pollen
- fleur de sel

Direction

- Slice bread into 1/4" slices, sandwich size
- With a sharp knife or scissors open up the links. It's okay to leave in the casing
- Do the same with the burrata
- Place the condiments in individual ramekins for the table
- Meanwhile grill your bread slices. Rub with garlic and drizzle with just a tiny bit of olive oil
- Be sure you have some knives, small spoons or spreaders out for the DYI part. This "sandwich" can be open faced or lidded. Everybody get down tonight.
- BTW encourage your guests to add a little fleur del to the bread while it's still hot off the grill.

4. 1975 Dick Taeuber's Brandy Alexander Pie

Serving: Serves 6 | Prep: | Cook: |Ready in:

Ingredients

- 1 1/2 cups gingersnap crumbs
- 1/4 cups melted butter
- 1 envelope unflavored gelatin
- 2/3 cup sugar
- 1/8 teaspoon salt
- 3 eggs, separated
- 1/4 cup Cognac
- 1/4 cup Crème de Cacao
- 1 cup heavy cream

Direction

- Preheat the oven to 350 degrees.
- Combine the crumbs with the butter. Form in a 9-inch pan and bake for 10 minutes. Cool.
- Pour 1/2 cup cold water in a saucepan and sprinkle the gelatin over it. Add 1/3 cup sugar, salt and egg yolks. Stir to blend.
- Place over low heat and stir until the gelatin dissolves and mixture thickens slightly (it won't be as thick as a custard). Do not boil! Remove from heat.
- Stir the liqueurs or liquor into the mixture. Then chill until the mixture starts to mound slightly (this means that if you push a spoon (or your finger) through the mixture, it will clump up into a mound rather than stay flat as a liquid would).
- Beat the egg whites until stiff, then add the remaining sugar and beat until the peaks are firm. Fold the meringue into the thickened mixture.
- Whip the cream, then fold into the mixture.
- Turn the mixture into the crust. Chill for several hours or overnight.

5. 3 Ingredients Gnocchi Gratin

Serving: Serves 3 | Prep: 0hours5mins | Cook: 0hours30mins |Ready in:

Ingredients

- 2 cups tomato and basil sauce
- 17 ounces patate gnocchis
- 1 cup Italian cheese mix
- 1 tablespoon canola oil
- salt and pepper

Direction

- Preheat the oven at 400°F.
- In a big pan, add the oil and add the gnocchi, sauté for 3 minutes and cover for 7 minutes. Add the tomato sauce and mix. Then, add 1/3 cup cheese and mix. Salt and pepper.
- Remove from the heat. Add the rest of cheese on the top and place in the oven for 15 minutes.

6. A Pear Of Apples Pie With Gruyere Crust

Serving: Serves 8 | Prep: | Cook: |Ready in:

Ingredients

- Crust
- 2 ½ cups unbleached all-purpose flour
- 2 tsp. salt
- 2 sticks unsalted butter
- 1 tbsp. cider vinegar
- about 1/3 cup ice cold water
- 1 cup shredded gruyere cheese
- filling
- 4 cored and peeled pears (I used 2 bosc and 2 bartletts)
- 3 cored and peeled golden delicious apples
- 1/2 stick unsalted butter
- 1/4 cup brown sugar
- 1/4 cup granulated sugar

- 1 vanilla bean (split open, seeds scraped)
- 1/4 tsp nutmeg
- 1/4 tsp cinnamon
- Pinch of salt
- 1/4 tsp vanilla
- 2 tbsp. and 1/2 tsp. corn starch

Direction

- Crust
- Place a medium sized bowl and fork in the freezer. Combine the flour, salt and shredded gruyere in a bowl, mixing the cheese into the flour mixture with your hands.
- Dice the butter into ¼ inch pieces. Place butter and the flour-cheese mixture in a large zip lock bag, seal and roll over with a rolling pin until the butter is combined. Place the bag in the freezer for at least 30 minutes.
- Pour the ingredients from the bag into the cold bowl and work together with your fingertips or/and the cold fork until the mixture becomes pebbly. Gradually drizzle the ice water (excluding the ice) and the vinegar over the mixture, blending with your fingertips and the fork. Add more water if necessary - a tablespoon at a time, until you achieve the right consistency.
- Form two discs out of the dough, working each in your palm. Wrap them each tightly with saran wrap and refrigerate for an hour.
- When the filling is ready, roll one of the discs out onto a floured surface, dusting it with flour as you work. Transfer to the pie pan, pressing the dough into it and leaving about an inch of overhang. Crimp or style however you like. Add the filling.
- Roll out the second disc the same way and place it over top the pie, making a few slits in the center or, if you choose to cut out decorative leaves, you can place them on top of the filling instead.
- Combine 1 egg yolk with a splash of milk and brush over the crust. Sprinkle with demura sugar. Wrap some foil on the edges of the crust (so they don't burn).Bake at 375 for about 45 minutes.

- Serve warm with vanilla ice cream
- Filling
- Cut the peeled and cored pears and apples into inch size pieces and place them in a bowl.
- Melt the butter in a large saucepan over medium heat and add the fruit, sugars, spices, salt, vanilla and vanilla bean seeds and pod.
- Stir and simmer on medium to medium-low heat for about 25 minutes, stirring occasionally. Then remove from heat, stir in the corn starch and let the filling cool to room temperature.

7. A Pistol For Paddy Garcia (with Apologies To The Pogues)

Serving: Serves 4 | Prep: | Cook: | Ready in:

Ingredients

- 2 medium white potatoes
- 1/2 of one head of savoy cabbage
- 8 medium sized flour tortillas
- 6 ounces Irish cheddar, grated
- 4 ounces cotija cheese, crumbled
- 1 cup Mexican or Salvadoran crema
- Hot sauce of your choosing (we like California Pepper Plant "Original California Style"), optional
- Grapeseed oil for frying
- Sea salt to taste

Direction

- Thinly slice the potatoes. Rinse in cold water and wrap in a towel until ready to use.
- Slice the cabbage into two wedges, cutting through the core to the top.
- Steam the cabbage just until tender but not squishy. When cool enough to handle slice crosswise into ribbons aka chiffonade.
- Grate your cheeses and set aside for you mise en place.
- In a hot skillet heat the grape seed oil and cook your potatoes in batches until brown and

slightly crispy (don't over crowd). Allow these to rest on paper towel to lose some of the oil.
- Take one tortilla and add a generous amount of cheddar. Top with potatoes and cabbage. Add cabbage followed by crumbled cotija. Add a dash of hot sauce if you like. Maybe a little more cheddar to help seal. Dip your finger in a bowl of water and run it around the edge of the bottom tortilla. Place another tortilla on top and press down the edges.
- Heat a large, dry skillet to medium high flame. Add your quesadilla. Allow time for the cheese to begin to melt. Turn it once (and only once---I hate "flippers"). When finished plate it, quarter it with a pizza wheel and add one tablespoon of cream to serve. Repeat with remaining tortillas.
- Garnish and hoist a pint.

8. A Tuscan Inspired Savory Bread Pudding

Serving: Serves 4 | Prep: | Cook: |Ready in:

Ingredients

- 1/2 cup heavy cream
- 1/2 cup organic whole milk
- 2/3 cup buttermilk
- 1/2 teaspoon fresh tender rosemary leaves, finely chopped
- 1 egg, beaten
- 1 tablespoon white wine, pinot grigio
- 1/2 teaspoon fresh ground black pepper
- pinch of kosher salt
- 1 1/2 cups baguette, chopped and cubed
- 2/3-1 cups fresh pecorino toscano, grated
- 1 cup cubed roasted beets dressed in a mix of tarragon vinegar, with a bit of honey and a few drops of white truffle oil
- sprinkle of freshly grated nutmeg
- 1/4 cup carmelized yellow onions
- sprinkle of freshly grated parmesan
- sprigs of rosemary

Direction

- Preheat the oven to 350 degrees.
- Whisk together the milk, cream, and buttermilk.
- Add the beaten egg and wine and whisk. Add the pepper, salt, and rosemary.
- Toss the bread cubes together with the cubed roasted, dressed beets and caramelized onions. Add these to a buttered baking dish (@10-12 inches by 2 inches deep).Gently add in the grated pecorino. Pour the liquid mixture over this.
- Sprinkle with nutmeg and parmesan. Bake for about 25 minutes until golden brown.
- Serve with sprigs of fresh rosemary and a glass of pinot noir.

9. A Very Short Cake

Serving: Makes 2 cakes | Prep: | Cook: |Ready in:

Ingredients

- Banana Cream
- 1 Medium Ripe Banana
- 4 Egg Yolks(room temperature)
- 1/4 cup Sugar
- 1 tablespoon Gelatin Powder
- 1/4 cup Cold Water
- 1/2 cup Almond Milk
- 1/2 cup Bailley's Irish Cream
- 1/2 teaspoon Vanilla Extract
- 1 cup Heavy Cream
- Cake
- 1 cup Almond Flour
- 1/2 cup Gluten Free Flour Blend w/ Xanthum Gum (I use Pillsbury's Multi-Purpose Blend)
- 1 3/4 cups Confectioners' Sugar
- 1 Overripe Pear
- 4 Egg Whites (room temperature)
- Pinch Salt
- 1/4 cup Granulated Sugar
- 1/2 teaspoon Vanillla Extract

- 1 Banana, cut in slices
- Handful Chopped Almonds
- Fresh Blackberries

Direction

- Banana Cream
- Combine Gelatin powder with the cold water and set aside so it can dissolve.
- Puree the banana in a blender or food processor until smooth.
- With an electric mixer, beat the yolks and sugar until fluffy, then gradually add the banana and beat until fully incorporated.
- Combine the milk and Bailley's in a saucepan and bring to the scalding point (when bubbles begin to form around the edge of the pan). Remove from heat and wait 5 minutes before pouring over the banana mixture and beat until combined.
- Return to heat and bring to the scalding point once again. Then remove from heat and let cool. You may want to transfer it to a new bowl. Stir occasionally.
- If the gelatin has dissolved, gently stir it and the vanilla into the mixture.
- In a separate bowl, whip the heavy cream into soft peaks. Gently fold the whipped cream into the mixture until fully incorporated.
- This makes a lot of cream and you'll probably have leftovers after the cake is finished. It can be used for banana cream pie, banana pudding or just spoon it over pound cake or fresh berries! I liked blackberries best.
- Cake
- Preheat oven to 350 degrees F
- In a bowl, whisk confectioners' sugar together with both flour types.
- Mash the pear with a fork or pastry blender then add the flour/sugar mixture and combine until fully incorporated.
- Beat the egg whites with the pinch of salt with an electric mixer until frothy, then gradually add the sugar. Beat into a meringue, when it will be stiff, shiny and form peaks.
- Transfer the meringue to the flour mix and with a rubber spatula, gently fold them into each other.
- Add vanilla and continue to gently fold the batter until smooth and everything is well mixed.
- Grease the bottom of the cake pans. Pour half the batter into each pan. The batter should cover the bottom and not be higher than a half-inch.
- Bake for 35-40 minutes. They are done when the tops are golden and the cake has pulled away from the sides of the pan.
- Pop the cakes out onto a cooling rack and allow to cool.
- For two single layer cakes, simply top the cakes with banana slices and a generous layer of cream and garnish with chopped almonds and blackberries. You can layer them on top of each other as well! Then refrigerate so the cream doesn't ooze when you cut the cake. If you can wait that long.
- Serve with extra cream on the side to allow everyone to have as much cream as they want!

10. A Little Bit Different Lasagna

Serving: Serves 12 | Prep: 1hours0mins | Cook: 0hours40mins | Ready in:

Ingredients

- Layering ingredients
- 8 cups Torn and despined kale and spinach
- 2 cups Washed and sliced porcini mushrooms
- 3 tablespoons Olive oil
- 1 teaspoon Seasoned salt
- 1 tablespoon Powdered garlic
- 1 teaspoon Dried basil
- 1 teaspoon Dried Italian seasoning
- 12 pieces Lasagna noodles
- 1 quart Marinara Sauce
- 1 pint Pizza sauce
- 2 ounces Tomato paste

- 4 pieces Eggs
- 1 cup Grated Parmesan cheese
- Cheese filling
- 4 cups Grated mozzarella cheese
- 3 pieces Eggs
- 2 pints Part Skim Ricotta Cheese
- 1 tablespoon Dried basil
- 1 tablespoon Dried parsley

Direction

- Layering ingredients
- Thoroughly tear and despite 5 cups of fresh washed kale, remove the stems from 3 cups of washed fresh spinach. Wash and slice 2cups of porcini mushrooms. Sauté the mushrooms separately in a pan with 1 tablespoon of olive oil and season salt until softened remove from pan and place mushrooms in a medium size mixing bowl. Continue to sauté the kale until limp and soft, then the spinach in the remainder of the olive oil sprinkling with garlic powder. Remove from pan and place in the medium size mixing bowl with the mushrooms, stir.
- In another pan while the vegetables are sautéing combine 1 large jar of marinara sauce, I small jar of pizza sauce and 1/2 can tomato paste. Stir until combined and simmer for a few minutes. Add a cup of the sauce to the sautéed vegetables. Sprinkle with Italian seasoning and dried basil. Remove the remainder of the sauce from the heat.
- Bring a pot of salted and olive oiled water to a rolling boil. Add 9 lasagna noodles, boil according to package directions.
- In a separate bowl combine 4 large organic eggs and 1 cup of grated Parmesan cheese. Set aside.
- Cheese filling
- Mix together all cheeses and eggs and basil in large mixing bowl and set aside. Prepare a 10x13 pan by coating with a few tablespoons of the red sauce.
- Layer three lasagna noodles length wise across pan
- Drop large dollops of all the cheese mixture on the lasagna noodles and spread the cheese with a spatula.
- Add another layer of lasagna noodles, spread all the sautéed vegetables across the lasagna noodles, spread more red sauce over the vegetables
- Add another layer of lasagna noodles, spread with the egg and Parmesan cheese mixture,
- Top with last layer of lasagna noodles, drizzle the red sauce over the noodles then sprinkle the noodles generously with mozzarella cheese and Parmesan cheese.
- The final steps are to sprinkle the top layer of noodles with parsley flakes, then bake for 40 minutes at 325 degrees pre-heated oven. .let cool for a few minutes then cut squares of lasagna into serving pieces.

11. Almond Crunch Halva Ice Cream

Serving: Serves 3 | Prep: | Cook: | Ready in:

Ingredients

- 200 milliliters heavy cream
- 200 milliliters whole milk
- 80 grams sugar
- 1 pinch salt
- 3 teaspoons cornstarch
- 100 grams sunflower seed halva
- 30 grams chopped roasted almonds

Direction

- Dissolve the cornstarch in 50ml whole milk, leave to rest.
- In a blender blitz together 50ml whole milk and the halva of choice (I use the sunflower seed one) until smooth and lump-free.
- Freeze in your ice cream maker according to the manufacturer's instructions adding the chopped almonds, walnuts, cashews or pistachios at the last couple of minutes of

churning. Store in an airtight container or spoon right away.

12. Anchovy Cheese

Serving: Makes about a cup (can be doubled, tripled or quadrupled) | Prep: | Cook: |Ready in:

Ingredients

- 4 ounces cream cheese (softened, at room temperature) or any similar cheese
- 4 ounces (1 stick, or 1/2 cup) unsalted butter, at room temperature (soft and easily spread)
- 3 tablespoons crème fraiche or sour cream
- 8-10 anchovies (more or less -- fewer if using large ones), plus more to taste and/or to garnish,
- 2 teaspoon of capers,, drained and coarsely chopped, plus a few more for garnish, if desired
- 1 tablespoon Dijon mustard, or more to taste
- 2 tablespoons finely chopped parsley, divided in half
- 10-12 chives, thinly sliced
- ½ teaspoon lemon zest
- Juice of 1/2 lemon
- Pine nuts, if desired, for garnish
- FOR SERVING
- Thin slices baguette, toasted, or water biscuits
- Radish rosettes

Direction

- Thoroughly cream together the butter, cream cheese and crème fraiche. Using a mortar and pestle, crush the anchovies with the chopped capers to make a fine paste. Add the anchovy paste and the mustard, chives, half of the chopped parsley (or all, if you plan to garnish with anchovies), and the lemon zest and juice. Stir well to blend thoroughly.
- Taste and add more lemon, mustard or anchovies, to taste. (You'll need to pound the additional anchovies, of course.) Shape into a mound onto a small plate surrounded by radish rosettes or plain crackers. I do this using a bowl that I've lightly rinsed with water beforehand. I stuff the spread into it, then turn it out, smoothing with a butter knife once it's on the plate. You can also serve this in several medium ramekins.
- Garnish with anchovies, radiating from the center, piling on a few capers at the intersection. Or sprinkle with the remaining chopped parsley. Or some toasted pine nuts. Whatever you like.
- Serve with water biscuits, thin slices of toasted baguette, or on radish rosettes.
- Enjoy!! ;o)
- If you really like paprika and caraway seeds, feel free to add a tablespoon or so of each. The result will be more complex, with the anchovies less dominant. You'll essentially have an anchovy-heavy Liptauer.

13. Anchovy Onion Butter

Serving: Makes 1 | Prep: | Cook: |Ready in:

Ingredients

- 1 large onion, diced
- 1 pinch sugar
- 6 anchovies
- 1 tablespoon anchovy oil
- 1/2 cup butter (1 stick)

Direction

- Caramelize the onions slowly over medium heat along with the sugar and anchovy oil. This will take an hour or so.
- Dice the anchovies and add to the onion mixture. Take off the heat and let everything cool.
- Whip up the butter in a mixer until fluffy.
- Add the onion mixture and mix to combine. Season with pepper and slather on bread.

14. Anytime Broccoli & Cheddar Fritters

Serving: Makes 8 fritters | Prep: 0hours20mins | Cook: 0hours30mins | Ready in:

Ingredients

- 1 cup flour in a shallow bowl

Direction

- Finely chop broccoli, garlic, & onion.
- Heat 2 tablespoons of the neutral oil in a skillet on medium-high, add broccoli, garlic, & onion to the pan.
- Wait 3-4 minutes until you start to hear a good sizzle, add 2 tablespoons of water and reduce heat to medium-low. Cook until broccoli is fork tender. Let it cool.
- Combine 3 cups cold mashed potatoes, 1 tablespoon flour, 1/2 cup grated cheddar cheese, broccoli/garlic/onion mixture, salt, & pepper.
- Place a wire rack over a parchment or paper towel lined baking sheet. Leave this near where you plan on frying your fritters.
- Pull off a small (nickel sized) test piece of the broccoli-potato mixture in the pan. (You are checking to see if it is hot enough, you want to hear an immediate sizzle)
- Fry patties 3 - 4 at a time, depending on how big your pan is! It's going to take about 3 minutes per side, flip when the edges are browned.
- Transfer your golden delicious fritters to the wire rack and salt while hot! Repeat the frying process until all of them are done.
- Optional Topping Suggestions- Poached Eggs- Pulled Chicken- Sour Cream or Greek Yogurt

15. Apostle's Fingers (lemon And Ricotta Filled Crepes)

Serving: Makes 8 to 10 crêpes | Prep: | Cook: | Ready in:

Ingredients

- For the crêpes:
- 1 3/4 cups (220 grams) flour
- 3 tablespoons (20 grams) of confectioner's sugar
- 3 eggs, beaten
- 2 cups (500 milliliters) milk
- Zest of 1 lemon or orange
- Butter, for greasing
- For the filling and assembly:
- 3 cups (750 grams) fresh ricotta
- 3/4 cup (150 grams) fine sugar
- Juice and zest of 1 large lemon
- 1/4 cup 60 milliliters of liqueur, such as limoncello or Borsci San Marzano (optional)
- 2 teaspoons ground cinnamon
- 2 tablespoons powdered sugar

Direction

- For the crêpes:
- For the crêpes, combine the flour and powdered sugar in a bowl. Add the eggs and mix with the dry ingredients, then add the milk, bit by bit, to obtain a creamy consistency. Add the lemon zest. Heat a flat pan over medium-high heat and grease it with some butter. Pour over a ladle of batter and tip the pan to cover the surface with a very thin layer of batter to make paper-thin crepes. Cook the crepes until the top looks dry, then flip over briefly and set to the side on a plate. Continue making crepes until batter is finished.
- For the filling and assembly:
- For the filling, leave the ricotta to drain overnight -- spoon the ricotta into a muslin cloth (or a clean linen tea towel) set in a strainer over a bowl in the fridge. The next day, discard the leftover liquid and combine the firmed ricotta, sugar, lemon zest and juice (and if desired, one of the additions mentioned

in the notes, like a handful of candied orange peel or chopped dark chocolate).
- With the help of two teaspoons, spoon the filling, about an inch wide, across the center of a crêpe. Roll it up tightly and cut the roll into three even pieces. Continue with the rest of the crepes and filling. Serve the crêpes with a splash of liqueur, if desired, and a dusting of powdered sugar and cinnamon.

16. Apple Küchl With Pistachios

Serving: Serves 8 | Prep: | Cook: | Ready in:

Ingredients

- 1 1/4 cups Flour
- 1 teaspoon Baking powder
- 2 tablespoons pistachio powder
- 1 pinch salt
- 100 milliliters milk
- 2 eggs
- 4 medium cooking apples
- 4 tablespoons sugar
- 2 teaspoons vanilla sugar
- Butter for frying
- Powder sugar
- 1 handful Pistachios, chopped

Direction

- Combine flour, baking powder, 1 tbsp. sugar, 2 tbsps. pistachio powder and salt in bowl. Stir in the milk, the eggs and mix gently with a mixer.
- Peel and core the apples without cutting them in half. Cut into thick, round slices. Sprinkle with 4 tbsps. sugar and 2 tsp vanilla sugar.
- In a skillet, melt enough butter to fry the Appleküchl properly. Dip the apple slices into the dough then fry for 2-3 minutes on each side until crispy.
- Dry the apples on paper towel. To serve, simply place a couple of Appleküchl of individual plate, sprinkle with powder sugar and chopped pistachios.

17. Apple Ricotta Pie

Serving: Serves 4 | Prep: | Cook: | Ready in:

Ingredients

- 2 cups ground graham crackers
- 4 tablespoons butter
- 4 medium apples, peeled and cut into small cubes
- 4 tablespoons brown sugar
- 1.5 cups ricotta cheese

Direction

- Preheat oven to 350 degrees F.
- Mix graham crackers and butter in a bowl until well blended.
- Transfer this mixture into a greased small or medium sized baking pan and press it down as this will serve as the base of our apple ricotta pie.
- Add apples, brown sugar and butter to a medium sized pan and cook over medium heat for about 7 minutes or until apples are slightly tender.
- Pour the apple mixture into the baking pan, over the graham cracker and butter base. Spread it out evenly.
- Put dollops of ricotta cheese on the top of the apple mixture.
- Bake in the oven for about 15 minutes and until the ricotta cheese is melted.
- Serve warm.

18. Apple And Goat Cheese Pizza

Serving: Makes 1 pizza | Prep: | Cook: | Ready in:

Ingredients

- 1 thin pizza dough
- 5-6 Granny Smith apples
- 1 clove of garlic
- 2 tablespoons walnut oil
- Parmesan shavings
- 4-5 tablespoons slices of fresh basil
- Salt and pepper

Direction

- Preheat oven to 400-425F
- Peel and cut the garlic. Heat walnut oil in a frying pan and fry the garlic for 5 minutes on low heat. Set aside
- Cut the apple into thin slices and crumble the goat cheese
- Roll out the pizza dough and transfer it a baking tray. Spread the garlic-olive oil sauce on the dough. Lay the apples on top and season to taste. Top with goat cheese and parmesan shavings.
- Bake for approx. 20 minutes. 5 minutes before the end sprinkle crumbled walnuts on top of the pizza. Be careful not to burn. Take out of the oven and top with fresh basil
- Serve with a side salad, such as spinach and arugula

19. Apple, Apple Butter And Cheese Crostata

Serving: Serves 8 | Prep: | Cook: | Ready in:

Ingredients

- pasta frolla (tart crust)
- 1/3 cup superfine sugar (or 1/2 cup powdered sugar)
- 1/2 cup unbleached all-purpose (regular) flour
- 1/2 cup whole-wheat pastry flour
- 1/4 cup almond meal
- 1/4 cup whole-grain barley flour or AP flour
- 3 ounces (6 tablespoons) cold unsalted butter, cut into small pieces
- 1 large egg, lightly beaten
- 1/4 teaspoon vanilla extract
- 1 pinch salt
- tart filling
- 1/2 cup [homemade] low-sugar apple butter
- 2 or 3 Stayman-Winesap apples (or other kind), thinly sliced using a mandoline
- 1/2 cup freshly grated [homemade] Cheshire cheese or Cheddar cheese

Direction

- Put sugar, flour, and salt in the bowl of the food processor and pulse a few times to mix.
- Add butter and pulse a few times until the mixture has the consistency of coarse meal.
- Empty food processor's bowl onto your work surface.
- Make a well in the center of the mounded flour and butter mixture and pour the beaten egg and vanilla extract into it.
- Use a fork to incorporate the liquid into the solid ingredients then use your fingertips.
- Knead lightly just until the dough comes together into a ball.
- Shape the dough into a flat disk and wrap in plastic wrap. Place the dough in the refrigerator and chill for at least two hours. You can refrigerate the dough overnight.
- When ready to make the crostata, heat the oven to 350°F [180°C]
- To help roll the pasta frolla, keep it on top of the plastic wrap that you had it wrapped in. This can also help when transferring the dough to your tart pan. You can also use parchment paper or you can roll the dough directly on a work surface.
- If the dough is very firm, start by pressing the dough with the rolling pin from the middle to each end, moving the rolling pin by a pin's width each time; turn the dough 90 degrees and repeat; when it softens, start rolling.
- Roll the dough into a circle about 1/8th inch (3 mm) thick.

- If you used the plastic wrap or parchment paper as rolling surface, flip dough over a 9 or 9.5-inch [23-24 cm] fluted round tart pan with removable bottom, about 1 inch [2.5 cm] high, centering it. Delicately press it all around so the corners are well covered. Peel away the plastic wrap.
- Trim the excess dough hanging over the edges of the pan. Press the remaining dough around the border into the sides of the pan making sure the border is an even thickness all the way around.
- Prick the bottom of the dough with a fork in several places.
- Distribute apple butter evenly over the pasta frolla.
- Make a layer of apples over the apple butter.
- Distribute cheese evenly over apples.
- Make a layer of apples over the cheese.
- Put the tart in the oven and bake for 35 minutes.
- After 35 minutes, check the tart, and continue baking (checking frequently) until the tart is of a nice golden hue (45 minutes or so, depending on the oven).
- When done, remove the tart from the oven and let cool slightly on a rack. If you have used a tart pan with a removable bottom, then release the tart base from the fluted tart ring.

- 1/4 -1/2 cups red walnut halves, broken into pieces
- 1 shallot, finely minced
- 1/4 cup grapeseed oil
- 3 tablespoons Meyer lemon olive oil
- 1 1/2 tablespoons honey
- 1 tablespoon Champagne vinegar
- 1/4 teaspoon honey mustard
- Salt and white pepper to taste
- 3 tablespoons pear nectar
- 1/2 pear, small dice
- crumbled Gorgonzola

Direction

- All of the salad ingredients can be prepared ahead of time, the pears being the exception and with all of the solutions for keeping them from turning them brown, I don't bother and slice them and add just before plating. The dressing is prepared ahead of time, even a day before, but keep refrigerated.
- The dressing ingredients: shallot, oils, honey, honey mustard, Champagne vinegar, nectar, and salt and pepper, whisk together and toss in the diced pear, refrigerate. Drizzle over individual salads or add some to a large bowl of salad, try not to over dress. The dressing makes about 2/3 of a cup. Top with crumbled gorgonzola.

20. Arugula And Spinach With Pears, Red Walnuts + Pear Dressing

Serving: Serves 4-6 | Prep: | Cook: | Ready in:

Ingredients

- 12 ounces clean spinach
- 6-8 ounces clean arugula
- 1-2 pears thinly sliced
- 4-6 fresh strawberries, sliced
- 1/4 red onion, thinly sliced

21. Asparagus, Egg And Roasted Tomato Salad With Pine Nuts

Serving: Serves 2 | Prep: | Cook: | Ready in:

Ingredients

- 1/2 bunch Asparagus, washed and trimmed
- 1/3 cup Roasted Tomatoes in Olive Oil
- 2 Eggs, Extra Large
- 6 tablespoons Olive Oil, Extra Virgin, Fruity
- 1 teaspoon Dill Weed, Dried
- Salt & Freshly Ground Pepper

Direction

- Pre-cook the asparagus just a little. I put mine in a microwave steamer, sprinkle with dried dill weed and steam for 4 minutes for thin asparagus.
- Use medium low heat to heat two sauté pans side by side on your stove with 1 - 2 Tbsp. of olive oil in each.
- In one sauté pan, add the asparagus, oven-roasted tomatoes in olive oil, pine nuts, salt and pepper. Toss to coat, turning occasionally
- In the second sauté pan, carefully pour in your two eggs making sure to keep the yolks intact. You want to end up with two separate eggs cooked over-medium or sunny side up. Toss the ingredients in the first pan at least a couple of times while the eggs cook.
- Divide the asparagus mixture and place on two plates. Place one egg on top of the asparagus mixture of each plate. Voila. The important thing about this dish is to be ready to sit down and eat once the food has been plated as it will cool quickly.

22. Austrian Almond Strietzel

Serving: Makes 4 | Prep: | Cook: | Ready in:

Ingredients

- 1000 grams Smooth Wheat Flour
- 0.5 liters Milk
- 3-4 Eggs
- 100 Butter
- 6 tablespoons Brown Sugar
- 21 grams Yeast
- Pulp of a Vanilla Pod (Only a small amount)
- Lemon Zest
- 2 extra Eggs
- Whole Almonds

Direction

- Warm up the milk together with the brown sugar and the yeast and when the sugar has melted let it cool down to room temperature. Put the correct amount of butter on a small plate and let it get soft.
- Weight the flour in a big bowl and add the mixture of milk, yeast and sugar first. When slightly blended, add the eggs, the lemon zest, the vanilla and the butter.
- Beat it up very well with a wooden spoon, it will be a very sticky dough. When the dough starts to loosen from the bowl and get very homogeneous, you have done it correctly. This takes some time so don't get worried. The longer you beat the dough the softer it will get.
- Now you put the bowl with the dough in a plastic bag, suck the air out and close it. Leave it on a warm spot until the dough has doubled its volume. This might take between 1 and 2 hours. I you have doubt, leave it a bit longer.
- After the dough has raised, put it out of the bowl on a floured surface and beat it up again with your hands but don't overdo it (10 seconds). Cut the dough into 4 equal parts, respectively 12 equal parts.
- Now take 3 parts and roll them out with your hands to a long "cylinder". All of those 3 parts should be approximately same in size and thickness. Align them next to each other and connect the 3 parts at one end. Now start to plaid those 3 parts. When finished connect them on the other end and put the plate on a baking tray with a baking sheet. You can squeeze the plate to adjust the length and thickness a little pad, but again don't overdo it. Continue with the other parts of the dough until you have 4 equal plaits.
- When the dough plaits increased, remove the towel and beat up the extra eggs. Spread them evenly on the dough plaits. Then you can softly stick the almonds into the dough plaids.
- That's it. Put the baking trays with the dough plaits into the oven and let them bake for about 20-25 minutes. They should get golden, brownish. You can test if they are done if you stick a thin and long knife into the plates and when pulled out, nothing stays on the blade.

Let them rest until cooled out and enjoy a perfect "Strietzel".

23. Avocado, Fried Egg And Gruyere On Country Bread

Serving: Serves 1 | Prep: | Cook: | Ready in:

Ingredients

- 1 dash Extra Virgin Olive Oil
- 1 pinch Coarse Salt and Fresh Ground Pepper
- 1 large Egg
- 2 pieces Country Bread
- 1 drop Dijon Mustard
- 2 pieces Guyere Cheese
- 1 bunch Arugula
- 1 ripe Avocado

Direction

- Rub a medium large pan in extra virgin olive oil and warm on medium heat. Pan fry your egg sunny side up and crispy around the edges seasoning with a small pinch of coarse salt and freshly ground pepper. Using the same pan toast the first side of your bread until brown. Flip and spread a thin layer of Dijon on one piece country bread and a layer of Gruyere cheese on the other piece. Once cheese is melted remove from heat and layer with arugula, sliced avocado and fried egg.

24. Baby Beet & Basil Spread

Serving: Serves 4 | Prep: | Cook: | Ready in:

Ingredients

- 20 Baby Beets
- 20 Fresh Basil Leaves
- 2 ounces Cream Cheese
- 2 tablespoons Lime Juice
- 1 teaspoon Salt
- 1/4 cup Grated Parmesan Cheese
- 1/2 teaspoon Pepper
- 4 pieces Rustic French Bread

Direction

- Boil baby beets until fork tender. Allow beets to cool then peel skin off.
- Place beets, 15 fresh basil leaves, cream cheese, lime juice, salt and pepper into food processor and pulse until somewhat smooth consistency.
- Toast or grill French bread.
- Smear each slice of bread with prepared Baby Beet & Basil Spread. Sprinkle with Parmesan cheese and left over chopped basil. Garnish with a sprig of more fresh basil and enjoy!

25. Baby Greens Greek Salad With Anchovy Crumbs

Serving: Makes 4 side salads | Prep: -1hours55mins | Cook: -1hours55mins | Ready in:

Ingredients

- For the lemon vinaigrette
- 1 clove garlic put through a garlic press or very finely minced
- 1 teaspoon dried oregano
- 3 tablespoons fresh lemon juice
- 1 teaspoon salt
- 1/2 teaspoon black pepper
- 1/2 teaspoon granulated sugar
- 1/3 cup extra virgin olive oil
- For the anchovy crumbs and salad
- 3 cups large fresh bread crumbs(I tore apart one half of a 12 inch baguette with my hands to make "large" pieces)
- 1/4 cup extra virgin olive oil
- 5   minced anchovy filets
- 6 cups dark green baby greens (spinach, kale or chard) or a combination
- 3/4 cup sliced red onion
- 3/4 cup small kalamata olives

- 1 cup grape tomatoes, halved
- 3/4 cup crumbled feta cheese
- The previously made vinaigrette

Direction

- For the lemon vinaigrette
- Whisk together the garlic, oregano, lemon juice, salt, pepper and sugar. Slowly stream in the olive oil while whisking constantly. Set the dressing aside.
- For the anchovy crumbs and salad
- In a large skillet over medium heat warm the olive oil and the minced anchovies and heat while stirring until the anchovies seem to disintegrate into the oil. Add the bread crumbs and continue to stir over the heat to thoroughly coat the crumbs and saute until the crumbs brown up. (Be careful not to burn them!) Once done, set aside.
- In a large salad bowl, combine the greens, onion, tomatoes, olives and Feta. Dress the salad with some or all of the vinaigrette.
- Divide the salad on to 4 serving plates and top each with as many of the anchovy crumbs as you like.

26. Bacon Cheddar Loaded Mashed Potatoes

Serving: Serves 4-6 | Prep: | Cook: |Ready in:

Ingredients

- 5 pounds Red potatoes
- 1 (12oz) can   Evaporated Milk
- 1/2 (16oz)   French Onion Dip
- 4 tablespoons Butter
- 1 packet Ranch dip
- 1 (16oz)   Sour cream
- 1/2 - 1 cups Whole Milk
- 2 cups Cheddar cheese
- 5-6 pieces Bacon strips
- 1/2 cup Cheddar cheese (for topping)
- Pinch Salt and pepper, to taste

Direction

- In a large stock pot, fill half way up with water and bring to a boil. Once at a boil, toss your potatoes in and let simmer until fork tender, about 30 – 45 minutes depending on the size and inner angst of your potatoes. After tender, drain potatoes.
- Preheat your oven to 350°F (182°C). Continue by mashing the potatoes, destroying all their hopes and dreams of a better life. After you have brutally destroyed your potatoes future, add the evaporated milk, French onion dip, butter, ranch, sour cream, milk, cheddar cheese, and bacon. Mix well to combine. Add salt and pepper to taste.
- Transfer your mashed potatoes to an oven safe dish. Sprinkle on the rest of the cheese. Bake at 350°F for 45 minutes to 1 hour, or until the cheese is melted and bubbly

27. Baked Bean And Cheese Burritos

Serving: Makes 6 burritos | Prep: 0hours10mins | Cook: 0hours15mins |Ready in:

Ingredients

- 6 tortillas
- 16 ounces refried beans
- 2 cups shredded sharp cheddar cheese
- 1 cup shredded rotisserie chicken, optional

Direction

- Preheat oven to 420 degrees.
- Line a baking sheet with foil. Spray baking sheet with nonstick spray.
- Place a tortilla on a plate. Scoop ¼ cup refried beans in closer towards one end of the tortilla. Add 4 pieces of chopped chicken - if using. Top with a handful of cheese - about ⅓ cup.
- Fold up like a burrito. Place seam side down. Spray the top with non-stick spray.

- Place in oven. Bake for about 7 minutes or until the bottom is crispy. Flip and continue baking for about 7 minutes or until crispy.

28. Baked Feta Cheese With Sun Dried Tomato And Capers

Serving: Serves 4 | Prep: | Cook: |Ready in:

Ingredients

- Sun dried tomato, oregano and thyme paste
- 1 cup sun dried tomatoes (the kind that need to be rehydrated before using)
- 1/2 cup olive oil
- 8 sprigs thyme, leaves picked and chopped
- 6 sprigs oregano, leaves picked and chopped
- salt and pepper to season
- Feta cheese
- 1 block of feta cheese
- 1 quantity of sun dried, oregano and thyme paste
- 2 tablespoons capers
- 1-2 sprigs thyme, leaves picked
- 1 sprig oregano, leaves picked and chopped roughly.
- crusty sourdough bread to serve

Direction

- Sun dried tomato, oregano and thyme paste
- Rehydrate your sun dried tomatoes by covering with boiling water and leaving to soak for about 20 minutes.
- Drain the sun dried tomatoes and pat dry. Use a hand held blender to blitz the sun dried tomatoes and olive oil to a smooth paste. When ready stir through the herbs and season to taste. (This can also be used as a marinade, spread, dip or to add extra flavor to pasta sauces- it will keep for 2 weeks refrigerated in an airtight jar.)
- Note: If you are using sun dried tomatoes that have been preserved in oil, use the oil from the jar rather than olive oil- it will give added flavor. You may not need the same quantity of oil, so start with a 1/4 cup. You are looking for a thick paste consistency.
- Feta cheese
- Lay a large piece of baking parchment on a flat surface. Spread 1/4 of the sun dried tomato paste in the center and place the block of feta cheese on top. Cover with 1/2 the remaining sun dried tomato paste (reserving some for later)
- Sprinkle with the extra herbs and a little olive oil, and wrap well with the baking parchment.
- Bake in a preheated oven (180'C, 350'F, gas mark 4) for 15 minutes.
- When ready, remove from the oven and tear away enough parchment to expose the cheese, making sure there is enough left to hold in all of the juices. Sprinkle with the capers and serve straight away with crusty bread and remaining sun dried tomato paste.

29. Balsamic Goat Cheese Stuffed Chicken Breast

Serving: Serves 2 | Prep: | Cook: |Ready in:

Ingredients

- 2 semi-thick chicken breasts (no skin)
- 4 teaspoons goat cheese (french)
- 2 tablespoons quality aged-balsamic vinegar
- salt to taste
- 1 tablespoon freshly shredded mozzarella cheese
- 1 dash fresh chopped chives
- 2 teaspoons Butter
- 1 tablespoon dry white wine
- 1/2 cup Baby Arugula
- 1/2 cup Romain
- 3 tablespoons dried cranberries
- 1 tablespoon oil and vinegar dressing mixture

Direction

- Begin, by slitting small line down each chicken breast with knife. About (1/2 the deepness through the chicken breast). Use fingers to separate the slit to form a well.
- Stuff each well with 2 tsp. goat cheese each. Salt the breasts to taste.
- Add the chicken breasts to pan along with the balsamic vinegar. Sauté until begins to appear white on side facing up. Add the butter and chives then flip.
- Allow about 5 minutes to cook. Deglaze the pan with wine scrapping bits of the bottom of pan. Cook a minute longer. Remove from heat and let stand for a few minutes prior to platting.
- Meanwhile loosely chop the greens and toss with the oil and vinegar dressing. Add the cranberries and toss.
- Season salad with salt, pepper, lemon zest, and goat cheese crumbled
- Place salad onto plate rounded out. Using a ladle form a well in center of salad. Place chicken over well and grate mozzarella on top.

30. Banana Gingerbread & Sweet Lime Frosting

Serving: Serves 12 | Prep: | Cook: |Ready in:

Ingredients

- Banana Ginger Bread
- 4 large bananas
- 0/5 tablespoon Stevia powder or 150g sugar (I used stevia, but in case of choosing sugar, reduce quantity of bananas to 2)
- 125 g butter
- 2 eggs
- 60 milliliters half & half cream
- 250 g flour (I used a mix of oat & corn flours)
- 2 teaspoons ground ginger
- 1 1/2 teaspoons cinnamon
- 1/2 teaspoon all spice
- 1/2 teaspoon ground clove
- 1 1/4 teaspoons Baking soda
- 1/4 teaspoon Sea salt
- Awesome Lime Frosting
- 100 g light cream cheese
- 30 milliliters half & half cream
- 60 g coconut sugar
- Zest & juice of 1 big lime

Direction

- Puree bananas. Beat eggs.
- Add cream, bananas and eggs to all the mixed dry ingredients. Stir well.
- Bake for 30 min @ 180°
- For the frosting simply beat all the ingredients until smooth paste. Let the bread cool down and cover.

31. Banana Pudding

Serving: Serves 8 | Prep: | Cook: |Ready in:

Ingredients

- 2/3 cup Sugar
- 1/3 cup Flour
- 1/2 teaspoon Salt
- 4 Egg Yolks
- 2 cups Half n Half
- 2 tablespoons Butter
- 1 teaspoon Vanilla
- 1 Banana
- 20-30 Nilla Wafers

Direction

- Mix 1st 3 ingredients (Dry)
- Mix egg & Half n Half (Wet)
- Mix Dry and Wet Together
- Heat mixture over Med-Hi heat (stirring continuously until thick)
- Remove Pudding from heat & add butter and vanilla. Mix to incorporate.
- Layer in serving dish: Wafers, Bananas, Pudding (x2)

- For an over the top experience: Beat the egg whites with 1/2 tsp Cr o Tarter, vanilla and 4 TBSP sugar, Top the pudding and bake in the Oven at 425 till meringue is brown!

32. Banana Yogurt Brownies

Serving: Makes 9 brownies | Prep: | Cook: |Ready in:

Ingredients

- 1 banana
- 1 cup yogurt
- 1 cup oat flour
- 1 tablespoon baking powder

Direction

- Preheat your oven to 180°C (350°F).
- Mash the banana in a large bowl using a potato masher or just a fork.
- Add the yogurt and the cocoa powder and mix well.
- Mix the baking powder with the oat flour and start adding it little by little while mixing well.
- Pour the mixture into a baking tray covered with baking paper. Decorate with some pecans or a few slices of banana. Bake for 30-40 minutes. Check the cake with a toothpick after 30 minutes; if it comes out clean, it's ready. Let it cool down before serving. It's great with a scoop of ice cream on top!

33. Basil Corn Cream & Goat Cheese Bake

Serving: Serves 4 | Prep: | Cook: |Ready in:

Ingredients

- 1 tablespoon butter
- 1/2 onion, finely chopped
- 1/2 teaspoon paprika
- 1/4 cup white wine
- 2 ears of corn
- 3/4 cup chicken broth
- 1/4 cup instant corn meal
- 1/4 cup whipping cream
- 1/8 teaspoon salt
- Dash freshly ground black pepper
- 1/4 teaspoon red chili flakes
- 1/4 cup black olives, finely chopped
- 1/4 cup fresh basil leaves, finely chopped
- 1/4 cup goat cheese, crumbled

Direction

- in a medium saucepan melt butter over medium heat, add chopped onion and paprika and cook for 3-5 minutes or until onion is soft
- add wine and cook 2 minutes; in the meantime cut kernels off the cobs, then add them to the pan and continue cooking for another 5 minutes
- Add chicken broth and cook on low heat for 15 minutes
- Remove from heat, pour into a food processor bowl and process until fairly creamy; return to pan on low heat
- Add instant corn meal and cook 1 minute, then add cream, salt and pepper and chili flakes and cook 3 minutes longer
- Remove from heat, add olives and basil and mix to blend ingredients
- Preheat oven to 400F; spoon cream into 4 individual small ramekins and top with crumbled goat cheese
- Bake for about 12 minutes or until cheese is golden, serve immediately

34. Basil, Mozzarella And Tomatoes

Serving: Serves 4 | Prep: | Cook: |Ready in:

Ingredients

- 2 Ripe tomatoes
- 1 pound Fresh Mozzarella

- 3-4 tablespoons Extra Virgin Olive Oil
- 1 pinch Sea Salt
- 1 bunch Fresh Basil

Direction

- Slice Tomatoes about 1/2 inch thick
- Slice mozzarella about 1/2 inch thick
- Arrange tomatoes and mozzarella slices and basil leaves on a serving plate in a circular manner. Alternate one slice of mozzarella, one slice of mozzarella and one basil leaf.
- Drizzle olive oil over tomatoes, mozzarella and basil.
- Sprinkle sea salt to taste.
- Garnish center with basil leaves.
- Note: Tomatoes must be fresh and either homegrown, vine ripe, heirloom or if you can all three. The tomatoes and mozzarella should be at room temperature and not taken directly from fridge. Use the best olive oil you can find.

35. Bay (or Rosemary) Scented Ricotta Infornata

Serving: Makes 1 | Prep: | Cook: |Ready in:

Ingredients

- 1 pound Fresh Whole Milk Ricotta Cheese (preferably homemade and with some heavy cream added to the whole milk- 1 cup cream to 4 cups milk)
- Fresh Bay Leaves or Rosemary, enough to cover the bottom of a small baking dish
- Coarse Salt
- Freshly Ground Black Pepper, optional
- Extra Virgin Olive Oil, enough to oil a small baking dish and coat the cheese

Direction

- Taste the ricotta, add a little salt if needed. Strain the ricotta in a mesh strainer in the refrigerator for 24-36 hours. The strainer is going to mold the cheese so use one that will give the depth of the strained cheese about 1.5-2 inches. A firm, dry ricotta is desired.
- Pre-heat oven to 350 degrees. Generously oil the bottom and sides of a shallow baking dish that is slightly larger than the diameter of the mesh strainer. Line the baking dish with either the fresh bay leaves or rosemary. Unmold the ricotta into the baking dish (invert the strainer onto the baking dish).Oil the cheese and sprinkle the top generously with coarse salt, and pepper (if desired)
- Bake for 1-1.5 hours until very nicely browned. Cool on a wire rack. Unmold after cooling.

36. Bean Soup (zuppa Di Fagioli) Toscana, Primo (First Course)

Serving: Serves 6 | Prep: | Cook: |Ready in:

Ingredients

- 300 grams dried cannellini beans
- 60 milliliters extra-virgin olive oil, plus extra for drizzling
- 1 onion, peeled and finely chopped
- 3 garlic cloves, 2 finely chopped and one bruised
- 2 carrots, rinsed, peeled, ends removed and finely chopped
- 2 celery ribs, rinsed, ends removed and finely chopped
- 4 sage leaves
- 10 grams grams ham or prosciutto fat or lardo, finely chopped (can substitute 20 mls olive oil)
- 1.5 liters vegetable stock or water
- 100 milliliters tomato sauce or 2 medium tomatoes rinsed, seeds removed and coarsely chopped
- 20 grams flat leaf parsley, rinsed and finely chopped
- 1 branch of rosemary, rinsed, leaves removed and finely chopped

- 300 grams cavolo nero, rinsed and sliced
- 30 grams Parmigiano-Reggiano cheese, finely grated
- 1 spring onion, rinsed, end removed and finely sliced
- sea salt
- freshly ground black pepper
- 6 slices grilled bread

Direction

- Soak the beans in cold water to cover by 5 cm overnight (minimum
- Drain the beans and place in a stockpot covered with fresh cold water by 5 cm. Add 10 grams of salt to the beans. Heat the pot over medium heat until it begins to simmer and then reduce the heat to low and cover. Let the beans cook for 1.5 to 2 hours until tender but not falling apart. Remove from the heat and let cool.
- Pour 30 mls of the olive oil into another stock pot and heat over medium heat. Add the onion, carrot, 2 cloves of minced garlic, celery, ham fat and sage and cook for 10-15 minutes, stirring occasionally until the vegetables have softened and begin to sweat.
- Add the water or stock to the pot. Remove a quarter of the whole beans with a slotted spoon and set aside. Place the rest of the beans and 300 mls of the cooking liquid in a food processor and blend until the beans have been pureed.
- Add the bean puree to the vegetables and then add the tomato sauce, rosemary, parsley, 5 grams of salt and black pepper to taste. Bring the mixture to a boil and reduce to a simmer. Let it cook for 3 hours, stirring occasionally. During the last 20 minutes of cooking, add the whole beans and taste the soup to adjust the salt and pepper if needed.
- In a frying pan, heat the remaining 30 mls of olive oil over medium heat.
- When the oil is hot add the cavolo nero with its washing water still attached. If there is not enough water, add 30 mls of water to the pan and cover.
- Cook for 10-15 minutes and taste to see if it is done.
- Ladle the soup into the serving bowls, top with the cavolo nero, a sprinkle of spring onions, 5 grams of the grated Parmigiano-Reggiano cheese, and drizzle olive oil over the top. Serve the soup with the grilled bread.
- Note: Eliminate the meat to make the dish Vegetarian.

37. Beet Crostata With A Pepper Parmesan Crust

Serving: Serves 6 | Prep: | Cook: |Ready in:

Ingredients

- Pepper-Parmesan Crust
- 1 cup all-purpose flour
- 1 teaspoon kosher salt
- 1 teaspoon pepper, freshly ground
- 2 tablespoons grated parmesan cheese
- 1/4 pound cold butter (1 stick), diced
- 2 tablespoons ice water
- Beet Filling
- 1 pound beets (any color/type)
- 1 garlic bulb
- extra virgin olive oil
- goat cheese
- walnuts, coarsely chopped
- salt and pepper
- 1/3 cup balsamic vinegar
- 1 egg, beaten

Direction

- Cut greens from beets. Rinse and dry beets. Then wrap in foil. Wrap garlic in foil after drizzling with olive oil. Bake beets and garlic at 350°F for 1 hour. Unwrap and let cool completely.
- For crust, put flour, salt, pepper, and parmesan in a food processor bowl fitted with a steel blade. Add the butter and pulse until the butter is the size of peas. With the motor

running, add the ice water while pulsing until just before the dough becomes a solid mass. Turn dough onto a floured surface and form into a disk. You can wrap with plastic and refrigerate while you prepare the filling.
- Preheat the oven to 400 degrees F.
- Reduce balsamic vinegar until it becomes syrupy (reduced to about 1/3). This happens pretty quick. Remove to small bowl.
- Remove peel from beets (they should easily slide off. You can peel directly into the foil and discard). Slice beets into rounds and set aside.
- Divide dough into 3 equal portions. Roll out one portion to ¼ in thick round about 6-8 inches in diameter. Transfer to a baking sheet.
- Cut roasted garlic bulbs cross-wise so each clove is halved. Squeeze out roasted garlic onto dough and spread around leaving a 1 in border. Sprinkle with salt and pepper.
- Arrange 1/3 of beets slices in a round on top of garlic. Generously tuck goat cheese and walnuts between slices. Sprinkle with salt.
- Drizzle with 1/3 of reduced balsamic vinegar. Finely grate a little orange rind evenly on top. Turn and pleat edges over toppings. Drizzle with olive oil.
- Brush dough with beaten egg. Bake at 400°F for 20-25 minutes until tops are golden brown. Let cool slightly.
- Drizzle with olive oil and serve. A squeeze of orange and/or a sprinkling of parmesan is nice too.

38. Beet, Pesto & Goat Cheese Flatbread With Basil & Dill { Whole Grain}

Serving: Makes 2 medium sized flatbreads | Prep: | Cook: | Ready in:

Ingredients

- Whole grain flatbread dough
- 1 1/4 cups Whole grain spelt flour
- 1/4 cup Millet Flour
- 1/4 cup Buckwheat Flour
- 1 tablespoon Quick drying yeast
- 1/2 cup Lukewarm water
- pinch   Sea Salt
- 2 tablespoons Olive Oil
- dusting   Organic cornmeal for rolling out the dough
- Toppings
- 3 tablespoons Pesto for each flatbread
- 1   decent chunk of soft local goat cheese
- 2 beets, steamed
- 1 bunch basil
- 1 handful chives, finely chopped
- 1 handful baby kale leaves (or other greens) per flatbread
- 1 pinch sea salt
- 1   drizzle balsamic crema (or regular balsamic) per flatbread
- 1   drizzle of good quality olive oil per flatbread

Direction

- Add the flours to a mixing bowl and blend well. Add the warm water to a bowl, and sprinkle in the yeast. Let the yeast proof for ten minutes, and then stir and add to the flour. Add one tablespoon of the olive oil. Add a pinch of sea salt, and start kneading. I kneaded for about five minutes. Add the remaining olive oil to the bowl and coat the inside of the bowl with it. Add the dough and cover with a dishtowel. Place the bowl somewhere warm for an hour or more.
- Preheat the oven to 350f.place the beets in a colander and steam until just tender (they should still have some texture). Once cooled, thinly slice and set aside. Sprinkle the cornmeal on a clean surface. Roll the dough out to desired thickness (I like mine really thin, and this makes a really crunchy crust if rolled out very thin). Spoon some pesto on top. Cut the goat cheese into thick slices, and spread out on the pesto. Place the beets in between the cheese. Place in the oven at 350f for fifteen minutes, or until the crust is golden

brown and the cheese has melted a bit. Once the flatbread is out of the oven sprinkle the chives, dill and basil on top. Add the baby kale leaves (pile them on!) drizzle some balsamic crema and the really, really good olive oil (seriously, buy the best you can afford. it really does make a world of difference) on top. Enjoy!

39. Beetroot Orange Ice Cream

Serving: Serves 3 | Prep: | Cook: | Ready in:

Ingredients

- 200 milliliters whole milk
- 200 milliliters heavy cream
- 85 grams sugar
- 1 pinch salt
- 3 teaspoons cornstarch
- 50 grams cream cheese
- 1 tablespoon agave syrup
- 1 orange
- 1 small beetroot

Direction

- Wrap 1 small washed beetroot in foil and bake for 1 hour at 375F. Remove from the oven, cool to room temperature.
- Peel the beetroot, cut it in small chunks and whizz in a blender until very finely ground. Measure out ½ cup of the beet mixture (you won't need the leftovers) and whizz in a blender once again but this time with a small addition of milk until purée like.
- Dissolve the cornstarch in 50ml whole milk, leave to rest.
- In a small saucepan combine the leftover whole milk, the heavy cream, sugar, agave syrup, pinch of salt and zest of 1 orange, mix, heat until boiling. Take off heat, cover with a lid and leave to rest for 10min. Strain through a sieve, return the mixture into the saucepan, heat once again until almost boiling. Add the cornstarch milk and cook on medium stirring constantly until thickened. Take off heat, mix in 50gr cream cheese and the beet purée until smooth and combined. Cool to room temperature and if willing whizz the custard in a blender once again for a smoother texture. Transfer to the fridge overnight.
- Freeze in your ice cream maker according to the manufacturer's instructions. Store in an airtight container in the freezer or spoon right away. Pair with a dark chocolate beetroot ice cream.

40. Best Chilaquiles With Roasted Tomatillo Salsa And Poblanos (and With Turkey Leftovers)

Serving: Serves 4 | Prep: | Cook: | Ready in:

Ingredients

- Chilaquiles
- 2.5-3 cups of shredded turkey leftovers (or chicken on any other time of the year)
- Cup of tomatillo salsa (recipe to follow)
- 8-10 yellow corn tortillas
- 3 oz of semi-soft yellow cheese that melt well, like mild cheddar, caciocavallo or Kasseri (just make sure you use a good one), shredded
- About 6 oz of queso fresco crumbled
- 2 poblano peppers
- Tomatillo Salsa - about a cup
- 10 tomatillos
- 1/2 a bunch of cilantro
- 1 big clove of garlic
- 1 jalapeno pepper
- 3 tablespoons of lime juice
- 1 tablespoon of oil
- 1/2 teaspoon of salt
- 1/8 teaspoon of black pepper
- Optional - 1/8 of a cup of water to thin it out a bit

Direction

- Chilaquiles
- Roast the poblanos: I char their skin on open stove flam, few minutes on each side until they look burned. Put them in a closed plastic bag for about 10-15 minutes. Then the skin will come of easily. Do not wash them to take the skin off to keep the smoky taste. You can also char them under the broiler, but watch them closely. Discard the seeds as well. Cut to small-medium cubes.
- Mix the poblanos with the shredded chicken.
- Put 2 tablespoons of the tomatillo salsa in the bottom of a squared dish (8 1/4" x 8 1/4"). Top it with tortillas (half them and use the straight part around the sides. About 2 1/2 tortillas for one layer).
- Spread 3 tablespoons of the salsa on the tortilla layer. Put on top half of the chicken and the poblano mixture. Scatter the 1/3 of the crumbled queso fresco on top and 1/3 of the shredded cheese.
- Repeat: layer of tortillas, salsa, chicken and cheese. Finish with a layer of tortillas, salsa and cheese.
- Bake in 360 degree oven for 20-25 minutes, until has a bit of color at top.
- Serve with pico de gallo, some of the tomatillo salsa and a dollop of sour cream.
- Tomatillo Salsa - about a cup
- Discard the tomatillos husks and wash them well. Cut the tomatillos to halves. Put them in a baking sheet and drizzle a bit of oil and salt. Bake in 400 degree oven for 25-30 minutes. Let them cool a bit.
- Chop the garlic. Discard the jalapeno seeds and cut to medium pieces.
- Put in a food processor the roasted tomatillos, garlic, jalapeno, cilantro, salt and pepper and process until you get a pretty smooth salsa.
- Put in a bowl and mix in the lime juice and oil. Taste for salt.
- (If you use it for the Chilaquiles and the salsa is pretty thick add water to thin it out a bit, so it will be more spreadable).

41. Best Stuffed Peppers

Serving: Makes 8 | Prep: 0hours10mins | Cook: 1hours0mins | Ready in:

Ingredients

- 4 large bell peppers, gutted and halved
- 1 tablespoon canola oil
- 1 teaspoon onion powder
- 1 teaspoon garlic powder
- 1 teaspoon kosher or sea salt
- 1 teaspoon ground black pepper
- 1 pound ground meat (turkey, chicken, or beef)
- 1 pound sweet longanisa sausage (can use honey garlic, or any sweet sausage, as a substitute)
- 2 cloves of garlic, minced
- 1 cup diced mushrooms, drained
- 1 cup mushrooms, diced
- 1 cup tomato sauce
- 1 cup Minute Rice
- 1 cup mozzarella cheese, shredded
- 1/4 cup parmesan cheese, grated
- Fresh parsley for garnish

Direction

- Heat grill on high heat.
- Place halved peppers on grill and grill until slightly charred with grill marks - approx. 5 minutes a side.
- Remove from grill and place on a plate. Set aside.
- In a large skillet, heat cooking oil.
- Add minced garlic and sauté until fragrant; make sure not to brown the garlic.
- Add the ground beef (or chicken/turkey) and the sausage. (If the sausage was in casing, make sure you squeeze it out of its casing).
- Add the onion powder, garlic powder, sea salt and ground black pepper.
- Stir well until meat is cooked.
- Add mushrooms, diced tomatoes, tomato sauce, and Minute Rice.

- Bring the heat to high until mixture reaches a simmer, and then bring the heat to low. Allow to simmer for approx. 5 minutes.
- Remove from heat and add 1 cup of shredded mozzarella cheese. Mix well and set aside.
- Pre-heat oven to 375F.
- With a tablespoon, carefully scoop the meat mixture into the peppers.
- Pack the peppers as much as you can and press down on the mixture to secure.
- Sprinkle each pepper with the remaining shredded mozzarella.
- Finish off by sprinkling each pepper with shredded parmesan.
- Place the peppers in the oven for approx. 15 minutes or until the mozzarella cheese melts and bubbles.
- Turn the broiler on to high heat and place the peppers under the broiler for approx. 2 minutes, or until cheese browns slightly.
- Garnish with fresh flat leaf parsley and serve.

42. Big Green Wheatberry Salad

Serving: Serves 2 | Prep: | Cook: | Ready in:

Ingredients

- Salad
- 2 cups Spinach
- 1 Carrot
- 1/2 Cucumber, halved and sliced
- 1/2 Avocado, diced
- 1/4 cup Crumbled feta cheese
- 1/4 cup Chopped fresh parsley or cilantro
- 1/2 cup Cooked wheatberries
- Citrus Dressing
- 1 Lemon, juiced
- 1.5 tablespoons Olive Oil
- 1 teaspoon Dijon Mustard
- Salt and Pepper, to taste

Direction

- Cook the wheat berries according to package instructions.
- Make the dressing by whisking together all the ingredients in a bowl. Set aside.
- Assemble the salads by dividing the spinach and filling 2 bowls.
- Shave the carrot into the bowls using a vegetable peeler. Add the diced cucumber and avocado. Top with crumbled feta cheese, chopped herbs, and cooked wheat berries.
- Split the dressing between the two salads. Enjoy!

43. Black Pepper And Parmesan Panna Cotta

Serving: Serves 4 | Prep: | Cook: | Ready in:

Ingredients

- 2 sheets gelatin
- 1 cup whole milk
- 1 cup heavy cream
- 1 cup grated Parmesan cheese
- Pinch freshly ground black pepper
- 3 to 4 tablespoons balsamic vinegar
- 1 tablespoon sugar
- 4 tablespoons olive oil, separated
- Handful cherry tomatoes, to serve
- Basil oil or premade basil pesto, to serve
- Pine nuts, to serve

Direction

- Bloom the gelatin sheets in a bowl of cold water while you make the base.
- Heat milk and cream in a saucepan. Bring it to boil, and mix in the Parmesan cheese and black pepper very thoroughly. Take the gelatin sheets (without the water) and add them in the hot mixture. Stir to combine completely.
- Pour this mixture into ramekins or glass cups. Place in the refrigerator to set, at least 5 hours or preferably overnight.

- Just before serving, assemble the garnishes: Prepare the balsamic reduction by heating balsamic vinegar with sugar until it reduces and looks thick.
- Cut cherry tomatoes in half. Toss them in 2 tablespoons of the olive oil and grill them in a grill pan until you see grill marks on them (or roast them in the oven for about half an hour at 350° F).
- You can serve the panna cotta with either premade basil pesto or with homemade basil oil: Process 1/4 cup of basil leaves with 2 tablespoons of olive oil. Process it in a way that it does not become a puree but is instead a coarse/rough mix. (You could also do this with a mortar and pestle.)
- To serve, spoon a little bit of basil pesto or oil on a plate. Unmold the panna cotta (directions below) and place it on it. Top it off with cherry tomatoes and drizzle some balsamic glaze on top of it. Garnish with pine nuts (or a Parmesan crisp!).
- To unmold the panna cotta, run a knife around the edges of the ramekins and then try to invert it on a plate before you place it on serving plate. I have found silicon muffin molds very useful for unmolding panna cotta. If you do not want to unmold them, you can serve them in small serving glasses and top off with the pesto, tomatoes, and glaze. Either way, it will taste great.

44. Black Sesame And White Chocolate Mousse Cake

Serving: Makes one 6-inch mousse cake | Prep: | Cook: | Ready in:

Ingredients

- For the sponge cake
- 35 grams all-purpose flour
- 15 grams corn starch
- 10 grams black sesame powder
- 2 large eggs
- 30 grams granulated sugar
- 30 grams whole milk
- 20 grams butter
- 1/2 teaspoon pure vanilla extract
- 1 pinch salt
- For the mousse layers
- 125 grams heavy cream
- 30 grams black sesame powder
- 1 large egg
- 20 grams granulated sugar
- 40 grams whole milk (for the sesame mousse)
- 25 grams whole milk (for the white chocolate mousse)
- 50 grams good quality white chocolate, chopped into small pieces
- 4 grams gelatin powder
- 1 tablespoon water (to soak gelatin)
- 1/2 teaspoon pure vanilla extract

Direction

- For the sponge cake
- Preheat the oven to 170°C (340°F). Line a 20-cm (8-inch) round cake pan with parchment paper.
- Sift the dry ingredients: flour, corn starch, and black sesame powder 2-3 times.
- Microwave butter and milk in a microwave-safe bowl for 20 seconds or until butter completely melts.
- Crack the eggs into a mixing bowl placed over a pot of simmering water, make sure the bottom of the bowl does not touch the water. Gradually add in sugar and beat the eggs with a hand mixer on high speed. Stop beating once the mixture becomes foamy and warm to touch. Take the bowl off the pot and place it on a tea towel on the countertop.
- With your mixer on high, continue to beat the egg. When it starts to thicken, turn speed to low and add salt and vanilla extract. Stop beating once the mixture thickens and forms ribbons.
- In 3 batches, gently fold the sifted dry ingredients into the egg mixture.

- Gradually drizzle the butter and milk mixture into the batter in a few batches. Quickly but gently fold it in with a spatula. Make sure you incorporate the milk and butter well with the batter for each batch before pouring in the next.
- Pour the batter into the prepared cake pan. Drop the pan a few times on the countertop to knock out any large air bubbles.
- Bake at 170°C (340°F) for 15-20 minutes. The cake is ready when a toothpick inserted into the center comes out clean.
- Remove the cake from the oven once it is done, and drop the pan from a height of 20 cm to prevent it from shrinking. When it is cool enough to handle, carefully turn the cake out (top down) onto a piece of plastic wrap. Remove the parchment paper. Wrap the cake in plastic wrap and let it cool at room temperature.
- When the cake has cooled completely, place a 6-inch round pan in the middle of the cake. Using a serrated knife, trace the bottom of the pan to cut out a circle. You should have a 15 cm x 1.60 cm (6" x 0.6") sponge cake layer. Place the sponge layer in the bottom of the 6-inch cake pan, flat side up. Gently press it down, so that you'll have a smooth surface for the mousse layers.
- For the mousse layers
- Whip the heavy cream in a mixing bowl until soft peaks form, mix in vanilla extract. Take out 75 grams of the cream and reserve it in a separate bowl for the white chocolate mousse. Now you have one bowl of 75 grams whipped cream and one bowl of 50 grams whipped cream. Chill both bowls in the fridge until ready to use. Label them if you want.
- Soak gelatin in 1 tablespoon of water. Separate the egg and reserve the white in a clean separate bowl for the chocolate mousse. We will be working with the yolk first.
- For the black sesame mousse: Whisk egg yolk with sugar until thick and pale.
- Mix sesame powder with 1 tablespoon of hot water. In a small saucepan, stir together the sesame mixture and 40 grams milk over low heat. When the mixture starts to bubble, remove from heat, stir in HALF of the soaked gelatin to dissolve.
- Slowly drizzle the hot sesame milk mixture into the egg in a thin stream while whisking continuously.
- Take out the 50 grams of whipped cream you have chilled in the fridge. Fold the sesame-egg mixture into the chilled whipped cream to combine. Pour this on top of the sponge cake layer and let chill in the fridge.
- For the white chocolate mousse: Heat the rest of the milk over low heat, once it starts to boil, turn off the heat and stir in the white chocolate chunks. Keep stirring until chocolate melts completely. Add the rest of soaked gelatin, stir to dissolve. If the gelatin does not dissolve, warm the mixture up a little bit. Be careful not burn the chocolate.
- Whip egg white until stiff peaks form.
- Take out the 75 grams of whipped cream you have chilled in the fridge. Fold the white chocolate mixture into the cream to combine. In 3 batches, fold the egg white into the chocolate-cream mixture, try not to break the foamy texture of the egg white.
- Take the chilled mousse out from the fridge and pour the white chocolate mousse directly on top. Return the mousse cake to the fridge again, let it chill for at least 2 hours.
- When the mousse cake has set, dust a little bit of black sesame powder on top if you want. Wrap a warm wet towel around the pan sides and hold for 20 seconds. Carefully remove the cake; smooth the mousse with a spatula if necessary. Cut and serve!

45. Blueberry Zucchini Lemon Cake

Serving: Serves 12-16 | Prep: | Cook: |Ready in:

Ingredients

- Cake
- 3 eggs
- 1 cup oil
- 2 1/4 cups sugar
- 1 tablespoon vanilla extract
- 1 lemon, juice and zest
- 2 cups shredded and drained zucchini
- 3 cups all-purpose flour
- 1 teaspoon salt
- 1 teaspoon baking powder
- 1/4 teaspoon baking soda
- 2 cups blueberries (tossed with 1 tablespoon flour)
- Frosting & Topping (optional)
- 8 ounces cream cheese, softened
- 1/2 cup butter, room temperature
- 3 1/2 cups powdered sugar
- 1 teaspoon vanilla extract
- 1 tablespoon lemon juice
- for candied zucchini (optional):
- 1 1/4 cups sugar
- 1 medium zucchini

Direction

- Cake
- Preheat oven to 350 degrees Fahrenheit. Grease and flour two 8-inch round cake pans.
- With an electric mixer, beat the eggs, oil, sugar, vanilla, lemon zest, and juice until blended. Fold in the zucchini.
- In a small bowl, whisk together the flour, salt, baking powder, and baking soda. Add the dry ingredients to the wet mixture in batches, mixing to blend. Gently fold in the blueberries. Divide the batter evenly between the cake pans.
- Bake 40-45 minutes or until a toothpick inserted in the center of a cake comes out clean. Cool in pans for 10 minutes then invert onto a wire rack to cool completely. Using a serrated knife cut off the cake dome. You want an even surface or your frosting is going to run right off the cake.
- Frosting & Topping (optional)
- Beat together the cream cheese and butter until smooth. Add powdered sugar, salt, vanilla, and lemon juice. Mix on low until sugar is well incorporated, then turn the mixer to high. Beat for 2-3 minutes then add more lemon juice if you'd like softer frosting.
- Candied zucchini. Slice zucchini lengthwise into thin strips using a mandolin slicer.
- In a small saucepan bring water and sugar to a boil, stirring until sugar dissolves. Add zucchini strips. Reduce heat to medium and simmer, until zucchini is translucent, 15 to 20 minutes. (Placing a round piece of parchment paper on top of zucchini will keep them submerged).Let zucchini cool in syrup. Arrange zucchini in a single layer on a wire rack set over a baking sheet. Let dry for 30-60 minutes.
- Layer the cakes and frosting then garnish with blueberries, candied zucchini, and lemon if desired.

46. Blueberry And Baked Ricotta Cheesecake

Serving: Makes 2 10 cm x 30 cm tarts or 1 round 9" inch cake | Prep: | Cook: |Ready in:

Ingredients

- For the crust
- 1/2 recipe Homemade Graham Crackers dough - by Martha Stewart
- 100 g unsalted butter, soft
- For the filling
- 2 cups creamy ricotta cheese
- 1 1/2 cups spreadable cream cheese
- 1/2 cup sugar
- 3 eggs
- 1 tablespoon lemon zest
- 1 teaspoon vanilla extract
- 1 cup blueberries
- 2 tablespoons assorted berry marmalade
- boiling water for the reduction

Direction

- For the crust
- Make the Homemade Graham Crackers dough according to the recipe, without cutting the dough into pieces
- Allow to cool. Cut into pieces and process the baked dough with the butter until well blended
- Butter and line a chosen baking tin and fill in with the dough, pressing it with your fingertips against the walls of the tin
- Refrigerate for 20 minutes
- For the filling
- In a bowl combine the creamy ricotta cheese, the cream cheese, sugar and lemon zest
- Add the eggs one by one and mix with a hand beater. Add the vanilla extract
- Pour the mixture over the dough in the baking tin
- Preheat the oven to 180 ° C / 350 ° F and bake for 40 minutes or until the filling is firm. Allow to cool on a rack
- Make a reduction with the marmalade and boiling water and stir gently over a low fire
- Glaze the blueberries in the sauce and pour on the cheesecake. Refrigerate
- Take out of the refrigerator a few minutes before serving

47. Boozy Beer Float (Peppered Honey Pear Ice Cream With Saison DuPont)

Serving: Makes 2 to 4 floats | Prep: | Cook: | Ready in:

Ingredients

- For the honey-pearl swirl:
- 10 grams freeze-dried pears, ground into a fine powder
- 55 grams honey
- 20 grams apple juice
- 10 grams turbinado sugar
- 25 grams toasted walnuts, chopped
- For the ice cream base and assembly:
- 5 grams corn starch or tapioca starch
- 220 grams whole milk, divided
- 225 grams cream
- 50 grams turbinado sugar
- 30 grams nonfat dry milk
- 20 grams corn syrup or tapioca syrup
- 4 to 5 turns black pepper, to taste
- Zest of one small orange
- 1 bottle Saison DuPont
- 1 orange peel, for garnish
- Nutmeg, for garnish (optional)

Direction

- For the honey-pearl swirl:
- Combine the freeze-dried pears, honey, apple juice, and sugar in a small sauce pan and whisk to combine. Bring the mixture to a simmer over medium heat, stirring with a rubber spatula until the sugar and pear powder have dissolved. Simmer until it reduces to a syrup, about 10 to 15 minutes, then stir in the walnuts and set it aside to cool.
- For the ice cream base and assembly:
- In a small bowl, whisk together the starch and 20 grams of the whole milk until smooth to make a starch slurry. Set aside.
- In a sauce pan, combine the remaining 200 grams of whole milk with the cream, sugar, nonfat dry milk, corn syrup, and pepper. Whisk vigorously until the dry ingredients are well-incorporated, then set it over medium heat. Prepare an ice bath for your finished mix.
- Bring the mixture to a boil, then lower it to a simmer for 4 to 5 minutes. Remove from the heat and add the starch slurry (you may need to whisk the slurry again prior to adding it to ensure the starch is still suspended in the milk and not stuck to the bottom of the bowl). Return the pan to heat and return to a simmer while stirring. After a few minutes, the mixture will begin to thicken.
- Once it starts to thicken, remove it from the heat and pour it into a bowl over your prepared ice bath — be careful that the ice bath doesn't overflow into the cream mixture. Blend well with an immersion blender and

- allow the mix to fully cool. Age in the refrigerator overnight, or for a minimum of four hours.
- Remove the mix from the refrigerator, add orange zest, and blend again with immersion blender. Pour into an ice cream machine and freeze according to manufacturer's instructions.
- Once frozen, alternate scoops of the ice cream base with the honeyed pear swirl into an airtight container. Freeze for another six hours or overnight.
- To build the floats, place two generous scoops of the ice cream in a tumbler. (I prefer low, wide rimmed tumblers as opposed to beer mugs or pint glasses. This allows a more equitable ice cream-to-beer ratio per bite or sip.) Because this beer is highly carbonated, tilt and pour a quarter to a half of the bottle gently down the side of the glass, allowing for a thick head to settle on top of the ice cream. You'll get a little beer volcano if you pour too aggressively. Repeat with 2 to 3 more glasses.
- Garnish with an orange peel and, if you're feeling spicy, a little grated nutmeg. Serve with a straw and a spoon, and enjoy!

48. Boozy Dark Chocolate Cookies N' Cream Ice Cream

Serving: Makes about 1.5 quarts | Prep: | Cook: | Ready in:

Ingredients

- 1 pint heavy whipping cream
- 1 cup whole milk
- 1/2 cup sugar
- 1/4 teaspoon good sea salt
- 8 ounces good dark chocolate, 60% cacao or higher (we recommend Valrhona or Woodblock)
- scant 1/8 teaspoons xantham gum
- 1 1/2 tablespoons bourbon or rye whiskey
- 10 Oreos, crumbled

Direction

- In a heavy bottomed 2-quart pan, heat cream, milk, sugar, and salt until simmers and the sugar and salt completely dissolve. Set aside, but move quickly. You need this mixture to be warm for the next step.
- Place chocolate into the bowl of a large food processor. Pulse until broken into small chunks, the smaller the better. Add 1 cup of the hot cream-milk mixture while the food processor is running. Blend until chocolate is melted, making a rich ganache.
- In a medium bowl, pour the rest of the cream-milk mixture. Add the ganache to the cream and whisk until fully incorporated. Add the whiskey. Add the xantham gum, and stir until dissolved. Chill mixture for at least 2 hours (or until cold) before churning.
- In your ice cream machine, churn the mixture for 25–30 minutes or until it thickens enough to stick to the churn or a spoon. Right before you stop churning, slowly add the cookies and churn for about a minute. Quickly transfer to a freezer-safe container. Cover with plastic wrap and the lid, and freeze until desired hardness is achieved. We recommend overnight, but this depends on how cold your freezer is.
- Scoop, then devour.

49. Breakfast Panini

Serving: Serves 4 | Prep: | Cook: | Ready in:

Ingredients

- Breakfast panini
- 8 thick slices of cinnamon swirl bread
- butter
- 8 tablespoons or so, mascarpone cheese
- 6 tablespoons apricot compote (or more if desired)
- Dried apricot compote

- 1 cup unsulphered, dried apricots, chopped
- 1/2 cup dried cherries (unsweetened)
- 1/2 teaspoon orange zest
- 3/4 cup apple juice
- 2 tablespoons sugar
- 1 teaspoon chopped candied ginger
- 1 tablespoon brandy (optional)

Direction

- Breakfast Panini
- Butter one side of each bread slice and place the bread buttered side down on a piece of wax paper or another nonstick surface.
- Spread two tablespoons of mascarpone on 4 of the bread slices leaving a decent size border between the cheese and the edge of the bread. Spread about a tablespoon and a half of the apricot spread on the other 4 slices, leaving a border on these as well.
- Unite the complementary halves with one another! Making 4 mascarpone-fruit compote sandwiches with butter on the outside.
- Grill each sandwich until it is golden and crispy on the outside and the spreads are oozing - 3-4 minutes in a Panini press, or 3 minutes per side if you are cooking them in a frying pan.
- Allow to cool for a few minutes, then cut each sandwich in half (this is messy and requires a serrated knife) and serve, sprinkled decoratively with a bit of powdered sugar.
- Dried apricot compote
- Combine everything except the ginger and brandy in a small saucepan, bring to a simmer and cook gently until thick and all the dried fruits are soft and plumped, about 15-20 minutes. Then, stir in the ginger and brandy, cook for another couple of minutes, then allow to cool.

50. Bresaola Surprise Rolls

Serving: Serves 4 | Prep: | Cook: | Ready in:

Ingredients

- 20   slices of bresaola
- 1 teaspoon mustard
- 2 cups fresh whole milk ricotta
- 1/2 cup Gorgonzola
- 1/4 cup pistachios – roasted, pealed and chopped
- 10   radishes julienned
- 10   sprigs of chives, chopped finely
- Extra Virgin Olive Oil
- Salt
- Pepper
- 4   Sicilian oranges
- Salad or arugula to serve
- 15   Cherry tomatoes
- Vinaigrette sauce

Direction

- In a bowl, using a whisk or a fork, beat the ricotta with 2 tablespoons of Extra Virgin Olive Oil until very, very smooth. Crumble the Gorgonzola in small pieces and add to the ricotta. Add salt and pepper to taste and mix. Add the chives, the julienned radishes and the chopped pistachios,
- Last, peel the pear, remove the core and julienne.
- To assemble the bresaola surprise rolls:
- Spread the slices of Bresaola on a chopping board and brush lightly with a tiny dot of mustard. Put 2 to 3 teaspoons ricotta mixture on one end, add on top some julienned pear and roll gently.
- To serve:
- Peel and thinly slice the navel oranges.
- On a plate put some slices of orange. On top put 5 Bresaola Surprise rolls. Finish with some arugula or salad and cherry tomatoes. Drizzle the Bresaola Surprise Rolls with Extra Virgin Olive Oil and the salad with a simple vinaigrette sauce.
- Enjoy!

51. Brie Fig Ice Cream

Serving: Makes "generous 1 quart" | Prep: | Cook: | Ready in:

Ingredients

- Brie Ice Cream Mix
- 2 cups whole milk
- 1 tablespoon 1 tsn cornstarch
- 6 ounces brie cheese, rind removed
- 2 tablespoons Naefchatel cheese
- 1.25 cups heavy cream
- 2/3 cup sugar
- 1/4 cup light corn syrup
- 1 fig sauce
- Fig Sauce
- 3/4 cup fresh fig seeds (druplets)
- 2 tablespoons sugar

Direction

- Mix about 2 tbsp milk with cornstarch in small bowl to make a smooth slurry," divide brie and Naefchatel cheese into tiny pieces and mix together in a large bowl
- Combine remaining milk, the cream, sugar, and corn syrup in a 4 quart saucepan, bring to a rolling boil over m-h heat and boil for 4 min. Remove from heat & gradually whisk in cornstarch slurry, bring mixture back to boiling over m-h heat, stirring with a rubber spatula until thickened, about 1 min. remove from heat"
- Gradually whisk hot milk mixture into cheese mixture until smooth." whisk well with each small addition of the hot milk mixture to ensure smoothness. Cover and chill in refrigerator while ice cream make in freezer overnight.
- Pour ice cream based into frozen ice cream maker until thick and creamy. Pack... into storage container, alternating with" fig sauce. "Do not mix. Press a sheet of" wax paper "directly against the surface, and seal with an airtight lid." Freeze overnight
- Fig Sauce
- Heat in small saucepan over medium high heat until well combined, remove from heat and allow it to cool before use. If making for brie ice cream, it's best to make before ice cream is put into ice cream maker. It can cool as you are spinning the ice cream.

52. Broccoli, Blue Cheese And Leek Quiche

Serving: Makes 1 9"-10" tart | Prep: | Cook: | Ready in:

Ingredients

- Butter pastry
- 1.5 cups all-purpose flour
- 0.5 cups unsalted butter, cubed and chilled
- 0.5 teaspoons salt
- 3-7 tablespoons ice water
- Broccoli, blue cheese and leek filling
- 10 ounces broccoli florets, about 1" wide at top
- 2 tablespoons unsalted butter
- 8 ounces washed, thinly sliced leeks (I used 3)
- 3 ounces blue cheese, crumbled
- 4 eggs
- 1 cup half and half cream
- 2 tablespoons fresh chopped dill (optional)
- salt and pepper

Direction

- Butter pastry
- Combine flour and salt in a food processor and pulse to combine. Add butter and pulse until it is broken up and partly incorporated. When some pieces are tiny, but some are still the size of peas, it is ready.
- Add 3 tablespoons water and pulse. You do not want the pastry to form a ball in the food processor. Open it and grab a handful of the crumbs. If you can squeeze them to form a ball it is ready. If not, add more water in small increments.

- Flatten dough into a disc and wrap in plastic. Refrigerate for a few hours.
- Roll dough on a lightly floured surface to a 13" circle. Transfer to a 9" or 10" springform pan/deep tart pan/deep dish pie plate. If using a springform, trim dough so it is 2" high. If using a tart pan, trim dough so edges extend just past top of dish. Chill for 30 minutes.
- Preheat oven to 375F. Place a greased sheet of foil (greased side down) over pastry and fill with dried beans. Bake for 15 minutes. Remove foil and beans carefully and bake crust for another 10 minutes or so, until set and pale golden. Set aside to cool on a rack while you prepare filling.
- Broccoli, blue cheese and leek filling
- Blanch the broccoli florets for 3-4 minutes* in boiling salted water. Drain and rinse well with ice water to stop the cooking. Drain again and blot dry with paper towels. Set aside. *You don't want crunchy broccoli here--I like mine tender but still firm.
- Heat butter over medium-low heat and add leeks, along with a pinch of salt. Saute until very tender but not browned, about 10 minutes. Set aside to cool slightly.
- Beat eggs, cream, dill, 1/4 teaspoon salt and a generous grinding of pepper together. Spread leeks evenly in bottom of tart shell, cover with broccoli florets and top with cheese. Carefully pour custard mixture over top (I do this while it's in the oven to minimize spilling).
- Bake at 375F for 40-50 minutes. I mistakenly used a 9" pan for mine, so it took the longer time. When done, the centre will still be a bit wobbly, but it will set as it cools.

53. Bruschetta With Plums, Serrano Ham And Ricotta

Serving: Serves 4 | Prep: | Cook: | Ready in:

Ingredients

- 4 half-inch slices of crusty country bread
- 2 Red plums, pitted and sliced into thin half moons
- Fresh Italian ricotta (i used the amazing stuff from Salvatore Brooklyn)
- 1 handful arugula
- 1/8 pound Serrano ham, sliced
- 4 tablespoons Extra virgin olive oil

Direction

- Grill the bread on one side
- Slather 2-3 tablespoons of ricotta on each slice of grilled bread
- Layer a few slices of serrano ham on each toast. Sprinkle arugula leaves on top of the ricotta. Do the same with the plum slices.
- Drizzle a tablespoon of olive oil on each toast. Grind black pepper on top.

54. Butternut Squash Ravioli With Caramelized Onions, Browned Pecans, Soaked Cranberries, And Apple Cider Reduction

Serving: Serves 4 | Prep: | Cook: | Ready in:

Ingredients

- Wonton wrappers
- 1 medium butternut squash
- 1/3 cup grated parmesan
- Salt & pepper to taste
- 3 medium onions
- 4t Olive Oil (divided)
- 1/4 cup sugar
- 1 cup Mascarpone cheese:
- ground sage
- 3 cups Apple Cider
- 1/2 cup cider vinegar
- 1/3 cup real maple syrup
- 1 cinnamon stick
- 1/2 teaspoon ground nutmeg
- 1 cup dried cranberries

- 2 ounces good bourbon (I used Jefferson Bourbon)
- 1 cup crushed pecans
- 1 tablespoon butter

Direction

- Peel, deseed, cut squash into chunks. Roast squash at 400 degrees until soft, 45mins to 1 hour.
- While squash is cooking, make the onions, cranberries, cheese, and apple cider reduction. (See below)
- Soak cranberries in bourbon for 45 mins. Strain the cranberries, saving the bourbon to drink, if you like.
- Thinly slice onions. Heat skillet over medium heat with 2T Olive oil. Add onions and cook until soft, stirring frequently, adding sugar if necessary until onions are golden brown. About 25 mins.
- Mix 1 c Mascarpone Cheese in medium bowl with salt, pepper, and ground sage until a sage-green color. Refrigerate.
- Mix apple cider, cider vinegar, maple syrup, cinnamon stick and nutmeg in a small saucepan and boil, stirring frequently until sauce is reduced by half.
- Remove from squash from oven to cool. Transfer to a small saucepan and mash over medium heat. Stir frequently to remove all the water from the squash and add in parmesan cheese. Stir until incorporated. Let cool.
- Fill wonton wrappers by adding a small dollop of squash to the middle of the wrapper. Fold into a triangle, wetting the edges with water to seal. Bring a pot of salted water to boil.
- Heat pecans with 1T butter until browned and hot. Set aside.
- Heat a skillet over medium heat with 2T olive oil.
- Add ravioli to boiling water and boil for 2-3 minutes, until blanched. Immediately remove ravioli from water with a slotted spoon and dry quickly on a paper towel. Add ravioli to the skillet and fry for 2 mins each side, until browned in some spots.
- Put ravioli on a plate. Top with caramelized onions, pecans, cranberries, dollop of mascarpone cheese. Spoon apple cider reduction over ravioli. Enjoy!

55. Cacio E Pepe Biscuits

Serving: Makes 12 biscuits | Prep: | Cook: | Ready in:

Ingredients

- 2 3/4 cups all-purpose flour
- 1/2 teaspoon kosher salt
- 1 tablespoon baking powder
- 1 cup (2 sticks) unsalted butter, very cold
- 1 cup grated Pecorino Romano cheese, plus extra for topping
- 2 tablespoons freshly ground black pepper, plus extra for topping
- 1 cup milk

Direction

- Preheat your oven to 425° F. Line two baking sheets with parchment paper.
- In a large bowl, whisk together the flour, salt, and baking powder.
- Cut in the cold butter using a fork or pastry cutter. The mixture should have pea-sized lumps.
- Stir in the grated cheese and black pepper with a fork and pour in the milk. Stir until the dough is a shaggy, wet mess. Once it mostly comes together, use your hands to fold in the dry bits that haven't been incorporated. You want to be very gentle and use your hands as little as possible. Focus on folding the dough over onto itself until it mostly comes together.
- Turn the dough out onto a lightly floured surface and pat it into a 1 1/2-inch-thick disc. Using a sharp biscuit cutter (or a round cookie cutter), cut out circles. I used a 3-inch inch

cutter. Place the dough circles onto your prepared baking sheets.
- Sprinkle a generous amount of black pepper and grated cheese over the top of each biscuit.
- Bake for 10 to 12 minutes, or until just golden brown on the edges. Remove from the oven and let cool slightly.

56. Cacio E Pepe Polenta

Serving: Serves 1 | Prep: 0hours5mins | Cook: 0hours20mins | Ready in:

Ingredients

- 1/4 cup polenta or grits
- 1 cup water or broth
- 1/4 cup pecorino romano
- 1 tablespoon fresh cracked pepper
- salt to taste
- 1 tablespoon butter

Direction

- Bring water or broth to a boil (I prefer chicken broth). Add polenta and stir to ensure there are no clumps. Bring temperature to low and simmer for 20 minutes.
- While the polenta is cooking, finely grate pecorino romano. Pay extra for the authentic, it matters.
- When the polenta is done, remove from heat and add butter, cheese and pepper and stir vigorously to combine well. Transfer to a bowl that brings you joy and top with extra cheese and pepper.

57. Caesar Salad Stuff And Dressing Recipe

Serving: Serves 4 | Prep: | Cook: | Ready in:

Ingredients

- 2/3 cup Parmesan cheese
- 1/2 cup EVOO (extra virgin olive oil)
- 4 tablespoons fresh lemon juice
- 2 tablespoons Dijon mustard
- 1 tablespoon Worcestershire sauce
- 1/4 teaspoon salt
- 1 teaspoon fresh ground pepper
- 8 anchovy fillets
- 2 large cloves garlic
- 2 heads Romaine lettuce
- 1 cup Caesar croutons or homemade croutons
- 3-4 Parmesan cheese fresh grated for garnish A few anchovy fillets for garnish if so desired
- Enough Parmesan cheese to make four crisps if desired

Direction

- Mix the dressing ingredients in a blender until smooth. Reserve and let stand for at least thirty minutes to warm up.
- Select enough of the best looking and most tender leaves in the lettuce for your salad. The other less appealing ones can be used in sandwiches where you can't see them.
- Cut off the white lower ends of the selected lettuce and cut the lettuce to the size you want to serve or serve, or leave whole, and arrange on plates.
- Sprinkle on the dressing or toss the lettuce with the dressing. Add the croutons artfully and garnish with grated Parmesan and an anchovy or two if desired.
- Parmesan Crisps are made by baking grated Parmesan cheese, placed in 2-3 inch circles and flattened to 1/8 inch thickness on a slightly oiled cookie tin at 350* F for about 6 minutes or until the edges are browned to about 1/4 inch in.

58. Camembert And Bacon Sandwiches With Apple And Fennel Slaw

Serving: Makes 2 | Prep: 0hours10mins | Cook: 0hours0mins | Ready in:

Ingredients

- 1 small Pink Lady apple, cored and shredded
- 1 baby fennel, thinly shaved
- 1 teaspoon extra-virgin olive oil
- Salt and pepper, to taste
- Butter, for spreading
- 4 slices of sourdough bread, lightly toasted
- 4 slices shortcut bacon, fried or roasted until browned and crispy
- 8 slices of your favourite Camembert cheese
- Crisps, to serve (optional)

Direction

- To make the apple and fennel slaw, place the apple, fennel and oil in a small bowl. Season with salt and pepper. Toss to combine.
- Spread butter onto one side of each slice of bread. Divide bacon, cheese and the slaw between two slices of bread. Cap with remaining bread slices, butter-side down.
- Serve cut in half with crisps on the side, if using.

59. Caprese Panini

Serving: Serves 4 | Prep: | Cook: | Ready in:

Ingredients

- 1 loaf focaccia bread
- 2 cups fresh basil leaves, packed
- 2 garlic cloves
- 1/4 cup pine nuts
- 1/2 to 2/3 cups extra virgin olive oil, divided. Plus extra for brushing.
- kosher salt and freshly ground pepper
- 2 8 ounce balls buffalo mozzarella, sliced 1/4-inch
- 3-4 plum tomatoes, sliced 1/4
- 1 bunch arugula

Direction

- Preheat a Panini maker to medium heat.
- Place sliced mozzarella in a single layer between several paper towels. Place a cutting board on top of the covered mozzarella and add 2 pounds of weight for 15 minutes, unopened soup cans work well. Doing this will remove the excess moisture and will prevent your Panini from becoming soggy while in the press.
- While the mozzarella is being lightly pressed, make the pesto. Add to the bowl of a food processor, the basil, garlic, pine nuts, and parmesan. Pulse while slowly adding 1/2 cup olive oil to start. Add more if needed until smooth and desired consistency. Add salt and pepper to taste and pulse a few more times to incorporate.
- Using a sharp bread knife, slice your focaccia loaf down the middle vertically and then down the middle horizontally, creating 4 servings. Slice each section in half to create a top and bottom of your sandwich and lightly brush the outside of each piece with olive oil. Oiled side down, liberally spread the pesto on the inside of each half. On the bottom half, add the sliced mozzarella, tomato, and arugula. If desired, add a little extra salt and freshly ground pepper to taste. Place the tops of the bread on each sandwich and place in the Panini Press. (If you do not have a Panini press, you can heat a heavy skillet over medium-high heat and cook each side for several minutes, using a lid or another skillet to press the sandwich while cooking).
- Cook 3 to 5 minutes, or until the cheese has melted and the bread is golden brown. Transfer the Panini to a cutting board and cut in half. Serve immediately.

60. Caramelized Carrots With Herbed Goat Cheese "Snow"

Serving: Serves 4-6 | Prep: | Cook: | Ready in:

Ingredients

- Goat Cheese "Snow"
- 4 ounces goat cheese
- 1/2 cup milk
- 1 tablespoon chives
- 1 tablespoon fresh thyme
- black pepper
- Caramelized Carrots
- 2 pounds carrots, peeled
- 3 tablespoons olive oil
- 1 teaspoon cumin seed
- 1 teaspoon coriander seed
- 1/2 teaspoon fennel seed
- 1/2 teaspoon urfa or other chili pepper
- 2 tablespoons apricot jam (or orange marmalade)
- 1 tablespoon orange juice
- maldon or other flakey salt

Direction

- Blend cheese with milk until smooth. Fold in pepper, chives and thyme. Pour into a 9x9 baking dish, cover and freeze. You may either scrape and stir with a fork every 15 minutes until frozen granita-style or allow it to freeze in one piece and break into chunks.
- Heat oven to 425. Toast cumin, coriander, fennel and pepper in a dry skillet until fragrant. Let cool then grind in a mortar and pestle. Cut carrots in half, toss with olive oil. And a generous sprinkling of spices. Arrange on a baking sheet so they are not too crowded and bake about 15 minutes or until starting to brown. Meanwhile, heat jam (I did 20 seconds in microwave) until syrupy and mix with juice. Flip carrots, drizzle with jam and roast until edges are browned and starting to crisp.
- Place carrots on a platter and scatter "snow" on top. Garnish with fresh thyme and chives and a sprinkling of maldon salt.

61. Caramelized Fennel Pizza With Leeks, Ricotta And Orange

Serving: Serves 4 | Prep: | Cook: | Ready in:

Ingredients

- 1 portion pizza dough (or baguette)
- 2 fennel bulbs with stalks
- 3 garlic cloves with skin
- 2 tablespoons olive oil
- 1 tablespoon butter
- 1 leek
- 1 cup ricotta, part skim
- 1 egg
- 1 orange
- 1/2 cup parmesan, finely grated
- Urfa or aleppo pepper for garnish
- 4 fried eggs for garnish (optional)

Direction

- Preheat oven to 425°. Trim stalks from fennel and cut in half lengthwise. Cut slices 1/4" thick across each bulb half leaving a bit of the root end intact. Drizzle on some olive oil and salt and carefully rub between slices and all over bulbs. Rub garlic with oil as well. Put all in a baking dish in the oven. Flip the garlic after about 10 minutes and spread the fennel slices out slightly. Check the garlic after another 5 minutes or so and remove when soft, then chop. Continue to roast fennel another half hour (or until nicely browned), flipping over about half way.
- Cut the fennel stalks in half and then crosswise into thin slices to measure 1/2 c. Do the same for the leeks to make 3/4 c. Rinse well and blot dry. Sauté in 1 T each butter and olive oil until softened and just starting to brown. Let cool.

- When fennel is done, crank heat to 500°. Roll out pizza dough until it is very thin and brush with a bit of oil. If using baguettes, cut in half and brush with oil. Cook until crisp and just starting brown.
- Mix ricotta, egg, leek mixture, garlic, salt and pepper. Zest the orange and fold in 1 T zest and parmesan. Mix 2 T orange juice, 1 t zest and 1T olive oil and set aside.
- Spread ricotta mixture on pizza dough. Carefully cut root end off fennel bulbs and arrange slices on top of ricotta mixture. Put back in oven for 5-8 minutes until ricotta mixture starts to brown and feels set. Remove from oven, drizzle with orange juice mixture. Garnish with fennel fronds and black pepper. Also great with urfa or aleppo pepper.
- Cut into four wedges and serve with a simple salad. At this time you can also add a fried egg, over medium per portion.

62. Caramelized Pear And Gruyère Torta

Serving: Makes 1 8" torta | Prep: | Cook: |Ready in:

Ingredients

- 3 tablespoons unsalted butter
- 1/3 cup granulated sugar
- 6 large D'Anjou pears, diced
- 4 (8-ounce) packages cream cheese, softened
- 2 cups finely grated Gruyère cheese
- 1 pinch of kosher salt
- 1 cup finely chopped pistachio nuts

Direction

- In a large non-stick sauté pan, melt butter over medium-high heat. Add pears and sugar and stir until combined. Cook for 12-15 minutes until liquid thickens and pears begin to caramelize, stirring occasionally. Remove from heat. Transfer pears to a bowl and cool completely.
- In a medium mixing bowl, combine the cream cheese, Gruyère, and salt using a hand held mixer. Beat on medium speed until well combined.
- Line an 8-inch round cake pan with plastic warp. Spread half the cheese mixer on the bottom of the pan. Spread half of the cooled pear mixture over the cheese. Spread the remaining cheese mixture over the pears. Refrigerate until firm, about 1 hour.
- Invert the torta on a serving dish. Carefully remove the pan and the plastic wrap. Cover the sides of the torta with the chopped pistachio nuts and top with the remaining pears. Cover and refrigerate until ready to serve. Serve with plain or rosemary crackers and a crisp white wine. Enjoy!

63. Caramelized Onion And Cheddar Palmiers

Serving: Makes about 50 pieces | Prep: | Cook: |Ready in:

Ingredients

- 1 packet Puff Pastry
- 4 Onions, thinly sliced
- 1/2 cup Good Cheddar (something not too dry) or gruyere
- Pinch Thyme (optional)
- 3-4 tablespoons Olive Oil
- Kosher Salt

Direction

- Defrost the puff pastry. Heat the oil in a pan, add the thinly sliced onions, sprinkle generously with kosher salt, and cook them on low, stirring intermittently, until the onions are nicely browned and caramelized (this can take a good 45 minutes, do not rush it). While the onions are caramelizing, roll out the defrosted puff pastry on a lightly floured surface. You want it to be about 9 1/2 x 11. Spread the puff with the caramelized onions (but taste the onions first to make sure they are properly salted)--you want the surface covered, but you might have extra; use your discretion. Then lightly dot the onions with the cheese, you still want some onions peeking through, but this is naturally to taste. (Note, I often use Cabot Clothbound--broken into small chunks or shredded). Sprinkle with thyme, if using. Starting from the short end, fold each side of the dough halfway to the center, then again halfway to the center so that both sides are nearly touching. Finally, fold one side over the other. Refrigerate the roll, covered in plastic wrap for at least 40 minutes. Repeat with the second piece of puff. Before you begin slicing, preheat the oven to 400 F. Slice each roll into 1/4 inch pieces and place the pieces (face up) on parchment covered baking sheets. Bake for 12-15 minutes until golden brown.

64. Caribbean Cream

Serving: Serves 2 | Prep: | Cook: | Ready in:

Ingredients

- 3/4 cup coconut yogurt
- 3/4 cup heavy cream
- 1 tablespoon coconut rum (optional)
- 1 banana
- 2 tablespoons dark brown sugar
- shredded coconut (optional)

Direction

- Stir together the yogurt and cream with the rum, if you're using it, and whisk until slightly thickened.
- Slice the banana and then divide the slices between two -1 cup ramekins to form a layer at the bottom of each one. Spoon the thickened yogurt and cream mixture filling the ramekins equally.
- Sprinkle 1 tablespoon of sugar over each ramekin, and then wrap them in plastic wrap and refrigerate for a couple of hours, or until sugar has dissolved. Garnish with shredded coconut if desired.

65. Carrot Cupcakes With Cream Cheese Frosting

Serving: Serves 24 | Prep: | Cook: | Ready in:

Ingredients

- The Cupcakes
- 1 3/4 cups (8.75 ounces) unbleached all-purpose flour
- 1 3/4 teaspoons baking soda
- 1 3/4 teaspoons cinnamon
- 1/2 teaspoon salt
- 4 large eggs
- 1 1/4 cups sugar
- 1 cup organic canola oil
- 1 3/4 cups (10 ounces) finely shredded carrots
- 3/4 cup Zante currants
- 3/4 cup finely chopped walnuts or pecans
- The Frosting
- 4 ounces cream cheese, room temperature
- 4 tablespoons unsalted butter, room temperature
- 1 teaspoon vanilla extract
- 1/8 teaspoon salt
- 1 pound powdered sugar, unsifted
- 1 tablespoon milk
- 2 drops red food coloring, optional
- 2 drops yellow food coloring, optional

Direction

- Preheat oven to 350 degrees. Put 2½-inch paper bake cups in two standard muffin tins. In small bowl, whisk together flour*, soda, cinnamon and salt. In another small bowl, stir a tablespoon of flour mixture into chopped nuts and currants to coat and separate. *It is important to note that this is a packed measure of unsifted flour.

- In large bowl, beat eggs; beat in sugar, then oil. Beat in flour mixture. Stir in carrots, raisins and nuts.
- Using a 1/4-cup measure, fill the bake cups with a scant 1/4 cup of batter. Bake at 350 degrees for about 24 minutes or until they are golden and test done with a toothpick.
- Immediately remove from pans and cool on wire rack for an hour. They must be thoroughly cool before frosting.
- In bowl of stand mixer, or with a hand mixer, cream together the cream cheese, butter, vanilla extract and salt. Gradually add powdered sugar (no need to sift) and mix until thoroughly combined, adding milk and food coloring at the end. I usually oppose food coloring, but I like to give a slight peach tint to the frosting if there's going to be more than one kind of cupcake, just so I know which is the carrot. You may need to add a little more milk, a teaspoon at a time, for proper piping consistency. With a pastry bag fitted with a 2D (sometimes I use a 1M) tip, pipe frosting on cupcakes in a classic swirl.

66. Cavatelli With Bacon, Corn, Mushrooms, And Parmesan, A La The Red Hen

Serving: Serves 4-6 | Prep: 0hours30mins | Cook: 3hours0mins | Ready in:

Ingredients

- For the roasted mushrooms, the parmesan broth, and the corn brodo:
- 1 pound shiitake mushrooms
- olive oil, for roasting
- salt, pepper, and chopped fresh thyme to taste
- 6 ears sweet corn, husked and de-silked (or 4 cups frozen sweet corn kernels, defrosted)
- 3 tablespoons unsalted butter, divided
- 1 head garlic, halved, plus 1 garlic clove, halved
- 1 medium-large onion, chopped
- 2 or 3 carrots and celery stalks (each), chopped (combined, they should roughly equal the quantity of onion)
- 1/4 ounce dried mushrooms (porcini, shiitake, mixed wild...go nuts)
- 1 bay leaf
- 1 pinch black peppercorns
- a few (each) parsley and thyme sprigs
- 1 pound parmesan cheese rinds
- 1 cup dry white wine
- 2 quarts water, brought to a simmer
- 1/2 cup yellow onion, diced
- 2 garlic cloves, chopped
- creme fraiche, to taste
- For the finished pasta:
- 1/2-1 pounds cavatelli (the Red Hen uses housemade whole wheat cavatelli, but regular pasta is fine, too; use the lesser amount of pasta if you want a more equitable ratio of pasta to the rest of the components, otherwise use the whole box)
- olive oil, for sauteing
- 4 ounces bacon, preferably double-smoked, diced
- 8 green onions, thinly sliced
- roasted shiitakes, reserved corn kernels, and corn brodo (see above)
- 2 tablespoons unsalted butter, for finishing
- 1 cup freshly grated parmesan cheese
- chopped fresh parsley and thyme, for garnish

Direction

- For the roasted mushrooms, the parmesan broth, and the corn brodo:
- Heat oven to 500F. Stem the shiitakes, reserving the stems. Slice the caps 1/8" thick. Toss with olive oil, salt, and pepper to taste, and roast 5-7 mins. Remove to a bowl. Using a micro plane, grate 1/2 a clove of garlic (or more/less to taste) over, and season with fresh thyme and more salt and pepper if necessary. Toss and set aside until ready to use.

- Cut the kernels from the 6 ears of corn. (You should get ~4 1/2 - 5 cups.) Set two cups kernels aside for the brodo, and the rest for the pasta. Scrape the cobs over the reserved brodo kernels with the back of your knife to extract the sweet corn "milk." Reserve the cobs. (NOTE: If fresh corn is out of season, skip this step and use defrosted frozen kernels--2 cups for the brodo and 2 for the pasta--instead.)
- Heat a little olive oil and 1 tbsp. butter in a large pot over medium heat. When the butter melts, add the scraped corn cobs and reserved shiitake stems, along with the halved garlic head, onions, carrots, celery, mushrooms, herbs, and spices. Let the aromatics soften, 8-10 mins, stirring occasionally. (Look for browning of the garlic and translucence of the onions.) As in the Cowgirl recipe, add the cheese rinds next, allowing them to sit at the bottom of the pot for short periods of time (10 seconds between scrapes) to get some nice browning going. Deglaze with white wine, stirring to scrape up all the good stuff stuck to the bottom of the pan, and reduce by half, then add the 2 quarts of simmering water. How long you let it go on the stove depends how robust a flavor you want--about two hours at a gentle simmer will reduce the broth by half, yielding a quart. A shorter simmer (say an hour), will yield a less-concentrated quart and a half. In either case, be sure to stir often (every five minutes, give or take), as the rinds will stick to the bottom and scorch otherwise. When reduced to the desired amount, strain and cool. Season to taste with salt. If making far enough in advance, refrigerate overnight so a fat cap forms and is easily removable. Otherwise, do your best to skim fat from the surface once the broth has cooled. You will only need 2 cups broth for the corn brodo; reserve the rest for another use.
- Next, make the corn brodo. Melt the remaining 2 tbsp. butter in a large saucepan over medium heat, and sauté the 2 cups reserved corn kernels with 1/2 cup chopped onion and 2 chopped garlic cloves until corn is tender. Remove from heat and let cool, then puree with 2 cups of the parmesan broth until smooth. Put through a fine-mesh sieve, then whisk in a few tbsps. of crème fraiche and season with salt to taste. Set aside till ready to use.
- For the finished pasta:
- Bring a pot of well-salted water to a boil, and cook the cavatelli according to package directions, draining it just shy of the recommended cook time, as it will finish cooking in the sauce. (Reserve some of the cooking water--a cup should do.)
- While the pasta is cooking, film a large skillet with olive oil and sauté the bacon and green onions over medium heat, until bacon starts to brown and crisp at the edges. Add the remaining reserved corn kernels and roasted shiitakes--about a 1/2 cup of each per person. (You may have some leftover mushrooms.) Toss. Add corn brodo and lower to a simmer.
- When pasta is ready, toss it in the sauce with a little of the pasta water and allow it to finish cooking. Add more water if too dry. Remove from heat and stir in butter and parmesan. Garnish with parsley, thyme, and a little extra parmesan, and serve.

67. Chard Wrapped Grilled Mozzarella With Kalamata Olives

Serving: Makes 8 | Prep: | Cook: | Ready in:

Ingredients

- 4 large, whole, outside leaves of swiss chard
- 8 pieces of mozzarella sliced into 2-inch wide triangles, 1/2-inch thick
- 8 kalamata olives, pitted and halved lengthwise
- 8 pinches dried oregano
- 8 pinches red pepper flakes
- salt, as needed
- olive oil, as needed

- 4 slices rustic italian bread about 1/2-inch thick

Direction

- Lay the chard leaves out in front of you. Using the tip of a sharp knife cut on either side of the center vein of all 4 leaves. Discard veins. You should have 8 segments of chard leaves approximately 8"x3".
- Put the leaves in a large heat-proof bowl and cover them with boiling water. Let the leaves sit about 3 minutes then drain and dry them with paper towels. Take care to keep them intact.
- Lay a leaf out flat on the surface in front of you, shiny side down. Place a slice of cheese at the wider end of the leaf. Top that with two halves of kalamata olives, a pinch of oregano, a pinch of red pepper flakes and a few grains of salt.
- The next step is just like folding a flag. Fold the leaf over the cheese creating and angle which becomes one side of a triangle. Alternate this fold left and right creating a tight little triangular bundle. Brush the triangle with olive oil on both sides and sprinkle it with a bit more salt. Repeat with the remaining leaves and cheese.
- The triangles may be made ahead several hours and kept covered in the refrigerator. Bring them to room temperature before continuing.
- To grill: Place the triangles, seam side down, on an outdoor grill over indirect heat. Cook uncovered about 6 minutes, turning once. Make sure the cheese is completely melted by pressing on each one gently with your finger.
- While the triangles cook, lightly brush the bread slices with olive oil on both sides. Give one side a light sprinkle of salt. Place them on the grill and toast them on both sides directly over the coals (no flame). Remove them from the grill and cut them in half on an angle.
- To serve: Top each piece of toast with a grilled mozzarella triangle. Serve immediately with a drizzle of olive oil.

68. Cheddar Corn Spoon Bread

Serving: Serves 6 | Prep: | Cook: | Ready in:

Ingredients

- 1 tablespoon unsalted butter
- 2 cups whole milk
- 1 1/2 cups fresh or frozen corn kernels
- 2/3 cup yellow cornmeal
- 1 teaspoon sea salt
- 1/4 teaspoon white pepper
- 1 pinch cayenne pepper
- 1 pinch nutmeg
- 1 cup sharp white cheddar cheese, grated
- 2 scallions, chopped
- 4 large eggs, separated

Direction

- Preheat oven to 400°. Butter or spray a 2 quart casserole dish and set aside. In a medium saucepan, melt butter and add corn kernels. If using fresh corn, cook for a few minutes to soften kernels up. Add milk, cornmeal, salt, pepper, cayenne and nutmeg. Bring to boil, then reduce heat to medium-low, stirring frequently until mixture has thickened slightly, about 3-4 minutes.
- Remove from heat and stir in cheese and scallions. Let cool until warm to the touch, about 15 minutes. Stir in egg yolks until combined.
- Meanwhile, beat egg whites with a pinch of salt until soft peaks form. Stir in 1/2 of the whites to corn mixture until combined, then gently fold in remaining whites. Pour into prepared dish and place in oven, reducing temperature to 375°. Bake until browned on top but slightly loose in the center, 25-30 minutes. Let cool for a few minutes before serving.

69. Cheddar Cheese Biscuits With Bacon Jam

Serving: Serves 12-16 | Prep: | Cook: |Ready in:

Ingredients

- Cheddar cheese biscuits
- 3 cups all-purpose flour
- 1 1/2 tablespoons baking powder
- 1 teaspoon salt
- 1/3 cup sugar
- 1 1/2 stick butter, divided
- 1 1/2 cups grated sharp cheddar, or cheese(s) of your choice
- 1 1/2 cups milk
- Bacon jam
- 1 pound good smoked bacon
- 1 medium onion, diced
- 3-4 cloves garlic, minced
- 1/4 cup brown sugar
- 1/2 cup strong black coffee
- 1/4 cup maple syrup
- 2 tablespoons apple cider vinegar
- 2 tablespoons balsamic vinegar
- 1/2 teaspoon allspice

Direction

- Cheddar cheese biscuits
- Preheat oven to 375. Sift all dry ingredients together. Cut one stick butter into tablespoon-sized pats, and cut into dry ingredients with a fork or pastry blender until it looks like coarse crumbs.
- Toss with grated cheese (I often use a combo of whatever kinds of firm cheeses I have in my fridge).
- Add milk, and stir just enough for dry ingredients to all come together. If dough is too dry and crumbly add a little more milk.
- Turn out onto a floured board and knead only two or three times -- enough to incorporate everything. Form into a ball and pat or roll out to about 1 inch thick.
- Use a small biscuit cutter -- I find a small tomato paste can, both ends cut out, makes a great cutter for cocktail sized biscuits -- to cut out biscuits. Place on ungreased baking sheet. At this point, if you're making in advance, you can freeze the biscuits on the baking sheet, then remove to a plastic bag. Allow to thaw before baking.
- Melt remaining half-stick of butter and brush tops of biscuits. Bake until golden brown, and cool on a rack.
- Bacon jam
- Cut bacon into 1-inch pieces and toss into heavy Dutch oven. Cook over medium high heat, stirring periodically, until starting to crisp.
- Dice onion and mince garlic, and add to bacon. If you're concerned about the fat content (It IS bacon, after all), drain off some of the fat first, leaving 3 tablespoons or so. Lower heat to medium and cook until onion starts to brown, about 8 minutes or so.
- Add remaining ingredients. Reduce heat to a simmer, cover, and cook for an hour or two. Stir occasionally, and add water if it gets too thick.
- When bacon is very tender, remove from heat and let cool for 30 minutes or so. Transfer to food processor -- you may need to do this in batches, depending on the size of your processor -- and pulse until mixture is the consistency you want.

70. Cheese Latkes

Serving: Makes 15 3-inch pancakes | Prep: | Cook: |Ready in:

Ingredients

- 3 ounces cream cheese
- 3 eggs
- 3/4 cup all-purpose flour
- 3 tablespoons sugar
- 1/2 teaspoon baking powder

- 1/2 teaspoon kosher salt
- 1 teaspoon vanilla extract
- 1 1/2 cups ricotta cheese
- Unsalted butter or vegetable oil, for frying
- For serving: cinnamon sugar, jam, sour cream, or maple syrup

Direction

- Add the cream cheese, eggs, flour, sugar, baking powder, salt, and vanilla extract to a food processor and process, scraping down the sides of the bowl as necessary, until the mixture is completely smooth and the consistency of loose pancake batter. Transfer the mixture to a large bowl and fold in the ricotta cheese until combined.
- Heat about 1 tablespoon of butter in a large skillet over medium heat, swirling the pan to coat. Working in batches of 5 or 6, drop the batter by the heaping tablespoon into the skillet, nudging it into a circle with the back of a spoon. Fry until golden brown on the bottom, 2 to 3 minutes; flip and continue frying until the latkes are cooked all the way through, another 1 to 2 minutes. Transfer latkes to a plate and serve immediately with desired toppings.

71. Cheese Strata

Serving: Serves 6 | Prep: 7hours20mins | Cook: 1hours0mins | Ready in:

Ingredients

- For the strata:
- 8 eggs
- 3 cups milk
- 3 tablespoons melted butter
- 1 teaspoon Kosher salt
- 1 handful fresh thyme, chives, and parsley
- 1/2 teaspoon black pepper
- 2 1/2 cups grated cheese (Cheddar or anything you like)
- 1/2 cup Parmesan cheese (to top)
- 8 cups bread cubes (typically Challah)
- 1 dash mustard (dry or regular)
- Plus add any of the following:
- 1 packet cooked and chopped bacon (or sausage or cubed ham)
- 1 packet sausage
- 1 packet cubed ham
- 1 cup halved cherry tomatoes
- 1 cup chopped red pepper
- 1 cup mushrooms

Direction

- Beat eggs and milk.
- Add all other ingredients and stir.
- Pour into buttered 9x13 glass dish.
- Refrigerate overnight.
- Preheat oven to 350 degrees.
- Sprinkle Parmesan on top.
- Bake for about 1 hour.

72. Cheese And Lobster Bites

Serving: Serves 2 | Prep: | Cook: | Ready in:

Ingredients

- 1 lobster
- 1/2 cup gouda
- flour
- 1 egg
- bread crumbs
- Pinch cayenne
- salt
- pepper
- 1/2 lemon
- oil (for frying)

Direction

- Melt the cheese in a bowl.
- Chop the lobster meat and mix with the melted cheese. Season with cayenne, salt,

pepper and lemon. Let it cool and then shape into smaller balls.
- Roll them in flour, then dip in egg and last bread crumbs.
- Fry in vegetable oil. Let them drain on paper towels.

73. Cheesy Corn Y Scones

Serving: Makes 8 scones | Prep: 0hours30mins | Cook: 0hours25mins | Ready in:

Ingredients

- 1 3/4 cups All purpose flour
- 1 tablespoon Plus 1/2 tsp baking powder
- 1 teaspoon Kosher salt, plus extra for sprinkling
- 1 teaspoon Granulated sugar
- 1/2 cup Extra sharp cheddar, grated on a box grater
- 1/2 cup Corn kernels, cut off approximately one cobb
- 1 teaspoon Dried thyme
- 1 cup Heavy cream, plus 2 tbsp for brushing scones

Direction

- Preheat your oven to 375. Combine the flour, baking soda, sugar, salt, thyme, paprika and butter in the bowl of a stand mixer. Place in the refrigerator for at least 15 mins, longer if it is warm in your kitchen.
- Once all the ingredients are cold, using the paddle attachment mix the ingredients on low speed, until the butter is cut into small pebbles.
- Add the cheese and corn. If your mixture has warmed up at all, place the bowl back on the refrigerator. Keeping your ingredients cold is key to the flakiness of the scones. Mix until the cheese is evenly incorporated into the butter mixture. Now slowly stream in the cold cream on low speed, just until your dough comes together.
- Turn the dough onto a lightly floured surface. Form into a round flat disk approximately 9" in diameter. Cut into 8 equal pizza-like wedges, and transfer to a cookie sheet lined either with parchment or ideally a silpat. Freeze for 15 minutes.
- These scones will keep for 3-4 days in an airtight container at room temperature. Fully formed and unbaked scones keep very well in the freezer for about a month or so if properly sealed in a freezer bag.

74. Cheesy Greek Style Baked Quinoa

Serving: Serves 8 | Prep: | Cook: |Ready in:

Ingredients

- 2 1/2 cups Cooked Quinoa
- 1 1/4 cups Fat Free Feta Cheese
- 1/2 cup Reduced Fat Shredded Mozzarella or Cheddar
- 1 cup Marinated Artichoke Hearts (in Oil)
- 1 cup Chopped Spinach
- 1 cup Diced Cherry Tomatoes
- 1/2 cup Skim Milk
- 1 teaspoon Crushed or Minced Garlic
- 1 teaspoon Lemon Juice
- 1 teaspoon Parsley
- 1 teaspoon Onion Powder
- 1/4 teaspoon Sea Salt & Coarse Black Peppercorn - approx.

Direction

- Prepare the quinoa as directed (preferably with chicken broth instead of water - this gives it more flavor). While quinoa cooks, dice cherry tomatoes and chop spinach leaves, then set aside. Next, in food processor combine 1 cup feta, skim milk, garlic, lemon juice, and parsley, blending until smooth.

- When ready, stir artichoke hearts, cherry tomatoes, and spinach into quinoa, plus 1 tbsp. oil from artichokes, stirring well. Pour over with feta sauce, then season with onion powder and salt & pepper, combining thoroughly.
- Transfer mixture to oven safe casserole dish, spreading evenly. Top with remaining feta and mozzarella (or cheddar), then bake at 400F for 15 minutes until top has melted. Immediately plate and serve.

75. Cherry Tomato & Homemade Chèvre Tart

Serving: Makes 1 tart | Prep: | Cook: | Ready in:

Ingredients

- French Tart Shell, modified from David Lebovitz
- 3 oz unsalted butter, cut into pieces
- 5 oz of unbleached all-purpose flour and whole wheat pastry flour blend (I just really try to find any excuse to use my pastry flour)
- 1 tbsp extra virgin olive oil
- 2 tbsp warm water
- scant 1 tbsp sugar
- pinch of salt
- Chèvre & the rest of the tart
- 1 liter unpasteurized or pasteurized goat milk (you cannot use ultra-pasteurized because of the intervals of hot/warm/cold it has already been through)
- 1/4 c fresh lemon juice
- 1/4 tsp salt
- 1 clove garlic, finely minced
- fresh ground black pepper
- Cheesecloth & thermometer required
- 10 large cherry tomatoes, sliced width-wise about 1/4 inch apart
- 6-8 fresh basil leaves, roughly chopped

Direction

- French Tart Shell, modified from David Lebovitz
- Preheat oven to 400°F. In a large oven-proof bowl, add all the tart ingredients, except for the flour. Place into the oven for 10 minutes. Take out, and be careful! The bowl is very hot. Add in the flour, and immediately mix. You should have a ball, in which you will place onto the tart pan. Using your utensil of choice, begin to spread the dough along the pan. Once the dough is warm enough to touch, use your fingers and palms to even out. Bake for 15 minutes, just enough time for the edges to brown.
- Chèvre & the rest of the tart
- Begin to heat the goat milk slowly until the temperature reaches 160°F. Once this is achieved, take the pot off the heat and add the lemon juice. Once the curds have formed and the whey is clearly distinct from the curds (a yellowish color), gently pour the curds (along with the whey) into a cheesecloth covered colander. Allow to drain, then pull all ends together and tie with twine. Hang from faucet to allow the whey to drip into the sink. Hang for 1 hour, in order to retain some moisture (after all, you want to have spreadable chèvre).
- In a large mixing bowl, add the chèvre, along with the ingredients listed: garlic, salt, fresh ground black pepper. Mix well, and spread over tart shell. Add the sliced cherry tomatoes meticulously.
- Add the basil. Bake in oven for 30 minutes at 350°F. Serve at room temperature with a drizzle of extra virgin olive oil.

76. Chicken Meatball Sub With Gobs Of Fresh Mozzarella

Serving: Serves 4 | Prep: | Cook: | Ready in:

Ingredients

- For the chicken meatballs:

- 1 tablespoon olive oil
- 1 sweet onion, minced
- 3 cloves garlic, minced
- 1 pound ground chicken
- 2 tablespoons tomato paste
- 1 teaspoon oregano
- 2 tablespoons chopped fresh basil
- Salt and pepper, to taste
- 1 pinch red pepper flakes
- 1 egg
- 3/4 cup breadcrumbs, or more as needed
- Olive oil, as needed for cooking
- For the tomato sauce and the finished sandwich:
- 1 tablespoon olive oil
- 1 small onion, minced
- 2 cloves garlic, minced
- 1 tablespoon tomato paste
- 4 to 5 tomatoes, roughly chopped (or one 15-ounce can)
- Salt and pepper, to taste
- Chopped fresh basil, to taste
- 1 baguette, halved and cut into 4 pieces
- 8 ounces fresh mozzarella, thinly sliced
- Pepperoncini or other hot peppers, optional

Direction

- In a small sauté pan, heat the olive oil over medium heat. Sauté the onions until translucent, about 4 to 5 minutes. Add the garlic and sauté until fragrant, 1 minute more. Set aside, and let cool.
- In a large bowl, combine the cooled onion mixture with all the other meatball ingredients. Mix well to combine. Using your hands, roll the mixture into small balls.
- Heat the olive oil over medium heat. Place the meatballs in the hot pan, and allow to cook until nicely browned on each side and cooked through, about 8 to 10 minutes (you can also sear the meatballs and finish them in the oven, if desired).
- To make the tomato sauce, heat the olive oil in a small pot. Add the onion and sauté until translucent, about 4 to 5 minutes. Add the garlic and sauté until fragrant, 1 minute more.
- Deglaze the pan with the tomato paste, then stir in the tomatoes. Season the sauce with salt and pepper, and bring to a simmer. Simmer until a good flavor develops, then stir in the basil just before serving.
- Place the mozzarella on half of the bread slices (if your bread is stale, you can toast it first; I used a fresh baguette, so it didn't need toasting). Run the bread under the broiler until the cheese is melted and bubbly, about 2 minutes.
- Toss the meatballs in the tomato sauce, and spoon some meatballs onto the bread. Garnish with hot peppers, if desired, then serve!

77. Chicken, Pepper, And Bean "Mexitalian" Casserole

Serving: Serves 8-16 | Prep: | Cook: | Ready in:

Ingredients

- Red Sauce
- 2 cups low sodium chicken broth
- 1 tablespoon cornstarch
- 1 large jalapeno pepper, quartered with seeds left in
- 1/8 cup currants
- 12 ounces lower sodium tomato paste
- 2-3 tablespoons chili powder
- 1 tablespoon cumin seeds
- 1 teaspoon dry mustard
- 1 teaspoon garlic powder
- 1 teaspoon onion powder
- 1 teaspoon oregano leaves
- 1/2 teaspoon jalapeno powder
- 1/2 teaspoon ground cinnamon
- 1/2 teaspoon ground cloves
- 1 bay leaf
- 4 ounces cream cheese
- 1/2 cup sour cream
- Chicken, Pepper, and Bean Casserole
- 2 cups red sauce (above)

- 1.5 pounds boneless-skinless chicken breast, sliced into strips, boiled in water for 15 minutes, cooled and shredded
- 24 ounces roasted red peppers, drained
- 15 ounces black beans, drained and rinsed
- 16 ounces refried black beans
- 2 cups Mexican cheese mix
- 2 cups shredded mozzarella

Direction

- RED SAUCE: In a quart saucepan, mix a little water with the starch to make a slurry.
- RED SAUCE: Then add all of the other ingredients. Bring the mixture to a boil. Reduce and simmer uncovered for 20 minutes.
- RED SAUCE: Strain and discard the solids. Before it is done cooling, blend in the cream cheese and sour cream. Refrigerate until needed.
- NOTE: Prepare the chicken and red sauce ahead of time. At the time of preparation, combine the beans with the refried beans.
- In each of two 9x9 baking dishes, layer half of each, in order: (Bottom) red peppers, chicken, red sauce, Mexican cheese mix, bean mixture, mozzarella (top)
- Bake uncovered at 375F for 40 minutes. Let sit for a few minutes before serving (tent with foil for the first 20 minutes to prevent the top layer of cheese from getting too toasty unless, of course, you like toasty cheese)

78. Chili Verde Totchos

Serving: Serves 6 to 8 | Prep: | Cook: | Ready in:

Ingredients

- For the baked tater tots:
- 2 pounds (about 2 large) Russet potatoes
- 1 teaspoon salt
- 1/2 teaspoon black pepper
- 1 tablespoon chopped flat-leaf parsley
- 3 tablespoons peanut oil
- For the chili verde and nacho béchamel:
- 1 tablespoon olive oil
- 1/2 pound ground pork (substitute ground chicken if you prefer)
- 1 small can green chilies
- 1/2 medium onion, diced
- 3 tomatillos, husked and cut in half
- 2 cloves garlic
- 1/4 cup chicken stock
- Salt and pepper, to taste
- 2 tablespoons butter
- 2 tablespoons flour
- 1 1/4 cups milk
- 1 1/2 cups shredded sharp cheddar cheese, divided
- 1/4 cup grated Parmesan cheese
- 1 to 2 tablespoons pickled jalapeños, depending on heat preference
- 1 pinch salt
- 2 tablespoons sour cream, for garnish
- 1/2 tablespoon piment d'espelette, for garnish
- 2 tablespoons chopped cilantro, for garnish

Direction

- For the baked tater tots:
- Place potatoes (skin and all, they are super easy to peel after boiling) in a pot of water, bring to a boil, and boil for 30 minutes (if your potatoes are small, check after half the time). Turn off the heat and let the potatoes sit in the water 10 to 15 minutes.
- Drain potatoes over a colander and run under cold water. Peel potatoes with your hands: The skin literally rubs off and there is very little wasted potato. Preheat oven to 450° F.
- When potatoes are cool, grate on the medium size hole of a box grater into a medium bowl. To the bowl add salt, pepper, and parsley and combine with hands. The natural starch in the potatoes will hold the mix together. When well blended, shape into "tots." I used about 1 1/2 teaspoon of the mixture for each tot, but I stopped measuring halfway through and eyeballed the rest.
- Place peanut oil on a Silpat- or parchment-lined half sheet pan, place in oven for a minute

or two. Place the tots on the hot pan, then bake 15 minutes, turn the tots, and bake another 15. They should be golden brown and crunchy.
- For the chili verde and nacho béchamel:
- Start by making the chili verde: Add olive oil to a skillet and brown the ground pork over medium-high heat, until golden.
- In a blender or processor, add green chilies, onion, tomatillos, and garlic. Blend until you form a thick salsa, then add to pork, cook until bubbly, add stock, reduce heat to medium-low, and let simmer for 20 minutes, frequently stirring and add salt and pepper to taste. While it simmers, prepare béchamel.
- Make béchamel by heating butter in a saucepan over medium-high heat. Add flour then stir and cook for about 2 minutes. Reduce heat to medium and slowly whisk in milk, cooking until thick and bubbly.
- Add 1/2 cup cheddar and the Parmesan, stir until melted, then add jalapeños. Check for salt and add a pinch if needed. Turn heat down to low.
- Preheat broiler. Place baked tater tots on a broiler-safe tray or platter, drizzle béchamel over the top, add chili verde, and top with 1 cup remaining shredded cheddar. Broil until golden.
- Top with sour cream and sprinkle with piment d'espelette and cilantro. Enjoy this with cerveza while watching football with friends.

79. Chive, Herb Goat Cheese, And Tomato Frittata

Serving: Serves 6 | Prep: | Cook: | Ready in:

Ingredients

- 1 tablespoon Olive Oil
- 1/2 cup Onion, chopped
- 2 cups Cherry Tomatoes, halved
- 3/4 teaspoon salt
- 1/4 teaspoon pepper
- 8 eggs, lightly beaten
- 2 ounces herb goat cheese

Direction

- Preheat oven to 425 degrees.
- In a 10-inch ovenproof nonstick skillet, heat oil over medium-high. Add onions and tomatoes, season with salt and pepper, and cook about 5 minutes.
- Add eggs and season with salt and pepper, and stir to combine. Sprinkle goat cheese throughout, crumbling with your fingers.
- Cook, undisturbed, until edges are set, about 2 minutes. Transfer skillet to oven and bake until top of frittata is just set, 10 to 13 minutes. Invert or slide frittata onto a plate and cut into 6 wedges. Serve warm or at room temperature.

80. Chocolate Chip Chocolate Cake With Raspberry Cream Filling And Orange Almond Drizzle

Serving: Serves 12 | Prep: | Cook: | Ready in:

Ingredients

- 2 cups flour
- 2 cups sugar
- 1 cup unsweetened cococa powder
- 1 teaspoon baking powder
- 1/2 teaspoon salt
- 1 1/2 cups milk
- 2/3 cup vegetable oil
- 2 eggs
- 2 cups semi sweet chocolate chips
- 1 cup cream cheese, softened
- 1/4 cup shortening
- 1 1/2 tablespoons water
- 2 3/4 cups powdered sugar
- 1/4 cup raspberry jam
- 2 tablespoons raspberry jam
- 2 cups powdered sugar
- 1/2 teaspoon almond extract

- 2 tablespoons fresh squeezed orange juice

Direction

- Preheat oven to 350 degrees F. Grease and flour two 9 x 1 ½ inch round cake pans and set aside.
- In a large bowl combine flour, sugar, cocoa powder, baking soda and powder and salt. Add milk and oil and beat on low just until combined. Add eggs, one at a time, until thoroughly mixed, about 2 minutes. Pour batter evenly into each prepared cake pan and smooth tops with a spatula.
- Bake 30 to 35 minutes until toothpick comes out clean. Cool cakes in pans on a rack about 10 minutes. Carefully remove cakes from pans and continue cooling on rack until completely cool.
- In a medium bowl combine ingredients for filling and beat until smooth. Let chill in fridge at least 30 minutes.
- Combine ingredients for drizzle until desired consistency is achieved. Assemble cake by slathering filling on top one of the cakes and topping with the other. Evenly pour drizzle over top and return to fridge to set and let flavors meld another 30 minutes.

81. Chocolate Chip Chouquettes

Serving: Makes 3 dozen | Prep: | Cook: | Ready in:

Ingredients

- 6 tablespoons unsalted butter, diced
- 1 cup water
- 1/2 teaspoon sea salt
- 2 teaspoons granulated sugar
- 1 cup all purpose flour
- 4 large eggs at room temperature
- 1 egg yolk plus 1tbs water for egg wash
- mini chocolate chips
- pearl sugar

Direction

- Preheat oven to 425°. Line 2 baking sheets with parchment paper.
- In a medium saucepan bring butter, water, salt and sugar to a boil. Reduce heat to low and add flour all at once. Stir vigorously until the mixture forms a smooth ball. Remove from heat and let cool for about two minutes. Add eggs one at time until the mixture is glossy and creamy in texture.
- Transfer batter to a pastry bag fitted with a medium tip and pipe small rounds onto the parchment lined baking sheet. Brush gently with egg wash and top with chocolate chips and pearl sugar.
- Bake for 12 minutes, or until chouquettes are golden brown and puffed.
- Hint: The puffs can be piped, frozen and stored in a freezer bag, ready for baking at your convenience.

82. Chorizo And Chard Pie

Serving: Serves 8 | Prep: | Cook: | Ready in:

Ingredients

- 1 ready made pie crust
- 1/2 pound raw pork chorizo
- 1 large onion, sliced
- 4 cloves garlic, minced
- 1 large head swiss chard, washed, chopped and deveined
- 1 tablespoon unsalted butter
- 1 tablespoon all-purpose flour
- 1 cup unsweetened vanilla cashew milk
- 2 tablespoons Dijon mustard
- 3 ounces sharp Irish cheddar, shredded
- 2 teaspoons Cholula hot sauce
- 1 pinch nutmeg, a few shakes
- salt and pepper, to taste
- 1 tablespoon olive oil
- 1/2 cup panko breadcrumbs

Direction

- Preheat the oven to 350F
- In a large skillet, remove the sausage from its casing, break up with a wooden spoon and let thoroughly cook through. Remove from skillet and set aside.
- To the same skillet, remove all the excess pork fat except for about 1 tablespoon. If there isn't enough, add enough oil so you have about 1 TB of fat in the skillet. Add the onions and cook about 5 minutes until softened. Add the garlic, salt and pepper to taste, and cook another 2 minutes. Add the chard and cover until it properly wilts, about 5 minutes. Remove the cover from the skillet and cook until all the liquid has evaporated.
- While the liquid evaporates, in a saucepan, add the butter and let it melt. Sprinkle the flour on top of the butter and let brown, about 1 minute. Add the milk and whisk until smooth. Add the mustard, nutmeg and hot sauce and let cook about 5 minutes until it boils. Add the cheese, and stir it in a figure-8 motion until it's all melted. Let the sauce thicken about 2 minutes and remove from heat.
- In a small skillet, add the olive oil and panko and let toast. This will only take about 5 minutes.
- Assemble the tart: In a proper tart pan or a pie plate, roll out the crust and, using a fork, poke a lot of holes all around to prevent the crust from bubbling up. Add the first layer of chard, followed by the chorizo. Pour the cheese sauce over the whole thing and then top with the panko breadcrumbs.
- Bake for 45-60 minutes until the crust has browned. Serve warm or room temp

83. Cider Glazed Sweet Potatoes With Bacon, Pecans And Blue Cheese

Serving: Serves 4 | Prep: | Cook: | Ready in:

Ingredients

- 3 sweet potatoes
- 1 onion
- 2 tablespoons olive oil
- 1 tablespoon butter
- 1/3 cup pecans
- 1 tablespoon brown sugar
- 1/4 teaspoon cayenne pepper
- 1/4 teaspoon salt
- 4 slices bacon, cooked and crumbled, reserving 2 Tablespoons drippings
- 2 teaspoons honey
- 1 tablespoon cider vinegar
- 3 tablespoons blue cheese, crumbled

Direction

- Peel sweet potatoes and onions. Cut into 2-inch chunks. Toss with olive oil. Season with salt and pepper. Spread onto foil-lined 10 x 15-inch baking dish. Bake at 375 degrees for 45 to 50 minutes or until fork-tender. Stir halfway through baking time.
- Melt butter in skillet and add pecans, brown sugar, cayenne pepper and salt, stirring constantly for about 5 minutes or until pecans are coated with sugar mixture. Pour pecans onto foil-lined baking dish to cool.
- To make glaze, add 2 cloves garlic to reserved bacon drippings. Cook 2 minutes. Whisk in honey and cider vinegar.
- Transfer potatoes and onions to serving platter. Drizzle with glaze. Top with pecans, blue cheese and crumbled bacon.

84. Clambake Quesadillas

Serving: Makes 2 large quesadillas | Prep: | Cook: | Ready in:

Ingredients

- 16 littleneck clams
- 1 bay leaf
- 2 strips bacon
- 1½ tablespoons butter (if you don't want to use the bacon drippings or if you don't have quite enough to saute the veggies)
- 1 cup 2 tablespoons chopped scallions
- 1/2 teaspoon kosher salt
- 4 flour tortillas (not the huge wrap size; just the standard size)
- 1 cup grated Monterrey Jack cheese
- 1 cup grated Asiago Fresco cheese

Direction

- Twenty or thirty minutes before you start cooking, place your clams in a bowl of fresh water to let them purge any grit from inside their shells. Just before cooking them, drain. Fill a medium-sized skillet (that has a lid) with water until you've got 1/4" or 1/2" in the bottom. Add the bay leaf, and set the skillet over medium-high heat. When the water is nearing a boil, carefully place the clams in, cover the skillet and steam 7-10 minutes. If some still haven't opened at that point, you can let them steam a bit longer. Ultimately, discard any that don't open. When the clams are cool enough to handle, remove the meat from the shells, coarsely chop it and reserve in a bowl with any juice you can save. You may then discard the cooking liquid and the shells.
- In an 8" or 10" skillet, fry the bacon until crisp. Remove to a paper towel-lined plate to drain and cool some; then chop and reserve. If there is roughly 1.5 tablespoons of drippings left, you don't need the butter. Or, if you don't want to saute your corn and scallions in the drippings, pour them off and add the butter to the skillet.
- Heat the skillet over medium-high heat, and when the butter is melted or the drippings are hot, add the corn, 1 cup scallions and salt. Toss to combine well and cook until the veggies have softened but are still nice and bright. Remove from heat.
- Set a cast iron skillet over medium heat. When hot, add one tortilla. Carefully place half the cheese, half the corn-scallion mixture, half the bacon and half the clams on tops. Add a second tortilla to make a "sandwich", pressing down gently with a large spatula. Pay attention to the heat- if your tortillas brown too quickly, turn it down some. After a couple minutes, carefully flip the quesadilla. After a couple minutes, you might want to flip it again. You want the cheese nicely melted, everything warmed through and the tortillas lightly golden. Garnish with remaining chopped scallions.
- Repeat with the remaining ingredients. Cut each tortilla into quarters or sixths and enjoy immediately.

85. Cocktail Samosa

Serving: Makes ~ 20-25 | Prep: | Cook: | Ready in:

Ingredients

- Potato peas & Paneer filling
- 1 medium-large idaho potato, boiled & peeled
- 1/4 cup baby peas, cooked
- 1/4 cup shredded paneer
- 1 tablespoon finely chopped cilantro
- 1/4-1/2 teaspoons Salt
- 1/2 teaspoon Garam Masala
- 1 teaspoon minced ginger root
- 2 teaspoons Lime juice
- 2 tablespoons Canola oil
- 3 teaspoons Roughly crushed Coriander seeds
- Samosa
- 1/2 package phyllo pastry sheets

- Oil for brushing
- Potato, peas & paneer filling

Direction

- Potato peas & Paneer filling
- Crumble the boiled potato. Add to the peas & paneer in a bowl and mash until the veggies are integrated, but not mushy.
- Heat the oil till smoking & add the crushed coriander seeds. Stir around till they barely begin turning brown and then add the minced ginger. Stir for 5-10 sec and then add the hot tempering mix to the potato mixture. Add the Salt, Garam masala, and cilantro and lime juice. Combine to disperse the seasonings evenly in the filling.
- Samosa
- Preheat oven to 350 F.
- Thaw the pastry sheets and keep them covered with a moist kitchen towel. Cut each sheet into app. 6 in X 10 in size.
- Place a single sheet onto the workspace and brush with oil. Fold longitudinally to get a strip that is 3 in wide. Brush the top surface again with oil.
- Place 1 tablespoon of filling at one end of the strip. Fold the pastry & seal.
- Lay the samosas on a baking sheet lined with parchment paper and brush the surface with oil. Bake at 350 C for about 15 min or until the surface has turned a light golden brown.
- Serve warm with a sweet & sour tamarind chutney or green cilantro mint chutney.
- You can prepare the pastries ahead of time, lay them on a baking sheet, cover with plastic wrap, and refrigerate until required. Simply pop into a preheated oven to bake & serve.

86. Cream Cheese Tart With Orange, Pistachios & Cardamom

Serving: Serves 8 | Prep: | Cook: | Ready in:

Ingredients

- Crust
- 15 Maria cookies
- 6 tablespoons unsalted butter, unsalted
- 1/4 cup suger
- 1 teaspoon cardamom
- 1/2 cup unsalted pistachios, toasted
- pinch salt
- Filling
- 3 tablespoons orange marmalade
- 8 ounces cream cheese, soften
- 1/2 cup heavy cream
- 3 tablespoons suger
- 1/8 teaspoon cardamom
- 1/2 teaspoon orange zest
- 1 orange, peeled & cut into segments
- pinch salt

Direction

- To make the crust, in a food processor, break Maria cookies into smaller pieces; add pistachios, cardamom and sugar. Pulse it until it becomes crumbs. Add melted butter and pulse it until mixture is moist.
- Press the crumb mixture into bottom and sides of tart pan. Cover the tart pan and freeze it at least for an hour. The crust should be solid before adding filling.
- To make the filling, in a stand mixture with a whisk attachment, whisk cream cheese until smooth. Add sugar, orange zest, cardamom and heavy cream. Whisk again until mixture is smooth and fluffy.
- Spread the orange marmalade on top of cooled crust. Pour the cream cheese filling. Smooth out the filling. Garnish with orange segments. Refrigerate for 4 to 6 hours before serving. Finish the tart within two days.

87. Creamy Bucatini With Seared Brussels Sprouts

Serving: Serves 4 | Prep: | Cook: | Ready in:

Ingredients

- 1 pound bucatini
- 1/2 pound brussels sprouts, trimmed and halved
- 2 tablespoons neutral oil (canola, vegetable, grapeseed, etc.)
- Sea salt
- Freshly ground black pepper
- Juice of one lemon
- 5 tablespoons butter, divided
- 1 clove garlic, minced
- 1/2 cup stock
- 3/4 cup finely grated pecorino
- 1 egg

Direction

- Place a pot of water over high heat and bring to a boil. While you are waiting for the water to boil, cook the Brussels sprouts.
- Set a large skillet over high heat. Add the oil, and wait until it begins to lightly smoke. Add the Brussels sprouts in a single layer (if you have to do it in batches, do). Leave them for a minute or two, and don't fuss with them too much—you want them to develop a nice golden color but not get soft. Toss, and continue cooking until the sprouts are just cooked through (imagine al dente pasta).
- Remove the Brussels sprouts from the pan and put them on a baking sheet. (This way, they won't continue to cook in the pan.) Season them with salt and freshly ground black pepper, and the juice of a lemon.
- Add the pasta to the boiling water. While the pasta is cooking, set a large skillet over medium heat, and add 1 tablespoon of butter and the garlic. Cook the garlic until it is soft and just beginning to brown around the edges. When the pasta is one minute away from being cooked al dente, transfer it to the skillet with the garlic.
- Add a little reserved pasta water and the stock to the skillet along with the rest of the butter and stir. When the stock has reduced, add the cheese and Brussels sprouts. When the cheese has melted, turn off the heat. Add the egg to the skillet and stir vigorously. You don't want the egg to scramble—you want it to add a creamy richness to the sauce. Taste the pasta and add more salt if necessary.
- Serve the pasta with an extra sprinkle of grated pecorino on top and a few cracks of freshly ground black pepper.

88. Creamy Chorizo Queso

Serving: Makes enough for a party | Prep: | Cook: | Ready in:

Ingredients

- 2 smoked chorizo links (casing removed, crumbled)
- 1 onion (diced)
- 2 Anaheim or Poblano chilies
- 2 tablespoons unsalted butter
- 1 teaspoon tumeric
- 1/2 teaspoon cayenne pepper
- 1/2 teaspoon paprika
- 2 tablespoons flour
- 1 - 1.5 cups milk or half and half
- 1.5 cups Pepper Jack cheese (grated)
- salt and pepper

Direction

- Start by prepping the chilies. Char the peppers on the stove top or under the broiler. Remove and place in a plastic bag to help steam the paper off. When cool enough to touch, remove skin, stem and seeds. Roughly chop and set aside.
- Heat a large sauté pan over medium heat. Add crumbled chorizo and sauté for 7-8 minutes,

until brown. Remove with a slotted spoon to a plate and set aside. Leave remaining oil in pan.
- Add 1 tbsp. olive oil to pan. Add onions, Anaheim chili, turmeric, cayenne, paprika, s&p. Sauté for 7-8 minutes, until veggies are soft. Add 2 tbsp. of flour to the pan, and stir to combine. Let cook for 3 minutes to ensure the raw flour flavor goes away.
- Add 1 cup of the half and half to the mixture, stirring until thickened, 3-4 minutes. Stir in the cheese until the cheese melts. Add more half and half to the mixture, a couple tablespoons at a time until the mixture is smooth, not "cheesy". I used almost the entire 1/2 cup.
- Add the chorizo back in, and stir the mixture over low heat for another 3-5 minutes. Transfer to a serving dish or mini-crock pot to keep warm for serving! Enjoy!

89. Creamy Indian Noodles

Serving: Serves 6 | Prep: | Cook: | Ready in:

Ingredients

- 1 box   Macaroni Elbow noodles
- 2 cups   grated carrots
- 2 cups   shredded cabbage
- 1 tablespoon   cumin seeds
- 1 1/2 tablespoons   ginger paste
- 1 cup   sour cream
- 1/2 teaspoon   tumeric powder
- 2   roma tomatoes diced
- 3 tablespoons   olive oil
- 2 tablespoons   salt or to taste
- 2   slit green Thai chillies
- 1   large onion diced
- 1   small container of grape tomatoes halved

Direction

- Boil macaroni noodles and keep to side.
- Crank stove up to medium high heat. Add 3 tablespoons of oil to wok. When oil is hot, add cumin seeds. When you get the aroma of the cumin seeds, add the onions.
- Halfway through frying the onions, add the green chillies. Fry everything till golden brown. Next, add the ginger paste. Fry for about 5-7 seconds making sure not to burn the ginger otherwise it will make the dish bitter.
- Add shredded carrots. Fry for about 5 minutes and then add shredded cabbage. Fry the cabbage halfway but make sure to leave it a bit crunchy for the fresh aspect.
- Add diced tomatoes, turmeric powder and salt, Cook until the tomatoes are completely cooked down.
- After the tomatoes have cooked down, add the cooked macaroni noodles. Combine everything thoroughly and then add the sour cream and combine again with heat for about a minute then turn stove off.
- Garnish with grape tomatoes and serve as an entree or as a side accompaniment to another entree. Delicious dish with an Indian, spicy flare. It is bound to please anyone's palate! Best when eaten hot!

90. Creamy Spinach Artichoke Dip

Serving: Serves a crowd | Prep: | Cook: | Ready in:

Ingredients

- 2 packets   frozen, chopped spinach, thawed
- 2   8-oz packages cream cheese, room tempature
- 2   cans mild rotel
- 2 cups   grated monterey jack cheese
- 1 cup   parmesan cheese
- 1   onion, diced
- 1   package frozen artichoke hearts, thawed and chopped
- 2 teaspoons   cumin
- 1/2 teaspoon   chili powder
- 3   cloves garlic, minced

- 1 tablespoon olive oil (or enough to lightly coat pan)

Direction

- Preheat oven to 450 degrees.
- Heat olive oil in a medium pan. Sauté onions until translucent but not browned. Add minced garlic and cook for another 2-3 minutes until soft. Remove from heat.
- Combine all ingredients in a medium bowl until thoroughly combined. Season to taste with salt and pepper.
- Transfer to a large baking dish. Bake for about 45 minutes or until bubbling and heated through.
- Serve with tortilla chips, salsa, sour cream (optional), or your dipping item of choice!

91. Creamy Spinach And Paneer

Serving: Serves 0 | Prep: | Cook: |Ready in:

Ingredients

- 0 tablespoons 0

Direction

- In a large pot, bring water to a boil. In a large frying pan, heat oil on a low - medium heat, then add in chunks of cheese and fry/brown them on several sides until slightly golden. Set them on a separate plate or dish. In the same pan, at the same temperature, add in cumin seeds, turmeric, coriander, and garam masala and heat them for a couple minutes then add in onions, tomatoes, garlic, and ginger and sauté them until the onions are translucent and the tomatoes have broken down some.
- Add spinach to boiling water, and blanch the leaves for 2- 3 minutes and then drain them well. Once drained and cooled enough to handle them, put them onto your chopping board and give them several rough chops with a big knife.
- Then add the cheese, spinach, and coconut milk back into the frying pan with everything else and let it simmer on a low heat for 10 - 15 minutes, so that all the flavors can marry together.
- Suggested Accompaniments: Brown or White Basmati or Long Grain Rice Naan Bread
- Serve and hope you Enjoy! xoxo

92. Cretan Tomato Salad

Serving: Serves 2 as a side salad, or 1 for a nice lunch. | Prep: | Cook: |Ready in:

Ingredients

- 2 pieces of barley rusks
- 2 fresh, ripe, garden tomatoes
- 2 - 3 tablespoons best quality extra virgin olive oil - Greek is perfect
- 1 generous pinch of sea salt
- Fresh Ground black pepper to taste
- 1/4 cup Fresh, greek sheep's milk feta - crumbled.
- 2 teaspoons Fresh greek oregano - lightly chopped (optional)

Direction

- Place the barley rusks in a plastic zip lock bag, and using a heavy pan or rolling pin crush them lightly. You want big chunks, not crumbs. Place on a plate or in two salad bowls.
- In a large bowl, grate your tomatoes using the largest holes on a box grater. It's messy, but worth it. Discard any leftover skins.
- Pour the grated tomatoes over the rusks.
- Sprinkle with salt and pepper from above, then drizzle the olive oil over all. Another reason to let the salad sit for a few minutes is to let the salt melt and bring out the flavor in the tomatoes.
- Sprinkle with the fresh feta cheese and oregano.

- Go do something for 10 - 15 minutes. Put in a load of laundry, make the bed, whatever.
- Get a fork and dig in to a wonderfully rustic, healthy salad.

93. Croque Monsieur Cigars

Serving: Makes 12 | Prep: | Cook: | Ready in:

Ingredients

- Gruyere cheese sauce
- 2 tablespoons unsalted butter
- 3 tablespoons AP flour
- 2 cups hot milk
- 1 teaspoon salt
- 1/2 teaspoon black pepper
- Pinch nutmeg
- 2 cups grated Gruyere cheese
- 1/2 cup grated parmesan cheese
- Croque Monsieur Cigar
- 1 package of puff pastry, 2 sheets, thawed
- Dijon mustard
- 1/2 pound ham, shaved
- 1 cup grated Gruyere cheese

Direction

- Melt the butter over low heat in a small saucepan and add the flour all at once, stirring with a wooden spoon for 2 minutes.
- Slowly pour the hot milk into the butter-flour mixture and cook, whisking constantly, until the sauce is thickened. Off the heat add the salt, pepper, nutmeg, grated Gruyère, and the Parmesan and set aside.
- Cut each sheet of puff pastry into 6 rectangle. Stretch out a little in length & width. Spread Dijon mustard on all 12 stretched out rectangles.
- Put ham on each puff pastry rectangle along the length of it. Follow with cheese and cheese sauce.
- Roll pastry up length wise and seal. Pinch ends.
- Place them on a baking sheet that has been lined with parchment paper. Make sure to leave space in between each cigar so they can crisp up.
- Bake in a preheat oven of 350F for about 25 minutes.
- Pull the cigars off the cookie sheet by the parchment. Let cool about 10-15 minutes. Wrap with wax paper then tie. Pack in insulated bag will keep them warm. I put the extra cheese sauce in a thermos, so your guests can dunk their cigars in it if they would like.

94. Crostini Alla Romana

Serving: Serves 2 | Prep: | Cook: | Ready in:

Ingredients

- 4 small slices of stale bread
- 1/2 to 1 cups milk (or soy milk)
- 2 tablespoons olive oil
- 8 slices of mozzarella cheese (to cover the bread)
- 4 anchovy fillets
- 1 teaspoon flat leaf parsley, finely chopped
- 1 pinch freshly ground black pepper
- 1 splash olive oil (optional)

Direction

- Soak the bread in milk. Depending on how dry the bread is, adjust the quantity of milk and the time for soaking. If the bread is only a day or two old, 1/2 cup of milk and 5 to 10 minutes of soaking should do. If it's quite stale, it can take a few hours in a cup of milk.
- Heat a frying pan on medium, add oil, and cook one side of the milk-soaked bread. When it has a nice golden color (about 2 minutes), flip the bread, top with mozzarella slices and anchovy fillets, cover, and cook until the cheese melts (2 minutes).
- Sprinkle parsley, a splash of olive oil (optional), and serve.

95. Crostini With Eggplant, Ricotta And Pears

Serving: Serves 2-4 | Prep: | Cook: | Ready in:

Ingredients

- 1 large pear
- 1/2 eggplant, cut into four slices
- 20 g pine nuts
- 2 clove of garlic
- olive oil
- 4 large slices of Ciabatta
- 1 tablespoon lemon juice
- 2 teaspoons sugar
- 50 g ricotta, soft or firm

Direction

- Heat a frying pan on high heat, heat 1 tbsp. oil and add the sliced eggplants. Fry for 5-8 minutes until soft and golden. Season to taste. Add the sugar and reduce heat to medium. Cook for another 5 minutes.
- Preheat the oven to 400F.
- Combine pine nuts with garlic and olive oil. Make a paste using an electric mixer. Season well. Spread paste on slices of ciabatta. Bake in the oven for about 10 minutes.
- Wash the pear. Cut into slices. Sprinkle with lemon juice and some sugar. Heat some olive oil in a pan. Once the pan in warm enough, cook the pears for one minute on each side.
- Crumble or slice ricotta cheese
- Take the ciabatta out of the oven. Lay one slice of eggplant, pear and ricotta. Set in the oven for another 2 minutes until cheese starts melting. Serve warm and enjoy!

96. Crostini With Ricotta, Truffle Honey And Smoked Salts

Serving: Makes 16 crostini | Prep: | Cook: | Ready in:

Ingredients

- 16 baguette slices, cut on the diagonal, 1/4" thick
- 1 1/2 cups ricotta
- 1/4 cup white truffle honey
- fine alder-smoked salts to taste
- 1 jellyroll pan

Direction

- Place the bread slices on the jellyroll pan and toast under the broiler on each side until golden-brown.
- Top each bread slice with 1 1/2 tablespoons of ricotta. Place the crostini on a serving platter. Drizzle each slice with a little truffle honey (about 3/4 teaspoon). Generously sprinkle the crostini with smoked salts and serve immediately, while the bread slices are still warm.

97. Crunchy Chicken And Brussel Sprouts In The Oven With A Melted Cheese And Wine Sa

Serving: Serves 1 person | Prep: | Cook: | Ready in:

Ingredients

- Chicken and brussel sprouts part
- 250 grams brussel sprouts
- 150 grams chicken breast (or any meat leftover)
- olive oil
- 1/2 lemon's juice
- rosemary, salt, pepper
- For the cheese and wine sauce
- 200 grams of melting cheese (I used goat and Brie)

- 2 tablespoons of dry red wine
- 2 tablespoons raspberry or pomegranate juice
- 1/2 tablespoon flour

Direction

- Clean the Brussels sprouts and cut them in 4 pieces. Cut the meat in little pieces and stir it with the sprouts (If you only have raw fresh meat, give it a boil for 15' before continuing.).
- Then drizzle the sprouts and the meat lightly with olive oil, lemon juice salt and freshly ground pepper and put them in the oven at 180C for 20'-30'. Stir frequently so all parts get golden brown; you want crunching meat and sprouts.
- In the meantime, take a pan and over low heat, add the wine and chopped cheese and start to stir. Mix it the juice with the flour and pour this uniform batter in the mixture that lightly boils. Continue to stir, season and add 2-3 chopped leaves of rosemary.
- Remove the food from the oven, pour your thick delicious sauce and enjoy while warm.

98. Crustless Pizza

Serving: Makes 24-wedge shaped pieces | Prep: | Cook: | Ready in:

Ingredients

- 2 cups coarsely shredded cheddar (or muenster, Swiss, or mozzarella — or a combination of such cheeses)
- oregano, garlic powder, red pepper flakes, and black pepper, as desired
- bits of sliced pepperoni, salami, cooked sausage, if available

Direction

- Use an 11- or 12-inch skillet (nonstick, preferably). Put the shredded cheese in the skillet and spread it evenly over the bottom. Turn heat to medium.
- As the cheese melts, sprinkle the seasonings on top and arrange the bits of meat as you like. (If you just happen to have a few sun-dried tomatoes around, cut them into slivers and include them as well; they make a fantastic addition.)
- Fry the cheese until the edges begin to become crisp and brown. Meanwhile, run about 1 inch of cold water into the kitchen sink.
- When the cheese is done (edges slightly crisp, but center not yet brown on top), remove pan from heat and set it in the sink to cool the bottom quickly. After 30 to 45 seconds, take a fork and lift the entire "pie" of cheese out of the skillet, transferring it to a cutting board. With a chef's knife or pizza cutter, cut it into about 24 wedge-shaped pieces and serve.

99. Crème Fraîche Cheesecake With Apple Cardamom Compote

Serving: Makes one 9-inch round cheesecake | Prep: | Cook: | Ready in:

Ingredients

- 1 1/2 cups cream cheese
- 1/2 cup fresh goat cheese
- 1/2 cup sugar, plus 3 tablespoons
- 1 1/2 cups crème fraîche
- 1 teaspoon vanilla extract
- 1/4 teaspoon black pepper
- 4 large eggs
- 3 large, red-skinned apples, chopped
- 1/4 tablespoon ground cardamom, plus more to taste

Direction

- To make the cheesecake, heat the oven to 325°F. Wrap the bottom of a 9-inch springform pan with foil and place on a baking sheet.
- Using an electric mixer, beat the cream cheese and goat cheese until very smooth. Add the 1/2 cup of sugar and continue beating until no

lumps remain. Beat in the crème fraîche, vanilla, and pepper. Beat in the eggs one at a time, scraping down the sides of the bowl between additions, and beat until combined.

- Pour the mixture into the pan and bake for 10 minutes, then reduce the temperature to 250°F and bake until the cake is just set (it will still wobble a little in the middle), 45 to 60 minutes. Transfer the pan to a wire rack to cool completely.
- While the cheesecake is cooling, make the apple cardamom compote. In a heavy-bottomed saucepan over medium heat, add the apples, cardamom, and sugar, and then cover three-quarters of the apples with water. Cook the liquid in the pan until the compote reduces by half and comes together, about 45 minutes. Set aside until the cheesecake is ready to serve.
- Run a knife around the edge of the pan to loosen the cake from the pan before removing and serving with the apple compote.

100. Crème Fraîche

Serving: Makes 3 1/2 cups | Prep: | Cook: | Ready in:

Ingredients

- 1/2 cup buttermilk
- 3 cups cream

Direction

- Whisk together buttermilk and cream. Let sit at room temperature for 24 hours, then refrigerate--will keep for up to two weeks.

101. Cucumber And Radish Salad With Harissa Yogurt

Serving: Serves 2 | Prep: | Cook: | Ready in:

Ingredients

- 1/2 cup plain whole milk yogurt
- 1 teaspoon harissa
- Maldon sea salt, to taste
- 2 Persian cucumbers, cut in a large dice
- 4 radishes, quartered
- 1/4 cup parsley leaves
- 1 tablespoon olive oil
- Salt and pepper, to taste
- 1 teaspoon toasted sesame seeds
- 1 teaspoon toasted nigella seeds

Direction

- For harissa yogurt, mix yogurt and harissa until well combined. Season to taste with Maldon sea salt. Set aside.
- In a mixing bowl, toss cucumbers, radishes, and parsley with olive oil. Season with salt and pepper to taste.
- To serve, dollop yogurt at bottom of bowl and use a spoon to spread it up the sides. Place cucumber-radish mix on top of yogurt. Garnish with sprinkle of sesame seeds and nigella seeds.

102. Curds & Whey Biscuits With Infused Honey & Ricotta Spread

Serving: Makes 8 3-inch biscuits & | Prep: | Cook: | Ready in:

Ingredients

- Homemade Ricotta and Infused Honey
- FOR THE RICOTTA (adapted from Cook's Illustrated)
- 2 lemons (enough for 1/3 cup juice)
- 1/2 gallon whole milk (not ultra-high temp. pasteurized)
- 1/2 teaspoon table salt
- FOR THE HONEY
- 8-inch sprig Rosemary

- 2 strips lemon peel (1/2-inch by 2-inch)
- 1/4 cup mild honey (e.g. clover)
- 1 tablespoon water
- 3/4 teaspoon dried lavender flowers
- Curds & Whey Biscuits and Infused Honey & Ricotta Spread
- FOR THE BISCUITS (Adapted from the Baking Illustrated recipe Buttermilk Biscuits)
- 1 stick unsalted butter (1/2 cup), refrigerator cold
- reserved ricotta and whey mixture, refrigerator cold
- 1 tablespoon barley malt syrup
- 1 teaspoon sugar
- 5 ounces all-purpose flour (1 cup)
- 4 ounces cake flour (1 cup)
- 1 tablespoon baking powder (non-aluminum containing if possible)
- 3/8 teaspoon table salt
- FOR THE INFUSED HONEY & RICOTTA SPREAD
- reserved ricotta
- 1/8 teaspoon fleur de sel
- infused honey

Direction

- Homemade Ricotta and Infused Honey
- FOR THE RICOTTA: Remove 2 ½ by 2" strips of peel with minimal white pith from one of the lemons, and set aside. (Feel free to zest the rest of the lemons to save the zest for another use.) Juice the lemons, and strain the juice to remove pulp.
- Heat the milk and salt in a stock pot over medium high heat to 185°F. This will take about 10 minutes, and the milk will start to steam as it approaches 185°. Scrape bottom of pot with spatula fairly frequently to prevent scorching. Once the milk is hot enough, remove from the heat. Stir in 3 T of the lemon juice and let the mixture sit for 5 minutes. If the whey is still white, add another T of lemon juice and wait an additional 5 minutes. Repeat once more if needed. The whey will become translucent yellowish or bluish when it is ready. Let the curds and whey rest in the pot for 15 to 20 minutes.
- Line a strainer with 2 layers of cheesecloth, and set strainer over a bowl. Use a slotted spoon to gently scoop curds from whey into the strainer. Once curds have been transferred use rubber spatula to gently toss the curds until no visible pools of whey remain. Scoop out ¼-cup of the curds at this point and transfer them to a 2-cup glass measure. Fold cheesecloth over remaining curds in strainer, and gently squeeze to remove more whey (for this application it's best if they are a little drier than typical ricotta.) Transfer curds into container, tightly seal, and refrigerate. Pour ½ cup plus 1 tablespoon of whey from the bowl into the 2-cup glass measure containing the ¼-cup curds you'd previously set aside. Cover and refrigerate. (If desired save the rest of the whey you've created)
- FOR THE HONEY: Remove the leaves from rosemary, and lightly crush with the side of a knife to help release the flavor. Tear the lemon strips in half. Mix honey and water in microwave safe container (I used a coffee mug). Heat to boiling (about 30 seconds.) Stir in rosemary, lemon peel, and lavender. Tightly cover and allow to sit at room temperature for 8 hour or overnight.
- Curds & Whey Biscuits and Infused Honey & Ricotta Spread
- FOR BISCUITS: Heat oven to 450° F with rack in center of oven.
- Cut stick of butter into quarters length-wise, then into approximately 1/4" thick pieces. Return to fridge. Combine ricotta & whey mixture with barley malt syrup and sugar using a stick blender or small whisk (if you use the whisk some tiny pieces of ricotta will remain - this is fine, but the biscuits will be freckled when they come out of the oven.) Return to fridge.
- Combine flours, salt, and baking powder in bowl of food processor with blade attachment. Pulse 6 or 7 times to combine. Scatter cold butter over flour mixture. Pulse to combine (12 to 14 1-second pulses.) Pour whey mixture

evenly over surface of dough. Pulse until clumping together, and very little dry flour remains (3 to 5 1-second pulses.) Dump dough onto lightly floured counter, and knead several times just until dough is cohesive. Form dough into a rectangle, then roll out to approximately ½-inch thickness. Try to make it so you can make 6 3-inch biscuits. Cut out biscuits. Briefly knead remaining dough, and shape so you can get 2 more biscuits. You should have very little if any dough remaining when you are done. (NB: alternately you can form the dough into a ½-inch thick round and cut it into 8 wedges.) Place biscuits on unlined baking sheet. Bake for 10 to 12 minutes, just until lightly brown. Remove from oven and serve hot, split and slathered with the Honey-Ricotta spread.

- FOR HONEY & RICOTTA SPREAD: While biscuits are baking, wash bowl and blade from food processor. Shake out excess water. Place reserved ricotta and salt in bowl of food processor. Turn on food processor. Strain honey through mesh strainer into ricotta mixture while running, adding honey little by little till you get the consistency you're looking for. Scrape down sides of bowl, and process until smooth and creamy. Transfer to serving bowl. (Will keep for several days, just make sure it's tightly covered or it will pick up off flavors!)

103. Curry Dip

Serving: Serves 6 | Prep: | Cook: | Ready in:

Ingredients

- 1 cup soft fresh cream chease
- 1 cup mayonnaise
- 3 tablespoons high quality curry powder
- chips, pita triangles, broken up papadums or cut fresh vegetables

Direction

- Whisk the mayonnaise and cream cheese together in a small bowl until completely blended. Add the curry powder, whisking it in slowly until it too is completely blended. (It will appear to be way too much curry powder, but it is fine.) The dip benefits from an hour's refrigerated rest but it is not essential.

104. Cyprus Easter Cheese Bread ("Flaounes")

Serving: Makes 12 flaounas | Prep: | Cook: | Ready in:

Ingredients

- For The Filling
- 3 cups   (226g) finely grated kefalotyri cheese
- 2.5 cups   (226g) parmigiano reggiano cheese
- 4 cups   (396g) pecorino romano cheese
- 2 tbs   ground dry mint
- 3/8 tbs   ground mastic powder
- 1/2 tbs   ground mehlep powder
- 10 tsp   baking powder
- 10 eggs
- 3/4 cup   sultana raisins
- For The Dough
- 7.5 cups   all purpose flour
- 7.5 tbs   vegetable shortening
- 1/4 tbs   salt
- 1/2 tbs   ground mastic powder
- 1/2 tbs   ground mehlep powder
- 2 small eggs
- 2 cups milk
- 1 & 3/4   tbs dry yeast
- 1/6 cup   white sugar
- sesame seeds
- 2 eggs for egg wash

Direction

- Prepare the filling the night before. In a large bowl mix together the cheeses, mint, mastic powder, mehlep powder and half of the baking powder with your hands.

- Add 3 eggs at a time, mixing the cheese mixture with your hands until it becomes medium-soft. You may only need 9 eggs.
- Cover the bowl with plastic wrap and let rest overnight at room temperature.
- In the morning, add the remaining baking powder, raisins and mix well with your hands. Cover the bowl with a kitchen towel.
- Prepare the dough. Mix together the flour, mastic powder, mehlep powder and salt in a large bowl. Add the vegetable shortening and rub the shortening into the flour mixture with your fingers.
- Dilute the yeast with 1/2 cup of warm milk and 1/2 tablespoon of sugar in a small bowl. Cover the bowl with plastic wrap and let rise in a warm place for about 15 minutes until a light foam has formed on top.
- In the meantime, warm the remaining milk with remaining sugar over the stove at low heat. Place in a large bowl.
- Beat the eggs and add them to the milk. Keep this mixture warm until the yeast mixture has risen.
- Once the yeast mixture has risen, add it to the flour mixture. Start adding the remaining milk mixture slowly while mixing the dough with your hands. If the flour mixture needs more water, have some warm water at hand and add a little warm water if necessary. (I added about 3 tablespoons of warm water.)
- Start needing the dough until it becomes smooth and elastic. (You may use an electric mixer with a dough hook.) This will take about 10 to 15 minutes.
- Place the dough in a bowl, cover the bowl with a blanket and let the dough rise for about 2 hours in a warm place.
- When the dough has risen, punch it down with your fists.
- Cut a piece of dough the size of a small lemon. Roll it into a circle approximately 20 cm in diameter. Place a small plate over the circle and trace around it with a knife forming a flat, circular piece of dough.
- Rinse about 1 cup of sesame seeds. Place the wet sesame seeds in a plate.
- Place the circular piece of dough onto the sesame seeds so that one side is covered with sesame seeds.
- Place a handful of the cheese mixture (about one cup) into the middle of the circle. Take a brush, and brush egg wash around the edge of the circular piece of dough.
- Fold the sides of the circle to form an open triangle. Ensure that there is a small opening on top. Lightly press the corner edges down with the prongs of a fork to secure the cheese inside.
- Place on baking paper on a pan. Prepare all the "flaounes" the same way. Once a pan is full, cover the same with a kitchen towel and let the "flaounes" rise again for about 1 hour. Do the same with each full pan.
- Preheat the oven to 160C. Lightly brush the top of each "flaouna" with egg wash and bake for 45 minutes. Pour yourself a drink and enjoy – it has been a long day!

105. Dark Meat Turkey Panini With Montasio Cheese Leftover Heaven

Serving: Serves 1 | Prep: | Cook: |Ready in:

Ingredients

- 2 tablespoons cranberry sauce
- 2 slices granola multi grain bread
- 1/2 cup dark turkey meat-in pieces
- 5 slices montasio cheese-enough to cover one piece of bread
- 3 ounces frisee
- fresh ground black pepper
- cooking spray

Direction

- Spread cranberry sauce on one side of each bread slice.
- Place turkey, montasio, and frisee on one of the bread slices and top with freshly ground

black pepper. Place the second piece of bread on top.
- Spray a panini maker with cooking spray and (once hot) place the sandwich in. This can also be done on the stove top, in a pan.

106. Devils On Hatchback

Serving: Serves 40 | Prep: | Cook: |Ready in:

Ingredients

- 20 fresh Hatch green chile peppers, or New Mexico green chile peppers
- 8 ounces cream cheese
- 20 slices of thin, center cut bacon
- 1 tablespoon honey, or maybe more, its just for drizzling
- black pepper

Direction

- Roast the Hatch peppers. To do this, put the peppers on a baking sheet and broil them until they are black on the outside, turning occasionally. Then, remove them from the oven, and put them in a ziploc bag so that they can steam for ten minutes. Then take out the peppers and rub them gently so that all the charred skin comes off of the peppers. This can be done ahead of time and they also freeze beautifully.
- Cut the peppers in half and cut the stem end off as well. Make one split lengthwise through the pepper halves and open them up so that you can see inside. Remove some of the seeds and vein (leave in more if you like your devils spicier).
- Put about a teaspoon of cream cheese in the center of each pepper half, wrap the pepper around it so that it closes, then place on a parchment lined baking sheet. Do not worry if your tender peppers tear and you can see the cheese come through a bit, the bacon will help contain everything.
- Cut the twenty strips of bacon in half and wrap around each little devil and place back on the baking sheet. Be sure to place them seam side down so that the bacon doesn't curl and open up in the oven. Crack black pepper over the devils and put them in a 350° F oven for 45 minutes. Some of your cheese may ooze out of your devils, but not to worry, because they will still be delicious!
- After 45 minutes, drizzle a generous amount of honey over the devils and bake for 5 more minutes. Take them out of the oven and pop them into your mouth.

107. Double Toasted Honey Dijon And Strawberry Grilled Cheese

Serving: Serves 1 | Prep: | Cook: |Ready in:

Ingredients

- 2 slices of a good textured bread (I like Milton's multigrain)
- 2 tablespoons butter
- 1 tablespoon coarse Dijon mustard
- 1 tablespoon honey
- 2 slices of gruyere cheese
- 2 slices of pepperjack cheese
- 2 medium sized strawberries (hulled and sliced)

Direction

- Melt 1 tablespoon of butter in a shallow medium sized pan over medium low heat and swirl it around to coat the entire pan.
- Lay both slices of bread in the melted butter and allow to toast for about 2-3 min or until deep golden brown. Add 1 more tablespoon of butter to the pan and flip to toast the other side.
- While you're toasting the other side, smear the mustard on one slice and squeeze the honey onto the mustard. Pick a cheese to lay on this

slice of bread. Place the other cheese onto the other slice of bread. Lay the sliced strawberries on either slice or close the sandwich (the melted cheese on both sides will help keep the strawberries from falling out).
- Give the sandwich a good press down with a metal spatula and continue to toast both sides until the cheese is melted and the bread is nice and crusty. Slice in half and serve!

108. Dreamy Greek Eggs

Serving: Serves 1 | Prep: | Cook: | Ready in:

Ingredients

- 4 eggs
- 1 handful chestnut mushrooms
- 10 black olives
- 6 semi sun dried tomatoes
- 1 small red onion
- 1 garlic clove
- 1 teaspoon dried oregano
- Fettah cheese (goat)
- pepper, salt, parsley

Direction

- Preheat the oven to 180C. Cut the onions in half rings, cut the garlic small, the mushrooms in quarters and the tomatoes in two.
- I use a terracotta oven dish which I also put on the fire to bake the onion before I put it in the oven (less dishes). Put some oil of the semi dried tomatoes in the dish and bake the onions until soft, add the mushrooms, the garlic and bake until the garlic smells lovely and the mushrooms have a little bit of a brown edge. Add the tomatoes and the olives and mix everything together.
- In a bowl mix the eggs with the oregano, pepper and salt. Be easy on the salt, we will add cheese later which makes the dish saltier already.
- Add the egg in the oven dish and mix everything together. Put nice chunks of feta cheese on the egg and place it in the oven. Bake until the egg is set, this will take about 10 minutes. Garnish with some parsley and eat with a nice and crunchy fresh bread or some rocket on the side.
- Make sure that when you put your terracotta dish on the fire that you start with the lowest fire or it will break. If you want to be really careful, you can put it in water one hour before you use it but always heat it slowly.

109. Dungeness Crab And Fire Roasted Corn Chowder

Serving: Makes 4 servings | Prep: | Cook: | Ready in:

Ingredients

- 1 tablespoon extra virgin olive oil
- 2 tablespoons unsalted butter
- 2 slices bacon, chopped small
- 1 large potato, peeled and chopped small
- 2 ribs celery, chopped small
- 1/2 medium onion, chopped small
- 1 small red jalapeno pepper, seeded and diced
- 2 bay leaves
- 1 tablespoon Crab and Shrimp boil mix (or something similar)
- 1 pinch red pepper flakes (optional)
- 1-2 tablespoons all-purpose flour
- 1 1/2 cups vegetable broth
- 1 1/2 cups fat free half and half
- Meat from 1 fresh Dungeness crab, cooked and cleaned or 12 oz. canned crab meat
- Corn stripped from 2 ears after roasting on BBQ or over gas burner or 1 can of fire roasted corn
- 2 tablespoons cooking sherry

Direction

- Remove the meat from the cooked and cleaned Dungeness crab body, legs and claws and refrigerate covered until needed for use.
- Remove the corn husks and roast the ears on your BBQ or put on skewers and roast over a gas burner on range until kernels turn golden and just start to develop brown spots (about 2-3 minutes). When cooled, slice the kernels from the cob and reserve until ready to use.
- Skin and cut potato into ½ inch cubes and microwave loosely covered for about 3 minutes and reserve. Cook chopped bacon in a 5 ½ Q Dutch oven over moderate heat then remove from pot and set aside.
- Add the onion, potatoes, celery, red jalapeno pepper and red pepper flakes to the pot and sauté in bacon fat for 5 minutes. Add corn after first 3 minutes. Add bay leaves and Crab Boil to the pot and cook 2 minutes, stirring constantly then deglaze with the sherry.
- Stir in broth and half and half and combine. Bring soup up to a boil and add back the crab meat and bacon and simmer soup about 8 minutes. While soup is simmering, add flour while whisking until thickness is right. Then remove the bay leaves.

110. Earl Grey Olive Oil Pound Cake

Serving: Makes one bundt cake | Prep: | Cook: | Ready in:

Ingredients

- 3/4 cup virgin olive oil
- 4 earl grey tea bags
- 12 tablespoons unsalted butter, room temp
- 2 1/2 cups granulated sugar
- 1 teaspoon salt
- 6 large eggs
- 3 1/2 cups all purpose flour
- 1 cup milk
- 1 1/2 teaspoons vanilla extract
- zest of half a lemon
- flour+butter for the pan

Direction

- Preheat oven to 350F (Celsius). Heat the tea bags with olive oil in a small saucepan for about 2 minutes on medium heat. Turn off heat, let it sit with the tea bags inside and cool almost all the way.
- In a large bowl with a beater, or in a stand mixer with paddle attachment, cream the butter on high speed for 30 seconds, slowly add sugar, salt, eggs, and continue to mix until well incorporated—about 1 minute. Scrape sides as needed. Then add 2 cups of the flour and mix with the beater just enough to get most of the flour wet on the lowest speed. Add 1 cup milk, the tea infused oil tossing out the tea bags, then add the remaining flour, vanilla, lemon zest, and once again mix on the lowest speed until roughly incorporated.
- Lightly butter the sides of the pan including the middle tube, sprinkle with flour, pour in the batter, and bake for approximately 1 hour. You may need to bake longer depending on your oven. Let it cool, slice, and serve with berries or ice cream.

111. Easter Bunny Bread Bowl With Grana Padano Kale Artichoke Dip

Serving: Makes 1 bread bowl | Prep: | Cook: | Ready in:

Ingredients

- For the dip:
- 1/2 cup drained canned or jarred artichoke hearts
- 1 1/2 cups de-stemmed and finely chopped kale
- 1 tablespoon minced garlic
- 3/4 cup shredded mozzarella cheese
- 3/4 cup milk
- 1/2 cup grated Grana Padano cheese

- 4 ounces cream cheese, room temperature
- 4 dashes Worcestershire sauce
- 1/4 teaspoon cayenne pepper
- 1/4 teaspoon salt
- For the bread bowl
- 1 round loaf of bread
- 1 round bun
- 2 chocolate chips or dried cranberries
- 1 soft candy or 1/8 inch thick slice of carrot

Direction

- To make the dip, heat kale, artichoke hearts and garlic over low heat until wilt and aromatic. Whisk in remainder of ingredients and cook until cheeses melt and dip is smooth.
- To assemble bread bowl, cut top (about 1/8-1/4 of loaf) and scoop out insides, leaving about an inch all the way around the edge of loaf.
- Cut bottom off of roll/bun. Cut two eye holes into the bun, a little smaller than the chocolate chips (or press the cranberries onto the tips of 2 whole cloves) and press into bun. Do the same with nose piece and press candy or carrot into place.
- From the bottom of bun, cut out two ears and push a toothpick halfway through the back of ears until they can stand up straight. Insert the end of toothpicks into the top of the bun to place ears.
- Using another toothpick or two, affix the bun to back of bread bowl.
- Pour dip into bread bowl and serve with cut up pieces of bread, crackers or carrots to dip.

112. Easy Broccoli Salad With Cheese Recipe

Serving: Serves 3 as a lunch | Prep: 0hours10mins | Cook: 0hours0mins | Ready in:

Ingredients

- 1 medium to large head of broccoli
- 8-10 pitted dates
- 3/4 cup walnut pieces, toasted or raw
- 1/4 cup dried sour cherries
- 5 ounces Cypress Grove Humboldt Fog, divided into 2 ounces and 3 ounces, at room temperature
- 1/4 cup extra virgin olive oil, plus 2 tablespoons
- 1 lemon, for 1 tablespoon freshly squeezed lemon juice and 1/4 teaspoon lemon zest
- 1/2 teaspoon kosher salt, plus more as needed

Direction

- On a cutting board, take the head of broccoli and cut off the florets with about 2 inches of stem attached to each. Slice these thinly (aim for between 1/8 inch and 1/4 inch), but roughly—no need to spend too much time getting everything the same size or thinness. Different textures are ideal. You want about 4 cups total of sliced broccoli pieces—add to a large bowl, where we'll build the salad. (Save the remaining stalks for another use!)
- Roughly chop the dates into pea-sized pieces—you should end up with about 1/3 cup. If the walnut pieces are large, give them a quick chop, too, so no piece is so chunky that it'd be unpleasant to get in a bite. Add the dates, walnuts, and dried sour cherries to the bowl of sliced broccoli. Crumble in the 2 ounces of goat cheese.
- In a food processor, blend the remaining 3 ounces of goat cheese with 1/4 cup extra virgin olive oil, 1 tablespoon freshly squeezed lemon juice, 1/4 teaspoon lemon rind, and 1/2 teaspoon salt, until the mixture is creamy. Pause the blending once or twice to scrape down the sides with a spatula, to ensure no cheese clumps are hanging around the perimeter. As it gets fully smooth and homogenous (this takes less than a minute), drizzle in the remaining 2 tablespoons of olive oil, until you have a dressing with the consistency of loose, thick yogurt. Taste and add additional salt and lemon juice if needed.

- Drizzle the dressing over your broccoli salad and toss to thoroughly coat. This salad is excellent right away, but can also sit in the fridge, fully dressed and covered, up to three days. (And it even lasts a few extra days if you prep everything, but wait to dress it until you serve.)

113. Easy Frittata Base Recipe

Serving: Serves 4 | Prep: | Cook: | Ready in:

Ingredients

- 2-3 pieces medium-sized potatoes, peeled
- 1 tablespoon olive oil
- 1/4 piece onion, sliced
- 1/4 cup milk
- 1/4 cup fresh parsley, chopped
- Sea salt and freshly ground black pepper
- 1/4 cup grated cheese

Direction

- Boil potatoes until just tender. Drain, cut into 3-4cm chunks and set aside.
- Heat oil in a small fry pan (approx. 20cm). Add onion and cook for 2 minutes until softened.
- Add potatoes and any other vegetables of your choosing, and toss to combine with onion.
- Whisk together eggs, milk, parsley, salt and pepper. Pour over the vegetables and cook on a low heat for 5-6 minutes.
- Sprinkle cheese over the top and place under a pre-heated grill for 3-4 minutes until golden.

114. Easy Homemade Ranch Dip

Serving: Makes 2 cups | Prep: | Cook: | Ready in:

Ingredients

- 2 cups sour cream
- 1 teaspoon dried dill
- 1 teaspoon dried parsley
- 1 teaspoon onion powder
- 1 teaspoon garlic powder
- 1 teaspoon kosher salt

Direction

- Combine all ingredients in a bowl. Stir well, and let sit for at least 15 minutes before serving.
- Can be kept in the fridge for up to a week.
- Serve with veggies, chips, wings, or any dipper you like.
- Enjoy!

115. Egg And Cheese Salad With Spicy Cilantro Pepitas Aioli

Serving: Makes makes 1 3/4 cups of the salad + enough aioli for one more portion | Prep: | Cook: | Ready in:

Ingredients

- • 3 extra-large eggs, hard boiled, (but the yolk should be still pretty soft), shredded on the large holes side of a box grater
- • 1 cup Aged Sharp White Cheddar or Parmesan cheese, shredded
- • 2 celery ribs with leaves, peeled and thinly sliced
- • Freshly ground black pepper to taste
- • 1/2 cup pepitas (raw pumpkin seeds), lightly toasted
- • 1 cup fresh cilantro leaves
- • 1 large garlic clove, peeled and chopped
- • 1/2 jalapeno chile, seeded and chopped
- • 1/4 teaspoon ground cumin
- • 1/2 teaspoon kosher salt
- • 2 tablespoons olive oil
- • 2 teaspoons each lime zest and juice

- • 1/4 cup Best Foods or Hellman's mayonnaise

Direction

- In a small skillet over medium heat, toast pepitas, shaking pan often, until they begin to pop and are fragrant, but not browned, 3-5 minutes.
- Transfer to food processor or blender. Add cilantro, garlic, jalapeno, salt and cumin. Process, scraping sides frequently, until well-minced. With machine running, gradually add oil, then lime juice, processing until as smooth as possible, and scraping down sides as needed. Transfer to a mixing bowl; whisk in mayonnaise and lime zest. Chill until ready to use.
- In another bowl toss to combine the eggs, cheese, celery and black pepper; gradually add spoonfuls of the aioli until desired consistency; I added about 3 and 1/2 or 4 tablespoons. Can be made ahead and kept refrigerated up to 3 days.

116. Endive With Bacon And Buttermilk Ranch Dressing

Serving: Serves 4 | Prep: | Cook: | Ready in:

Ingredients

- For the buttermilk ranch dressing:
- 1/4 cup mayonnaise
- 2 tablespoons sour cream
- 1 teaspoon minced shallot
- 1 clove garlic, crushed and minced
- 1 teaspoon lemon zest
- 1/4 teaspoon mustard powder
- 1/2 cup buttermilk, shaken vigorously
- 1 to 2 tablespoons lemon juice
- 1 splash sherry vinegar
- 2 tablespoons minced parsley, plus more for garnish
- 2 teaspoons minced chives, plus more for garnish
- 1 teaspoon thyme leaves, plus more for garnish
- ground black pepper to taste
- For the salad:
- 1/4 pound thick-cut bacon
- 6 Belgian endives
- sea salt, to taste
- ground black pepper, to taste
- 1 teaspoon minced fresh herbs

Direction

- In a medium bowl, combine mayonnaise and sour cream. Stir in shallot, garlic, lemon zest, and mustard powder. Slowly whisk in buttermilk. Next, whisk in 1 to 2 tablespoons lemon juice (until dressing reaches desired thickness) and the sherry vinegar. Finally, fold in herbs and black pepper. Cover bowl and set dressing in the fridge to chill for at least 20 minutes, but preferably overnight. Recipe makes approximately 1 cup.
- To prepare the salad, cook bacon over medium heat until edges have crisped. Briefly cool on a plate lined with paper towels, and then chop.
- Core endives, remove leaves, and cut into diagonal 1/2-inch strips.
- Set chopped endive in a serving bowl, drizzle with ranch dressing, and toss gently. Scatter bacon and spoon on a bit more dressing. Finish with a pinch each of sea salt and black pepper and a sprinkle of minced herbs. Serve immediately.

117. Farmer's Market Tomato And Ricotta Tart

Serving: Serves 6-8 people | Prep: | Cook: | Ready in:

Ingredients

- Tart Shell Ingredients
- 1 cup plus 2 tablespoons all purpose flour

- 1/4 cup fine polenta or cornmeal
- 1/4 teaspoon kosher salt
- 6 tablespoons cold unsalted butter, small diced
- 1 large egg
- 1 tablespoon room temperature unsalted butter
- Filling Ingredients
- 12 ounces whole milk ricotta cheese
- 2 1/2 ounces softened plain goat cheese
- 8 ounces finely grated parmesan cheese
- 1/2 teaspoon kosher salt
- 1/3 teaspoon ground black pepper
- 3/4 teaspoon minced fresh thyme leaves
- 1 pint heirloom, grape or cherry tomatoes
- 1/2 cup pesto (optional for serving)

Direction

- In a medium bowl mix together flour, polenta or cornmeal, and salt. Using a pastry cutter or fork work the diced butter into the dry ingredients until the butter is in very small pieces and the mixture is just starting to come together. Add the egg and mix in with a fork until the dough forms a rough ball. The mixture will be fairly dry, resembling shortbread.
- Turn the dough into an ungreased 9" tart pan with a removable bottom and using the floured, flat side of a measuring cup press into the bottom and along the sides of the pan in an even layer. Even the edges with a butter knife, or by flattening with the measuring cup.
- Remove the shell from freezer and place on a baking sheet. Using a brush or clean hands, spread the room temperature butter on a sheet of aluminum foil large enough to cover the tart shell with some overhang. Smooth the buttered side of the foil along the bottom of the tart shell and up the sides. Fill with pie weights or dried beans.
- Bake the foil covered tart shell for 10 minutes. Carefully remove the pie weights and foil from the shell and using a fork, prick the bottom of the shell – this will allow any air to release. Replace the uncovered tart shell in the oven and bake for an additional 5 to 8 minutes until it is lightly golden and crisp. Set tart shell aside on a baking rack and allow to cool completely.
- While the tart shell is cooling, assemble the ricotta filling. In a medium bowl, whisk together the ricotta and softened goat cheese until smooth, then stir in the finely grated parmesan, kosher salt, pepper, and fresh thyme. Cut the tomatoes – a serrated knife will work best – into 1/4 to 1/8" slices.
- Once the tart shell is completely cooled, spoon the ricotta mixture into the shell and smooth with a spatula or knife. Layer the sliced tomatoes on top of the cheese in any pattern or arrangement you like – this is a moment to be creative! If you're a perfectionist like me here's a tip: after the tomatoes are sliced practice layering on your cutting board or a piece of foil before you try to arrange them on the tart. Sprinkle with a few fresh thyme leaves, salt and pepper. Serve as is, or with a spoonful of pesto sauce.

118.   Farro Casserole With Cranberries, Squash, Kale And A Sage Béchamel

Serving: Serves 6-8 | Prep: | Cook: | Ready in:

Ingredients

- 1 cup Emmer farro, soaked overnight and drained
- 5 cups water or broth
- 2 Delicata squash
- 1 1/2 tablespoons olive oil
- 2 cups cranberries
- 2 tablespoons brown sugar
- 1 tablespoon olive oil
- 10 ounces Tuscan kale, roughly torn from stems
- 1 tablespoon olive oil
- 2 ounces walnuts

- 1 shallot, finely chopped
- 6-8 sage leaves, roughly chopped
- 2 tablespoons butter
- 2 tablespoons all-purpose flour
- 1 cup whole milk
- Dash freshly ground nutmeg
- salt and pepper to taste
- 3 ounces Gruyere cheese, grated

Direction

- Preheat the oven to 400 F, butter a medium-sized casserole dish and set aside. Then, line two baking sheets with parchment paper.
- In a medium saucepan, combine the drained farro and the water or broth. Bring to a boil and then lower the heat.
- Cover the pan and let cook for 50-60 minutes. The farro is ready when it has plumped up and softened, yet retains a somewhat chewy texture. The farro won't absorb all of the liquid, so be sure to drain off the excess.
- While the farro is cooking, halve and seed the squash, then cut it into half-moons. Quarter the larger half-moon slices into small cubes and cut the smaller ones into thirds. Spread the cubes on a parchment-lined baking sheet and lightly sprinkle them with salt and pepper. Drizzle the olive oil over the squash and lightly toss to coat.
- Place the cranberries in a small bowl and add salt, pepper and brown sugar. Stir, then add the olive oil and toss to coat. Spread the prepared cranberries out on the other parchment-lined baking sheet.
- Put the two baking sheets in the oven (cranberries on top rack, squash on the bottom) and let the cranberries roast for 20 minutes. Remove the cranberries from the oven, then toss the squash and leave it roast for another 10 minutes.
- While the squash and cranberries are roasting, soak the kale for a few minutes in a large bowl filled with cold water and 1 tablespoon of distilled white vinegar. Massage the kale, softening it and helping to remove any insects that have latched onto the leaves. Drain the kale and, if necessary, soak and drain again. Using a salad spinner, dry the kale.
- Heat a large frying pan (preferably cast iron) on medium heat, add enough oil to coat the bottom and add the kale. Sauté for five minutes or until the kale has wilted and become tender. Sprinkle with salt and pepper.
- After roasting the cranberries and squash, toast the walnuts in the preheated oven for 5 minutes. Remove from the oven, let cool for a few minutes and then roughly chop and divide into two even piles.
- Place the cooked farro in the grated casserole dish and add the cranberries, squash, kale and walnuts. Stir to combine, then sprinkle in half of the chopped walnuts. Stir again. Now that the casserole is assembled, turn to the Béchamel.
- Heat the butter in a small saucepan over medium-low heat until it melts. Once the butter is sizzling, add the shallot and chopped sage and cook until the shallot has softened and become translucent. Add the flour, stirring it in with a wooden spoon. It will become a smooth paste. Over low heat, slowly whisk in the milk, adding a little at a time. The sauce will gradually become thicker. Once fully thickened, remove from heat and sprinkle in both the nutmeg, salt, and pepper, then, stir in the grated cheese until it fully melts into the sauce.
- Pour the Béchamel over the assembled casserole and top with the remaining chopped walnuts.
- Place in the oven for 25-30 minutes and cook until the sauce is bubbling.

119. Fettuccine Alfredo For One

Serving: Serves 1 | Prep: 0hours0mins | Cook: 0hours20mins | Ready in:

Ingredients

- 4 ounces fettuccine, preferably fresh (but dried is good, too)
- Kosher salt, to taste
- 2 tablespoons unsalted butter, divided
- 1 small shallot, thinly sliced
- 1/2 cup grated Parmesan, plus more to taste
- Freshly ground black pepper, to taste

Direction

- Bring a pot of water to a boil and salt generously. Cook the pasta according to package instructions until al dente. Reserve 1/2 cup of the cooking water and drain pasta.
- In the same pot over medium heat, melt 1 tablespoon of the butter, then sauté the shallot for about 1 to 2 minutes, just until translucent and no longer raw. Add 1/4 cup of the reserved cooking water, bring to a simmer, then stir in the butter, followed by the cheese, until both are fully incorporated.
- Add the pasta to the sauce and continue cooking, stirring constantly and incorporating more of the water as needed to coat the noodles sufficiently. (The trick here is to amalgamate the pasta, butter, cheese, and starchy water until it comes together into a creamy emulsion.)
- Plate, then finish with a final smattering of Parmesan and freshly ground pepper.

120. Fig Jam Pizza

Serving: Makes 1 | Prep: 0hours30mins | Cook: 0hours20mins | Ready in:

Ingredients

- 1 large frozen pizza dough ball, thawed
- 4 tablespoons Strawberry Chipotle + Fig Jam
- 1 large mozzarella ball, thinly sliced
- 7-8 thin slices of prosciutto
- 1/2 cup arugula
- 1 egg (optional)
- Drizzle of good olive oil
- Pepper, freshly cracked
- Salt

Direction

- Preheat oven to 400 degrees Fahrenheit.
- Roll out the pizza dough on a lightly floured surface until you reach your desired size. Be careful not to roll too thin. Place on a large baking sheet or pizza stone.
- Spread the fig jam over the surface of the dough. Lay the slices of mozzarella on top and sprinkle the cheese lightly with salt and pepper. Top with prosciutto, carefully crack 1 egg over the top of the pizza (if using) and season the egg with salt and pepper.
- Bake the pizza until the crust is golden, the cheese is bubbly and the egg whites are fully cooked, 15-20 minutes.
- Pull pizza from oven and let cool for 10 minutes. Toss arugula with olive oil and pile on top.

121. Fig, Ricotta And Pear Galette

Serving: Serves about 8 - 10 people | Prep: | Cook: | Ready in:

Ingredients

- For the pastry base
- 105 grams (3.7 oz or 3/4 cup) plain flour
- 70 grams (2.5 oz or 1/2 cup) rye flour(you can also use any other flour you have on hand)
- 1 1/2 teaspoons sugar
- big pinches salt
- 113 grams (4 oz or 1/2 cup) unsalted butter, very cold and diced
- 1 egg, beaten
- ice water, if needed
- For the filling
- 185 grams (6.5 oz) dried figs
- 113 grams (4 oz or 1/2 cup) unsalted butter, melted

- 2 heaping tablespoons honey (you can also use any other sweetener you like)
- big pinches salt
- 1 pear
- 1 slice fresh ricotta, to crumble on top
- 1 egg beaten with a tablespoon of water (egg wash) and some demerara sugar

Direction

- Start with the dough, by placing both flours, sugar and salt in a bowl, along with the diced butter. Rub the ingredients together with the tips of your fingers, until the butter is broken into some small pieces and some bigger pieces. Add the beaten egg, and mix it until the dough is formed into a ball, no longer than that. If you feel like the mixture is too dry, add about 1 to 2 teaspoons of ice water, until you get the right consistency. Wrap the dough in cling film, and leave it to rest in the fridge for a minimum of 2 hours, or overnight, if making ahead.
- Meanwhile, make the filling. Add the dried figs to boiling water, cover it and leave it soak for about 20 minutes. Pour the melted butter, honey and soaked figs into a blender, and blend for a few minutes, until the mixture has fully incorporated into a paste. Taste for sweetness and, if you'd like, add more honey. Set aside. Cut your pear into quarters, take off the core, then slice it thinly, squeeze some lemon juice on top of it and set it aside as well (it's best if you do this only a few minutes before assembling the galette).
- Preheat your oven to 205ºC (400ºF) and line the bottom of a baking tray with parchment paper, set aside. After it's chilled, lightly flour your working surface, and roll the dough into a roughly 30 to 32cm (13 inches) circle (ish), and transfer it to the lined baking tray. Place it in the freezer for about 10 minutes. Then spread the fig paste on the middle of the dough, but don't reach the edges, leave a, approximately, 3cm (1.2 inches) border. Add the sliced pears, in a circle pattern, then fold the edges over the filling, brush the pastry with the egg wash and sprinkle some demerara sugar. Place it in the freezer for about 10 minutes, then bake it for 40 to 45 minutes, rotating the tray a few times, until it's golden brown all over. After it comes out of the oven, crumble the ricotta on top, leave it to cool for a few minutes and serve.

122. Fonduta Con Tartufi (Truffle Fondue)

Serving: Serves 4 | Prep: | Cook: | Ready in:

Ingredients

- 1 pound Fontina cheese, diced
- Some milk
- 5 egg yolks
- 1/4 cup (2 tablespoons or 50 gr) butter
- 3 ounces fresh truffles, shaved

Direction

- Place the diced Fontina cheese in a large bowl and cover with milk. Let rest in the fridge for several hours.
- In a saucepan, place the butter, egg yolks and cheese, along with all the milk. Place the saucepan on top of another saucepan containing boiling water (a bain marie or double broiler) and mix energetically until the cheese begins to melt.
- When you have a fondue with a dense, creamy consistency, remove from the bain marie. Keep the fondue warm and serve with the truffle scattered on top. Enjoy with plenty of grilled bread.

123. Fontina, Roasted Fennel & Spinach Seafood Tart

Serving: Serves 4-6 | Prep: | Cook: | Ready in:

Ingredients

- 17.3 ounces package puff pastry sheets
- 3 large eggs
- 10 ounces tub original cooking crème (locate in cream cheese section of grocery store)
- 1/4 cup low fat milk
- 1 Meyer Lemon, juice and zest
- 1 tablespoon all-purpose flour
- 2 ounces or 1 cup shredded Fontina cheese
- 2 ounces smoked salmon, chop in 1/8-inch pieces
- 5 ounces raw shrimp, shells removed, deveined, chop in 1/2-inch pieces
- 1 tablespoon olive oil
- 1 fennel bulb (white part), cut 1/8-inch horizontal slices to equal about 1-cup
- 4 ounces fresh spinach, shred in 1/4-inch strips
- 3 tablespoons fennel fronds (fern green part), chopped

Direction

- Remove pastry sheets from outer package leaving each sheet in the individual wrapper. Thaw for 30-40 minutes. Meanwhile prepare filling.
- In a large measuring bowl with pouring spout, whisk eggs, cooking crème, milk, 1-tablespoon lemon juice, 1-tablespoon lemon zest, and flour until smooth. Stir in Fontina cheese, smoked salmon pieces and raw shrimp. Set aside.
- Heat oil on HIGH in a large skillet. Toss the sliced fennel bulb into hot oil, don't stir, shake pan a little and cook 2 minutes or just until fennel is pan-roasted and just beginning to turn brown. Lower heat to MEDIUM and add spinach, stir and cook until wilted. Set aside. Heat oven to 400 degrees F.
- Line two 8-inch by 8-inch baking pans with parchment paper. Spray sides and bottom of pan with cooking spray. Unfold each thawed puff pastry sheet in its own baking pan. Gently stretch the short-sides up the pan wall to make a 1 ½-inch edge. Pastry corners will easily stretch to the top edge of pan. Divide fennel-spinach mixture in half and spoon over pastry sheet. Pour egg mixture evenly over fennel-spinach mixture. Bake for 25 minutes or until set in center. Cover with foil the last 10 minutes if needed to prevent over browning. Remove from oven and cool 5 minutes. To remove from pan, run a knife along the edges and gently slide out onto serving platter, removing parchment paper. Garnish with 1-tablespoon chopped fronds on top. Serve warm or cold.

124. French Onion Soup In A Hurry

Serving: Serves 1 | Prep: | Cook: | Ready in:

Ingredients

- Easy caramelized onions
- 3 pounds yellow or white onions
- 1 stick butter
- 1 teaspoon salt
- French Onion Soup
- 1 1/2 cups beef broth
- 1/2 cup red wine
- 1/2 cup caramelized onions
- 1/4 teaspoon dried rosemary, crumbled
- 1 slice French bread
- 1/2 cup grated Gruyere or other cheese of choice
- salt and pepper to taste

Direction

- To caramelize the onions: Peel onions, slice in half vertically and then slice thinly. Put in slow cooker, sprinkle with salt, top with butter cut into tablespoon-sized chunks, and cook on low for about 18 hours. Stir occasionally. Will make about 4 cups of caramelized onions.
- Heat together broth, wine and onions to a boil; reduce heat, add rosemary, and simmer about 10 minutes. Taste and correct seasonings. Pour

into ovenproof bowl, top with French bread and cheese, and run under broiler until cheese is melted, bubbly and starting to brown.
- In the alternative, just stir some grated Parmigiano into the soup and eat with crackers or crostini, or make yourself a grilled cheese sandwich. Oh, and drink the rest of the wine, since you had to open the bottle anyway.

125. French Onion And Endive Soup

Serving: Serves 4 | Prep: | Cook: | Ready in:

Ingredients

- 2 spanish onions, thinly sliced into 1/2-moons
- 2 endives, thinly sliced into 1/2-moons
- 2 teaspoons butter
- 1 tablespoon extra virgin olive oil
- 1 teaspoon salt
- 1 teaspoon cracked black pepper
- 1 tablespoon finely minced garlic
- 1 teaspoon ground coriander seed
- 2 teaspoons rosemary (dried or fresh)
- 1 teaspoon thyme (dried or fresh)
- 1 bay leaf
- 1/3 cup dry white wine, good enough to drink
- 2 tablespoons good balsamic vinegar
- 1 tablespoon raw sugar
- 3 cups low-sodium vegetable stock
- 4 handfuls parmigiano reggiano cheese: grated
- 1 piece parmigiano reggiano cheese: rind

Direction

- Prep! Thinly-slice onions and endives into 1/2-moons. Finely-mince 2 cloves of garlic.
- Preheat a soup pot with a thick bottom.
- Add butter, olive oil, and a moment later once the butter starts to melt, add the garlic.
- Once the garlic starts to work, add the onions and endives, salt and pepper; cook down on medium heat, always stirring, until they are very soft and caramelized but not burnt. (Approx. 7-10 minutes)
- Turn up the heat and add the white wine - cook it for a few minutes to get the alcohol out.
- Add balsamic vinegar, herbs, spices, and sugar, and let the mixture thicken and cook down on a medium-high heat, stirring occasionally. (Approx. 7-10 minutes)
- Add vegetable stock, and the RIND of the Parmigiano reggiano cheese. Bring to a boil, then lower the heat to simmer.
- Allow the soup to simmer for at least 10-15 minutes, but the longer the better! Always seasoning to taste.
- Serve. Each bowl should boast a handful of beautifully-grated Parmigiano reggiano cheese, and a crack of black pepper.

126. French Onion Rutabaga Baguette Au Gratin

Serving: Serves 6 (a serving is 1 baguette slice with rutabaga/onion mixture evenly divided into 6 portions). doubles easily. | Prep: | Cook: | Ready in:

Ingredients

- 6 stale baguette slices cut from 1/2 to 1 inch thick. Set aside until needed.
- 2 medium rutabaga, (about ½ pound) sliced 1/4 inch thin
- 3 medium sweet onion, thinly sliced
- 1 stick of salted butter, @ room temp. - assures you will have enough, will not use it all
- 1-1/2 cups shredded Gruyère cheese
- Salt and Pepper
- Sherry (Lustau Dry Amontillado is my favorite to use)
- Heavy cream
- 8x5 oven & broiling safe baking dish – this recipe can easily be doubled

Direction

- Preheat oven to 350 degrees.
- Sauté the onion in a couple tablespoons butter and a tablespoon of sherry, until browned and limp - set aside. NOTE: I always save 6 raw onion rings aside for garnish.
- Blanch the rutabaga slices in salted boiling water for 3 minutes. Remove from water and drain. (It's best to use young rutabaga; the older ones that are drier and tougher may need to blanch a little longer).
- Coat the inside of the baking dish with butter. Add the rutabaga slices; it's ok to overlap, season with salt and pepper. Sprinkle 1/2 cup cheese over the top and dot with cream – about 6-8 teaspoons.
- Top with the sautéed onion, season with pepper and dot with 6-8 teaspoons cream. Sprinkle 1 tablespoon sherry over the top.
- Add 6 stale baguette slices that have been buttered on both sides. Dot the top of each baguette slice with sherry and cream.
- Top with the remaining cheese. Optional - add a raw onion ring over each baguette slice.
- Bake for 30 minutes or until it starts to bubble; for the last few minutes broil a couple minutes to brown the top.
- Let cool for 15 minutes before serving.

127. French Baguette Sandwich

Serving: Serves 2 | Prep: | Cook: | Ready in:

Ingredients

- 1 baguette
- 3 leeks
- brie
- 2 tablespoons brown sugar
- 1 teaspoon butter
- salt and pepper

Direction

- Start by caramelizing the leeks. Add the butter in the pan to melt and then add the leeks with the brown sugar on low heat and stir. When they turn transparent and brown (but not burnt) they will be ready.
- Add some salt and pepper at the end.
- Cut the baguette lengthwise and fill it with the caramelized leeks, the brie and the beetroots in this order.

128. Fresh Fig And Goat Cheese Canapés

Serving: Makes 24 pieces6 | Prep: | Cook: | Ready in:

Ingredients

- 6 fresh Mission figs
- 6 ounces goat cheese
- 24 water crackers
- a few ounces honey
- a few leaves of fresh mint, as optional garnish

Direction

- Slice each fig into 4 disks, length-wise.
- Use a knife or spreader to put a thin layer of goat cheese on each cracker.
- Place a fig slice atop each goat cheese-topped cracker.
- Drizzle each fig and goat cheese-topped cracker with a bit of honey. (Easiest with a honey bear.)
- If desired, chiffonade mint leaves and sprinkle on top as an optional garnish.
- Serve immediately.

129. Fresh Figs For Breakfast

Serving: Serves 2 | Prep: | Cook: | Ready in:

Ingredients

- 6 Fresh Figs
- about 1/3 Wheel of Red Hawk Cheese from Cowgirl Creamery
- 4 fresh organic eggs
- 1/2 freshly baked baguette, sliced on the diagonal and toasted
- Extra Virgin Olive Oil
- Sea Salt
- Freshly Ground Black Pepper

Direction

- Preheat oven to 400F.
- Using a sharp paring knife, cut the small stem off the top of the fig.
- Cut an "X" into the top of the fig, going about an inch deep. Gently spread the fig open just a touch.
- Slice your cheese into small cubes. Drop one or two cubes into each fig.
- Arrange figs on an ovenproof dish. Drizzle olive oil and sea salt on top.
- Roast for about 10 minutes, or until cheese is bubbly.
- Meanwhile, crack your eggs into a hot cast iron skillet that's slick with olive oil. Cook for 2 minutes and gently flip. Cook for another minute. Top with black pepper and serve alongside the figs and toasted bread.
- Be sure to use the bread to sop up the glorious juices and olive oil left in the dish used to cook the figs!

130. Fresh Ricotta And Peach Pizza With Honey Drizzle

Serving: Makes 1 pizza | Prep: | Cook: | Ready in:

Ingredients

- 1 packet of pizza dough (approx 1 lb.)
- 3/4 of a ripe peach
- spoonfuls of fresh ricotta
- drizzle of honey
- drizzle of extra virgin olive oil
- sprinkle of kosher salt
- heavy sprinkle of black pepper
- sprinkle of ground parmesan

Direction

- Place 1/4 cup of whole wheat flour on a cutting board and coat all sides of the pizza dough (I like Birritella's) until no moist spot are left on the exterior. Roll out the dough, occasionally sprinkling the residual flour on both sides. I form the dough until it fits the circumference of the stone of my Breville pizza crisper (with shaped parchment paper on the stone to prevent sticking!). I make the circumference slightly thicker than the interior of the dough.
- Drizzle the dough with the olive oil, not too much and no need to rub in. Add a generous pinch of kosher salt, freshly ground black pepper and a sprinkle of ground parmesan cheese. Add a generous amount of peach wedges (around 1/2" thick) to the pizza (I like to place them in a nice pattern for presentation purposes). Place the dough in the pizza crisper after heating it up for roughly 10 minutes to make sure its hot (I set it to medium thickness on the dial). The dough should cook for approximately 12-15 minutes. You'll know when it's done, as it should be crisp golden in color, with an occasional char spot.
- Remove the dough. Place on a cutting board in front of guests. Spoon fresh ricotta on top. Add a generously drizzle of honey, especially to the exterior crust. Sprinkle with kosher salt and generous amounts of coarsely ground black pepper. Serve.

131. Fresh Summer Salad With Raspberry Lambic Dressing

Serving: Serves 4 | Prep: 0hours20mins | Cook: 0hours0mins | Ready in:

Ingredients

- 10 ounces bag Trader Joe's Organic Power Greens
- 1 1/2 cups fresh raspberries
- 5 ounces package of chèvre goat cheese
- 1/4 cup French's Caramelized Crispy Fried Onions, crushed
- 5 ounces package of Trader Joe's Candied Walnuts
- 1 medium red onion, sliced thin
- 4 teaspoons Chia seed
- 1/4 cup Raspberry Lambic Beer
- 1/2 cup extra virgin olive oil
- 1 tablespoon shallots, chopped fine
- 2 tablespoons Trader Joe's Aioli Garlic Mustard Sauce
- 4 tablespoons red wine vinegar
- salt and pepper to taste

Direction

- To make the dressing, combine lambic beer, 1/2 raspberries, olive oil, shallots, aioli, vinegar, salt and pepper in a blender and process until emulsified. Set aside.
- To make the goat cheese balls, divide the goat cheese into 16 portions and form into small balls. Add crushed fried onions to a plate and rolls the goat cheese balls over the onions until evenly coated. Set aside.
- To assemble the salad add greens, 1 cup of raspberries, goat cheese balls, walnuts and red onions to a large salad bowl. Top with dressing and chia seeds. Toss and serve immediately.

132. Fresh Tomato Tart

Serving: Serves 2 as a meal | Prep: | Cook: | Ready in:

Ingredients

- 1 sheet frozen puff pastry dough, thawed
- 4-5 ripe yellow tomatoes 'fist size"
- 3/4 - 1 pounds fresh mozzarella
- extra virgin olive oil
- kosher salt
- parmesan-reggiano cheese
- 1 sprig basil

Direction

- Pre-heat oven to 400 degrees F
- Place dough on a parchment lines sheet pan, cut a slight slit around edge about 1/2" in to create border
- Slice the mozzarella roughly 1/4" slices, you want enough to cover the puff pastry within the cut boundary you made
- Wash tomatoes and dry, cut enough slices (1/4" thick min.) to cover the mozzarella
- Drizzle the tomatoes with the extra virgin olive oil to liking, and sprinkle tomatoes with a little kosher salt.
- Use a vegetable peeler to shave the Parmesan cheese block over the tart just to cover the tomatoes.
- Place sheet pan with tart in oven, bake until edges are puffed and dark golden brown and cheese is melted and bubbling. Should be around 15 minutes. Chiffonade the basil leaves while tart in oven.
- Remove tart from oven and sprinkle basil over tart. Can be cut into desired serving sizes. Best with a pizza cutter. For 2 people, cut half, then each half into 2 or 3 slices. For a larger gathering, can be cut into bite size pieces.

133. Fresh Mozzarella Stuffed With Cranberries, Pecans, And Maple Syrup

Serving: Makes 4 people | Prep: | Cook: | Ready in:

Ingredients

- 2 fresh mozzarella balls
- 2 handfuls fresh cranberries
- Sugar (to cook the cranberries)
- 1 handful pecans chopped
- 1/2 handful fresh thyme leaves

- 1 tablespoon Olive oil
- 1 teaspoon maple syrup

Direction

- Rinse the cranberries with cold water. Place in large skillet and add some sugar. Cover with water and stir well. Cook the cranberries on medium heat, until the mixture starts to bubble. Taste and add more sugar if the cranberries are too sweet. Turn down to low heat and cook for five more minutes. Remove from heat and let cool.
- Cut each mozzarella ball in two. Remove a little bit of the base so you can place the mozzarella on a plate later on.
- With a small spoon, delicately scoop out the inside of the cheese. It should look like a well.
- In a bowl, stir together cranberries, chopped pecans, fresh thyme, oil and maple syrup. It should be quite "creamy". Fill each mozzarella with this mixture and serve!

134.   Freshies On Sticks

Serving: Makes 20 sticks | Prep: | Cook: | Ready in:

Ingredients

- 10 pieces Cherry Tomatoes
- 1 packet Rocket Leaves
- 3 packets 120gms Feta Cheese
- 3 teaspoons Balsamic Vinaigrette
- 2 tablespoons Olive Oil
- 1 teaspoon Coarsely Ground Black Pepper
- 20 pieces 4" Cocktail Sticks

Direction

- Halve the cherry tomatoes.
- Cut Feta Cheese into 20 2"inches cubes.
- Take a Cocktail stick and first insert halved Cherry Tomato, then 2 Rocket Leaves, followed by a square of Feta Cheese.
- Arrange these on a platter.
- Sprinkle the coarsely ground Black Pepper on top.
- In a small cup, lightly whisk together the Balsamic Vinaigrette with Olive Oil to make a light dressing.
- Just before serving, sprinkle the dressing on top and serve.

135.   Frittata With Leeks, Sundried Tomatoes, And Fresh Parmigiano Reggiano

Serving: Serves 6-8 | Prep: | Cook: | Ready in:

Ingredients

- 1 tablespoon organic butter
- 1 tablespoon olive oil
- 1 bunch leeks- white parts only, cleaned well and chopped (about 1 1/2 cups)
- 1 cup sliced mushroons
- 1 cup chopped fresh basil
- 1/2 cup fresh parsley, chopped
- 1/2 cup sun dried tomatoes in oil, drained and julienned
- 8-10 eggs, preferably organic and free-range
- 2 tablespoons ricotta cheese
- 1/2 cup freshly grated Parmigiano-Reggiano, plus more for serving

Direction

- Preheat oven to 350°F. In a cast-iron skillet, heat the butter and oil. Add leeks and the sliced mushrooms and fennel and cook over low until they are very soft, about 5 minutes.
- Add the herbs and the sun-dried tomatoes and continue to cook for a few more minutes.
- Crack the eggs into a large bowl. Add the ricotta and whisk well. Add the grated cheese. Pour egg mixture over the vegetables.
- Bake for 15-20 minutes or until the frittata is set (it may take a bit longer, but watch that it doesn't overcook). Allow to cool before slicing.

Serve with additional grated cheese on top, if desired.

136. Garlic Bread Soup With Clams

Serving: Serves 4 | Prep: | Cook: | Ready in:

Ingredients

- 1 pound onions, roughly chopped
- 1 cup garlic cloves, peeled and roughly chopped
- 1 tablespoon unsalted butter
- 1 tablespoon olive oil
- salt and white pepper, to taste
- 1 (4 inch) piece of parmgiano-reggiano rind only
- 1 tablespoon mixed herbs (parsley, thyme, etc)
- 4 slices stale garlic bread cut into 1-inch cubes
- 1 quart chicken stock, plus more if necessary
- 1 pound steamed clams per person (optional)
- 5 stems of thyme, leaves removed stems discarded
- additional parmgiano-reggiano for topping
- very good extra-virgin olive oil for drizzling

Direction

- In a medium-sized saucepan set over medium heat sauté onions and garlic in a mixture of butter and olive oil. Add a pinch or two of salt and a bit of white pepper. Do not let the mixture fry. Small gentle bubbles should form around the edge of the pan and are a good sign that the heat is just right. They will become a deep golden caramel color in about 30 minutes. Stir frequently, and watch them as they cook.
- Add the chicken stock, cheese rind, chopped herbs and the garlic bread cubes. Simmer another 15 to 20 minutes, stirring often. Taste for seasoning. It may need a bit more salt. If it does add a pinch and let it cook another 2 or 3 minutes. Remove what is left of the cheese rind and discard it.
- Puree the soup with an immersion blender. Adjusting consistency with more stock if necessary.
- You may make the soup a day ahead as it is often better on the second day. Serve this with steamed clams (optional) on the side and a hefty sprinkling of grated Parmigiano-Reggiano, a drizzle of good olive oil and some chopped thyme leaves.

137. Ginger Egg Cream

Serving: Serves 1 | Prep: | Cook: | Ready in:

Ingredients

- For the ginger syrup:
- 1/2 cup peeled, thinly sliced ginger
- 1/2 cup granulated sugar
- 1/4 cup packed light brown sugar
- 1 1/2 cups water
- 1/4 teaspoon vanilla extract
- For the ginger egg cream:
- 1 tablespoon chocolate syrup
- 4 tablespoons ginger syrup (recipe above)
- 1/3 cup half-and-half
- Seltzer water

Direction

- For the ginger syrup:
- Combine all ingredients except the vanilla in a saucepan. Bring to a boil, then simmer for about 15 minutes, until reduced to about 1 cup of liquid.
- Remove from the heat, stir in the vanilla, cool, and strain.
- For the ginger egg cream:
- In a 12- to 16-ounce glass, mix the chocolate syrup, ginger syrup, and half-and-half together.
- Pour in enough seltzer to come within an inch from the top of the glass. Stir and enjoy!

138. Glazed Shallot, Walnut, Sage, And Goat Cheese Pizza

Serving: Makes two 11 x 17-inch pizzas | Prep: 3hours30mins | Cook: 0hours10mins | Ready in:

Ingredients

- Pizza Dough (Adapted from Dorie Greenspan)
- 1 packet active dry yeast
- 1 3/4 cups warm water (80° F)
- 1/4 cup milk
- 2 tablespoons olive oil
- 4 1/2 cups all-purpose flour, divided (you may need less)
- 1/2 cup bread flour, divided
- 1 3/4 teaspoons fine sea salt
- For the Shallot Mixture (Enough for 2 Pies)
- 2 tablespoons olive oil
- 2 medium onions, quartered lengthwise and sliced thinly crosswise
- 4 large shallots, halved and sliced thinly lengthwise
- 3 fat cloves of garlic, crushed with the flat side of a knife and coarsely chopped
- 10 to 12 fresh sage leaves, coarsely chopped (3 to 4 tablespoons, loosely packed)
- 1 teaspoon fine sea salt
- Freshly ground pepper to taste
- Zest from 1/2 Meyer lemon (optional)
- Juice of 1/2 Meyer lemon (optional)
- Cornmeal for sprinkling the pan
- 3 ounces soft, fresh goat cheese, crumbled
- 1/4 cup walnut halves, toasted in a rimmed baking sheet in a 375° F oven for 8 to 10 minutes, cooled and coarsely chopped

Direction

- Pizza Dough
- Combine yeast, water, and milk in a large bowl. Whisk to combine, then set aside for about 5 minutes to proof.
- Whisk in olive oil, then add 1/4 cup of the bread flour and 2 cups of the all-purpose flour. Cover with plastic wrap and set aside to rise in a warm place for about 1 1/2 hours. Tip: I sometimes warm the oven very briefly on low, then switch it off and put on the pilot light before putting in the mixture to rise. After 1 1/2 hours, a bubbly soft sponge of about twice the volume of the original mixture should form.
- With a rubber spatula, stir and fold the sponge to deflate it. With a wooden spoon, gradually stir in the salt and the last 1/4 cup of bread flour. Slowly add in some of the remaining all-purpose flour: just enough for the dough to pull away from the sides of the bowl and form into a cohesive mass. You probably will not need all of it.
- Put the dough in the bowl of a stand mixer fitted with a dough hook and turn it on low. Gradually increase the speed to medium-high and beat about 5 minutes, until the dough is soft and elastic. Turn it out onto a lightly floured board, adding a little extra flour if necessary to create a workable dough, and knead for a few turns -- less than a minute.
- Cover a large bowl with a thin film of olive oil. Form the dough into a smooth ball and turn it into the bowl, coating it with the oil. Cover with plastic wrap. Set dough aside in a warm place to rise for another 1 1/2 hours. After this time, the dough should be bubbly. Tip: After deflating and dividing the dough (see step 5 below), you can wrap it in plastic wrap and put in the refrigerator overnight for improved texture.
- For the Shallot Mixture (Enough for 2 Pies)
- Preheat the oven to 500° F.
- In a large heavy sauté pan over medium-high heat, heat olive oil until it shimmers. Add onions, garlic, and shallots and sauté, tossing and stirring, until they turn golden. Add the salt and pepper. When the onions and shallots are very tender and well-browned, add the sage leaves and sauté until wilted. Add the Meyer lemon juice and zest, if using, and cook another minute.

- Remove from heat and cool to room temperature. This mixture makes enough for two pies, with some left over.
- Grease two rimmed 11 x 17-inch baking sheets with a bit of olive oil. Sift some cornmeal over them (a mesh tea strainer works well for this).
- When the dough is ready, deflate gently and divide in half. Form each half into a dome or disc. Keep one disc covered while you form the other to fit the measurements of the pan. Flatten the disc as much as possible, then stretch it into shape, keeping the edges a little thicker than the interior. You can aim for a large disc, or fit the dough into the rectangle of the pan. If a thin spot or two forms, that's okay -- it doesn't have to be perfect. Just call it rustic!
- Brush the edges of the dough with a little olive oil. Spread the shallot mixture lightly over the dough, leaving a 1-inch margin all around. Scatter some of the walnuts and cheese across the top, but make sure to keep the topping light. Cover with a tea towel or plastic wrap, and repeat with the other half of the dough. Remove the covering. Bake the pizzas in the bottom third of the oven for about 5 to 10 minutes, rotating the pan halfway through, until edges are golden. Watch carefully to make sure the walnuts don't burn too badly -- if they begin to, you may need to turn down the oven to 400° F or 450° F. There will be some burnt onion edges, which is perfectly fine.
- Remove from the oven, cut into squares, and serve hot.

139. Gluten Free Ritz Bits Style Crackers

Serving: Makes 80 mini cracker sandwiches | Prep: | Cook: | Ready in:

Ingredients

- Miniature Gluten Free Ritz-Style Crackers
- 2 cups (280 grams) all purpose gluten-free flour
- 1 teaspoon xanthan gum (omit if your blend already contains it)
- 1 tablespoon baking powder
- 1 1/2 teaspoons sugar
- 1 teaspoon smoked Spanish paprika
- 1 teaspoon (6 grams) kosher salt
- 8 tablespoons (112 grams) unsalted butter, chopped and chilled
- 2 tablespoons (28 grams) vegetable oil
- 1 cup (8 fluid ounces) cold water, with ice (ice does not count in the volume measurement)
- Cheese Filling
- 8 ounces Asiago cheese, cut into a large dice
- 6 ounces (1/2 can) evaporated milk
- 2 tablespoons (16 grams) cornstarch (or another starch, such as arrowroot or potato starch)
- 2 tablespoons (28 grams) unsalted butter

Direction

- Miniature Gluten Free Ritz-Style Crackers
- Preheat the oven to 375° F. Line rimmed baking sheets with unbleached parchment paper and set them aside.
- In a large bowl, place the flour blend, xanthan gum, baking powder, sugar, paprika, and 1/2 teaspoon of the salt, and whisk to combine well. Add the chopped and chilled butter to the dry ingredients, toss to coat and cut the butter in using either a pastry blender or two knives until the mixture resembles small pebbles. Add the vegetable oil and stir to combine. Add the water a bit at a time, stirring constantly until the dough begins to come together, discarding the ice. You may not need all the water. Wrap the dough in plastic wrap, and place in the refrigerator to chill for about 10 minutes.
- Remove the dough from the refrigerator, place between two large sheets of unbleached parchment paper, and roll out about 1/8-inch thick (about the thickness of a nickel). Using a fluted 1/2-inch round cookie cutter, cut out shapes. With a toothpick, poke 2 holes in each

cracker to help them rise. Place the shapes about 1 inch apart from one another on the prepared baking sheets, brush the crackers lightly with water, and sprinkle with the remaining kosher salt. Place the baking sheets, one sheet at a time, in the center of the preheated oven. Bake until just beginning to brown, about 7 minutes.

- Remove the baking sheet from the oven, and allow the crackers to cool completely.
- Cheese Filling
- In a medium-size, heavy-bottom saucepan, place the Asiago cheese and evaporated milk. Cook, whisking frequently, over medium-high heat, until the cheese is completely melted. Add the cornstarch, and whisk to combine well. Continue to cook, stirring constantly, for another 2 minutes. Remove the saucepan from the heat, and stir in the butter until it is melted. The cheese will be somewhat thick, but still easily pourable. Transfer the cheese mixture to a medium heat-safe bowl, and allow to sit at room temperature until cool (about 10 minutes).
- Once the cheese mixture is cool, place it in a pastry bag fitted with a medium-sized plain piping tip (or just place it in a large zip-top bag, seal the bag and snip off one corner). Turn half of the cooled mini Ritz crackers upside down. Pipe about 1/4 teaspoon of cheese filling onto the underside of those crackers. Top each with another cracker, right-side up, to close each sandwich.

140. Gorgonzola Grapes

Serving: Serves 4 | Prep: | Cook: | Ready in:

Ingredients

- 1 bunch seedless grapes
- 8 ounces creamy gorgonzola cheese
- 1/2 cup chopped pecans
- 1 packet toothpicks

Direction

- Put a dab of creamy gorgonzola cheese and one grape in your palms. Roll it around until the grape is mostly coated with the cheese.
- Roll the grape in chopped pecans.
- Stick a toothpick in it! Lovely served with a cocktail (or 2).

141. Gorgonzola Potatoes Au Gratin

Serving: Serves 12 | Prep: | Cook: | Ready in:

Ingredients

- 3½ pounds Russet potatoes, peeled and thinly sliced
- 1 Onion, small, thinly sliced
- 6 ounces Gorgonzola cheese, crumbled
- 3 tablespoons Flour
- 1 tablespoon Thyme, fresh, chopped
- 1½ teaspoons Salt
- 1 teaspoon Pepper, freshly ground
- ¼ cups Butter, melted
- 1½ cups Cream

Direction

- Preheat oven to 350F (175C). Arrange an overlapping layer of thinly sliced potatoes in bottom of lightly greased 9 in. by 13 in. baking pan.
- Place over potatoes: a few thinly sliced onions, about 2 oz. of Gorgonzola, about 1 Tbsp. of flour and the butter. Sprinkle with 1 tsp. thyme, ½ tsp. salt and pepper and about ½ cup cream. Repeat process until all the ingredients are used.
- Cover pan with foil and bake for 1 hour.
- Remove foil and bake another 20 to 30 minute or until the potatoes are soft and a golden crust forms.

142. Gorgonzola Tart With White Truffle Honey, Pears & Radicchio

Serving: Serves 6 | Prep: | Cook: |Ready in:

Ingredients

- Everything but the crust
- 1.5 cups Light cream
- 3 Eggs
- 1/4 pound Gorgonzola dolce
- 1 cup Marscapone
- 1 cup Ripe pears (medium dice). Peeled
- 1 tablespoon Chives
- 1 cup Shredded radicchio
- 2 tablespoons Or so White truffle honey
- 2-3 tablespoons Lemon juice (Meyer if ya got it)
- 2 tablespoons Olive oil
- Walnut Olive Oil Crust
- 2 cups 1 tbs white pastry flour (or 2 cup a/p)
- 1 teaspoon Fine sea salt
- 1/4 cup Olive Oil
- 1/4 cup Chopped toasted walnuts
- 3 tablespoons Grated pecorino
- A few healthy grind black pepper
- 1/2 cup Ice water

Direction

- Everything but the crust
- Heat cream to a bare simmer, whisk in gorgonzola & mascarpone until well combined & smooth season with salt & pepper
- Whisk eggs, temper in cream/cheese mixture slowly then whisk or blend with hand mixer or blender
- Stir in chives & pour into tart shell
- Bake 30 minutes in 375 oven, when top starts to set, drizzle on white truffle honey, bake another 15 minutes or so until just set (should quiver slightly)
- Toss pears in lemon juice and season lightly w salt & pepper
- Toss radicchio with pears and olive oil
- Serve tarts warm topped with pears & radicchio
- Walnut Olive Oil Crust
- Sift flour & whisk in cheese, walnuts, salt & pepper
- Pour in oil and blend with a fork, until the mixture resembles coarse meal
- Slowly add in ice water (you may not need all of it) until the dough comes together in a ball
- Roll out dough on a well-floured table (flour rolling pin as well) until you have a 13" circle (1/4" thick)
- Lay dough out in 10" Fluted tart pan with removable bottom tart delicately nudging in to the bottom with your knuckles, trim edges
- Chill for 30 minute
- Poke a few holes in the bottom with a fork Lay a parchment paper circle (I use the removable bottom as a guide) over the bottom , line with dried beans, pie weights, old rice ... Whatever you have bake in 375 oven for 20 minutes, remove paper & weights bake another 10 min

143. Green Eggs And Ham

Serving: Makes 1 quiche | Prep: | Cook: |Ready in:

Ingredients

- 2 bunches green onions
- 1 cup diced, cooked ham
- 1 tablespoon unsalted butter
- 1/2 cup mayonnaise
- 1/4 teaspoon celery salt
- 1/4 teaspoon lemon pepper
- 3/4 teaspoon cornstarch
- 1/2 cup milk
- 1 egg
- 1 1/2 cups shredded white cheddar cheese
- 2 tablespoons diced green chiles (optional)
- 1 9 inch pie shell

Direction

- Preheat oven to 350.
- Slice only the whites of both bunches of onions.
- Melt 1 tbsp butter in sauté pan. Sauté onions on low until they begin to brown. Add ham and increase heat to medium. Sauté 5 minutes. Remove from heat and set aside to cool.
- Chop the greens from one bunch of onions.
- Place the greens from the second bunch of onions into a food processor. Pulse until finely chopped. Add mayo, spices, and cornstarch. Blend until fully combined.
- Using a fork, whisk milk and egg into mayonnaise mixture. Once fully incorporated, add cooled ham, chopped onion greens, cheese, and green chiles (if using).
- Pour mixture into pie shell.
- Bake at 350 for 45-55 minutes. You'll be able to tell that it's done when the filling is set and the top is slightly browned.
- Remove from oven and let cool for at least 10 minutes before serving.

144. Greenest Goddess Dressing And Dip

Serving: Serves 2 1/2 cups/600ml | Prep: 0hours0mins | Cook: 0hours0mins | Ready in:

Ingredients

- 3/4 cup (180 grams) mayonnaise or Aioli
- 3/4 cup (180 grams) sour cream or Greek yogurt
- 3 tablespoons finely chopped tarragon
- 1/4 cup (5 grams) finely chopped flat-leaf parsley
- 2 tablespoons finely chopped chives or scallions
- Juice of 1 lemon
- 2 olive oil- or salt-packed anchovies, rinsed, finely chopped
- 1 ripe California avocado, halved, pitted, peeled, and cut into quarters
- 3 tablespoons finely chopped carrot tops
- 1/4 teaspoon sea salt
- Ground black pepper

Direction

- Combine the mayonnaise, sour cream or yogurt, tarragon, parsley, chives or scallions, lemon juice, and anchovies, avocado, carrot tops, and salt in a blender and blend until smooth. Taste and adjust the seasoning, adding pepper to taste. Serve immediately.
- Store in a jar with a tight-fitting lid in the refrigerator for up to 1 week.

145. Grilled Apple Salad With Maple Mustard Vinaigrette

Serving: Serves 2-3 | Prep: | Cook: |Ready in:

Ingredients

- Grilled Apple Salad
- 5-6 cups coarsely chopped spinach
- 1 apple, cored and sliced
- olive oil, for griling
- salt and pepper, to taste
- 2 ounces pecans, coarsely chopped
- 3 ounces shaved double gloucester cheese
- 1/4 small purple onion, thinly sliced
- Maple Mustard Vinaigrette
- 3 tablespoons olive oil
- 1 tablespoon apple cider vinegar
- 1 tablespoon tablespoon maple mustard or substitute
- 1 tablespoon maple syrup
- salt and pepper, to taste

Direction

- Chop spinach and place on serving platter. Top with sliced onion. Toast pecans in a frying pan until slightly browned, then coarsely chop and add to salad. Coat apple slices with olive oil and season with salt and pepper. Place in a

grill pan over medium heat and cook for 1-2 minutes per side, until grill marks appear and apples are slightly softened. Remove from heat, arrange on top of salad along with shaved cheese.
- To make the vinaigrette, simply mix all ingredients together and season to taste with the salt and pepper. Drizzle over assembled salad.

146. Grilled Flatbread With Peaches, Prosciutto, Mozzarella And Arugula

Serving: Serves 4 | Prep: | Cook: | Ready in:

Ingredients

- 2 packaged flatbreads or pitas
- 2 tablespoons olive oil
- 1 garlic clove, crushed
- 1 tablespoon salt
- 2 teaspoons pepper
- 1 shallot, chopped
- 8 greek black olives, chopped
- 12 fresh basil leaves
- 3 peaches, sliced thinly
- 8 slices prosciutto, torn into strips
- 8 ounces fresh mozzarella (I used bocconcini)
- arugula
- balsamic vinegar glaze

Direction

- Heat grill to low or preheat oven to 400 degrees.
- Mix olive oil, garlic, salt and pepper in a small bowl. Brush onto flatbreads. Scatter chopped shallots and olives around the bread.
- Place basil leaves on bread, then add the sliced peaches. Add fresh mozzarella balls.
- Grill on low heat until the cheese melts. In the oven, place on a pizza stone or directly on the rack and bake until the cheese melts.
- Remove from oven and place a big handful of arugula on top. Drizzle with balsamic vinegar glaze.

147. Grilled Foil Pack Chicken Nachos

Serving: Serves 4 | Prep: 0hours15mins | Cook: 0hours30mins | Ready in:

Ingredients

- 2 teaspoons olive oil
- 1 1/2 teaspoons salt
- 1 1/2 teaspoons ground cumin
- 1 teaspoon chili powder
- 1 teaspoon tomato paste
- 1/2 teaspoon dried oregano
- 1 pound boneless, skinless chicken thighs
- 8 cups tortilla chips (or two handfuls per packet)
- 1 cup shredded Monterey Jack cheese
- 1 cup shredded cheddar cheese
- Pico de Gallo, for topping
- Sliced avocado, for topping
- Cilantro, for topping
- Sour cream, for topping
- Hot sauce, for topping

Direction

- In a large mixing bowl, using a fork, mix together the olive oil, salt, cumin, chile powder, tomato paste, oregano and cayenne until thoroughly mixed. Add the chicken thigh and toss until the thighs are well coated in the spice mixture. Let marinate for at least an hour or up to 12.
- Preheat grill to high. Once hot, add the chicken to the grill and cook for 4-6 minutes per side or until cooked. Remove the chicken to a plate and let rest for 10 minutes. Turn the grill heat down to medium. Once the chicken has rested, chop the chicken into 1/2-inch pieces. Set aside.

- Tear off four big square piece of aluminum foil. Place about two cups (two big handfuls) of tortillas chips in the center of a sheet of foil. Top the chips with ¼ of the Monterey Jack cheese, ¼ of the chopped chicken and then ¼ of the cheddar cheese. To seal the packets, bring two sides of the foil together over top of the nachos and roll them together to create a seal. Roll up the open sides of foil packets to seal together all the edges. Repeat with the rest of the ingredients to make four foil packets. You could easily stretch the ingredients to make six foil packets, if you're serving this as a snack or a side dish.
- Place the foil packets onto the grill and let cook for 8-10 minutes or until cheese melts (it's OK to peek inside the pouch if you're unsure). When ready, remove from the grill, carefully open the packets and top with your favorite toppings.

148. Grilled Garden Sandwich

Serving: Serves 3 to 4 | Prep: | Cook: | Ready in:

Ingredients

- For the Gremolata Cheese Spread
- 8 ounces fromage blanc
- 1 small to medium clove garlic
- ¼ teaspoon kosher salt
- 1 ounce parmesan – microplaned
- zest from 1 lemon
- ½ to 1 jalepeño, (seeds removed) finely diced
- generous ¼ cup chiffonade cut basil
- ¼ teaspoon freshly ground black pepper
- 1 tablespoon olive oil
- For the Grilled Garden Sandwich
- 2 medium summer squash (elongated type)
- 1 small to medium eggplant (the oval to egg-shaped type)
- 1 red pepper
- ½-inch thick slice of a large sweet onion
- 1 loaf French batard
- olive oil
- juice from one lemon
- kosher salt
- ¼ teaspoon freshly ground black pepper

Direction

- Remove fromage blanc from refrigerator to soften.
- Cut ends off summer squash, and slice squash lengthwise into thirds. Cut stem end off eggplant and slice eggplant lengthwise into fourths. Sprinkle cut surfaces of squash and eggplant with kosher salt and arrange in a colander with as little overlapping as possible. Set colander aside over a bowl or in the sink for 30 minutes.
- Quarter red pepper from stem to blossom end. Remove stem, ribs and seeds. Set aside. Carefully thread onion slice onto a bamboo skewer. Set aside.
- Heat your grill or grill pan to medium. You'll be grilling over direct heat.
- Slice batard in half so the bottom half is about 1-inch thick. Use your fingers to pluck most of the bread from the inside of the top slice. Discard or better yet, save for bread crumbs or rustic croutons. Brush the cut surfaces with olive oil.
- Mince garlic and sprinkle it with the salt. Using the flat side of a chef's knife scrape the garlic and salt back and forth on your cutting board until it becomes a paste. Transfer garlic mixture to a bowl. Add remaining gremolata cheese spread ingredients, and mix well to combine. Set aside until ready to assemble sandwich.
- Grill bread on cut surfaces only for several minutes until grill marks form. Set aside and allow to cool to room temperature.
- Rinse eggplant and squash and pat dry with paper towels or a clean tea towel. Set aside. Place ½ cup olive oil, lemon juice, and black pepper in a bowl, and whisk until well-combined. Brush mixture on all sides of the eggplant and squash slices. Add ¼ teaspoon kosher salt to the olive oil mixture, and whisk

to dissolve. Brush all surfaces of the onion and the red pepper.
- Grill vegetables over medium heat until grill marks form on the first side, 3 to 4 minutes. Then flip until vegetables are softened and grill marks form on the second side, 3 to 4 minutes. Place red pepper pieces into a small paper bag, and crimp closed. Remove onion from skewer and coarsely chop. After pepper has steamed for several minutes, remove and discard the charred skin. Thinly slice the pepper.
- Spread the gremolata cheese spread in a thin even layer on both top and bottom halves of the bread. You should use all of the spread. Layer the eggplant and squash over the bottom half of the sandwich, distributing each in an even layer. Scatter an even layer of red pepper and onion over the other vegetables. Place the "lid" on the sandwich. Wrap the sandwich as tightly as you can with plastic wrap. You want the filling components to smoosh together and get really friendly. It's even okay if the sandwich gets a bit crushed in the picnic basket - the batard is quite sturdy and can take it! Allow to rest at room temperature for 1 to 2 hours or overnight in the fridge before slicing with a serrated knife and serving.

149. Grilled Lemon Tzatziki

Serving: Makes 2 1/2 cups | Prep: | Cook: |Ready in:

Ingredients

- 1 large or 2 small cucumbers, seeded and finely diced
- 2 cups plain Greek yogurt
- 2 lemons, grilled and juiced
- 1 tablespoon olive oil
- 2 tablespoons fresh dill, finely chopped
- 1 tablespoon garlic, minced
- 1/2 teaspoon salt
- 1/4 teaspoon black pepper

Direction

- Whisk together cucumber, yogurt, lemon juice, olive oil, dill, and garlic in a medium bowl. Season with salt and pepper and refrigerator until ready to serve. For a thinner tzatziki, blend 1/2 of the tzatziki in a food processor until smooth then reintegrate it with the rest. It's delicious right away, but the flavors gets better after a few hours.

150. Grilled Olathe Sweet Corn And Chicken Chowder With Goat Cheese

Serving: Serves 6 | Prep: | Cook: |Ready in:

Ingredients

- 1 tablespoon Olive oil
- 3 pieces Thick bacon, cut into 1/2-inch pieces
- 4 Chicken thighs, skinless/boneless, diced
- kosher salt +fresh ground pepper
- 1 pinch Crushed red pepper
- 1 Onion, medium, diced
- 3 Carrots, medium--trimmed, peeled, and sliced into 1/4-inch coins
- 3 Celery stalks--trimmed and sliced into 1/4-inch pieces
- 1 Garlic clove, minced
- 2 teaspoons Thyme, dried
- 1 Bay leaf
- 4 cups Chicken broth, low-sodium
- 1/2 cup Water
- 4 Red potatoes, small and unpeeled, cut into 1-inch pieces
- 4 Ears Grilled Olathe corn, husked, silks removed, kernels cut off (reserve cobs for broth)
- 4 ounces Colorado goat cheese, crumbled
- 3 Scallions, minced (green and white parts) for garnish
- 6 sprigs Fresh thyme for garnish

Direction

- In a 6-quart heavy pot, heat a tablespoon of oil over medium heat and sauté chopped bacon until crisp. Remove bacon to a paper towel-lined plate and reserve for garnish. Carefully pour out or spoon the bacon grease into a heat-proof container, leaving 2 tablespoons in the bottom of the pot.
- Add diced chicken to hot pot; season with 1/2 teaspoon kosher salt, 1/4 teaspoon freshly ground black pepper, and crushed red pepper. Cook, stirring often, until beginning to brown. Add onion, carrots, and celery; cook, stirring, until vegetables are softening and chicken is browned. Add garlic, thyme, and bay leaf.
- Pour in broth and water. Raise heat; bring to a boil. Lower to simmer; add potatoes and corn cobs to flavor broth. Cook 10 minutes; add corn kernels. Simmer another 10 minutes or until all vegetables are tender. Remove cobs and discard. With a potato masher, mash through soup lightly and briefly–just to thicken a bit, not to purée.
- Add goat cheese and stir until melted. Taste, adjust seasonings. Serve hot garnished with reserved bacon, green onions, and a sprig of fresh thyme for each bowl. (Diners should pull the thyme leaves off into the bowl before eating soup. This truly makes the soup!) Whoever gets the bay leaf does the dishes.
- COOK'S NOTE: While I've used leftover grilled corn here because I like the taste, you can use boiled corn or frozen corn for any season soup. Fresh corn would also work perfectly well as the cobs help make a tasty broth and the corn cooks very quickly.

151. Grilled Peach And Mozzarella Summer Stack

Serving: Serves 4 | Prep: | Cook: | Ready in:

Ingredients

- 5 Peaches
- 3 green onions sliced thin
- 3 tablespoons honey
- 1 teaspoon salt
- 1/2 cup lime juice
- 1 teaspoon lime zest
- 1/2 teaspoon cumin (toast cumin seeds and fine grind)
- 1/4 teaspoon chili powder
- 1/3 cup olive oil
- 1 bunch baby arugula
- 3/4 pound fresh mozzarella sliced 1/4 inch
- 1 handful cilantro as garnish

Direction

- Peel and chop 1 peach. Cut remaining peaches into 1/4 inch round pieces. Discard the pits.
- Place in a food processor, chopped peach, green onions, cilantro, honey, 1 tsp. salt, lime zest and lime juice. Add chili powder to taste. Process to smooth. Add oil, pulse several times until combined.
- Spray grill with cooking spray or oil. Preheat grill to medium high (350-400 degrees). Brush sides of peach round with some of the dressing.
- Grill peaches covered for 3-5 min on each side. Grill marks will appear.
- On platter, place baby arugula and layer grilled peach rounds and mozzarella cheese on top. Add another round of grilled peaches and stack several layers high. Finish with the peach dressing and garnish with cilantro. Enjoy!

152. Grilled Rye With Muenster, Avocado, And Sprout

Serving: Serves 2 | Prep: | Cook: | Ready in:

Ingredients

- 4 pieces sliced, thick rye, pumpernickel, or multi-grain bread
- 1 ripe avocado

- 2 tablespoons butter
- 1/2 cup alfalfa or broccoli sprouts
- 1/2 pound sliced Muenster cheese
- 2 medium tomatoes, optional

Direction

- Preheat toaster oven or conventional oven to 350F. Generously and evenly butter two thick slices of bread. Make sure the smear of butter covers the whole slice; this is how to achieve a crisp, golden, flavorful exterior. If your butter is unsalted, sprinkle a bit of salt over each buttered side.
- Preheat a non-stick or cast iron pan on medium heat for 4-5 minutes. While the pan preheats, slice the avocado and the tomatoes, if using. Lay two pieces of bread on the hot pan, butter-side down. The butter should sizzle, but not too much -- you don't want your pan so hot that it burns your bread. Top each slice of bread with ¼ lb. of Muenster cheese.
- Lay down the other two slices of bread on top of the cheese, buttered side up, and press down lightly with a spatula. You don't want to flatten the sandwich completely, but a little pressure helps the cheese melt and the butter sear. After a minute or so, begin to check the color on your bottom slices. Once it's beautifully browned, flip everything over, holding the sandwich together with your other hand to keep it from falling apart. Press down some more with your spatula, and cook until the bottom slices look like the top slices.
- Once you're happy with the color of your crusts, finish your sandwich on a baking sheet in the oven. If you're making more than two, use the oven as a way to keep everything warm. Let your sandwiches bake for at least five minutes, or until their cheese is completely melted.
- Add your extras. Now, it may seem sacrilegious to peel open a perfect-looking grilled cheese, but that's what we're going to do. Add the sliced avocado, sprouts, and tomato slices (if using), sprinkle with salt and pepper, and go to town.
- Serve with sliced tomatoes and a simple arugula salad with Dijon vinaigrette.

153. Grilled Taleggio Cheese, Salami And Truffle Honey Crostone Di Taleggio, Salami Con Miele Tartufato

Serving: Serves 6 | Prep: | Cook: | Ready in:

Ingredients

- 6 slices of Italian bread
- 12 tablespoons Taleggio cheese or Stracchino cheese for a milder taste
- 48 slices of salami or truffled salami
- 1 1/2 teaspoons Truffled Honey

Direction

- Pre-heat the oven grill on high and put the rack on the top shelf.
- Cut 6 slices of Italian bread the thickness of a standard sandwich slice.
- Cut 36 slices of salami paper thin.
- Spread 2 tablespoons of Taleggio cheese (or Starcchino if you want a milder taste) on each slice of bread, add 8 slices of salami on top of the cheese and drizzle a tiny amount of honey over the salami. I really mean a tiny quantity so it doesn't overpower the taste of the salami and cheese.
- Grill in the oven until the cheese has melted and the salami is slightly crispy on the edges (about 5 minutes) - don't overcook it as the salami will become very hard and salty.
- Serve immediately.
- At the enoteca in Florence they recommend a frutty, light red wine.

154. Grilled Watermelon With Tequila

Serving: Serves 4 | Prep: | Cook: | Ready in:

Ingredients

- 4 pieces watermelon
- 2 shots premium tequila
- 1 tablespoon coarse sea salt
- Zest and juice of 1 lemon
- 3 teaspoons chili powder (Ancho works great)
- 8 ounces crème fraîche
- Zest of 1 lime
- 1/3 cup cilantro, chopped

Direction

- Mix the crème fraîche, lime zest, and cilantro in bowl. Salt and pepper to taste. Cover and reserve in refrigerator.
- Mix the tequila, lemon juice, and lemon zest in bowl. Drizzle equal amounts of mixture over each watermelon slice. Top with chili powder and salt, patting gently into the slices.
- In a grill pan over high heat, grill the watermelon slices, chili powder side down, just until the powder's oils are released and grill marks are made, about 1 to 3 minutes.
- Remove the slices and assemble grilled side up. Top with cilantro lime crème fraîche and serve immediately.

155. Grilled Zucchini Orzo

Serving: Makes 4 servings | Prep: 0hours10mins | Cook: 0hours20mins | Ready in:

Ingredients

- Orzo
- 1 cup orzo pasta
- 3 zucchinis (any variety, halved)
- 1 vine ripened tomato (quartered)
- 1 spring onion (quartered)
- 5 cloves garlic (whole, in peel), more if you like garlic
- Olive oil, for brushing
- Salt and pepper, to taste
- 2 tablespoons unsalted butter
- 1 cup (125g) goat cheese
- Vinaigrette
- 1/4 cup plus 2 teaspoons sesame oil
- 2 tablespoons red wine vinegar
- 1/2 lemon (juice and zest)
- 1 tablespoon honey
- 1 tablespoon Dijon mustard
- 1/2 cup cilantro, parsley, dill, or mixed herbs chopped (plus more for garnish)
- Salt and pepper, to taste

Direction

- Heat grill or grill pan over medium high heat. Brush or rub zucchini, tomato, spring onions, and garlic cloves with olive oil. Season with salt and pepper. Add veggies to grill. (I used my grill pan, but if you use a grill you may want to wrap the garlic in foil.) Cook until the veggies have a nice brown crust and the garlic is soft, about 6 minutes on each side. When done and cool enough to handle, cut everything into bite-sized pieces and place in a large mixing/serving bowl.
- Cook the orzo according to the packet instructions and make sure to salt the water really well. In the meantime, whisk together the vinaigrette ingredients. Set aside. Drain orzo with a colander and add it to the mixing bowl.
- Add the butter and the vinaigrette to the orzo. Mix until the butter is melted. Taste and adjust ingredients as you see fit, but be wary of salt since goat cheese is salty and you haven't added it yet.
- Top with goat cheese. Mix lightly if you want chunks of goat cheese, and more vigorously if you want a more uniform, silky goat cheese taste. Add salt and pepper to taste. Garnish and dig in.

156. Grilled Cheese And Bacon

Serving: Serves 1 | Prep: | Cook: | Ready in:

Ingredients

- 3 strips slab bacon, fried crisp and drained
- 2 ounces Gruyere, shredded
- 2 ounces butterkase cheese, shredded
- 2 tablespoons butter
- 2 slices sourdough bread

Direction

- Butter both sides of both pieces of bread. Distribute one kind of cheese on one slice, top with bacon, and add second kind of cheese. (You may use any combination that you have on hand.) Top with other slice of bread, and grill with a press.

157. Halloumi, Cranberry And Stuffing Bites

Serving: Makes enough munchies for 4 or 5 | Prep: | Cook: | Ready in:

Ingredients

- 2 packets 500g halloumi
- cranberry sauce
- sage and onion stuffing

Direction

- Cook the stuffing according to the packet. Usually it needs about 20 minutes in a 180 oven, but whatever heats it through.
- In the meantime, slice and fry your halloumi in a dash of olive oil until golden brown and crispy. About 3 minutes each side on a medium heat should suffice.
- Now is time to assemble. Take each slice of ciabatta and spread enough cranberry sauce to cover the bread and moisten it a little. Then spoon on some stuffing. Quantities are up to your taste but make sure there is enough so that it can be tasted, as the other flavours are strong. Top with a slice of your warm halloumi.
- Serve and await the compliments. Enjoy!

158. Ham, Gruyère, And Caramelized Onion Galette With A Fried Egg

Serving: Makes 1 galette | Prep: | Cook: | Ready in:

Ingredients

- For the crust:
- 2/3 cup rye flour
- 1 1/2 cups all-purpose flour
- 1 teaspoon fine grain sea salt
- 1 cup unsalted butter, cold and cut into chunks
- up to 2/3 cups dark beer, cold
- For the filling:
- 1 medium or large onion, sliced
- Salt and pepper, to season and sprinkle
- 1 tablespoon balsamic vinegar
- 1 tablespoon grainy mustard
- 3/4 cup Gruyère, shredded
- 1/2 cup ham steak, diced
- Splash olive oil
- 1 tablespoon butter
- 1 large egg

Direction

- For the crust:
- In a large bowl, whisk together the flours and salt. Using a pastry cutter or knife and fork, cut in the butter until it is the texture of cornmeal and peas.

- Make a well in the center of the butter-flour mixture and pour in the beer. Using a wooden spoon, combine until the dough forms together into a flat ball (you may need to use your hands at the end). Fold the dough over itself and wrap in plastic wrap, then let chill in the fridge for about 30 minutes.
- For the filling:
- Preheat the oven to 375° F. Add 1 tablespoon olive oil and sliced onions to a cast iron skillet and place over medium heat. Stir to coat the onions with olive oil. Cook the onions, stirring occasionally, until translucent. Sprinkle them with salt and pepper and reduce heat to medium-low. Cook 25 to 30 more minutes, until the onions are caramelized.
- While the onions are cooking, prepare the rest of the galette. In a small bowl, whisk together the balsamic vinegar and mustard and set aside.
- After 30 minutes, remove dough from the fridge and unwrap. On a floured surface, roll it out into an elongated rectangle. Pick up the bottom of the rectangle, and fold the dough 2/3 of the way up. Now pick up the top third of the dough and fold it over the bottom. Sprinkle more flour over the dough, rotate it 90 degrees, and then repeat the same folding technique.
- Roll out the dough into a 10- or 11-inch circle on a sheet of parchment paper. Transfer the parchment and dough to a large cookie sheet.
- On top of the crust, brush on the mustard-vinegar mixture and spread evenly. Add the cheese, ham, and caramelized onions, scattering them evenly across the crust, but leaving a 1-inch border. Fold the edges over the top of the filling and press to seal. Brush olive oil on the crust edges and sprinkle the entire tart with sea salt and pepper.
- Place a sheet of aluminum foil over the filling, leaving the crust exposed (this will keep the filling from browning too quickly or burning). Bake for 35 to 50 minutes, until the crust is browned. Remove from the oven and cool on a rack while you fry the egg.
- Heat a pat of butter in a small skillet. Fry the egg, sunny-side up, until the white is no longer translucent and the edges have crisped. Using a skillet, transfer the egg to the tart. Serve immediately and enjoy with a glass of hard, dry cider -- I recommend Foggy Ridge First Fruit!

159. Healthy Stuffed Manicotti Shells

Serving: Serves 7 | Prep: | Cook: |Ready in:

Ingredients

- 3/4 cup dried garbanzo beans
- 1 box manicotti pasta shells
- 15 ounces Ricotta cheese
- 2 egg whites
- 1/2 cup fresh parsley minced
- 1/3 cup Parmesan cheese, grated
- 1 small onion, quartered
- 2 cloves garlic, minced
- 24 ounces jar of tomato sauce
- 1 1/2 cups mozzarella, shredded

Direction

- Soak garbanzo beans overnight and boil for 60 minutes or until soft. Drain and set aside.
- Cook Manicotti pasta shells according to package directions.
- Place garbanzos and egg whites in a food processor and process until smooth. Add ricotta, parsley, parmesan, onion and garlic; continue processing until well blended.
- Spread 1 ½ cups of Bertolli sauce on the bottom of a 9x13, ungreased baking dish (or make two 8x8 dishes and freeze one for later) and set aside.
- Drain the pasta shells and stuff with the garbanzo mixture. Put remaining Bertolli sauce on top of the pasta shells, if you have some left over garbanzo mixture put a dollop on top of each shell.

- Bake uncovered at 350° for 30 minutes.
- Sprinkle with the shredded Mozzarella and bake another 5-10 minutes until melted and until the sauce becomes a bit bubbly.

160. Heavenly Kanafe.... A Syrian Dessert Made With Ricotta & Shredded Filo Dough

Serving: Serves 12-14 | Prep: | Cook: | Ready in:

Ingredients

- For the kanafe
- 1 pound kanafe (shredded phyllo dough)
- 2 1/2 pounds ricotta cheese
- 1/2 cup cream of rice cereal
- 3 sticks of sweet butter melted
- 4 tablespoons sugar
- 1 tablespoon rosewater
- 2 cups milk
- 1/4 cup pistachios, peeled & chopped
- For the Syrup
- 2 cups sugar
- 1 cup water
- 1 teaspoon rosewater
- 1 teaspoon orange blossom water
- 1 teaspoon lemon juice

Direction

- Drain the ricotta in a strainer. Prepare the cream of rice according to the box directions using the 2 cups of milk, add the 4 Tbsp. sugar and the rosewater. When the cream of rice mixture is cool add the ricotta and mix well.
- In a large bowl shred the kanafe with your hands, tearing apart the strands of dough so there are no clumps. Mix in the melted butter, continuing to shred the kanafe till it is well coated with the butter.
- Spread 1/2 the kanafe in a 9 x13 Pyrex or large pan. Press down firmly and press the kanafe 1/2 way up the sides of the pan. Add the ricotta mixture, spreading evenly over surface. Top with the other 1/2 of the kanafe. The kanafe may be frozen up to this point.
- For the syrup, bring the sugar, water and lemon juice to a boil and then simmer for 15 minutes. Add the rosewater and orange blossom water. This syrup may be made ahead and refrigerated.
- Bake in a 350 oven for one hour or till golden. Pour the cold or room temperature syrup over the hot kanafe. Garnish with the chopped pistachios. Serve warm or at room temperature.

161. Herby Sweet And Savory Bread Pudding

Serving: Serves 6 | Prep: | Cook: | Ready in:

Ingredients

- Raspberry Sauce
- 1.5 cups frozen unsweetened raspberries
- 1/2 cup water
- 1/3 cup sugar
- 2 teaspoons cornstarch
- 1 tablespoon water
- Bread Pudding
- 1 16 ounces good-quality baguette (about 1 foot long and 3 or 4 inches diameter)
- 1 round of Boursin cheese
- 1.5 cups milk
- 4 eggs

Direction

- Raspberry Sauce
- In a small saucepan, combine the raspberries, water and sugar and bring to a boil. Lower the heat and simmer until the raspberries are broken down, about 8 minutes.
- Whisk together water and cornstarch. Add to raspberry mixture and simmer until a bit thickened, about 3 or 4 minutes. Refrigerate until ready to use, if making ahead.

- Bread Pudding
- Cut the baguette into 1/2 inch chunks.
- Place the Boursin in a 9 x 13 inch baking dish. Mash it up and flatten it out with a fork. Add eggs and milk and whisk until pretty well combined - a few lumps of cheese are not a problem. Mix in bread chunks and squish them down to make sure they are well covered with the custard. Cover with plastic wrap and refrigerate overnight.
- When it's time to make breakfast, preheat the oven to 350. Take the plastic wrap off the bread pudding and give it another squish down to make sure all the bread is well-soaked in custard. Bake bread pudding for 35 to 40 minutes, until the top is golden and slightly puffed. Scoop out and serve with warm raspberry sauce.

162. Homemade Milk Kefir

Serving: Makes 1/4 gallon | Prep: | Cook: | Ready in:

Ingredients

- 4 to 6 tablespoons milk kefir grains
- 1 liter milk

Direction

- Pour the milk into your glass jar and add the kefir grains. Cover the top of the jar with muslin and secure it in place with a rubber band. Next, place the jar in a dark place (I put mine in the pantry), and leave it for 12 to 24 hours, until you see that the liquid is beginning to separate into curds and whey. Keep in mind that the mixture will ferment quickly in the summer, but at colder temperatures, this process will take longer. Avoid making the kefir in rooms hotter than 90° F; at this temperature, the milk might spoil before the grains can culture it.
- After the mixture has been sitting, pour the entire contents of jar into a plastic sieve placed over a bowl. Gently shake the sieve from side to side to encourage the kefir to drain through. If I have left the jar a little bit too long and really solid bits have formed, I let the sieve rest in the bowl of drained whey. I mix the solid parts gently back into the grains until the really firm curds are loosened, and then I re-strain the liquid.
- The strained kefir is then ready to use. Drink it plain or sweetened, or use it in place of milk, yogurt, or buttermilk in your baking and cooking. It can also be stored in the fridge for up to a week.
- Then, use the strained kefir grains to make your new batch in a clean jar. There's no need to rinse the grains between batches.
- NOTES: You can make as little or as much kefir as you want: I usually make 1/2 liter every other day. If you want to slow things down a bit, let the mixture ferment in the fridge instead of in the pantry.
- If you only have a tablespoon or two of grains to begin, just use a cup or two of milk until your grains have multiplied enough to ferment more milk.
- Excess kefir grains can be frozen: Rinse them well, pat them dry on a clean cloth, coat them lightly in in milk powder, and then freeze them in a double-lined plastic bag. Keep in mind, however, that frozen kefir grains may take up to three months of fermentation before they produce consistently good batches of milk kefir.

163. Homemade Nutella Frozen Yogurt

Serving: Makes 1 quart | Prep: | Cook: | Ready in:

Ingredients

- 2 cups full-fat plain yogurt
- 1 cup full-fat Greek yogurt
- 3/4 cup Nutella

- 1/2 cup sugar
- 1/4 teaspoon kosher salt

Direction

- Combine all of the ingredients in a blender and blend until smooth (you don't want big lumps of Nutella).
- Chill the mixture until it's 45° F or cooler. You can use an ice bath to expedite this process.
- Churn in the ice cream machine according to the manufacturer's instructions. Eat right away as soft serve or transfer to an airtight container and freeze for at least 4 to 5 additional hours, until hard enough to scoop.

164. Homemade Paneer

Serving: Makes ~ 10 oz block | Prep: | Cook: |Ready in:

Ingredients

- 1/2 gallon organic whole milk
- 1/2 cup Fresh squeezed Lemon Juice (~ 3-4 lemons)
- 1/2 cup water

Direction

- Add the water to a heavy bottom 5 quart pan and set to heat on medium-high. Add the milk into the pan (adding the milk directly to the pan & heating it tends to scorch the bottom resulting in brown bits of caramelized milk solids. adding the milk to water tends to minimize that))
- Squeeze out the juice from 4 lemons. Strain to remove pulp and seeds. Set aside. Moisten a large piece of cheesecloth & set over a mesh strainer. Set the strainer over a large container to contain the whey.
- When the milk boils over, remove from heat & IMMEDIATELY add the lemon juice. Stir the milk to ensure that the acid is well mixed. You should see the milk curdle almost instantly. Allow to cool for about 5 minutes. Pour the curdled mix into the cheesecloth covered strainer. Gather the corners of the cloth & Twist to squeeze out as much whey as you can. Take care, the whey is still scalding hot!
- Once most of the whey has been squeezed out and the cheese is cooled down to a point where you can handle it with your bare hands, gently untwist the cheesecloth and cover the ball of cheese with it. Place a container over the cheese and weigh down with a heavy can until it completely cools. Walk away from the contraption, leave it alone to its own devices for the next 2 hrs.!
- Unwrap the cheesecloth, the texture will now be set, but yielding. This is great if you're looking to crumble & shred it for your recipe. To get a firm consistency for cutting into cubes & frying, wrap the round block of Paneer with some sturdy kitchen paper towel (to wick away any stray moisture) then tightly in plastic wrap and refrigerate overnight.

165. Homemade Gnocchi With Coriander And Roasted Almond Pesto

Serving: Serves 2 | Prep: | Cook: |Ready in:

Ingredients

- For the Gnocchi
- 4 Large Desirée potatoes
- 300g/10½oz Rock Salt
- 65g/2¼oz '00' flour, plus extra for dusting
- 50g/2oz Parmesan, finely grated, plus extra for serving
- 1 Large Free-range egg yolk
- 1 teaspoon Olive oil
- Salt and pepper to taste
- For the Pesto
- 1 Large bunch of fresh coriander
- 1 Clove of garlic
- 1/4 pint Olive Oil
- 2 oz Roasted flaked almonds

- Salt to taste

Direction

- To make the gnocchi, prick the potatoes several times with a small knife and place onto a bed of rock salt in a baking tray in a hot oven. Bake for about 1½ hours, or until the inside is soft when tested with a knife. When cooked, remove from the oven and set aside to cool. The salt bed helps to dry out the potatoes even more resulting in really nice gnocchi. Remove the cooked potato from the skins and pass through a potato ricer or sieve into a large bowl. Add the flour, parmesan, egg yolk, olive oil to the potatoes. Season, to taste, with salt and stir until the mixture comes together into a dough. Working on a floured surface, divide the dough into four and roll each quarter into a long sausage shape. Cut into 2cm/1in pieces. I like to chill the gnocchi at this stage to firm them up before cooking, at least half an hour covered with cling film in the fridge.
- When you are ready to cook the gnocchi, bring a large saucepan of boiling water to the boil with a good pinch of salt. Add the gnocchi in to the water gently and cook for a minute or two until the gnocchi pop to the surface, this means they are cooked. Remove the cooked gnocchi with a slotted spoon. Now make the pesto by blending all ingredients together until they form a paste, heat a frying pan with some olive oil, when hot add in the cooked gnocchi and toss around the pan until golden brown, take out and serve mixed with the pesto.

---

166. Hot And Spiced Butternut Squash, Goat's Cheese, Caramelized Onion And Pistachio Parcels

---

Serving: Serves 36 triangles approximately | Prep: | Cook: | Ready in:

Ingredients

- 1 large butternut squash
- 1 teaspoon cinammon
- 1 1/2 teaspoons cumin
- 1 teaspoon cardamom
- 1/2- 1 teaspoons dried red chili flakes
- 1 teaspoon demerara brown sugar
- 2 cloves garlic, finely minced
- 1 dash coarse sea salt
- 2 dashes cracked black pepper
- 1/8 cup fine freshly grated parmesan cheese
- 2 splashes extra virgin olive oil
- 1/2 red onion, finely chopped
- 1/2 cup shelled salted pistachios, chopped
- 1 package soft goat's cheese
- 1 pound (about 18 sheets) commercial phyllo, defrosted and at room temperature
- 1/4 cup olive oil for brushing pastries
- 1 jar good quality hot mango chutney for serving

Direction

- Line a cookie sheet with aluminum foil. Preheat oven to 350 degrees Fahrenheit.
- Peel, de-seed, and chop the butternut squash into small chunks. Place in a large mixing bowl with one splash of olive oil and all the spices on the ingredient list before stopping with cracked pepper. Mix well. Pour out and arrange evenly on the cookie sheet. Place the sheet in the oven. Bake for 40 minutes approximately, or until squash pieces are fork-tender.
- Remove baked squash from the oven and empty into bowl from cookie sheet. With a potato masher, mash the squash pieces to a rough mash consistency. Grate approximately 1/8 cup Parmesan cheese over the squash mixture and stir in. Set aside.
- In a frying pan heat one splash olive oil over medium-high heat. Add chopped red onion. Saute the onion gently until it is quite wet and caramelized (approximately 5-10 minutes). Take off heat and set aside.

- Finely chop the shelled salted pistachios. Place in a small bowl and set aside.
- PHYLLO-TIME: .Have the phyllo ready. Place the sheets in front of you and, using a sharp knife, cut lengthwise into 4 equal columns. Stack them, and keep the stack covered with a dry kitchen towel and then over that a damn kitchen towel. Preheat the oven to 350°F, and lightly oil 2 baking sheets.
- Remove 1 strip of phyllo, brush it lightly with olive oil, and place another strip on top. Brush that with oil, too. Place 3/4 teaspoon of the SQUASH filling in the lower right-hand corner of the phyllo, about 1/2 inch from the edge. Top the filling blob with a tiny dob of the caramelized onion, a 1/2 teaspoon dob of soft goat's cheese and a pinch of the chopped pistachios.
- Fold up the right corner to form a right triangle, and continue folding, the way one folds a flag. Place seam side down on the baking sheet. Continue until the phyllo and filling are used up. Bake in the center of the oven for 12 to 15 minutes, or until puffed and golden.
- Serve the triangles warm either alone or with a good hot mango chutney. Enjoy!

167. How To Make Ghee At Home, Pure And Simple

Serving: Serves 10-12 | Prep: | Cook: | Ready in:

Ingredients

- 250 grams butter

Direction

- Take a heavy bottom saucepan. Put your block of butter in it and heat over medium-low heat.
- Let the butter melt slowly and then come to a boil.
- Let it boil for some minutes, occasionally scrape a spoon over the bottom of the pan to check the color of the residue that's collecting at the bottom of the pan.
- When it has turned a nice nutty brown color, like walnut shells (this might take about 10 minutes), then turn off heat and remove your pan from the stove.
- The darker the color of the residue, darker will be your ghee, nuttier will be the taste. But careful! Don't let it burn.
- Let it sit undisturbed for five minutes.
- Strain the ghee into a clean and dry jar through a tea-strainer or a piece of fine cheesecloth.
- Store in the fridge for unlimited shelf-life. Will keep on the counter-top for at least a month.

168. Incredibly Easy Jalapeno Pop 'Ems

Serving: Serves 6 | Prep: | Cook: | Ready in:

Ingredients

- 12 medium jalapenos
- 4 ounces cream cheese
- 4 ounces grated cheddar or jack cheese
- Healthy squeeze of sriracha
- 4 slices proscuitto

Direction

- Wearing gloves, split jalapenos lengthwise and scoop out the seeds. Leave the stem, if possible.
- Mix together cheeses and sriracha sauce to taste.
- Stuff the jalapeno halves with the cheese. Drape a piece of prosciutto over the top.
- Bake at 400 for about 10 minutes. Allow to cool a minute or two before serving.

169. Italian Rice Pie

Serving: Serves 8-10 | Prep: 1hours0mins | Cook: 1hours30mins |Ready in:

Ingredients

- For the crust
- 1 1/2 cups all-purpose flour
- 1/4 cup sugar
- 1/2 teaspoon salt
- 1/2 teaspoon baking powder
- 3/4 stick unsalted butter (chilled)
- 1 extra large egg or 2 small eggs
- 1 tablespoon tablespoons ice water, or as much as needed
- For the rice filling
- 1/2 cup uncooked Arborio rice
- 4 cups water OR whole milk
- 7 large eggs
- 1 cup sugar
- 2 teaspoons lemon extract (or the zest and juice of 1 small lemon, preferably Meyer)
- 2 teaspoons pure vanilla extract
- 1 pound ricotta cheese, drained (minimum of 2 hours or preferably overnight)

Direction

- For the crust
- Combine flour, sugar, salt and baking powder in the work bowl of a food processor fitted with a metal blade. Pulse several times to combine. Add the butter and pulse about 10 times until the dough becomes pebbly in texture. Add the eggs and pulse repeatedly until the dough begins to stick together. Slowly add the ice water by the tablespoonful, while using a few long pulses. Add more drops of ice water as necessary, until the dough holds together well. Invert the dough onto a floured work surface. Form the dough into a ball, flatten into a disc, wrap in plastic wrap, and refrigerate while preparing the filling. (Dough can be refrigerated for up to 2 days before continuing.)
- If you don't have a processor, then combine the dry ingredients in a bowl. Add chunks of chilled butter, and using a pastry blender or two forks, chop the butter until it resembles little pebbles. At this point, add the eggs and ice water, and stir with a spoon until the dough begins to form. Using your hands and working the dough as little as possible, transfer it to a lightly floured surface. Knead until the dough holds together. Form the dough into a ball, flatten into a disc, wrap in plastic and refrigerate while preparing the filling. (Dough can be refrigerated for up to 2 days before continuing.)
- For the rice filling
- Place the rice and water OR whole milk in medium heavy-bottom saucepan and bring to a boil. Reduce the heat to low and cook the rice, uncovered, stirring occasionally for about 15 to 20 minutes, or until the water is absorbed and the rice is sticky. The rice should still be firm as it will finish cooking in the oven. Remove from heat and set aside.
- Add the eggs and sugar to a large bowl. Using a hand-mixer, beat until well combined. Add the lemon extract (or zest and juice) and vanilla, and beat on low for about 10 seconds. Add the drained ricotta, and beat on low for a few seconds until just combined. Stir in the cooked rice. Mix with a rubber spatula until well combined, making sure there are no clumps of rice. Place in the refrigerator.
- Place a rack in the lower third of the oven and preheat to 375 degrees. Coat a 10 1/2-inch pie plate with cooking spray. Turn out the dough onto a lightly floured surface and roll into an 11 1/2-inch circle. Transfer the dough to the prepared pie plate, gently pressing it into the bottom and sides. No fluted crust is necessary. At this point, set the crust in the freezer for about 10 to 15 minutes to get it really chilled, which will make for a flakier crust.
- Remove the chilled crust from the freezer and pour the filling to about 1/4 of an inch below the top of the crust, as it will puff up slightly when baking. Bake for 1 hour or until the filling puffs up, turns golden, and is "set,"

meaning it should be firm, not jiggly when you gently move the pie plate. Remove from the oven and let cool on a rack. Serve at room temperature or chilled.
- Note: If you have some extra filling left over, you can pour it into a small baking dish or ramekins for a crustless version, and follow the same baking instructions. Leftover rice pie can be stored in an air-tight container in the refrigerator for 3 to 4 days.

170. Italian Sausage Strata

Serving: Serves 8 | Prep: | Cook: | Ready in:

Ingredients

- 1 day-old French baguette
- 1 medium-large yellow onion, chopped
- 3 scallions, green and white parts chopped
- 3 mild Italian sausage links
- 2 cups Swiss cheese, shredded
- 1 cup Parmigiano-Reggiano cheese, shredded
- 1/2 cup feta cheese, crumbled
- 14 eggs
- 1 1/2 cups milk
- 1/4 cup 2% Greek yogurt or heavy cream
- 1/2 teaspoon cayenne pepper
- 2 tablespoons Dijon mustard
- 1 teaspoon rosemary, chopped
- Salt & Pepper

Direction

- Preheat oven to 325º F. Cut your loaf into cubes and bake for about 10 minutes or until slightly browned and dried out.
- Heat a pan over medium heat and drizzle olive oil in the bottom. When hot, add your chopped onion with a generous amount of salt and reduce heat to low. Cook slowly for about 30-40 minutes. When soft and browned, remove from heat.
- Meanwhile, in another skillet warm 3 tablespoons of water over medium heat. Place your sausages in the pan and cover. Cook for about 10 minutes until warmed through. Take the sausage out and pour the water out if any remains. Return the skillet to the heat and drizzle in some olive oil. Put the sausages in the skillet once more and fry briefly in the oil until browned on the outside, about 1-2 minutes each side. Remove the sausages from the pan and slice when slightly cooled.
- Mix the chopped scallions, onions, and rosemary in a bowl and the shredded parmesan and Swiss cheese in another bowl.
- Grease a deep cast iron Dutch oven or a 9x13 glass dish in a pinch. Layer a third of the bread cubes followed by the onion mixture, one sliced sausage, and cheese mixture in the dish. Repeat two times to use up all of the bread, onion, sausage, and cheese. Sprinkle the feta on top of the last layer.
- Whisk together the eggs, milk, yogurt, cayenne, Dijon mustard, and lots of salt and pepper.
- Pour the egg mixture on top of the bread layers, cover, and refrigerate overnight. Don't skip this step! It lets the bread soak up the egg mix and the flavors meld.
- In the morning, preheat the oven to 350º F. Check your strata and make sure your bread has not soaked up all of the liquid. This differs for each bread type, but if your strata seems too dry, beat a couple extra eggs and a splash of milk together and pour it on top of the strata.
- With your Dutch oven lid on, bake your strata. After 30 minutes, remove the lid and continue to bake for about an hour or until the top is nicely browned and it no longer wiggles. If you are using a casserole dish, forgo the lid and bake for an hour and a half. Your top may just be more browned. If you are worried about under-heating, heat until the middle of your strata reaches 165º F.
- Let your strata cool for about 15-20 minutes before cutting pieces out. Eat while warm with extra shredded parmesan if you desire!

171. Italian Sweet Sausage Stuffed Shells With Four Cheese Cream Sauce

Serving: Serves 4-6 | Prep: | Cook: | Ready in:

Ingredients

- 2 tablespoons unsalted butter
- 1/4 cup whole wheat bread crumbs
- 1 tablespoon olive oil
- 1 1/2 pounds Italian sweet sausage
- 14 1/2 ounces can artichoke hearts, drained and chopped
- 1/4 cup sundried tomatoes, finely chopped
- 16 ounces jumbo pasta shells
- 6 cups water, for boiling
- 2 tablespoons unsalted butter
- 1/4 cup flour
- 1 clove garlic, grated
- 2 cups milk
- 1/4 teaspoon salt
- 1/8 teaspoon white pepper
- 1/8 teaspoon nutmeg
- 1/2 cup parmesan, asiago, romano blend
- 1 cup mozzarella, shredded

Direction

- Preheat oven to 350 degrees F. In a small skillet melt butter over medium and add bread crumbs. Cook until slightly toasted stirring often, about 5 to 7 minutes. Remove from heat and set aside.
- Heat oil over medium heat and add sausage, removed from casing. Using the back of a wooden spoon, break down the sausage and cook until browned, about 8 to 10 minutes. Drain and return to skillet along with artichoke hearts and sundried tomatoes. Stir to combine, remove from heat and set aside.
- In the meantime bring a large pot of salted water to a boil and add shells. Cook just until almost al dente, or tender, about 7 minutes. Drain and set aside to cool. Place shells in a greased 9x13 baking dish.
- In a medium sauce pot melt butter over medium heat. Whisk in flour and cook 2 minutes. While whisking add garlic, milk, salt, white pepper and nutmeg. Bring to a boil, reduce heat to low and simmer until thickened, about 3 to 5 minutes. Stir in parmesan, asiago, Romano blend until smooth.
- Begin stuffing shells with sausage mixture until gone and pour cheese sauce over top. Sprinkle with mozzarella and bread crumbs, cover and bake for 25 to 30 minutes. Remove cover last 5 minutes of cooking until golden and bubbly.

172. Jalapeño Cream Cheese Dip

Serving: Makes 1 large serving bowl | Prep: | Cook: | Ready in:

Ingredients

- 16 ounces softened cream cheese
- 1 cup sour cream
- 2 cups shredded sharp cheddar cheese
- 1/2 cup chopped jalapeño (jar, drained)
- 4.25 ounces chopped black olives
- 2 teaspoons onion powder
- 1 teaspoon garlic powder
- 1/2 teaspoon smoked paprika
- 1/2 teaspoon white pepper

Direction

- Place all ingredients in a bowl and mixed with a hand held mixer until mixed thoroughly. Place in a serving bowl and garnish with jalapeños, shredded sharp cheddar cheese and smoked paprika! Serve with crackers!

173. Jasmine Scented Raspberry Breakfast Tiramisu'

Serving: Serves 2 | Prep: | Cook: | Ready in:

Ingredients

- Jasmine Syrup
- 1/2 cup sugar
- 1 cup water
- 1 cup jasmine flowers (or a tea bag)
- Tiramisu'
- 2 cups Greek yogurt
- 2 tablespoons honey
- 1 package savoiradi (lady fingers)
- 1 cup raspberries

Direction

- Make the jasmine syrup: In a small pan, bring the water and the sugar to a boil. Once all the sugar has dissolved, turn off the heat and add the flowers to the pot. Let steep for 2 to 3 hours, or overnight.
- Once the syrup is done steeping, drain the flowers and put the syrup back in a small pot. Turn on the heat and add in the raspberries. Boil them for about 5 minutes, or until the syrup has turned bright red.
- Strain the syrup to eliminate the seeds, and pour it into a deep plate. Dip the lady fingers into the syrup and let them absorb it for about 10 seconds, then line the bottom of your serving dish with them.
- Mix the yogurt with the honey and spread half of it on top of the lady finger layer in your dish. Top the yogurt with more soaked lady fingers, and add the second half of the yogurt on top. Garnish with some raspberries and jasmine flowers, and enjoy!

174. Jersey Pizza With Roasted Garlic And Arugula

Serving: Serves 1 pizza dough | Prep: | Cook: | Ready in:

Ingredients

- 1 head of garlic
- 1/4 cup olive oil
- 1 /2 cups very hot tap water
- 1 packet active dry yeast
- 1 tablespoon honey
- 1.5 cups all purpose flour
- 1/2 teaspoon salt
- 1 tablespoon cornmeal
- 1 bunch arugula
- 1/3 cup shaved parm
- 1/3 cup diced Italian fontina
- fresh ground black pepper
- 1/2 teaspoon Italian seasoning

Direction

- Preheat oven to 400 degrees. Cut off the top of a head of garlic, drizzle with some olive oil, wrap in foil, and roast for 30-40 minutes, or until soft. Once cool, squeeze out roasted garlic into a bowl and set aside.
- Whisk honey into hot tap water (or nuke filtered water to 100 degrees), and mix in one packet of yeast. Allow yeast to proof (foam up) for about 5 minutes. In the meantime, add one cup of the flour and salt to a food processor and pulse several times. Once yeast mixture is foamy and thick, turn on the food processor and drizzle yeast mixture into the flour in a slow and steady stream until the flour just starts to stick together into a cohesive ball. You might not need all of the yeast mixture, and you do not want to add more liquid than needed, Remove the dough from the food processor and knead the dough on a floured surface for 2-3 minutes, Once dough is elastic and no longer sticky, place it in a small bowl and drizzle with olive oil until the entire dough ball is covered. Cover the bowl with plastic wrap, and allow to rise for 1-2 hours.

- While dough is rising, heat the oven to 500 degrees, and place your pizza stone in the bottom of the oven. Once the dough has risen, punch it down, and press dough out on a floured surface into the shape of a circle. Place cornmeal onto your pizza peel, and place the dough on top. Drizzle dough with some olive oil, and spread with roasted garlic and season with salt, pepper and Italian seasonings. Add cheese. Place dough onto heated pizza stone and bake for 5-10 minutes or until cheese is melted and crust is brown.
- Remove pizza from oven onto pizza peel. Toss arugula with olive oil, salt and pepper, and cover the pizza with the arugula mixture and allow to wilt. Serve hot.

175.   Joan Nathan's Chosen Cheese Blintzes

Serving: Makes 30 blintzes | Prep: | Cook: |Ready in:

Ingredients

- Filling
- 1 pound farmer cheese (2 cups)
- 1/4 cup cream cheese
- 1 large egg
- 1/4 cup sugar
- dash salt
- Batter
- 1 cup milk
- 1 1/2 cups water
- 5 large eggs
- 2 cups unbleached all-purpose flour
- 6 tablespoons salted butter (for frying)
- dash salt
- Sour cream (for garnish)
- Blueberries, raspberries, or strawberries (for garnish)

Direction

- In a medium bowl, mix together thoroughly the ingredients for the filling: farmer cheese, cream cheese, egg, sugar, and salt. Set aside in the refrigerator at least half an hour.
- Now make the batter: Put 1 1/2 cups of water, 1 cup of milk, and eggs in a blender, and pulse until well mixed. Next, add the flour and salt and mix until all lumps are dissolved. Let the batter rest for half an hour. It does not have to be refrigerated.
- Heat a non-stick 8-inch skillet or omelet pan over a medium-low heat. When the pan is hot, add about a scant teaspoon of butter or coconut oil to melt. Lift the pan off the heat, and pour about 1/4 of a cup of batter onto the frying pan. Tilt the pan so the batter just covers the bottom. Return the pan to the heat and cook until the crepe blisters, about 1 to 2 minutes. Do not flip. Turn the crepe gently onto waxed or parchment paper, cooked side up. You might need a spatula to help you. Continue cooking the crepes, adding more butter or coconut oil between every 2 to 3 times. Stack the finished blintzes on top of each other.
- Take one crepe and spread 2 tablespoons of cheese filling along the end closest to you, leaving an inch of space. Fold that inch over the filling, then turn the sides over so they meet in the middle. Roll up the filled end away from you until the blintz is completely closed. Repeat with the remaining filling and crepes.
- In a large frying pan, melt about a tablespoon of butter or coconut oil a medium heat. Place the filled blintzes in the pan, leaving about an inch of space between them. Fry until golden brown, then flip and repeat. Remove to a paper towel-lined cookie sheet. You will have to do this in batches. Serve immediately with sour cream and fresh berries.
- NOTE: Blintzes can also be frozen and reheated in a 425-degree oven for about 30 minutes.

176. Juniper And Honey Pot De Créme

Serving: Serves 4 to 6 | Prep: | Cook: | Ready in:

Ingredients

- 1 1/2 cups heavy cream
- 1/2 cup whole milk
- 1/2 cup mild-flavored honey
- 2 tablespoons dried juniper berries, lightly crushed
- 6 large egg yolks
- Whipped cream, sea salt, and toasted pine nuts to serve

Direction

- In a medium saucepan combine the heavy cream, milk, honey, juniper berries, and salt. Bring to a low simmer and turn off the heat. Let steep for 30 minutes then strain out the berries.
- While the cream steeps, preheat the oven to 300° F, put a kettle of water on to boil, and arrange 4 to 6 ramekins in a baking dish.
- Whisk the egg yolks until well combined, then whisk the warm cream mixture into the egg yolks. Divide the mixture into ramekins.
- Put the baking dish onto the oven rack and fill the dish with about 1 inch of boiling water; the water should reach about halfway up the ramekins. Tent the dish with foil and bake for 40 50 minutes or until the custards are set, but jiggle slightly in the center. Cool the custards for at least 2 hours and up to overnight before serving.
- Garnish with a light sprinkle of sea salt, a dollop of whipped cream, and a sprinkling of toasted pine nuts.

177. Kabocha Squash (Japanese Pumpkin) Braised In Milk

Serving: Serves 4 as a side dish | Prep: | Cook: | Ready in:

Ingredients

- 1 pound kabocha squash (Japanese pumpkin)
- 3/4 cup (180 ml) whole milk
- 1 tablespoon soy sauce
- 1 tablespoon sugar
- 1 splash rice wine vinegar, optional

Direction

- Chop the squash into 1-inch pieces. Kabocha is a very soft squash once cooked, so you can choose to leave the skin on if you want it to retain its shape better and create contrast in color and texture. Otherwise, you can cut off the skin and discard it along with the seeds.
- In a small saucepan, mix the squash, milk, soy sauce, and sugar and bring to a simmer. Cook uncovered for 15 minutes, then half-cover with a lid until the pumpkin is soft but not falling apart and the milk has turned into thick, curdled flecks a little bit similar to ricotta or cottage cheese.
- Serve warm or cold with a splash of rice wine vinegar stirred through it.

178. Kitty's Latin Tart

Serving: Serves 4 as an appetizer or 2 for a meal | Prep: | Cook: | Ready in:

Ingredients

- 1 pre-made pie crust (the kind that comes chilled/rolled) or home made
- 2 teaspoons minced sundried tomato (the kind packed in oil works well)
- 1 fresh jalapeno that has been minced and seeded

- 3 thinly sliced scallions
- 4 pieces of cooked bacon that have been crumbled
- 6 medium sized shrimp that have been grilled and cut into thirds (grill on grill pan if you don't have an outside grill)
- 3/4 cup shredded cheddar cheese
- 1/2 cup sour cream
- 3/4 teaspoon ground cumin
- 1 dash your favorite hot sauce

Direction

- Preheat oven to 400 deg.
- Spray a non-stick baking sheet with a light coat of canola oil
- Place pie crust in center of baking sheet and spread the shredded cheese to an even layer -- leave a 1 1/4 inch border so you can roll the edge later.
- Sprinkle the jalapeno and tomato over cheese.
- Sprinkle crumbled bacon on top.
- Fold up the edges of crust one section at a time. Each section folds over and presses into the next to form a rustic rounded and pleated edge.
- Bake the tart at 400 deg. for 12 to 15 minutes (every oven is different). The edges should look golden brown.
- Mix the sour cream, cumin and hot sauce together and place in a squeeze bottle if you have one.
- Slide the tart off the baking sheet onto a cutting board. Add the shrimp.
- Drizzle or squeeze the sour cream mixture heavily onto the tart in a wagon wheel or star pattern. Sprinkle scallions on top.
- Cut the tart with a pizza wheel and serve!

179. Kunafa With Mango Cream Filling

Serving: Serves 6 | Prep: | Cook: | Ready in:

Ingredients

- For layering & Honey Syrup
- 100 grams Thin vermicelli (Readymade) Or Kaitiafi
- 30 grams Butter (Melted)
- 1 cup Water
- 3-4 tablespoons Sugar
- 3-4 tablespoons Honey
- 3-4 drops Rose water
- 1 tablespoon Lemon juice
- For Filling:
- 1 1/2 cups Full cream milk
- 1 cup Mango Puree (Alfanzo)
- 50 grams Cottage cheese (Paneer)
- 1/4 tablespoon Cornflour
- 1 tablespoon All purpose flour (Maida)
- 2-3 tablespoons Sugar free (You can use the same amount of white sugar)
- 3-4 drops Kewra
- 1/4 cup ¼ cup dry fruits or more for garnish(Almond + Pistachio roasted in butter)

Direction

- For layering & Honey Syrup
- Break the vermicelli with fingers in a large bowl adding butter to it.
- Now grease 6 muffin molds, always grease upward (I used silicon mold as it's easy to demold).
- Pre – heat the oven on 200 degrees.
- Now mix water sugar, honey, rose water and lemon juice and boil for 10-15 mins, till you get a syrup
- For Filling:
- Take a deep sauce pan and pour milk into it,
- Now mix corn flour, custard powder & maida with some cold water. Mix well till there are no lumps in the mixture
- Top the remaining vermicelli over the mixture lightly, don't press the vermicelli too much.
- Now bake for 45-50 mins or till the top layer of vermicelli becomes golden
- Now pour the honey syrup and top it with roasted dry fruits, serve the way you want

180. LAMB SOUVLAKI WITH ZUCCHINI TZATZIKI

Serving: Serves 2-4 | Prep: | Cook: |Ready in:

Ingredients

- SOUVLAKI
- 500g (approx. 7) lamb fillets
- 3 tbsp extra virgin olive oil
- 2 cloves garlic, crushed
- ¼ tsp freshly grated nutmeg
- ¼ tsp cinnamon
- 1 tbsp greek oregano (rigani)
- Zest & juice of half a lemon
- Pinch murray river salt flakes
- Freshly ground black pepper
- ZUCCHINI TZATZIKI
- 1 ½ cups zucchini, grated or shredded
- 4 tbsp Greek yogurt
- 1 small clove garlic
- ½ tsp dried dill
- 1 tsp dried Greek oregano
- 1 tsp lemon juice
- Pinch murray river salt flakes
- Freshly ground black pepper

Direction

- For the zucchini tzatziki, place grated zucchini in a strainer lined with a clean tea towel, add a pinch of salt and mix salt through using your hands. Leave it sit for 10 minutes.
- Meanwhile, chop lamb fillets into bite size pieces and place into a bowl. Add all remaining souvlaki ingredients to the lamb, mix well with your hands, cover and refrigerate to marinate for an hour or overnight.
- To finish the zucchini tzatziki, gather the sides of the tea towel and squeeze out all the liquid (you should be left with about half a cup of grated zucchini). Place in a bowl with all remaining tzatziki ingredients, stir to combine, cover and refrigerate until needed.
- Thread the lamb onto skewers (I like to use metal skewers so they don't burn). You can cook the souvlaki on the barbeque, grill or griddle pan. Either way, cook over a med-high heat, turning them occasionally for 4-5 minutes until golden or to your liking.
- To serve, place lamb on a platter, squeeze lemon juice all over and serve alongside your zucchini tzatziki.

181. Labneh Grilled Cheese

Serving: Makes 2 | Prep: | Cook: |Ready in:

Ingredients

- Olive oil
- 4 thick slices seedy wheat bread
- 2 ounces shaved white Cheddar
- 2 ounces shaved Parmesan
- 1/4 cup labneh or plain full-fat Greek yogurt
- Za'atar
- Sumac
- Tomato soup, for serving

Direction

- Heat a thin layer of olive oil in a large skillet over medium heat. Toast the bread slices on one side until lightly browned and then flip them over. Top two slices with cheddar and two slices with parmesan and then spread two of the slices with the labneh and sprinkle with a pinch of za'atar and sumac. Carefully sandwich them together, cover with a lid, and cook until the bottom is toasted. Flip, cover, and cook until the bottom is toasted and the parmesan and cheddar are melted. Transfer to a plate, cut diagonally, and serve with tomato soup.

182. Lasagna Aperto

Serving: Serves 4 | Prep: | Cook: | Ready in:

Ingredients

- Fresh Ricotta
- 6 cups whole milk
- 3/4 teaspoon salt
- 2 tablespoons fresh lemon juice
- 4 tablespoons distilled white vinegar
- Lasagna
- 2/3 cup all-purpose flour
- 1/4 teaspoon salt
- 1 egg
- 6 roma tomatoes
- 6 tablespoons chopped garlic, about 6-8 cloves
- 3 tablespoons oil
- salt and pepper to taste
- 2 cups loosly packed basil leaves
- 2 cloves garlic
- salt and pepper to taste
- 2 tablespoons toasted pine nuts
- 1/3 cup olive oil
- 1/2 cup parmesan
- fresh ricotta, recipe above
- 4 ounces fresh mozzarella, sliced

Direction

- Fresh Ricotta
- Line a colander with cheesecloth or food safe paper towels and put in the sink.
- Heat the milk and salt in a non-reactive pot over medium heat until it reaches 165 degrees, or until it starts to bubble around the edges.
- Add the lemon juice and vinegar and stir until the milk separates into curds and whey. Scoop the curds into the colander and let drain for 15-20 minutes, until you have a soft, moist cheese, but firm enough that it holds its shape. Less like cottage cheese, more like soft goat cheese. It will keep in the refrigerator for 2-3 days.
- Lasagna
- Preheat the oven to 450 degrees.
- Begin by making the pasta. Combine the flour and salt in food processor, and pulse once or twice. Add egg and process until a ball begins to form, about 30 seconds. Knead by hand (with a little flour if necessary) for a minute or two. You want a not-sticky, firm dough. Cover with plastic wrap and let rest for 30 minutes
- While the dough rests, slice the tomatoes into 1/4-1/2" slices. Toss with the olive oil, garlic, and a generous helping of salt and pepper and place on a baking sheet in a single layer. Roast the tomatoes 35 minutes.
- Make the pesto. Combine the basil, salt, garlic, nuts and about half the oil in a food processor. Process, adding the rest of the oil gradually. You may not want to use all the oil, or you may prefer a little more. Stir in the parmesan and set aside.
- Roll out the pasta. Cut the ball in half and press each half down with your hand. Feed each half of the pasta roller starting on the largest setting, going down to the smallest setting. Cut each sheet into thirds.
- At this point, the tomatoes probably have about 10 minutes left, so heat a large pot of salted water to a boil. Cook the lasagna noodles for three minutes and drain well.
- When the tomatoes are done, turn on the broiler and assemble the lasagna. On a baking sheet put down a little oil, so the lasagna won't stick. Place one of the pieces of pasta on the oil. Spread a tablespoon or so of the pesto on the pasta, top with a couple of tablespoons of the ricotta, a pinch of salt and pepper, and a generous helping of tomatoes and garlic. Top with another piece of pasta and repeat. Top with a third piece of pasta and spread another tablespoon of pesto. Top the lasagna with 1/2 of the mozzarella. Repeat with the remaining ingredients. Put under the broiler for 1-2 minutes, until the cheese melts.

183. Lasagne Alla Bolognese

Serving: Makes 4 generous portions | Prep: | Cook: | Ready in:

Ingredients

- For the ragu:
- 1 pound (500 gr) total of mince beef and pork
- 2 slices of rigatino or pancetta, chopped
- 1/2 carrot, finely chopped
- 1/2 celery stalk, finely chopped
- 1 small onion, finely chopped
- a handful of parsley, leaves and stalks finely chopped
- 2-3 pinches salt
- white wine to cover (about half a bottle)
- 8 ounces (250 ml) of tomato puree
- For the bechamel and assembly:
- 3 1/2 tablespoons (50 gr) butter
- 1/2 cup (50 gr) flour
- 2 cups (500 ml) cold milk
- 3 1/2 ounces finely grated Parmesan cheese
- 1 pound (500 gr) pasta sheets (fresh, dried or homemade)

Direction

- For the ragu:
- Brown the meat in a hot pan with some olive oil. Don't overcrowd the pan – if you don't have a large pan, do it in two batches. This is to avoid the meat losing too much liquid and boiling in it instead of searing.
- Remove the meat when browned, turn down the heat to low and add the pancetta. Once the pancetta begins to melt, add the carrot, celery, onion and parsley. Season with a pinch of salt then let sweat and cook until the vegetables are soft.
- Return the meat to the pan, season with another pinch of salt and add the wine to cover.
- When the wine has reduced, add the tomato and a splash or two of water. Cover and cook slowly until you have a thick, glossy, tasty ragu. The longer you cook it, the tastier it will be -- at least two hours as an indication. If the liquid reduces too quickly, add water or stock and continue cooking.
- For the béchamel and assembly:
- Make the béchamel sauce: melt butter in pan. Before it begins to color, add flour and stir with a wooden spoon, cooking the flour for a few minutes. Add the milk, stir until smooth. Cook until it just coats the back of the spoon. It should be just a little looser than usual for lasagne.
- To assemble the lasagne once the ragu and béchamel are ready, blanch the pasta sheets in plenty of boiling, salted water for 1 minute, making sure they don't stick together. Drain, pass through cold water and drain again. Lay them flat on clean tea towels.
- Use a rectangular or square casserole dish (such as an 8x8 inch pan) – keeping in mind that a larger one will produce less layers and a smaller one will produce more. Begin with a dollop of ragu on the bottom, roughly spreading to all edges. Lay down your pasta sheets; a little overlapping is fine. A layer of ragu - just enough to cover - followed by a layer (or several dollops) of béchamel and a sprinkle of Parmesan cheese. Continue layering this way until you finish with ragu, béchamel and a final heavier layer of Parmesan cheese.
- Bake at 350°F for about 30-45 minutes, depending on the thickness, depth and size of your lasagne. It should be golden brown on top and you should see sauce bubbling at the edges. Let rest for 10-15 minutes before cutting and serving.

184. Layered Croissant Sandwich Casserole

Serving: Makes 7 large croissant sandwiches | Prep: | Cook: | Ready in:

Ingredients

- 7 Croissants
- 14 Slices of Deli Ham
- 7 Slices of Swiss Cheese
- 6 teaspoons Dijon Style Mustard
- 10 Large Eggs
- 1.5 cups Milk
- 1/2 teaspoon Pepper

Direction

- Spray a 9x13 inch oval baking dish with cooking spray.
- Slice the croissants and assemble sandwiches by spreading each with mustard and filling with ham and cheese. Each croissant gets 2 slices of ham and 1 slice cheese.
- Arrange croissant sandwiches by shingling them into the casserole dish.
- In a medium bowl beat eggs, add milk and salt and pepper, and mix well. Pour over the sandwiches and cover the dish with foil. Weight the top with a plate or cookie sheet to submerge sandwiches in the custard and refrigerate at least 4 hours or overnight.
- Preheat oven to 350º F. Bake, covered with the foil, for 30 minutes. Remove foil and bake an additional 30 minutes.

185. Layered Grapes And Bread With Chèvre And Balsamic

Serving: Serves 6 to 8 as a side | Prep: | Cook: | Ready in:

Ingredients

- For the bread:
- 10 ounces day-old sourdough, cut into 1-inch cubes (8 to 9 cups)
- 2 tablespoons olive oil
- 2 teaspoons minced garlic
- 2 teaspoons fresh thyme
- 1/2 teaspoon fresh ground black pepper
- For everything else:
- 2 large sweet onions (1 pound total)
- 2 teaspoons olive oil, plus extra for the dish
- 3 tablespoons port, divided
- Kosher salt
- 1/3 cup balsamic vinegar
- 1 pound organic seedless black grapes, de-stemmed and halved (about 4 cups), divided
- 1 1/2 cups homemade or low-sodium chicken stock or vegetable broth
- 4 1/2 ounces chèvre
- 1/4 cup grated Parmesan

Direction

- For the bread:
- Heat oven to 400° F.
- Place bread cubes on a large rimmed baking sheet and drizzle with olive oil. Using your hands, toss the cubes to distribute the oil. Add garlic, thyme, and black pepper and toss again to evenly coat. Toast bread in the oven for 10 minutes, stirring cubes with a wooden spoon at the halfway point. Remove from oven and set aside to cool. Turn oven down to 325° F.
- For everything else:
- Trim ends from onions and peel papery skin. Cut onions in half. With the cut side down, thinly slice lengthwise. Repeat until you have cut all of the onion.
- Heat the oil in a large skillet over medium heat, until shimmering. Add onions and stir to coat. Spread onions out evenly across pan. Turn heat down to low and allow onions to cook, undisturbed, for 10 minutes. Add 2 tablespoons port and a pinch of salt and continue to cook for 40 minutes more, occasionally stirring to promote even coloring and prevent burning. As you are cooking and stirring, add a teaspoon or two of water if the onions seem dry. Onions are finished when they are fragrant and deep golden brown. Add remaining tablespoon of port, stir, and transfer to a bowl.
- In a small saucepan, combine balsamic vinegar with 2 cups of halved grapes. Bring mixture to a boil and turn down to maintain a simmer.

- Cook for 10 minutes. Transfer to a bowl or 1-cup Pyrex measure.
- Warm the chicken stock in a small saucepan over low heat.
- Oil the bottom of a rectangular ceramic roaster (about 2-quart capacity). Spread 1/3 of the caramelized onions in the bottom of the dish, followed by 1/3 of the reserved toasted bread, drizzle 1/3 of the cooked grape-vinegar mixture, spread 1/3 of the remaining raw grapes, and dot with 1/3 of the chèvre. Repeat layering ingredients, starting with onions and ending with chèvre, until you run out. The top layer can incorporate a little of everything. Finish the top by evenly sprinkling the Parmesan.
- Ladle the warmed stock around the edges of the dish. Cover with foil and bake for 30 minutes. After 30 minutes, remove foil and turn heat up to 375° F. Continue baking for an additional 10 minutes. Remove from oven and allow dish to cool slightly before serving. Enjoy!

186. Lazy Greek Pizza With Shrimp

Serving: Serves 2 small pizza | Prep: | Cook: |Ready in:

Ingredients

- 1 piece Sea Salt Ciabatta Bread from Whole Foods
- 1 cup feta cheese, crumbled
- 2 cups Mozzerella, shredded
- 1 cup tomato sauce
- 1 bunch basil, roughly chopped
- 1 handful anchovies
- 1 tablespoon capers
- 1 pound shrimp, peeled and deveined, no tail
- 1 handful grape tomatoes
- 1/2 cup olive oil

Direction

- Heat oil in a cast iron skillet. Slice bread lengthwise (like a hamburger bun) and toast in olive oil about 2-3 minutes each side.
- Spread tomato sauce on toasted bread.
- Sprinkle the cheeses on top of the tomato sauce.
- Top with tomatoes, shrimp, anchovies and capers.
- Decorate pizzas with the chopped basil, and any extra mozzarella that you might have laying around.
- Bake in preheated oven at 500 degrees for 30 minutes. Let cool before serving or you will burn your mouth and not taste anything for several days.

187. Lebanese Maftoul Couscous With Roasted Butternut Squash, Mint And Feta

Serving: Serves 6 | Prep: | Cook: |Ready in:

Ingredients

- 1/2 cup fresh orange juice
- 2 tablespoons lemon zest
- 4 tablespoons fresh lemon juice (from approximately 2 med lemons)
- 1 medium butternut squash, peeled and seeded, cut into 1/4 inch-dice
- 3 tablespoons olive oil
- 1 large red onion, chopped
- 1 cup maftoul pearl couscous (Isreali couscous)
- 1 1/2 cups vegetable broth
- 2 cinnamon sticks
- 1 dried bay leaf
- 2 star anise
- 1 cup chopped fresh flat-leaf Italian parsley
- 1/2 cup toasted pine nuts
- 1/2 cup dried cranberries
- 1 Granny Smith apple, diced (approximately 1 1/2 c)

- 1/2 cup fresh chopped mint
- 1/2 cup crumbled feta

Direction

- Preheat oven to 475 degrees F.
- Toss squash with 2T olive oil and salt to taste in large baking pan and spread in single layer. Roast in oven for 15 minutes until squash is just tender and transfer to a separate bowl.
- Cook onion in 1T olive oil in skillet over medium heat stirring occasionally until golden brown and add to bowl with squash.
- Add star anise, bay leaf, cinnamon sticks and vegetable broth to a pot and bring to a boil. Add couscous and reduce heat to a simmer then cook for approximately 12 minutes until just tender. Remove star anise, bay leaf and cinnamon sticks, then add couscous to squash and onions in bowl.
- Add orange juice, lemon zest, lemon juice, parsley, pine nuts, cranberries, apples, mint and feta to bowl with squash and onions. Toss and serve at room temperature.

188. Lemon Goat Cheese Cheesecake

Serving: Serves 10 | Prep: | Cook: |Ready in:

Ingredients

- 1/4 cup unsalted butter, plus 1 teaspoon (for greasing the pan)
- 8 ounces cookies (lemon, shortbread, vanilla wafers, or your favorite cookie)
- 1/2 teaspoon kosher salt, divided
- 10 ounces cream cheese, room temperature
- 6 ounces creamy fresh goat cheese, room temperature
- 1/2 cup sugar
- 3 eggs, room temperature
- 1/2 cup crème fraîche or sour cream
- 2 tablespoons lemon juice
- 2 teaspoons firmly packed lemon zest (not strips, make sure it's very finely zested)
- 8 ounces cookies, enough to circle the cake (preferably the same kind you used for the crust)
- 2 tablespoons of your favorite jam or honey (for gluing on cookies)

Direction

- Heat oven to 350° F. Butter the interior of your springform pan. Cut a piece of parchment to fit the bottom of the pan and press it into the pan. Butter the parchment. Set aside. Place butter for the crust in a medium-sized pan over medium heat. The butter will melt, sizzle, and foam up. Once it smells nutty and the noise stops, watch closely. Turn off the heat once the brown bits drop down to the bottom of the pan. Set aside. Pulverize your cookies in the food processor. Pulse in the brown butter and a 1/4 teaspoon of the salt. Press into the bottom and up about 1 inch of the greased spring form pan. Bake until just starting to brown (about 10 minutes). Remove from the oven to cool. Turn oven down to 300° F.
- Place cream cheese and goat cheese in the bowl of a standing mixer, and beat until light and smooth (about 3 minutes). Scrape down the sides. Add the sugar and beat for another minute. Scrape down the sides. Add the eggs one at a time, scraping down between each addition. Add the remaining salt, crème fraîche, and lemon juice and zest. Beat for another 30 seconds. If you see any lumps, beat for another 30 seconds or so.
- Pour into the crust in the prepared springform pan. Bake for 40 minutes. Don't peek. Not even once. After 40 minutes, turn off the oven and open the door. Leave the cake to cool for an hour in the oven. After an hour, remove from the oven to cool completely. (Otherwise, the cake will sweat in the fridge.) Cover and place in the fridge for 8 hours or overnight.
- To serve, place the bottom of the pan over a medium flame on the stove. Move it around for about 5 seconds over the flame. Use a

warm paring knife (warmed under hot water or over the flame) to separate the cake from the side of the pan. Remove outer ring from the spring form pan. Don't stress if it looks like a mess because you will be covering the sides up with cookies. Try to slide the cake off of the bottom of the pan. If it won't budge, put it over the flame for a few more seconds and/or use a spatula to loosen things up. I've found that once the cake is off the base and on the plate, you can easily slide out the circle of parchment paper. Sometimes, the parchment will even stay behind on the pan.
- Encircle the side with the same cookies you used for the crust. They will need a little help sticking; you can use any kind of jam or honey.
- Eat immediately, or store in the fridge until serving -- though be warned, the cookies might get a big stale the longer it sits.

189. Lemon Souffle Pancakes With Raspberry Syrup

Serving: Makes 12 three-inch pancakes | Prep: | Cook: | Ready in:

Ingredients

- Pancakes
- 3 eggs, separated
- 1/3 cup all-purpose flour
- 3/4 cup ricotta cheese
- 1/4 cup butter, melted
- 2 tablespoons sugar
- 1/4 teaspoon salt
- 2 tablespoons grated lemon zest
- Raspberry Syrup
- 3/4 cup light corn syrup
- 3/4 cup fresh raspberries
- 3 teaspoons fresh lemon juice

Direction

- Pancakes
- Beat the egg whites until they form stiff peaks.
- In another bowl, stir together the egg yolks, flour, ricotta, butter, sugar, salt and lemon zest. Mix well.
- Gently fold the whipped egg whites into the egg yolk batter. There should be small pieces of egg white showing when mixed.
- Heat skillet or griddle over medium heat. Grease lightly.
- Spoon out approximately 3 large tablespoons of batter for each pancake. Cook slowly for about 1.5 minutes, then turn the pancake over and cook for 30 seconds.
- Keep the pancakes warm in a 250 degree (F) oven until ready to serve.
- Serve with raspberry syrup and fresh raspberries.
- Raspberry Syrup
- Combine corn syrup and raspberries in a small saucepan, and bring to a boil.
- Simmer for five minutes, and remove from heat.
- Allow to cool, then add lemon juice.
- Strain through a fine mesh strainer, pushing hard to remove the seeds.

190. Lemon And Honey Cheesecakes

Serving: Makes 3 | Prep: 0hours10mins | Cook: 2hours0mins | Ready in:

Ingredients

- Base
- 4 Shortbread fingers
- 10 grams Unsalted Butter
- Filling and topping
- 180 grams Light Philadelphia cheese
- 1 tablespoon Double cream
- 1/2 tablespoon Icing sugar
- 2 tablespoons Lemon zest
- 5 milliliters Lemon juice
- 3 tablespoons Honeycomb pieces

Direction

- In a food processor pulse the biscuits until they become crumbs
- Melt the butter and mix it with the shortbread crumbs.
- Push it at the bottom of some cake rings and leave in the fridge
- Whisk together the cream cheese, sugar, lemon juice, double cream and half of the lemon zest
- Spoon the filling over the shortbread crust, smooth it out and leave in the fridge to set for 2 hours
- Decorate with the rest of the lemon zest and the honeycomb pieces just before serving

191. Lemon Mint Peas With Burrata And Breadcrumbs

Serving: Serves 2 | Prep: | Cook: | Ready in:

Ingredients

- 1 handful mint
- 1 lemon
- 1/2 bag frozen peas
- 1 tablespoon butter
- 1 tablespoon olive oil
- 1/3 cup breadcrumbs
- 1 pinch chile flakes
- Salt and freshly ground black pepper
- 8 ounces burrata

Direction

- Coarsely chop the mint and juice the lemon. Steam or microwave the peas.
- Once the peas are cooked, remove them from the heat and mix in a bowl with the butter, mint, and lemon juice. Season with salt and pepper to taste.
- Drizzle olive oil in a small pan. On a medium heat, toast the breadcrumbs with the chile flakes until crispy. Lightly season with salt and pepper.
- Pour the peas into a serving bowl and place the burrata in the center of the peas. Scatter the breadcrumbs over everything and eat immediately.

192. Lemony Cheese Blintzes

Serving: Serves 6 to 8 | Prep: | Cook: | Ready in:

Ingredients

- The Pancakes
- 1 cup milk, plus more if needed
- 2 large eggs
- 1 tablespoon vegetable oil, plus more for frying
- 1 pinch salt
- 1 cup all-purpose flour
- 1 piece Butter for frying
- The Filling
- 2 7.5-ounce packages (Avi's grandmother recommends Friendship brand) farmer cheese, salted
- 1/4 cup sugar
- 2 egg yolks
- 1 lemon, zested
- 1 teaspoon lemon juice
- 1 teaspoon vanilla extract
- 1/8 teaspoon salt

Direction

- To make the pancake batter, whisk together the milk, eggs, oil and salt in a large bowl. Add the flour gradually, whisking constantly until the batter is smooth. Set aside.
- Stir together all of the filling ingredients in a small bowl. Set aside.
- Set an 8-inch frying pan (I used a non-stick crepe pan) on medium heat. When the pan is hot, add a swipe of butter. Pour in 2 to 3 tablespoons of the pancake batter, swirling the pan to create a thin pancake. (If the batter seems too thick and you have trouble swirling it evenly in the pan, whisk in a little more

milk.) Cook the pancake about 30 seconds, until the top looks dry and the edges start to curl. Use your fingers or a spatula to remove the pancake and set aside on a plate to cool. Then, make as many more pancakes as the batter will allow.

- Let the pancakes cool a little. Lay out about 4 pancakes, pale side up, and put about 1 1/2 tablespoons of the filling in the center of each. Fold each of the pancakes up into a square package, making sure the corners are completely closed.
- Heat 2 teaspoons vegetable oil and 1 1/2 tablespoons butter in a large frying pan over medium heat. Cook the blintzes in batches until deep golden brown and warmed through, 2 to 3 minutes per side. Sprinkle with powdered sugar and serve with applesauce on the side if you like.

193. Lentil Meatballs With No Meat And A Surprise Center

Serving: Serves a crowd | Prep: | Cook: | Ready in:

Ingredients

- 1 pound green lentils
- 2 tablespoons finely minced garlic
- 4 tablespoons finely minced cilantro
- 1 + teaspoon cumin (to taste)
- 2 tablespoons lemon zest
- 1 eggs, lightly beaten
- feta cheese(about 1/2 tsp for each fritter)
- 4 tablespoons panko/bread crumbs
- olive oil
- Greek yoghurt

Direction

- Rinse and check the lentils for foreign objects (like rocks!).
- Cook in enough water to cover the lentils by about an inch. Cook until very tender. 30 min to an hour depending on age of lentils, etc. Watch them carefully.
- Cook until very dry, stir with a wooden spoon.
- Mash completely with a wooden spoon. Don't make a smooth paste...you should see some whole lentils in the mix.
- Add the egg, garlic, cilantro, cumin, zest, and panko. Mix completely, taste, and add more cumin if needed.
- Form the "dough" into golf ball sized fritters. As you are forming the fritters, put a piece of feta (about 1/2 tsp) into each and form the fritter around the cheese center.
- Roll the fritters into panko that is in a dish or flat surface and coat the entire fritter.
- Fry the fritters in olive oil that is about 1/2 inch deep. I use a high sided pan to minimize splatter of oil. Fry the fritters until all sides are golden browned.
- Serve with Greek yoghurt that is garnished with lemon zest and chopped cilantro. Or, use them instead of meatballs with a nice tomato sauce and pasta.

194. Lime Cado Bites

Serving: Serves 6 | Prep: | Cook: | Ready in:

Ingredients

- 1 pound fresh mozzarella that can be sliced into shapes
- 1 egg, beaten
- 1/2 cup plain Greek yogurt
- 1/2 avocado, mashed
- 1 teaspoon fresh ground cumin
- 1 tablespoon chopped green chiles (mild)
- salt and pepper to taste
- 1 rind grated of lime
- 2 cups panko bread crumbs
- 1 tablespoon each of the following fresh chopped herbs- mint, flat leaf parsley, scallions, and chives
- salt and pepper to taste

- oil for skillet
- 1 cup plain Greek yogurt
- 1 1/2 mashed avocado
- 1 cup chopped English cucumber
- 1 tablespoon mild green chiles
- 1 tablespoon ground cumin
- salt and pepper to taste
- herbs for garnish

Direction

- Slice the mozzarella into bit size pieces. An inch square is a good size, or a bit larger.
- Mix the beaten egg with 1/2 c. yogurt, half an avocado, half the rind of a lime, green chiles, cumin, salt, and pepper in one bowl.
- In another bowl mix the panko crumbs with other half of the lime rind, the chopped fresh herbs, salt and pepper.
- Dip and coat the mozzarella morsels with the egg, yogurt, and avocado mixture.
- Next roll the coated morsels into the panko mixture, trying to retain a generous coat.
- Heat a good vegetable oil (grape seed oil works well here) coating the entire bottom of a skillet.
- Add the coated morsels into the skillet, making sure you hear a definite sizzle upon contact. Quickly brown and serve.
- Serve with chopped cucumbers, mixed together with yogurt, mashed avocado, chopped fresh herbs, cumin, green chiles, salt, pepper, and fresh herb garnish.

195. Loaded Cream Cheese Cookie Bars With Animal Cookie Crust

Serving: Makes 1 pan of bars | Prep: | Cook: | Ready in:

Ingredients

- Crust
- 8 ounces animal cookies
- 1 stick butter
- 1 tablespoon honey
- 1 teaspoon cinnamon
- Icing & Batter
- 1/2 stick butter (for icing)
- 1/2 package cream cheese (for icing)
- 1/2 cup powdered sugar (for icing)
- 1 and 1/2 cups flour
- 1/2 cup sugar
- 2 eggs
- 1/2 stick butter (for cookie layer)
- 1 teaspoon vanilla
- 1 tablespoon baking powder
- 1/2 cup white chocolate chips
- sprinkles - to taste

Direction

- Preheat oven to 425 degrees. Then crush the 8 oz. of animal crackers in a bag until fine and grainy. Pour into a bowl and add in the stick of melted butter, honey, and cinnamon to make crust. Stir and then place in the bottom of a baking pan.
- Then place the crust in the oven until its golden brown (I put it in there for approximately 10 minutes).
- Next, move onto the icing and take the 1/2 stick butter, 1/2 package of cream cheese and 1/2 cup of powdered sugar and stir mixture over low heat until melted together. Place in freezer or fridge for 5 or so minutes to cool slightly.
- While that is cooling you can make your cookie batter. Mix the flour, sugar, and baking powder together in a bowl. Then mix in the two eggs (lightly beaten together), vanilla, and butter (I use melted but not super hot so as to not affect the eggs too much.)
- Then add in the white chocolate chips and sprinkles to the cookie batter.
- Now comes the fun part – layering. You can really mix the cookie dough and the icing anyway you want. I thought it would be fun to have the icing layer in-between the crust and the cookie mixture so I spread it on very thinly right over the baked crust. Then I spread out

the cookie dough in an even layer on top of the icing (careful or some of the crust will mix in).
- Place in oven for 10-15 minutes or until golden brown.

196. Mac And Cheese Pie

Serving: Serves 6 | Prep: | Cook: | Ready in:

Ingredients

- Filo Crust
- 1/3 cup parmesan cheese, grated
- 5 tablespoons unsalted butter, melted
- 6 pieces filo dough, 12x12 inch sheets (ok to patch some together)
- Pasta, Sauce and Crumb topping
- 8 ounces elbow macaroni
- 1 tablespoon unsalted butter, melted
- 2 ounces American cheese, grated
- 2 ounces sharp cheddar cheese, grated
- 1 can evaporated milk
- 1 egg
- ¼ - ½ teaspoons hot sauce (use your favorite, and the larger amount if you like your food a little spicy)
- ¼ teaspoons ground black pepper
- 1 teaspoon mustard powder
- 1 clove garlic, minced
- 1 teaspoon salt
- 2 tablespoons unsalted butter, melted
- 1/2 cup fine dry bread crumbs
- 1/4 cup parmesan cheese, grated

Direction

- Filo Crust
- Preheat oven to 400 degrees
- Brush a deep dish 9" pie pan with a little of the butter and set aside.
- Cut 6 sheets of filo, measuring 12x12 inches. It's ok to patch some smaller pieces together to make a sheet, but be sure to have at least 2 whole pieces. Cover with plastic wrap to prevent drying.
- Starting with a whole sheet, lay it flat on the counter and brush with some of the melted butter from step b. above. Don't soak the dough, but do be sure to coat the entire piece. Sprinkle 1/5 of the cheese from step a. lightly and evenly over the sheet
- Lay on another sheet of filo, rotated slightly so that the corners don't line up. Brush with butter and sprinkle with cheese as above.
- Repeat with remaining layers. Butter, but do not sprinkle cheese on the 6th and final layer.
- Lift crust and gently press into pie pan. Be sure to press firmly into the pan, but try not to tear the filo sheets. Fold outward and tuck in the filo that sticks up over the pie pan to make a neat edge.
- Bake for 20 minutes on middle rack. Remove and set aside. Leave oven on, set to 400 degrees.
- Pasta, Sauce and Crumb topping
- While crust is in the oven: Make Crumb topping: Mix bread crumbs, ¼ cup Parmesan cheese, and 2 TBS butter in a small bowl, set aside.
- Bring 2 qt. of water and 2 tsp salt to a boil. Add pasta and cook until very al dente (about 6 minutes). The pasta should be slightly undercooked. Drain and return to pan, adding the remaining 1 TBS butter.
- Mix milk, egg, garlic, mustard, pepper, salt, and hot sauce, whisking until smooth.
- Return pasta to heat, and add the milk mixture and grated cheeses. Warm over medium heat, stirring gently, until cheese begins to melt. Cook for another minute and remove from heat.
- Pour pasta mix into prepared filo crust and top evenly with bread crumb mixture.
- Bake for 15 minutes, or until crumbs are toasted golden and crunchy.
- Rest for 5 minutes and then cut into wedges and serve.

197. Mamma Linda's Cheesecake With Fresh Raspberries

Serving: Serves 8 | Prep: | Cook: | Ready in:

Ingredients

- 3 cups Graham cracker crumbs
- 8 tablespoons Butter
- 24 ounces Cream cheese at room temperature
- 4 Eggs
- 1 cup Sugar
- 2 tablespoons Vanilla extract
- 12 ounces Sour cream
- 1 pint Fresh raspberries

Direction

- Preheat the oven to 350 degrees.
- Combine the ground graham cracker crumbs with melted butter until it's a light crumble. Mash it down the sides and bottom of a tart pan, or baking dish.
- In a separate bowl combine the cream cheese, eggs (one at a time), 3/4 cup of sugar and one tablespoon of vanilla until whipped and smooth.
- Pour over the crust and smooth the top.
- Bake for 25-30 minutes until the center isn't liquid.
- Remove from oven and set aside.
- In a separate bowl, combine remaining 1/4 cup of sugar, 1 tablespoon of vanilla and the sour cream.
- Mix until ingredients are combined.
- Top the cheesecake with a thin layer of sour cream and return to the oven to bake for 10 minutes.
- Remove and refrigerate overnight.
- Top with fresh raspberries and eat as breakfast like I did the next morning.

198. Mango Coconut Burfi (fudge)

Serving: Serves 9 | Prep: | Cook: | Ready in:

Ingredients

- coconut powder cups 1
- mango pulp cups 1/2
- milk cups 1
- milk powder cups 2/3
- sugar tablespoons 3
- clarified butter teaspoons 1
- almonds blended and separated inth almond meal and tiny pieces cups 1/2 cup

Direction

- 1. Set a wide shallow no-stick pan at medium heat.
- 2. Warm clarified butter in the pan and add coconut powder. Mix well. Roast for 30-40 seconds while tossing continuously.
- 3. Add milk and stir occasionally till all milk dries up.
- 4. Sprinkle milk powder and mix thoroughly.
- 5. Add almond meal and 1/3 of the almond pieces. Mix well and roast till it becomes dry.
- 6. Add mango pulp, Stir and increase heat to high. Keep stirring.
- Add sugar and keep roasting till the mix becomes dry.
- Switch off the heat when the mix lumps together.
- Allow the mix to cool and then transfer to a greased plate.
- Using a table knife/spatula/hands, shape the mix to a square.
- Mark cuts in the square for easy cutting later. Once cooled down, cover with a cling film and refrigerate for 2 hours. Finally cut into small squares and enjoy homemade mango coconut burfi.

199. Maple Balsamic Kale And Egg Brunch Tart With Canadian Bacon And Sharp White Cheddar

Serving: Serves 4 | Prep: | Cook: | Ready in:

Ingredients

- flour for dusting
- 1 sheet frozen puff pastry (from a 17.3 oz package), thawed according to package directions
- 2 tablespoons olive oil
- 1 tablespoon finely chopped shallot
- 3 ounces Canadian bacon, rind removed, diced (about 5 slices)
- 5 cups chopped kale (tough stems removed), rinsed and drained
- 2 tablespoons maple syrup
- 2 tablespoons balsamic vinegar
- pinch of salt and freshly ground black pepper
- 2/3 cup grated sharp white cheddar cheese
- 1 egg, beaten
- 4 large eggs
- salt and freshly ground black pepper to taste

Direction

- Preheat oven to 400 degrees F.
- On a lightly floured surface, roll out each pastry sheet into a square measuring approximately 10" x 10". Place pastry sheet on a large, parchment-lined baking sheet.
- In a large skillet, heat olive oil over medium high heat. Add shallots and bacon and cook, stirring, for 2 minutes. Add kale, maple syrup, balsamic vinegar, salt and pepper and cook until kale is bright green and wilted, about 2 minutes. Remove from heat.
- Using a slotted spoon, removed kale mixture from pan, squeezing out as much of the liquid as possible (discard liquid). Place in a bowl and refrigerate until cool.
- Spread kale mixture over the center of pastry sheet, leaving an approximate 1" border. Sprinkle cheese evenly over kale mixture. Brush pastry border with beaten egg.
- Bake in a 400 degree F oven for 8-10 minutes or until pastry is light golden. Remove from oven, and gently break one egg onto each quadrant of the kale mixture (taking care not to break the yolks). Return to the oven and bake for an additional 5-7 minutes, or until egg whites are set and yolks are partially cooked (but still a little runny). Pastry should be golden brown.
- Remove from heat, sprinkle to taste with salt and freshly ground black pepper, and serve warm.

200. Margherita Naan Pizza

Serving: Makes 2 individual pizzas | Prep: 4hours30mins | Cook: 0hours10mins | Ready in:

Ingredients

- Margherita Naan Pizza
- Dough of 1 recipe Naan (see below)
- 2 teaspoons all-purpose flour, plus more for rolling out the pizza
- 2 teaspoons coriander seeds
- 2 teaspoons nigella seeds
- 2 teaspoons dried red chili flakes
- 2 teaspoons cornmeal or semolina
- 1 cup [185 g] cherry tomatoes, halved crosswise
- 1 cup [160 g] grape tomatoes, halved lengthwise
- 1 cup [80 g] shredded mozzarella
- 1 tablespoon chopped fresh chives
- 1 tablespoon flaky sea salt, such as Maldon
- Naan
- 1/2 cup [120 ml] whole milk, heated to 105 to 115°F [41 to 46°C]
- 1 large egg
- 2 tablespoons plain full-fat Greek yogurt
- 1 tablespoon unsalted butter, melted
- 1 tablespoon sugar

- 1 teaspoon fine sea salt
- 1 tablespoon active dry yeast
- 2 cups [280 g] all-purpose flour or whole-wheat pastry flour, plus more for rolling out the naans

Direction

- Margherita Naan Pizza
- Place a baking steel or pizza stone on a rack in the middle of the oven and preheat the oven to 500°F [260°C] for 30 minutes. Divide the dough into two equal parts and shape into balls. Cover one ball with a kitchen towel. On a clean, lightly floured work surface, roll the remaining ball into a circle 1/8 in [4 mm] thick and 12 in [30 cm] in diameter. Cover loosely with a kitchen towel. Repeat with the second ball of dough.
- Crack the coriander lightly with a mortar and pestle, add the nigella seeds and chili flakes, and set aside.
- Prepare one pizza at a time: Flip over a baking sheet, wrong-side up, and place a sheet of parchment paper on the baking sheet. Sprinkle 1 tsp of the flour and 1 tsp of the cornmeal on the parchment to coat evenly. Place rolled-out circle of dough on top of the paper and drizzle with a little melted ghee. Spread out half of the tomatoes over the dough. Sprinkle with half the mozzarella and 1 Tbsp. of the spices in the mortar. Slide the circle of dough onto the preheated baking steel, discard the parchment paper, and shut the oven door. Lower the heat to 425°F [220°C] and bake until the edges of the crust start to turn golden, 10 to 12 minutes. Garnish with half the chopped chives and flaky salt, and drizzle with a little extra ghee. Repeat with the remaining circle of dough and serve the pizzas hot.
- Additional notes: Get a baking stone or baking steel sheet to get a fantastic crust with the nice char. For the last 2 minutes, set the broiler on to get a nice blistered char to recreate that fire oven finish. Otherwise, this recipe can be used on a grill or smoker. I usually line the base of the grates with foil or use a baking stone or steel and then proceed as usual.
- Naan
- Using a fork, whisk the milk, egg, yogurt, butter, sugar, and salt in a small bowl. Sprinkle with the yeast and let sit for 5 minutes. The mixture should be bubbly on the surface.
- Put the flour in a large bowl or mound on a clean work surface and make a well in the center. Pour the yeast mixture into the middle of the well. Using clean hands or a large wooden spoon, gradually mix the flour from the inside wall of the well into the liquid to form a sticky dough. Knead well for 4 to 5 minutes.
- Fold the dough by grabbing it from the underside and stretching it and folding it back over itself. Rotate a quarter of a turn and repeat three or four times. Brush a large bowl with a little oil and put the dough in the bowl. Cover with plastic wrap and allow to rise in a dark, warm place until doubled in size, about 4 hours.
- Proceed with above recipe for Margherita Naan Pizza.

201. Marinated Feta Cheese

Serving: Serves 2-4 | Prep: | Cook: | Ready in:

Ingredients

- 100g feta cheese, cubed
- 1 Blood orange
- 2 tablespoons olive oil
- 1 tablespoon mint, chopped
- Cayenne pepper, to taste
- 50g olives (ooptional)

Direction

- Zest the blood orange and reserve a tablespoon. Using a knife, cut the white pith away and carefully remove segments, placing

- over a bowl to catch the juices. Reserve 4 tablespoons of the juice
- In a bowl, combine the orange juice, zest and olive oil. Whisk till slightly thickened and then add the feta cubes, the orange segments and the mint. If using the olives, add them too.
- Sprinkle with some cayenne and let marinade for a few hours - up to a week in the refrigerator.

202. Mascarpone Stuffed French Toast Fritters

Serving: Serves 4 | Prep: | Cook: | Ready in:

Ingredients

- 1 cup Grade B dark amber pure maple syrup
- 1 Vanilla bean, split in half, and seeds scraped
- 8 slices Italian bread
- 4 tablespoons butter, room temperature (for the skillet)
- Organic Powdered sugar for dusting
- 3 eggs
- 2 tablespoons Heavy cream
- Zest of 2 Clementines
- 1 Vanilla bean, split in half, and seeds scraped (use other half for filling)
- 1 teaspoon Organic sugar
- 1 cup Mascarpone cheese, room temperature
- 2 teaspoons Organic powdered sugar
- 1 teaspoon orange juice concentrate
- 1 teaspoon Amaretto liquor
- Zest of 1 Clementine, tangerine, navel orange, or grapefruit
- Vanilla bean seeds (use other half from batter)

Direction

- Preheat oven to warm (200 F degrees)
- In a small sauce pan, heat the maple syrup with scraped vanilla bean on low. Do not boil.
- Make the batter: In a pie dish, whisk together the eggs, cream, zest, vanilla bean seeds and sugar. Set aside
- Make the filling: In a bowl, combine Mascarpone, powdered sugar, orange juice concentrate, Amaretto liquor, zest and vanilla bean seeds. Set aside.
- Make the fritters: Cut the crust off the slices of bread. Lay 4 of the bread slices on a baking sheet, in a row. Add 1/4 of the Mascarpone mixture to each slice of bread. Top with other slice of bread to make a sandwich. Heat a nonstick skillet on medium-low heat. Add 2 tablespoons of butter and coat entire pan. Working quickly, dip all sides of each sandwich in the egg mixture to coat. Add each sandwich to the pan and cook until golden. Adjust heat as needed to brown, but prevent burning. When the first side is golden, flip the sandwich. Add more butter to the pan if needed for browning. Remove any sandwiches from the heat that may have finished browning before the others, place on a baking sheet and slide into a warm oven until the other sandwiches are ready. Dust with powdered sugar. Serve with citrus wedges and warm vanilla maple syrup for dunking.

203. Mayo Free Caesar Dressing

Serving: Makes about half a cup | Prep: | Cook: | Ready in:

Ingredients

- half cup Natural plain yogurt*
- 3 Anchovy fillets
- 1 teaspoon Dijon mustard
- 2 garlic cloves, roasted
- 1 tablespoon Lemon juice
- 1 teaspoon Extra virgin olive oil
- 1 tablespoon Grated parmesan (EXTRA)**

Direction

- Start by roasting the garlic cloves with the skin on in a 200 C? (390 F?) for 10 minutes, until tender. Squish it out of the skin in a jar (or to the bowl where you're preparing your salad). Roasting the garlic will make the dressing less harsh and more digestible. If you're fine with raw garlic, just chop it very finely and skip the cooking.

- Finely chop the anchovy fillets and add them to the vessel you're using, together with the other ingredients. Mix well. It will keep in the fridge for 2-3 days. Spoon over Caesar salad. Poached eggs version aside, I find it lovely with flaked steamed salmon.
- * To save on calories, you can use skim. Still, full-fat yogurt will get you an even tastier dressing.** I am only using a tbsp here, assuming you'll add more cheese to the final salad. Add more Parmesan to taste if you like.

204. Mediterranean Pressed Sandwich

Serving: Serves 6 as part of a picnic | Prep: | Cook: | Ready in:

Ingredients

- For the Sandwich
- 1 ciabatta loaf
- 8-10 sundried tomatoes
- 2 balls of mozzarella
- 6-8 slices of prosciutto
- For the Pesto
- 1 handful of basil leaves
- 1 handful of pine nuts
- 1 handful of grated parmesan cheese
- 1 clove of garlic
- Olive oil
- Salt and Pepper
- (or use a jar of pesto)

Direction

- Make the pesto by putting the basil, pine nuts (toast them first in the oven if you have time) and cheese in a processor. Grate in the garlic, then blend, adding olive oil through the hole in the top to make a thick paste. Season well
- Slice the ciabatta lengthwise, spread both cut sides with the pesto, then build up the filling in layers, ham then cheese slices, then sundried tomatoes, more cheese slices etc., seasoning each layer
- Sandwich the bread together again, wrap tightly in plastic wrap and put in the fridge with cans on top of it to weight it down (it might balance better to put a baking tray on top, then the cans on the tray). Refrigerate overnight.
- Slice cross-ways into sandwiches

205. Melt In Your Mouth Stuffed Spinach Manicotti With Fresh Marinara Sauce

Serving: Makes 12 manicotti | Prep: | Cook: | Ready in:

Ingredients

- CRESPELLE BATTER & RICOTTA SPINACH FILLING
- 3 Large Eggs
- 1- 1l2 cups Whole Milk
- 3 tablespoons Melted Butter
- 1 cup All-Purpose Flour, or more if needed
- Pinch Sea Salt
- Canola Cooking Spray
- FILLING:
- 1 pound Whole Milk Ricotta Cheese
- 1/2 pound Whole Milk Mozzarella Cheese, shredded
- 1 Large Egg
- 1 teaspoon EACH, sea salt, sugar, ground pepper and ground nutmeg
- 1/2 cup Fresh Italian Parsley, finely chopped
- 5 ounces Bag, Fresh Baby Spinach, chopped
- FRESH MARINARA SAUCE
- 1/4 cup Extra Virgin Olive Oil
- 1 Small, Sweet Onion, chopped fine
- 6 Cloves Fresh Garlic, peeled & chopped fine

- 2- 28 ounces Cans, Crushed Tomatoes, preferably San Marzano type
- 1/2 cup Fresh Basil Leaves, chiffonade
- 1 teaspoon Each, salt and pepper, more if taste necessary
- TOPPING:
- 1/4 cup Extra Virgin Olive Oil
- 1/2 cup Grana Padano Cheese, grated or more if you like
- 12 Whole Fresh Basil Leaves

Direction

- CRESPELLE BATTER & RICOTTA SPINACH FILLING
- MAKE THE CREPES (CRESPELLE): In a large bowl, whisk together the eggs, milk and melted butter. Gradually whisk in the flour and salt until the mixture is smooth. Cover with plastic wrap and refrigerate for about 1 hour until slightly thickened. Bring to room temperature before making the crepes. If the room is cool, cover with plastic wrap and store at room temperature to thicken for about 1 hour. Spray a 10" non-stick skillet with cooking spray. Place the pan over medium heat. With a small ladle, pour about 4 tablespoons (1/4 cup) of the batter into the pan. Turn the pan at a 45 degree angle to coat the pan evenly so the batter forms a perfect circle. Cook the crepe only until set; do not brown, about 30 seconds or until the top is set. Slide the crepe onto a 12- inch flat plate and continue the process with the remaining batter. Spray the pan with cooking spray when making each crepe. Stack the crepes between waxed paper so they don't stick. You can prepare these crepes a day in advance covered in plastic wrap in the refrigerator. No need to reheat the crepes before filling and baking. You can also use an electric crepe maker.
- MAKE THE RICOTTA FILLING: In a large bowl, add all the ingredients for the ricotta filling. With a large wooden spoon or spatula, stir all the ingredients until well blended. Store covered with plastic wrap in the refrigerator until ready to stuff the manicotti. You can make this filling the day before.
- FRESH MARINARA SAUCE
- MAKE THE MARINARA SAUCE: In a large heavy non-reactive saucepan with a lid, heat the olive oil on medium heat. Stir in the onion and garlic and cook until fragrant but NOT browned. Add the crushed tomatoes to the pan, use a potato masher if there are any tomato chunks. Add 1/2 the basil leaves and parsley. Simmer 30 minutes, slightly covered, on medium-low heat, stirring every so often as not to burn the bottom of the pan. Add the remainder of the basil leaves and salt and pepper to taste; simmer for another 10 minutes until the sauce is slightly reduced. Taste and reseason as necessary. You can make this sauce the day before; store in a plastic container in the refrigerator. No need to reheat when assembling the dish.
- PUT IT ALL TOGETHER: Preheat the oven to 375 degrees (350 degrees convection). Evenly coat the bottom of a 13 X 9 glass or ceramic baking dish with 2 cups of the prepared marinara sauce. Spoon 4 tablespoons of the prepared ricotta filling 1 inch from the edge of each crepe. Roll evenly into a log, keeping the filling even as you roll. Repeat with the remaining crepes. Trim each end of the manicotti about 1/2" so they fit in the pan neatly and don't overlap. Place manicotti seam side down. Spoon 2 cups of sauce over the middle of the manicotti. Sprinkle with grated Grana Padano cheese. Top each manicotti with a whole basil leaf. Spray the top with cooking spray. Cut a 13x9 piece of foil or parchment and coat one side with cooking spray. Cover the baking dish loosely with the sprayed side down. Bake about 20 minutes. Uncover and bake another 15- 20 minutes until the topping is golden brown and the sauce is bubbling on the sides. Let rest about 15 minutes before serving to firm up the manicotti filling.

206. Middle Eastern Grilled Cheese

Serving: Serves 1 sandwich | Prep: | Cook: | Ready in:

Ingredients

- 1 pita pocket
- 1 ounce cheddar cheese
- 1/4 cup crumbled feta cheese
- 1 teaspoon zatar
- 1/2 tablespoon butter or non-hydrogenated vegetable spread

Direction

- Carefully, open up the pita pocket and arrange cheddar cheese, making sure it doesn't get too close to the edges.
- Add feta cheese on top and sprinkle with zatar.
- Melt butter on a skillet at medium low heat. Place sandwich and cook until golden brown, for about a minute or two.
- Turn the sandwich over and let it cook until the bread is golden brown and the cheese has melted.
- ENJOY!!!

207. Mike Lepizerra's Polenta

Serving: Makes 4-5 cups | Prep: | Cook: | Ready in:

Ingredients

- 1/4 cup virgin olive oil

Direction

- Ingredients: 1/4 cup virgin olive oil1/2 pound (2 sticks) unsalted butter (can cut down to 1 stick, 4 ounces.) 1 1/2 to 2 tablespoons chopped garlic 2 cups chicken stock, preferably homemade [optional: can use part or all of any stock, including mushroom] 1 1/2 quarts half-and-half (yes!) 2 1/2 cup water1 1/2 to 2 teaspoons kosher salt 12 turns of a pepper grinder1 teaspoon crushed red pepper flakes2 cups cornmeal [Anson Mills preferred] pinch sugar 1 1/2 to 2 cups freshly grated high quality pecorino romano [optional sliced and sautéed shiitakes or other mushrooms]
- Directions
- 1. Heat the oil and butter in a large, heavy stockpot. Add the garlic and sauté over low heat until it is golden.
- 2. Add the stock, half-and-half, 2 1/2 cups of water, salt and black and red peppers, and stir to combine. Raise the heat and bring to a boil.
- 3. Very slowly, add the cornmeal, stirring constantly. Lower the heat to maintain a gentle boil. After all the cornmeal has been added, [optional: add mushrooms now] continue to stir until it is thick and creamy, [and spoon can stand up straight in it] about 20 minutes.
- 4. Off the heat, stir in the sugar and Romano. Serve right away with any sauce or side of your choosing. I like it with braised short ribs, roast chicken or a killer red sauce. [If you want to serve it with a rich dish, like osso bucco, use less butter and cream and more stock or water.] Notes: I prefer stoneground cornmeal from traditional mills like Anson in South Carolina or Gray's in Rhode Island.

208. Milk Soup

Serving: Serves 2 | Prep: | Cook: | Ready in:

Ingredients

- 2 cups low fat milk
- 2 cups water
- 1 cup orzo
- 2 tablespoons dried thyme
- 1 pinch salt
- 1/2 tablespoon butter (optional-I didn't use)

Direction

- Combine milk, water and orzo in a soup pot.

- Bring them to boil stirring constantly. (You don't want to end up with clotted milk :))
- When it starts boiling, you can add the salt and thyme (and if you want to add butter it is the best time). (Keep stirring!)
- After 3-5 mins of boiling, check orzo and if it is cooked ready to go to your favorite bowl!

209. Minted Zucchini Soup

Serving: Serves 4 | Prep: | Cook: | Ready in:

Ingredients

- 4 zucchini
- 2 shallots, chopped
- 1/2 yellow onion, chopped
- 4 cups low sodium chicken or vegetable broth
- 1/3 cup fresh mint leaves
- 5 ounces fresh baby spinach
- 1 lemon, juiced
- 1/2-1 teaspoons salt
- 1/4 teaspoon ground black pepper, plus more to serve
- goat cheese or yogurt, to serve
- mint, torn into pieces, to serve

Direction

- Throw zucchini, shallots, onion and broth into a pot and bring to a boil. Once boiled, turn heat to medium-low and simmer until vegetables are soft.
- Stir in mint leaves, spinach, lemon, salt and pepper. Purée in blender or with an immersion blender. Adjust lemon, salt and pepper.
- Serve immediately and top with goat cheese or yogurt, pepper and a sprinkling of torn mint. (Great cold too!)

210. Mmmmascarpone Mashed Potatoes With Dill And Chives

Serving: Serves 4 | Prep: | Cook: | Ready in:

Ingredients

- 3 pounds Russet potatoes, peeled and cubed
- 1/2 cup Mascarpone cheese
- 2 tablespoons fresh dill, minced
- 2 tablespoons fresh chives, minced
- 1 teaspoon salt
- 1/2 teaspoon white pepper
- 1-2 tablespoons white wine

Direction

- Boil the potatoes until tender and drain.
- Add remaining ingredients and mash by hand or with electric mixer until smooth, thinning them with the white wine.
- Enjoy!

211. Moussaka In Four Parts

Serving: Makes 8 to 10 ample portions | Prep: 0hours0mins | Cook: 0hours45mins | Ready in:

Ingredients

- 2 large eggplants, skins on, sliced lengthwise into 1/3" slabs
- olive oil
- salt and pepper
- 2 large Yukon Gold potatoes, peeled and sliced lengthwise into 1/3" disks, and placed in a bowl of cold water
- vegetable oil, or neutral oil of your choice
- coarse salt for seasoning
- 1 medium onion, finely chopped
- 1/4 cup water if needed
- 1 1/3 pounds 85/15 organic ground beef
- 2 tablespoons tomato paste

- 15 ounces diced San Marzano tomatoes and their juice
- 1/2 cup red wine
- 1 large bay leaf
- 1 large cinnamon stick
- Pinch fresh grated nutmeg
- salt and pepper, to taste
- 3 1/2 cups whole milk
- 1/4 cup olive oil
- 1/4 cup flour
- 1 small bay leaf
- Pinch freshly grated nutmeg
- salt and pepper
- 2 egg yolks
- 6 ounces finely grated gruyere cheese

Direction

- Preheat oven to 350 degrees. Lay the eggplant slices on half sheet pans brushed with olive oil, and then use a pastry brush to lightly coat tops of slices with more olive oil. Salt lightly. Bake in the oven, rotating the sheet pans, until the slices are lightly brown and soft. Remove from the oven and set aside. Turn off the oven.
- Pour about 1 inch of vegetable oil in 2 sauté pans. Heat over medium to high heat. When the oil is ready, pat dry the potato slices and fry. Flip the potato slices and fry until golden brown. Pierce slices with a fork to determine doneness- - there should be no resistance when pierced.
- Place fried potato slices on paper towels and pat to absorb as much oil as possible. Lightly salt the potatoes. Set aside.
- Make the meat sauce. Add about 3 TBS. olive oil to a Dutch oven over medium heat. Sauté the chopped onion, being careful not to brown the onion. After about 8 minutes, pour the water into the onions, and stir and cook until all water is evaporated.
- Add the ground beef. Cook until the meat is no longer pink, and use two forks to completely break down the meat so no chunks of meat are evident. You may want to spoon off any fat that accumulates in cooking.
- Stir in the tomato paste, and cook for a few minutes until the raw tomato taste disappears. Then, add the red wine, stirring until all the wine evaporates.
- Add the tomatoes, the bay leaf, the cinnamon stick, the grated nutmeg, and salt and pepper, Cook over low heat for about 25 minutes. Taste to correct seasonings. Set aside, covered. Allow the bay leaf and cinnamon stick to remain in the sauce until you are ready for assembly of the moussaka.
- Make the béchamel sauce. Heat the milk over a low fire in a medium sauce pan. While the milk is heating, make a roux in a larger saucepan by heating up the 1/4 cup olive oil, and then whisking in the flour. Allow the roux to cook, stirring constantly, until it develops a light tan color.
- Slowly add the heated milk to the roux. Keep stirring with the whisk to prevent lumping. Add the small bay leaf, the grated nutmeg, and salt and pepper. Stir until the sauce is thick enough to heavily coat a wooden spoon. Adjust seasoning. Take off the heat and allow to cool for about 20 minutes.
- While the béchamel is cooling, begin assembly. Preheat the oven to 400 degrees. Place the potato slices on the bottom of a 9 x 15 glass baking dish. Make the potatoes fit tightly. Then, add a layer of eggplant slices.
- Return to the béchamel sauce. Add the egg yolks to the cooled sauce, stirring constantly. Take one ladleful of the béchamel and add to the meat sauce, (you will have removed the bay leaf and cinnamon stick) and stir in well to combine.
- You will have two layers of meat sauce in the moussaka. Spread a layer of sauce on top of the eggplant layer. Sprinkle some gruyere over the meat sauce.
- Add a second layer of eggplant slices, then the second layer of meat sauce. Then sprinkle with cheese. If there is any eggplant left, place randomly on top of the meat sauce layer.
- Pour the remaining béchamel over the top of the casserole, and then a final sprinkling of cheese. Bake uncovered in the oven for 45

minutes, until the béchamel is bubbly and golden with a few brownish areas.
- Allow the moussaka to cool for about 30 minutes before serving.

212. Mozzarella

Serving: Makes 1 large or 2 small mozzarella balls | Prep: 1hours0mins | Cook: 0hours40mins | Ready in:

Ingredients

- 1/4 rennet enzyme tablet
- 1/4 cup cold filtered water (to mix with the rennet)
- 1 1/2 teaspoons citric acid
- 1/4 cup cold filtered water (to mix with the citric acid)
- 1 gallon whole milk (non-homogenized is best)
- 1 teaspoon sea salt, plus more to taste

Direction

- In a small bowl, mix the rennet with 1/4 cup water to dissolve. In another small bowl, mix the citric acid with 1/4 cup water to dissolve.
- Place a 5-quart pot into a large bowl with enough room to pour water around the sides. Pour your milk into the pot and add warm water to the bowl—you're creating a water bath to gently heat up the milk. Once it reaches 86°F, add the citric acid solution and give it gentle stir with a slotted spoon to evenly distribute. Allow the mixture to sit for about 10 minutes at 86°F.
- After 10 minutes, add more warm water to the bowl to bring the temperature of the milk up to 90°F. Once the milk reaches 90°F, add the rennet mixture. Very gently stir the milk in an up and down motion to disperse the rennet for about 1 minute, taking care not to stir too vigorously. Allow the mixture to sit for about 30 minutes.
- At this point, the curds will have come together into a solid-looking mass. Add more warm water to the bowl to bring the mixture up to 105°F and allow to sit for about 10 minutes.
- After 10 minutes, it's time to drain the curds. Place a colander on top of a bowl. Using a slotted spoon, lift the curds and place them into the colander to let the whey drain off. Lift the colander to keep draining. Using your hands, very gently press the curds into the colander to release more whey. You want to remove as much whey as possible while handling the curds as gently as possible. They should feel firm when they're ready for kneading.
- Add a few cups of hot water (we think 180°F is best) to a large bowl. Food-safe gloves can help protect your hands from the heat if you're sensitive.
- Break up your drained curds into evenly-sized pieces. Gently drop the curds into the hot water. Use all the curds to make one large mozzarella ball, or divide them in half to make two smaller ones.
- Using a large spoon, lift the curds to see if they're ready for kneading. They're ready when they are melty and stretching off the spoon.
- Now it's time to stretch and knead, salting your cheese as you go. If the cheese starts to get cold and stiff, dunk it back into the hot water. Keep stretching, kneading, and dunking until the cheese starts to feel smooth. This can take anywhere from 5-20 minutes.
- Form your cheese into a ball, or any other shape you'd like.

213. Mushroom And Sourdough Crusted Cremini Mini Quiches

Serving: Serves 6 | Prep: | Cook: | Ready in:

Ingredients

- CRUST
- 3-4 slices day old sourdough bread to make 2 1/2 cups crumbs
- 1 cup finely chopped Cremini mushrooms
- 1 teaspoon lemon pepper
- 2 tablespoons grated Parmesan cheese from canister
- 3 tablespoons extra virgin olive oil
- FILLING
- 2 tablespoons extra virgin olive oil
- 1 clove garlic, chopped
- 1 slice prosciutto, chopped or 2-teaspoons crumbled crisp bacon
- 1 cup chopped Cremini mushrooms and 1-2 large (2-inch) Cremini mushrooms sliced 1/8-inch thick
- 1 teaspoon Italian seasoning
- 3 large eggs
- 1/2 cup fresh ricotta cheese
- 1/2 cup shredded Italian blend cheese
- 1 tablespoon grated Parmesan, if desired, to garnish

Direction

- Heat oven to 400 degrees F. In a food processor, or by hand, finely mince bread to measure 2 1/2-cups crumbs resembling Panko crumbs. Add mushrooms, lemon pepper, and Parmesan; pulse 5 times, or stir to combine. Add olive oil and pulse 5 times or stir until evenly mixed. Coat 6 muffin cups with cooking spray. Press 1/3-cup crumbs over bottom and up sides of each cup. Bake for 10 minutes. Remove from oven and fill with filling.
- Meanwhile, heat olive oil in a large frying pan on medium heat. Add chopped garlic, chopped prosciutto, and mushrooms to one side of pan and sliced mushrooms to the opposite side, do not mix. Sprinkle both sides of mushrooms with Italian seasoning, stir and cook, continue to keep mushrooms separate. Cook mushrooms for 3 minutes or until tender. Transfer chopped mushroom mixture to medium bowl and stir in eggs, ricotta, and Italian cheese until well blended. Reserve sliced cooked mushrooms in pan.
- Pour egg mixture into baked sourdough-mushroom cups, top each cup with a slice of mushroom. Bake for 15-17 minutes or until set. Cool 3 minutes. Run a knife along the inside edge of the muffin cups, gently remove quiches with a large spoon. Sprinkle with Parmesan cheese, if desired, and serve. Yields: 6 mini muffin size quiches.
- Variations: *For vegetarian quiches simply omit the prosciutto. *The lemon pepper used in this recipe contained lemon peel, black pepper, salt, sugar, garlic, onion, and thyme; adjust seasoning if desired. *The Italian seasoning contained marjoram, thyme, rosemary, savory, sage, oregano, and bail; adjust seasoning if desired *Substitute 1-tablespoon fresh herbs in the filling for the dried seasoning when possible.

214. Mushroom Stuffed Eggplant

Serving: Serves 2 | Prep: 0hours30mins | Cook: 1hours0mins | Ready in:

Ingredients

- 2 eggplants
- salt
- extra virgin olive oil
- 1/4 pound mushrooms, sliced
- freshly ground Pepper
- 1-2 yellow onions, finely diced
- 1 teaspoon herbes de provence
- 4 pieces toasted white bread, cut into 1/2 inch dice
- 1 tablespoon unsalted butter
- 3/4 cup grated cheese medley (mozzarella, emmental & tomme de caractère)
- 1/2 cup vegetable broth
- 1-2 cloves of garlic, minced

Direction

- Halve the eggplants lengthwise and cut out the flesh, leaving 1/4-inch shells. Cut the flesh into 1/2-inch dice. Salt the eggplant shells and let stand for 30 minutes. Pat the shells dry.
- Preheat the oven to 160°C. Rub the eggplants with oil; set them on a rimmed baking sheet, cut side down. Add 1/4 cup of water, cover with foil and bake for 30 minutes.
- Meanwhile, in a skillet, heat olive oil. Add the mushrooms. Season with salt and pepper, cover and cook over moderate heat until tender; transfer to a bowl.
- Heat more olive oil in the skillet. Add the diced eggplant. Season with salt and pepper, cover and cook until tender and browned, 3 minutes; remove and put in the same bowl.
- Add the garlic, onions and more olive oil to the skillet. Cover and cook, until softened.
- Add the herbes de provence and the butter and stir until fragrant, 1 minute. Add to bowl with the eggplant mushroom mixture.
- Stir in the bread cubes, ½ cup of cheese, and the vegetable broth. Season the stuffing with salt and pepper.
- Increase the oven temperature to 210°C. Turn the eggplant shells cut side up and fill with the bread stuffing. Sprinkle with the rest of the cheese and bake for about 15 minutes (until browned)

215. Nathaniel's One Dish, An Easy Toast With Greens, Tomatoes And Cheese

Serving: Serves 4 | Prep: | Cook: | Ready in:

Ingredients

- Roasted Tomatoes
- 2 heirloom tomatoes, halved
- glug of olive oil
- 2 garlic cloves
- a few branches of fresh thyme
- Toasts
- 1/2 cup cooked bitter greens, warmed in a little olive oil
- 1/2 cup soft cheese, goat or Brie or ricotta
- 1/4 cup walnuts
- 4 shots small pieces wholegrain bread, thickly sliced

Direction

- Roasted Tomatoes
- Seed the tomatoes. Put them in a foil lined baking dish with a generous amount of olive oil.
- Sliver the garlic cloves and stick them into the tomatoes. Lay the thyme branches on top of the tomatoes. Make sure they have some of the olive oil on them, too, so they don't burn or dry out. You can roll them around in the tomatoes or press them into the tomatoes.
- Place the baking dish in a very low oven ideally about 250 and let them cook gently until the tomatoes are very soft and shrunken, likely at least 3 hours. If you don't have enough time to wait that long, turn up the temperature but the tomatoes will not be as richly flavored. They should still be quite moist and there will be olive oil in the pan. Add more olive oil during cooking if the tomatoes start to dry.
- Toasts
- Warm the walnuts with a smidge of olive oil or butter in a small frying pan and salt lightly. Chop into small pieces.
- Toast the bread.
- Top each slice of bread with about 2 T of the greens. They should be fairly dry. Top the greens with half a roasted tomato.
- Add a little bit of cheese and a sprinkle of walnuts to each toasts. Enjoy!

216. Nectarine And Avocado Caprese

Serving: Serves 2 | Prep: | Cook: | Ready in:

Ingredients

- 2 ripe nectarines, cut into wedges
- 1 ripe avocado, sliced
- 2 tomatoes of your choice, cut into wedges
- 1-2 balls buffalo mozzarella
- 2 sprigs of basil
- 1 small red chili, deseeded and thinly sliced
- olive oil
- balsamic vinegar
- salt and pepper

Direction

- Arrange the nectarine, avocado and tomatoes on a platter, with each overlapping the other. Then tear the mozzarella into pieces and nestle into the nooks. Tear the basil and scatter over the top, along with the chili.
- Season with salt and freshly cracked black pepper. Drizzle liberally with olive oil and balsamic vinegar.

217. No Churn Ben & Jerry's Style Core Ice Cream

Serving: Makes 1 pint ice cream | Prep: | Cook: | Ready in:

Ingredients

- Equipment you will need:
- 1 pint container
- 1 piece cardboard
- 1 piece wax paper
- Tape, as needed
- 1 zipper bag
- For the ice cream:
- 1/4 cup plus 1 tablespoon unsalted butter, divided
- 1 cup plus 5 tablespoons heavy whipping cream, divided
- 2 tablespoons brown sugar
- 1/2 teaspoon plus 1 big pinch sea salt, divided
- 2 1/2 teaspoons vanilla extract, divided
- 5 tablespoons sweetened condensed milk, divided
- 2 1/2 teaspoons vanilla bean paste, divided
- 4 ounces dark chocolate, divided
- 1 handful pretzels
- 1 egg
- 3/4 cup confectioners sugar
- 1/4 cup all-purpose flour

Direction

- To prepare the pint container, cut a rectangle of cardboard so that it fits across the center of your container. You want it to fit snugly against the sides and bottom and reach the top. To make this easier, measure the diameter of the container from the bottom to determine the width of your cardboard before cutting.
- Next, cover the cardboard piece with wax paper, securing it down with tape. Place it in the center of the container, dividing it in half. To keep the divider in place, place a zipper bag into one side of the container, pushing it into the bottom edges, then fill the zipper bag with something malleable to weigh it down (I used sugar) to keep the divider up for when you pour ice cream into the other side later. Set aside.
- To make the butterscotch-vanilla ice cream, in a small saucepan over medium-low heat, melt 1 tablespoon of butter. Add 2 tablespoons of heavy cream, the brown sugar, and one big pinch of sea salt. Stirring constantly, allow the mixture to come to a low simmer, then cook for 2 to 3 minutes.
- Remove the saucepan from the heat and let it cool for a few minutes. Add 1 teaspoon of vanilla extract and stir to combine. Set aside to cool to room temperature.
- While you wait, in a small bowl, whip 1/2 cup of the heavy cream into stiff peaks. Set aside.

- In a large bowl, whisk together the cooled brown sugar mixture with 2 tablespoons of sweetened Whisk together the brown sugar mixture that has cooled with 2 tablespoons of the condensed milk and 1 1/2 teaspoons of vanilla bean paste. Add 1/3 of the whipped cream into the large bowl and whisk to combine. Using a rubber spatula, fold in the rest of the whipped cream into the brown sugar mixture. Transfer the mixture into a glass measuring cup.
- While holding onto the cardboard divider with one hand and stabilizing it against the zipper bag, pour the brown sugar ice cream mixture into the other half of the container. Cover the container with the lid and freeze for 6 to 8 hours.
- Once the half-pint of ice cream has solidified, remove the sugar-filled zipper bag from the container. Peel the cardboard divider from the ice cream and discard it. If any ice cream mix crept through to the other side, use a spoon to scrape it from the edges and/or sides. Return the container to the freezer while you make the chocolate ice cream.
- In a small bowl, whip 1/2 cup of the heavy cream into stiff peaks and set aside.
- In a small bowl, heat the remaining 3 tablespoons of sweetened condensed milk with 2 ounces of dark chocolate in the microwave, stirring every 15 seconds until melted, or in a double boiler. Add the remaining 1 teaspoon of vanilla bean paste to the chocolate mixture as well as 1/4 teaspoon of sea salt. Stir to combine.
- Using your hands, crush the pretzels into small chunks and add them to the chocolate mixture. Whisk 1/2 of the whipped cream into the pretzel-chocolate mixture until well combined. Using a rubber spatula, fold in the rest of the whipped cream into the brown sugar mixture. Transfer the mixture into a glass measuring cup.
- Pour the pretzel-chocolate mixture into the empty half of the pint container until level with the butterscotch ice cream half. Freeze for 6 to 8 hours.
- Once the ice cream is firm, use an apple corer or swivel peeler to create a cavity in the center of the two ice creams. Depending on how large of a core you prefer, you may choose to continue this process to make the center core as big as you want. (The recipe for the brownie batter center will yield leftovers so there will be enough to fill almost any size core.)
- To make the core, melt the remaining 1/4 cup butter with the remaining 2 ounces of dark chocolate in a small or medium saucepan over medium-low heat. Set aside. Crack 1 egg into a bowl and whisk briefly to scramble it.
- Once the chocolate and butter is melted together, remove from the saucepan from the heat and allow to cool for 1 minute. Adding 1 tablespoon at a time while constantly whisking, temper the egg by adding 3 tablespoons of the chocolate mixture into the egg.
- Allow the remaining chocolate mixture to cool for another 5 minutes then add the tempered egg to the saucepan and whisk quickly to combine. Add the confectioners' sugar and the remaining 1/4 teaspoon salt and whisk to combine.
- Return the saucepan to medium-low heat and stir constantly, scraping across the bottom and edges for 5 minutes. Remove from the heat and add the remaining 1 1/2 teaspoons of vanilla extract, the remaining 3 tablespoons of heavy cream, and the flour. Mix well to combine and let cool.
- Once cooled, pour the brownie batter into a piping bag and pipe it into the core you created in the ice creams. Freeze for 4 hours. Store any remaining brownie batter in the refrigerator for later use.
- Once the core is solid, the ice cream is ready to eat! Spoon it directly out of the pint or serve yourself a double scoop.

218. No Bread Savoyard Croque Monsieur

Serving: Serves 4 people | Prep: | Cook: | Ready in:

Ingredients

- 500g   potatoes, peeled
- 250 g   Green cabbage
- 250g   parsnip, peeled
- 1   onion
- 2   cloves of garlic
- Parsley
- 2   eggs
- 50g   grated cheese (Emmental, Edam etc)
- 4   slices of raclette cheese
- 4   slices Bayonne ham or other cured meat
- 1   tomato
- Salt and pepper

Direction

- Grate the potatoes, cabbage, parsnip and onion. In a bowl, combine vegetables with garlic, eggs, grated cheese, salt and pepper, and parsley.
- Pour in brownie dish covered with parchment paper. Bake for 30-40 minutes, until veggies are cooked
- Carefully remove from pan and cut into 8 squares
- Make you Croque-monsieur: take one vegetable square, put one slice of Bayonne ham first, one slice tomato, one slice of raclette cheese, then close your "sandwich".
- Grill in a pen or in the oven for about 10-15 minutes on 350F, just to let the cheese melt and the vegetable are rather crispy.
- Use a tooth-pick to hold your croquet-monsieur together if necessary. Serve immediately.

219. Not Budapest Mushroom Soubise

Serving: Serves 4-6 | Prep: | Cook: | Ready in:

Ingredients

- 3 ounces dried mushrooms - I've used porcini, chanterelle, morels. Alternatively, about 1 cup wild mushrooms sauteed in butter
- 4 tablespoons butter
- 8 cups chopped sweet onion
- 2/3 cup uncooked rice
- 1 cup grated Gruyere or Swiss cheese
- 1 cup cream
- 3 tablespoons white wine
- Salt and Pepper
- 1 teaspoon fresh thyme
- 1/2 cup almonds, optional

Direction

- Preheat the oven to 325. Butter a casserole dish. If using almonds, I like to pop them in the oven a few minutes to toast.
- Soak the mushrooms in boiling water until hydrated, about 20 minutes. Drain, reserving liquid.
- Melt the butter in a large skillet and cook the onions slowly, stirring often, until soft, about 20 minutes. If using fresh mushrooms, add them for the final 5 minutes of cooking.
- Now, par-boil the rice in boiling water for 5 minutes.
- Mix everything together, including 2-3 Tablespoons of reserved mushroom liquid (avoiding grit.) Bake until crusty, 1 - 1.25 hours. Garnish with toasted almonds, if desired.

220. Old Fashioned "No Short Cuts" Strawberry Ice Cream

Serving: Makes 1.5 quarts | Prep: | Cook: | Ready in:

Ingredients

- Macerated Strawberry Pieces
- 1 pint fresh strawberries (cleaned, hulled, air-dired, sliced and finely chopped into little pieces)
- 1/4 cup granulated sugar
- 1 tablespoon freshly squeezed Meyer lemon or Valencia orange juice
- 1 tablespoon sweet liqueur (such as orange liqueur, Frangelico or Creme de Casis) or rum, port or ice wine (optional)
- Vanilla Custard Base
- 2 cups heavy cream
- 1 cup whole milk
- 1/4 cup granulated sugar
- 1-2 eggs
- 1/2 cup granulated sugar
- 1 teaspoon vanilla extract

Direction

- To make the macerated strawberries, mix together the strawberries, 1/4 cup sugar, 1 Tbsp. lemon or orange juice and 1 Tbsp. liqueur (if using any) in a large bowl. Cover and refrigerate for at least 1 hour (preferably overnight). Keep chilled until ready to churn with the vanilla custard base.
- To make the vanilla custard base, beat the eggs for 2 to 3 minutes, until light and airy and pale yellow. Whisk in 1/2 cup of sugar and the vanilla extract and beat for another minute or two. Set aside at room temperature.
- Combine the heavy cream, whole milk and 1/4 cup of sugar in a clean, dry saucepan. Heat on medium, whisking from time to time, dissolving the sugar, until the cream mixture just reaches 175 deg F (or barely simmering).
- Remove the saucepan from heat and add a tiny stream of the hot cream mixture into the egg mixture while whisking the egg mixture quickly and continuously, until about 1/4 cup of the hot cream mixture has been incorporated into the egg mixture.
- Gradually return all of the warmed egg-cream mixture back into the saucepan containing the remaining cream mixture, whisking the cream mixture quickly and continuously.
- Return the saucepan to medium heat, whisking continuously, until the custard mixture just reaches 180 deg F (barely boiling). Immediately remove from heat and give the custard mixture another few good whisks.
- Strain the custard mixture through a fine sieve (lined with cheesecloth if you want) into a large mixing bowl. Allow the custard mixture to cool to room temperature. Then refrigerate for at least 4 hours (preferably overnight). Prepare your ice cream maker if you need to pre-freeze the canister.
- When you are ready to churn the ice cream, drain the macerated strawberries of their excess juices (the sugar and alcohol will have drawn out these excess juices from the strawberries) ~ this allows the strawberry pieces to take on a chewy consistency once frozen (instead of freezing like ice). You can reserve the excess juices to make little flavored ice cubes for cocktails. Add the drained strawberry pieces to the chilled custard and mix well. Refrigerate the strawberry custard mixture until your ice cream maker is all set up and ready to churn.
- Set up the ice cream maker to start churning. Carefully and slowly add the chilled strawberry custard mixture into the canister through the opening in the lid. Churn for approximately 20 minutes, or until the texture of the mixture thickens into a soft-serve consistency.
- Turn the machine off and unplug it (safety first!). Using a wooden spoon or rubber spatula, quickly transfer the ice cream into freezer-safe airtight container(s) and freeze for at least 4 hours (preferably overnight).
- Serve scoops of the ice cream with slices of fresh strawberries.

221. Olive CHA! Penade Goat Cheese Spread

Serving: Serves 1 tbsp-- yeild 1 cup | Prep: | Cook: | Ready in:

Ingredients

- 3/4 cup Goat cheese, whipped
- 1/4 cup Olive tapenade
- 1 tablespoon CHA! by Texas Pete
- 1 Salt and Pepper -- TO TASTE

Direction

- Place the goat cheese into a small mixing bowl and lightly whip the cheese.
- Add the olive tapenade, CHA! by Texas Pete® and a pinch of salt and pepper and mix well.
- Place in an airtight storage container and keep refrigerated until ready to use.

222. Oma's Bavarian Cheesecake Bites

Serving: Makes 20 bite size pieces | Prep: | Cook: | Ready in:

Ingredients

- Base
- 1 1/2 sticks unsalted butter, cubed
- 2 large eggs
- 1/3 cup granulated sugar
- 2/3 cup all-purpose flour
- 1 teaspoon baking powder
- 1 vanilla bean cut length wise and scraped
- Cheesecake
- 3 large eggs, separated. set egg yolks aside and beat egg whites until stiff, chill
- 1 pound cream cheese, cubed
- 1 vanilla bean cut length wise and scraped
- 1/2 teaspoon fresh lemon juice
- 1 small handful lemon zest
- 1/2 cup granulated sugar
- 1 package vanilla sauce mix
- 1 12 oz log goat cheese, cubed

Direction

- Preheat oven to 325 degrees Fahrenheit. In a bowl, cream butter, 2 eggs and 1/3 cup sugar until fluffy. Add half of flour, mix well. Add remaining flour, baking powder and 1 vanilla bean. Mix until smooth. Pour mixture into a greased spring form pan.
- In a separate bowl, cream 3 egg yolks, cream cheese, 1 vanilla bean, lemon juice, lemon zest, 1/2 cup sugar, vanilla sauce mix and goat cheese. Mix until smooth. Gently fold in 3 chilled egg whites. Pour on top of base and bake 50 minutes. Let cool and refrigerate overnight. Before serving, cut into bite size pieces.

223. Parmesan And Truffle Popcorn With Chives

Serving: Serves four to six | Prep: | Cook: | Ready in:

Ingredients

- 1 Bag organic, unseasoned microwave popcorn
- 1/2 cup Finely grated parmesan cheese - plus a little extra to freshly grated over the top
- 2 tablespoons Truffle butter
- 1/4 cup Chives, finely chopped
- 2-4 teaspoons Truffle salt

Direction

- Cook the popcorn according to instructions. I use organic, unseasoned microwave popcorn since it's so convenient and because I don't mind the taste, but of course you can pop the kernels conventionally in oil over the stove.
- In a large bowl, add the popped popcorn. Slowly pour the butter over it while stirring it around with a rubber spatula. Then, stir in the

parmesan and chives and season with truffle salt to taste. Grate some more parmesan over the popcorn as the finish touch, and serve!

224. Parmesan Cheese "chips"

Serving: Makes ;start with one and then there is no limit | Prep: | Cook: |Ready in:

Ingredients

- Parmigiano Reggiano or Grana Padano rinds

Direction

- Preheat oven to 400 F.
- Place rind on the baking sheet.
- Cook for 5-6 minutes depends on how tick rind is.
- Cut into the smaller pieces when it comes straight from the oven.
- Another option is to cut into the smaller pieces, let it cool and ground in small food processor or in a spice grinder.
- Use like you will use regular Parmesan. It has nice nutty flavour.

225. Parmesan, Oregano And Pine Nut Melts

Serving: Serves 3 | Prep: | Cook: |Ready in:

Ingredients

- 2 cups Parmesan, finely grated
- 1 tablespoon flour
- 1 tablespoon oregano
- 1 tablespoon pine nuts

Direction

- Preheat oven to 200C. Line two large baking sheets with parchment paper
- If your Parmesan is fine enough, start by pulsing it a few seconds in your food processor. In a large bowl, combine Parmesan, flour and oregano
- Place a cookie cutter on a prepared sheet
- Carefully sprinkle a tablespoon of cheese mixture into the cutter and smooth the surface
- Remove the cutter
- Bake in oven for 5-7 minutes or until light golden
- Transfer to a wire rack to cool

226. Parmesan Panko Fried Summer Squash With Buttermilk Ranch

Serving: Serves 4 | Prep: | Cook: |Ready in:

Ingredients

- Panko-Parmesan Summer Squash
- 3-4 summer squash (zucchini and yellow squash)
- 2 cups panko bread crumbs
- 3/4 cup freshly grated Parmesan or Asiago cheese
- 2 teaspoons kosher salt
- 3 eggs (whites only)
- 1 1/2 cups buttermilk
- 1 cup vegetable oil
- Buttermilk Ranch
- 2 tablespoons buttermilk
- 2 tablespoons Greek yogurt 2%
- 2 1/2 tablespoons mayonnaise
- 1 tablespoon apple cider vinegar
- 2 tablespoons chopped fresh basil
- 2 tablespoons chopped fresh chives
- 1 tablespoon chopped fresh thyme
- 2 teaspoons fresh black pepper
- salt to taste

Direction

- Panko-Parmesan Summer Squash

- Removing ends, slice squash into 1/4 inch disks.
- Add next three ingredients in small bowl and mix.
- Separate egg whites into their own bowl, and buttermilk as well, respectively.
- Dip disks into buttermilk, then egg whites, and finally panko crumbs/cheese mixture. Get aggressive with your dredging to make sure squash disks are at their panko-max.
- Heat 3/4 cup of vegetable oil in a heavy skillet. When hot, carefully add squash disks. Turn when browned, about 3 minutes on each side. Remove and drain on plates covered in paper towel. Do in batches, and cover finished squash to keep warm. Add more oil if necessary.
- Buttermilk Ranch
- Pulse first four ingredients in food processor. Stir in remaining ingredients. Pulse once or twice more (if you lose control and over-pulse, dressing will be green.)

227. Pasta Ponza

Serving: Serves 8 | Prep: | Cook: |Ready in:

Ingredients

- 2 cups red chcherry or grape tomatoes, halved
- 2 cups yellow cherry or grape tomatoes, halved
- 1/4 cup capers, rinsed and drained
- 1 tablespoon extra-virgin olive oil, plus extra for drizzling
- 1/2 teaspoon kosher salt, plus extra for seasoning
- 1/4 teaspoon freshly ground black pepper, plus extra for seasoning
- 1/2 cup Italian-style seasoned breadcrumbs
- 1 pound ziti or other short tube-shaped pasta
- 1 1/4 cups Pecorino Romano cheese, grated
- 1/4 cup chopped fresh flat-leaf parsley

Direction

- Preheat the oven to 375 degrees F. Butter an 8 by 8-inch glass baking dish. Set aside.
- Place the tomatoes, capers, 1 tablespoon olive oil, 1/2 teaspoon salt, and 1/4 teaspoon pepper in the prepared baking dish. Toss to coat. Sprinkle the breadcrumbs over the tomato mixture. Drizzle the top with olive oil and bake for 30 to 35 minutes until the top is golden. Cool for 5 minutes.
- Bring a large pot of salted water to a boil over high heat. Add the pasta and cook until tender but still firm to the bite, stirring occasionally, about 8 to 10 minutes. Drain and reserve about 1 cup of the pasta water.
- Place the pasta in a large serving bowl. Spoon the tomato mixture onto the pasta. Add the cheese and toss well. Thin out the sauce with a little pasta water, if needed. Season with salt and pepper, to taste. Sprinkle with the chopped parsley and serve immediately.

228. Pastrami Rueben Mac & Cheese

Serving: Serves 6-12 | Prep: | Cook: |Ready in:

Ingredients

- 1 Box Elbow Macaroni (1#)
- 3 cups Light Cream (or Heavy)
- 1.5 Cup Shredded Gruyere
- 1.5 Cup Shredded Monterey Jack
- 1 cup Yellow American Cheese, chopped in to bits
- 2 tablespoons Grainy Mustard
- 1 tablespoon Smoked paprika
- 2 cups Cubed pastrami (medium dice)
- 4 slices toasted seeded rye
- 2 tablespoons melted butter
- 1.5 cups drained sauerkraut
- 3/4 cup additional- Shredded gruyere or if you can find it Dry Jack (pref Vella)

- 1/4 cup Russian Dressing

Direction

- Butter Rye Topping (can be done day ahead) Grind rye toast in food processor to medium fine crumb. Mix with melted butter, set aside. Boil 4 quarts heavily salted water. Add pasta. Bring water back up to boil, boil 4 minutes. Pasta should be slightly less than al dente…not soft with the tiniest bit of white visible when you bite into it. Reserve 1.5 cups pasta water. Drain pasta
- Boil 4 quarts heavily salted water. Add pasta. Bring water back up to boil, boil 4 minutes. Pasta should be slightly less than al dente…not soft with the tiniest bit of white visible when you bite into it Reserve 1.5 cups pasta water. Drain pasta
- In same pot add heavy cream, bring to a simmer over a medium flame
- Let cook a few minutes until reduces slightly, adjust flame to low Whisk in mustard & paprika
- Add cheese in 3 parts whisking each time to incorporate. Sauce should be creamy, if it is too thick add reserved pasta water slowly until velvet-y. Gently stir in pasta Add more pasta water if needed End result should be a smooth slightly liquid sauce; the pasta will absorb the liquid as it bakes.
- Butter or Spray an ovenproof casserole dish. Pour in Pasta/Cheese mixture in to prepared dish. Gently stir in pastrami Strew Sauerkraut evenly across the top. Sprinkle Reserved Gruyere/Dry Jack over top. Cover with Buttered Rye Crumbs. Bake @ 350 till bubbly (@ 20 - 30 minutes). Let rest 5-10 minutes before serving Drizzle Russian Dressing across top to serve
- Great sides include: Cole Slaw, Broccoli Salad, Cucumber Salad or Just Big Green Crunchy Salad… anything with lots of crunch and acid to balance out the richness

229. Peach Basil Goat Cheese Galette

Serving: Serves 6 | Prep: | Cook: |Ready in:

Ingredients

- Lemon Pate Brisee (adapted from the Bouchon cookbook)
- 2 1/4 cups flour
- 1 teaspoon kosher salt
- 8 ounces cold unsalted butter, cubed
- 1/4 cup ice water
- 1/2 teaspoon lemon zest
- flour
- Cheese Filling and Peaches
- 4 ounces goat cheese
- 6 tablespoons whole milk ricotta
- 1 extra large egg
- 2 tablespoons basil, chopped
- 2 large peaches, skins removed
- 1 1/2 teaspoons sugar
- juice of 1/2 a lemon
- 1 tablespoon basil, chopped
- 1 egg white. beaten

Direction

- Make the dough a day ahead. Place 1 cup flour in salt in standing mixer with dough hook attachment, turn on low and add the butter in a handful at a time, in about 4 batches, increase to medium speed and when butter is incorporated, stop machine, scrape down sides or dislodge dough from mixing arm, turn on to low again and slowly add in remaining flour, followed by the water, mix until just incorporated.
- Remove and divide in to two, wrap one disk in plastic wrap and freeze for later use.
- Return the other half to the mixer and add in the lemon zest, turn on low until incorporated. Shape in to a disk, wrap in plastic wrap and refrigerate overnight.
- Boil a small pot of water. Score an 'X' in the bottom of each peach place them in boiling

water turn off the heat, put the lid on and let them sit in the hot water for 2 minutes.
- Remove the skins from the peaches. Slice the peaches in quarters, slice in to 1/8" slices and place in a bowl, toss with sugar, lemon juice and basil.
- Using a mixer combine the goat cheese, ricotta and egg. Fold in the basil.
- Roll out the dough on a floured surface to 10'-12" in diameter, place on parchment on a baking sheet, spread the cheese mixture in the center of the dough staying clear of the outer 1.5". Arrange peaches on top. Roughly fold over the edges and brush with the egg wash. Bake at 375 for 35 minutes. Remove from oven let cool on the baking sheet on wire rack. Take care when transferring it to a plate or cutting board, the pastry is very flaky.

230. Peachy Buttermilk Sherbet

Serving: Makes 3 cups | Prep: | Cook: | Ready in:

Ingredients

- 1 cup buttermilk
- 1/3 cup (66 grams) sugar
- 3 cups (12 ounces/340 grams) peeled peach slices
- 1 to 3 tablespoons peach preserves or sugar (optional)

Direction

- Freeze the peach slices on a shallow baking sheet lined with foil or parchment paper. Stir the 1/3 cup sugar into the buttermilk and set aside for a few minutes to dissolve the sugar. Pour the buttermilk mixture into a foil- or plastic wrap-lined loaf or other shallow pan; cover and freeze until solid.
- Dump the frozen peach slices into a food processor fitted with the steel blade. Assuming the peaches are rock hard, let them sit for 15 minutes so they are slightly less than rock hard, and meanwhile leaving the frozen buttermilk in the freezer. After 15 minutes, remove and cut the frozen buttermilk into chunks the size of ice cubes. Add chunks to the processor and process until the mixture is completely blended and lightened in color. You will need to stop the processor from time to time to scrape the mixture from the side of the bowl or spread and redistribute it to better engage with the processor blades; inspect for lumps of peach when you do this. When the sherbet is smooth and free of lumps, taste and pulse in preserves or additional sugar, to taste, if necessary.
- Serve the sherbet immediately or scrape it into a container and store in the freezer until needed. Sherbet will retain its scoopable and spoonable texture for 2 or 3 hours before it hardens. Once it's hard, you will need to soften it for 10 to 20 minutes in the fridge before serving, or zap it for a few seconds at a time in a microwave on defrost.

231. Persian Style Ice Cream (Bastani)

Serving: Serves 8 | Prep: | Cook: | Ready in:

Ingredients

- 3 cups Milk
- 2 cups Clotted Cream
- 3 tablespoons Rosewater
- 1 cup Sugar
- 1 teaspoon Saffron
- 6 Egg Yolks
- 1 cup Pistachio Nuts
- 1 teaspoon Vanilla Extract
- 2 tablespoons Zest of a Pink Grapefruit

Direction

- In a non-stick pan, on medium to low heat, warm the milk and keep stirring. Add the saffron (crushed), vanilla and grapefruit zest.
- Add the sugar and keep stirring until it dissolves. Be patient and careful not to burn the milk. Add the rosewater, keep mixing and bring the temperature to low.
- Whisk the egg yolks, pour the eggs into the mixture and whisk quickly so the mixture unifies and the egg doesn't cook separately.
- Refrigerate for an hour. Combine clotted cream to the custard mix. Mix in the pistachio nuts. Put in the container you would like to store it in and freeze for a half hour.
- Mix well. Reseal and place container in a plastic bag. I don't know the science/witchcraft behind this but this stops all of my ice cream from frosting over. Freeze for at least 4 hours before serving.

232. Persimmon Snap Cannoli

Serving: Makes 10 cannoli | Prep: | Cook: | Ready in:

Ingredients

- Cannoli shells
- 2 tablespoons raw honey, slightly rounded
- 6 tablespoons unsalted, grass-fed butter
- 1/2 cup soft light brown sugar, lightly packed
- 2 teaspoons ground ginger
- 1/8 teaspoon ground cardamom
- 1/2 cup unbleached all purpose flour
- 1/8 teaspoon sea salt
- Spiced Hachiya persimmon filling
- 2 8 oz containers of mascarpone
- 1 1/2 cups Hachiya persimmon pulp, pureed (approximately 5-6 large persimmons, making sure to remove any skin or seeds)
- 2 teaspoons vanilla extract
- 1 teaspoon Vietnamese cinnamon
- 1 teaspoon ground ginger
- 1/4 teaspoon ground cardamom
- 1/4 teaspoon ground clove
- 1/2 teaspoon sea salt
- 1 tablespoon raw honey

Direction

- Add all persimmon pulp to a blender and blend until completely smooth.
- Measure out 1 1/2 cups of persimmon puree and add to a chilled metal bowl.
- Add all remaining filling ingredients to the bowl and mix with a hand mixer until completely smooth (the mixture will begin to ribbon).
- Refrigerate filling until ready to use.
- Pre-heat oven to 350°F.
- In a heavy bottomed saucepan, combine butter, honey and brown sugar.
- Over very low heat, stir ingredients until butter melts and the mixture is well combined.
- Remove from heat and sift all remaining ingredients directly into the pan. Stir until thoroughly combined.
- Line two baking sheets with parchment paper.
- Using a measuring tablespoon, measure out one level tablespoon of the mixture and pour onto the left side of a lined baking sheet. Repeat on the right side. Leave at least 3" on all sides for the batter to spread out. Two cookies will fit on an average baking sheet.
- Working one sheet at a time, bake for about 6 minutes (you can prep a sheet while one is in the oven). The cookies will be bubbling, begin to slightly darken at the edges and will appear lacy.
- Remove from oven and place on cooling rack for 30-60 seconds. Using a bench scraper and a spatula (VERY gently), transport the cookies to a piece of parchment on a cool surface.
- Using a cannoli mold (or any other one-inch metal tube), very gently roll the cookie around the form. Work quickly, as the sugars will begin to harden. Let the cookie rest on the form for 60-90 seconds to retain the cylindrical shape. Set on a cooling rack until all cookies are done.
- Repeat the above four steps until all batter has been used. Yield is about 10 cookies.

- Once completely cooled, add filling mixture to a prepared pastry bag. Pipe filling into one end of the cooled shell (filling will reach the halfway point), then pipe from the other end. Serve immediately.

233. Philadelphia Style Peach Ice Cream

Serving: Serves about 12 | Prep: | Cook: | Ready in:

Ingredients

- 2 cups heavy cream
- 1 cup whole milk
- 1/2 cup honey
- 1 teaspoon vanilla extract
- pinch of salt
- 2 very ripe peaches

Direction

- Peel and slice one of the peaches. Reserve everything but the pit (the color of the skin helps give your finished product a slight peach color.)
- In a saucepan, combine heavy cream, honey, vanilla, salt, and reserved peach. Bring to the first sign of a boil, then turn off immediately. Let peaches steep for at least an hour.
- Add whole milk to the cream mixture, and place in the refrigerator to cool. While this is cooling, peel and slice the second peach. Place in food processor and pulse until just pureed, with a few small chunks. Set aside, covered, in refrigerator.
- Strain cream mixture and pour into ice cream machine. Spin ice cream according to manufacturer's instructions, about 25 minutes. Right before the ice cream looks set (about 5 minutes before), swirl in the peach puree, using as much or as little as you like.
- Pour into an airtight container and store in the freezer. To serve, keep in refrigerator about 10 minutes before scooping to soften.

234. Pizza Appetizers

Serving: Serves 12 | Prep: | Cook: | Ready in:

Ingredients

- 2 cups shredded sharp cheddar cheese
- 1 cup chopped black olives
- 1 cup Hellmann's mayonnaise
- 2 tablespoons finely chopped onion
- 1 packet cocktail party rye bread
- bacon pieces (I use bottled Hormel, but you could crisply cook and crumble your own bacon)

Direction

- Preheat oven to 350 degrees F. In a large bowl, mix together the cheese, olives, mayonnaise, and onion.
- Spread about a tablespoon of the mixture on each piece of cocktail rye bread. Place the pieces on a baking sheet lined with parchment paper, making sure to not crowd them too close together. Sprinkle the bacon pieces on top of the pieces.
- Bake in the preheated oven for 10 minutes. Allow to cool a minute before transferring to a plate with a spatula. Enjoy!

235. Pizza Piccante

Serving: Serves 2 | Prep: | Cook: | Ready in:

Ingredients

- 1/8 pound Hot Soppressata, sliced, and chopped into bite sized pieces
- 8 Small Jarred North African Sweet/Hot Peppers or 4 Hot Cherry Peppers, seeds removed, chopped
- 1 tablespoon Fresh Oregano, chopped

- 1/3 pound Fresh Mozzarella, thinly sliced
- 1 small can plain Tomato Sauce (we used Del Monte brand) or Homemade
- 1 Standard round of store-bought Pizza Dough, preferably from a bakery or pizza shop
- 2 tablespoons Flour, for dusting
- Salt to taste
- Pepper to taste

Direction

- Place pizza stone in the oven. If not using a stone, prepare pizza as normal in a pizza pan. Turn oven on to 525 with the rack placed in the middle. Preheat the stone for 30 minutes.
- Flour a clean counter top and your hands. Place extra flour nearby. Form Pizza Dough into a ball. Press it down onto the counter and continue pressing until you have a flat round.
- Form dough into your desired pizza shape, making it as thin as possible - ideally an eighth of an inch thick. Pinch the edges of the dough all the way around to form a crust.
- Once Pizza Crust is formed, carefully transfer it onto parchment paper that is cut to a size just slightly bigger than the dough shape
- Now you are ready for toppings: Drizzle a Tablespoon or two of Oil onto the dough. Using a paper towel, spread the Oil around the entire surface of the dough. Using a Tablespoon, slowly spoon on Tomato Sauce and spread it around. The dough need not be totally covered (your pizza will be too saucy)
- Next, add the Fresh Oregano, Hot Peppers, Soppressata, and Crushed Red Pepper. Nestle slices of Mozzarella all over the Pizza, leaving some space in between them. You want some sauce and toppings to show through! Sprinkle the entire pizza with Salt and Pepper to taste. Lift the Pizza and the Parchment onto the pizza stone. You may leave the parchment in the oven while cooking.
- Cook for 10 minutes or until crust is crispy, puffed, and golden.

236.   Plum & Ricotta Crostini

Serving: Serves 24 crostini | Prep: | Cook: |Ready in:

Ingredients

- 1 baguette, cut into 1/4" rounds
- 3/4 cup balsamic vinegar
- 12 cherry plums (or any other "bite-size" variety), halved and pitted
- 1 cup sheep's milk ricotta
- fresh ground black pepper, to taste
- approx 1/2 cups fruity olive oil
- 12 mint leaves, chiffonade
- salt, to taste

Direction

- Preheat oven to 425 degrees. Place baguette rounds on parchment paper lined baking sheet and drizzle with oil and salt. Bake until rounds are golden, approximately 10 minutes. But check periodically because they can burn quickly.
- Place balsamic vinegar in sauce pan and reduce by half. You want to create a syrup. Once desired consistency is reached remove from heat.
- Remove baguette rounds and let cool on rack.
- Preheat grill pan until hot. Drizzle plums with olive oil and place on hot grills, cut side down, for less than 1 minute. You want grill marks to form but you do not want to soften the plum.
- Once baguette rounds have cooled, spread approximately 1 tablespoon of fresh sheep's milk ricotta on each round.
- Top each round with grilled plum, cut side facing up (to show grill marks.)
- Next, drizzle each crostini with balsamic syrup reduction.
- Lastly drizzle with some fruity olive oil, freshly ground pepper and salt.
- Right before serving, sprinkle each crostino with mint.

237. Polenta, Parmesan, And Prosciutto Spoon Breads,

Serving: Serves 6 | Prep: | Cook: |Ready in:

Ingredients

- 1 cup polenta, preferably fine mill
- 2 cups water (more if needed)
- 1 teaspoon salt
- 1 teaspoon freshly ground black pepper
- 2 sprigs thyme, intact
- 1 1/2 cup buttermilk, divided
- 2 tablespoons butter
- 1 1/2 cups Parmigiano Reggiano, divided
- 3 eggs, separated
- 1 teaspoon baking powder
- Pinch cayenne
- 1 1/2 ounces thinly sliced proscuitto (about 3 pieces), cut crosswise into 1/2 inch ribbons

Direction

- Preheat oven to 400. In a large heavy saucepan, combine water, salt, pepper, thyme; bring to boil and let simmer for 2 minutes. Bring it back to a boil and slowly add the polenta, whisking constantly, until you have a smooth porridge. Stir in 1 cup of the buttermilk, and continue to cook over medium heat, for 2 more minutes. Remove the thyme; reduce heat to low and continue to cook, whisking occasionally, for 35 minutes. It should bubble like a tar pit. If it gets too thick, stir in hot water as necessary. You want it to remain very thick, however.
- Remove polenta from heat and let cool slightly. Stir in remaining half cup of buttermilk, butter, and 1 cup of the Parmesan. Beat the egg yolks; stir into mixture.
- Meanwhile, beat egg whites in a separate bowl, until soft peaks form. Fold a spoonful of the egg whites into the polenta mixture; sprinkle baking powder into polenta mixture and mix well by hand. Fold in remaining egg whites.
- Spoon mixture (about one cup) into prepared 1 1/3 cup ramekins or soufflé dishes. Bake for 25 minutes. Once the spoon breads have puffed and browned, sprinkle with remaining cheese and the prosciutto shreds. Turn on broiler and let the cheese brown and the prosciutto crisp. Let cool slightly before serving.

238. Pork And Pear Galette With Bleu Cheese And Brown Sugared Pecans

Serving: Serves 6 | Prep: | Cook: |Ready in:

Ingredients

- 1 1/4 cups all-purpose flour
- 1/4 teaspoon baking powder
- 1 teaspoon kosher salt, divided
- 1/2 cup cold butter, cut into 1/2-inch pieces
- 4 - 6 tablespoons ice water
- 4 ounces cream cheese, softened
- 1 teaspoon prepared horseradish
- 1/2 pound deli roast pork, shaved
- 2 scallions, chopped
- 1 Bosc pear, cored, thinly sliced
- 1 ounce bleu cheese, crumbled
- 2 tablespoons butter
- 1/3 cup pecan pieces
- 2 tablespoons light brown sugar

Direction

- Sift together flour, baking powder, and 1/2 teaspoon salt in a large bowl. Using a pastry blender, cut in the butter until coarse crumbs form. Add in the water, a little at a time, until dough comes together. Place onto a floured work surface, knead for 30 seconds to one minute. Shape into a flat disc, wrap in plastic wrap and refrigerate for 30 minutes.
- Preheat oven to 400 degrees. Spray a large baking sheet with non-stick cooking spray; set aside.

- On a floured work surface, roll out dough into a 12-inch circle. Place onto the prepared baking sheet.
- In a small bowl, mix together the cream cheese and horseradish. Spread onto dough leaving a border of approximately 2 inches on all sides. Top with the roast pork, scallions, and pear slices. Carefully fold the border over the edges of the filling to create a rustic crust. Place galette into preheated oven and bake for 30 - 35 minutes until cooked through and crust has browned. Immediately top pears with bleu cheese crumbles, let galette rest for 2 - 3 minutes to allow bleu cheese to begin to soften.
- Meanwhile, melt the butter in a small skillet over medium-low heat. Add pecans, remaining 1/2 teaspoon salt and brown sugar, stirring until brown sugar has melted. Cook for 2 - 3 minutes, until pecans have become coated in the brown sugar mixture, stirring occasionally. Remove from heat; set aside to cool.
- To serve, cut galette into 6 slices, top with brown sugared pecans and enjoy!

239. Potato Cheese Perogies

Serving: Makes 7 dozen | Prep: | Cook: |Ready in:

Ingredients

- Garnish and Filling
- 1/2 cup canola oil
- 6 cups finely chopped white onions
- plain yogurt or sour cream
- 1 tablespoon salt
- 2-1/2 pounds Yukon gold potatoes, peeled and cut into 1-inch cubes
- 2 cups grated old or extra-old cheddar cheese
- Dough
- 8 cups unbleached, all-purpose flour
- 1 tablespoon salt
- 3/4 cup margarine
- 3 eggs
- 3 cups potato water (reserved from making filling; you might not need all of it)

Direction

- Make the garnish: Heat canola oil over medium heat in a large skillet. Add onions and fry slowly until they are very soft and just begin to caramelize, taking on a deep golden color. Reserve. (Also reserve the yogurt or sour cream separately until ready to serve.)
- Make the filling: Bring a large pot of water to the boil; add the salt and cubed potatoes. Cook until potatoes are tender, approximately 20 minutes. Drain potatoes well (reserving 3 cups of the cooking water) and return them to the pot. Mash until they are very smooth (if potatoes are dry, you can add up to 1/2 cup of milk to achieve proper consistency). Add the grated cheese to the mashed potatoes and stir until it has melted and is well blended. Let filling cool to room temperature before stuffing the dough.
- Make the dough: Stir together flour and salt in a large mixing bowl. Cut in margarine until dough comes together, resembling dried peas. Beat eggs together in a measuring cup and fill with potato water to measure 1 cup. Add the egg mixture to the dough and stir until dough comes together. Turn dough out onto a lightly floured surface and knead until it is smooth and pliable, adding more flour if dough is too soft and more potato water if it is too dry. After kneading, let dough rest, covered, for 1 hour.
- Assemble perogies: Cut dough into six pieces, keeping unused pieces covered so dough does not dry out. On a lightly floured surface, roll a piece of dough out into a thin sheet, approximately 1/8-inch thick. Cut dough into 2-inch squares or rounds. Place 1 tablespoon filling in the center of each square. Fold square into a triangle, pinching edges together firmly around the filling. Lay finished perogies on a tray covered with a tea towel until cooking

time. Repeat with remaining 5 pieces of dough.
- Cook perogies: Bring a large pot of water to the boil and slide in perogies, several at a time, cooking them until the skins start to blister slightly and they float to the surface of the water. Remove perogies from boiling water with a slotted spoon, draining them well. Toss perogies with fried onions and top each serving with a dollop of plain yogurt or sour cream. (You can also fry the boiled perogies in a little bit of canola oil until the skin starts to crisp and brown before adding garnish.)

240. Princess Pasta

Serving: Serves 8 | Prep: | Cook: |Ready in:

Ingredients

- 500 grams beetroot
- 400 grams overcooked fatty ham as a piece
- 300 grams blue cheese (mild / medium)
- 1 large sweet onion (or several chalottes)
- 300-400 grams pasta (fusilli, penne, etc.)

Direction

- Dice ham and simmer on low/medium temp until golden and crispy and remove from pot. Smoky is good and should
- Peel & dice beets and put in pot. Cover with water and let boil on medium temp under lid until tender (20-30min, depends on size).
- Add pasta to pot and add water to almost cover pasta (not too much) and boil until pasta almost done (not yet al dente). Mix once and while to make sure no dry pasta remains and add a bit water if needed.
- Chop onion to large chunks and add to pot. If onion is not sweet, let cook for a few minutes.
- Dice and add blue cheese and cook until it melts. Blue cheese should not very strong or salty as it's used a lot to give creaminess (cheap is good).

- Remove from heat and add ham. Garnish with spring onion if available.

241. Prosciuto & Eggplant Rolatini

Serving: Serves 6-9 | Prep: | Cook: |Ready in:

Ingredients

- Ricotta Filling:
- 1 cup ricotta cheese
- 1 lg. egg
- 2 tablespoons flat leaf parsley, minced
- 1/4 cup grated parmesan cheese
- 1/4 cup sliced black pitted olives
- 1 roasted red pepper, seeded & diced (store bought can be used) * Recipe follows*
- Preparation
- 3 long chinese eggplants
- 1 lg. egg
- 1 cup flour for dredging
- 1 teaspoon black pepper, ground
- 9-12 thin slices of prosciutto
- 2 cups preferably homemade tomato sauce

Direction

- Mix together all of the filling ingredients. Set aside.* Taste for seasoning but the cheese and prosciutto have plenty of salt.*
- Preheat oven to 350FSlice eggplants 1/4" - 1/2" slices making 3-4 lengthwise pieces = making 9-12 slices. Dredge both sides in flour. In a pie plate beat egg & pepper with a fork. Dip each floured eggplant slice into the egg mixture and place on a greased parchment lined baking sheet. Large enough to hold all of the slices. Bake for 15min turning over once, halfway of the cooking time. Just until eggplants are pliable. Remove and allow to cool to the touch.
- Assembly: Place 1 prosciutto slice on a clean flat surface. Lay a slice of eggplant over it. Add a large dollop of filling on the end closest

to you. Begin to roll up, push any loose filling back into the roll. The egg will hold it in place when cooking. Place in a large enough casserole dish seam side down with the tomato sauce spread over the bottom. Continue until all of the rolls are finished in the same manner. *You could switch the presentation by placing the eggplant on the bottom then laying the prosciutto on top if you desire*
- Bake in the center of a preheated 350F for 30-40 min until prosciutto is crisp. Top with the sauce

242. Prosciutto & Fig Stuffing

Serving: Serves 4-6 | Prep: 0hours0mins | Cook: 0hours0mins | Ready in:

Ingredients

- Prosciutto & Fig Stuffing
- 2 cups Dried figs, tough stems removed
- 1 cup Italian red wine, sweet
- 1/4 pound Prosciutto di Parma
- 1 Stick of butter
- 1 cup Fresh minced Italian Parsley
- 1 cup Chopped celery stalks
- 2 teaspoons Dried Thyme
- 1 teaspoon Dried Sage
- 1 teaspoon Dried Rosemary
- 8 cups Homemade breadcrumbs -- use egg or butter-type bread
- 1/3 cup Chicken broth
- Frittata Mixture

Direction

- Preheat the oven to 300°.
- Prepare the breadcrumbs. To do this, take fresh bread loaves and cube them. I leave the crusts, but you can remove them if you prefer. You'll need 8 cups. Place the bread cubes on a cookie sheet. Let them bake for about 25 minutes. They'll be lightly browned, so toss them around to get the ones underneath that haven't browned yet. Bake for an additional 20 minutes. You want them golden and brown, like toast. Baking them on a lower heat for a longer time makes it less likely you'll burn them accidentally and helps dry them out.
- Cut the stems off of the dried figs. Here I'm using figlets, which are smaller. Then, in a non-reactive sauce pan simmer them in the wine for about 15 minutes to plump them. Let them cool, pat them dry and roughly chop them. Place them aside in a bowl with the minced Prosciutto di Parma.
- Chop the onion, celery and parsley. I use the food processor. In a skillet over medium heat, melt the stick of butter. Add the parsley, celery, salt, pepper, thyme, rosemary and sage and cook for about ten minutes or until the onions are translucent.
- Place the mixture in a large bowl. (I actually use the tin that I'm going to bake it in because it's big and it's easier to toss everything together in.) Add the cubed bread and the 1/3 cup of chicken broth. Add the fig and Prosciutto di Parma mixture. Toss and combine.
- Now you can either stuff the turkey or bake as you usually do. Or, you can preheat the oven to 350° and bake the stuffing in a casserole dish until lightly browned, about 40 minutes. That's what I did here and this is what it looked like when it was done.

243. Prosciutto, Roasted Asparagus, Parmigiano Reggiano & Mozzarella On Ciabbata

Serving: Serves 1 | Prep: | Cook: |Ready in:

Ingredients

- Prosciutto
- Roasted asparagus

- Parmigiano-reggiano
- Mozzarella
- Ciabbata bread
- Unsalted butter

Direction

- To make this grilled cheese sandwich, place a heavy skillet (cast-iron works best) over medium heat to pre-heat. Spread sandwich with softened butter and cook until golden brown, about 3-4 minutes per side. If the bread is browning too quickly, simply turn the heat down until cheese has melted. Cut on the diagonal and serve hot.

244. Pumpkin Bread With Brie

Serving: Makes 1 loaf | Prep: | Cook: | Ready in:

Ingredients

- 1 2/3 cups all purpose flour
- 1 1/2 teaspoons baking powder
- 1/2 teaspoon baking soda
- 1 tablespoon ground cinnamon
- 1 teaspoon freshly ground nutmeg
- 1/4 teaspoon ground cloves
- 1 cup 2 Tbs. pumpkin puree
- 1 cup melted coconut oil (or you can replace this with vegetable oil)
- 3/4 cup sugar
- 1/3 cup dark brown sugar
- 3/4 teaspoon salt
- 3 large eggs at room temperature
- 1 wedge of Brie - enough for everybody eating to have a couple thin slices

Direction

- Heat your oven to 350F. Grease a 9X5 loaf pan.
- In one bowl, combine the flour, baking soda, baking powder, cinnamon, nutmeg, and cloves.
- In a large bowl, beat together the pumpkin, oil, sugars, and salt until well blended. Beat in the eggs one at a time, beating until completely incorporated. Stir in the dry ingredients just until blended.
- Scrape the batter into the prepared loaf pan and bake until a toothpick stuck into the bread comes out clean, about an hour.
- Allow the bread to cool in the pan for about 20 minutes before removing it. Serve thick warm slices topped with pieces of the Brie. You can also toast leftovers and serve with Brie.

245. Pumpkin Breakfast Parfait

Serving: Serves 1 | Prep: | Cook: | Ready in:

Ingredients

- 1/2 cup pumpkin purée (I use canned)
- 1 teaspoon maple syrup, plus more to taste
- 2 pinches ground cinnamon
- 1 pinch ground ginger
- 1 pinch ground nutmeg
- 1/2 cup plain yogurt (or vanilla if you prefer)
- Granola for sprinkling on top, if desired

Direction

- In a small mixing bowl, stir together the pumpkin, maple syrup, and spices. Taste and add a little more maple syrup if you want.
- In a bowl or glass, make alternating layers of the pumpkin-spice mix and the yogurt until you've used them up. Then, sprinkle a little granola on top if you want a touch of crunch. Serve.

246. Pumpkin Kale Mac And Cheese

Serving: Serves 3 | Prep: | Cook: |Ready in:

Ingredients

- 2 cups dry pasta (shell, rotini, penne)
- water
- 1 1/2 cups milk
- 1 teaspoon cornstarch
- 2/3 cup pumpkin puree
- 2/3 cup shredded cheddar cheese, more to taste
- 1/2 cup kale, torn into bite size pieces
- 1/4 teaspoon garlic powder
- 1/4 teaspoon salt, more to taste

Direction

- Boil water in a medium sized pot. Once the water comes to a boil, pour in the pasta. Cook the pasta for about 7-9 minutes until the pasta become al dente. The pasta will be soft but still firm. Drain the pasta and run it through cold water to prevent the pasta from continuing to cook.
- Add half of the milk and cornstarch into a small bowl. Stir to dissolve the cornstarch in the milk. Make sure that the cornstarch has dissolved completely. Otherwise, clumps may form.
- Pour the cornstarch milk mixture into a large skillet or saucepan over medium heat. Stir to evenly heat the mixture. Add in the rest of the milk, pumpkin puree, and cheese. Stir to evenly distribute and to evenly melt the cheese.
- Add in the kale and cook for about a minute.
- Then add in the pasta. Stir to evenly coat the pasta with the pumpkin cheese mixture. If needed, add more milk until the consistency is to your liking.
- Season the pasta with garlic powder and salt. Add more to taste.
- Serve the mac and cheese warm.

247. Pumpkin Swirls

Serving: Makes 12 | Prep: | Cook: |Ready in:

Ingredients

- 1/4 cup pure canned pumpkin
- 2 ounces softened cream cheese
- 4 tablespoons granulated sugar, divided (3/1)
- 1/8 teaspoon cinnamon
- 1/8 teaspoon ground ginger
- 6 gratings of nutmeg
- 3 tablespoons very finely chopped pecans
- 1 teaspoon of your favorite bourbon
- 1 sheet puff pastry from a 17.3 ounce package
- 1 egg beaten with 2 tablespoons water

Direction

- Beat the pumpkin, cream cheese, cinnamon, ginger, nutmeg and 3 tablespoons of sugar together until creamy. Stir in the finely ground pecans and the bourbon.
- On a clean work surface, sprinkle 1 tablespoon of the sugar over about the size of your puff pastry sheet and lay the sheet over. Roll the sheet to form a 10x12 inch rectangle.
- Spread the pumpkin mixture over the pastry sheet to within 1/2 inch of the edges. Starting at the short end, roll the sheet to the middle and then do the same with the other end. The twin rolls should be touching.
- Place the roll in the freezer while you pre heat the oven to 425F. At this point you can also wrap and freeze the roll to bake another day. Just slightly defrost before baking.
- Once the oven is pre heated, take the roll out of the freezer, trim the ends and cut crosswise into 12 equal pieces. Place the pieces, cut side down, on a parchment lined baking sheet. Brush each piece with a little of the egg wash and bake for 14 to 18 minutes. Best served warm.

248. Quiche In Winter White And Blue

Serving: Makes one 10 inch quiche | Prep: | Cook: |Ready in:

Ingredients

- for the tart crust
- 1 1/4 cups all purpose flour
- 1/2 teaspoon salt
- 1 stick unsalted butter
- 2 tablespoons ice cold water
- for the filling
- 3 slices thick, applewood smoked, uncured bacon
- 1 1/2 cups cauliflower, cut into individual florets (halving large ones)
- 2 teaspoons minced garlic
- 1 tablespoon apple cider vinegar
- 1 tablespoon water, plus more if necessary
- 1/3 cup Fuji apple, peeled, cut into ¼ inch dice (can substitute another late season variety) drizzled with juice from 1 lemon wedge to prevent oxidation
- 1/3 cup finely grated Emmentaler (grate right before adding to quiche)
- 1/4 cup finely grated Buttermilk Blue Cheese (grate right before adding to quiche)
- 1 cup half-and-half
- 3 large eggs
- Freshly ground black pepper

Direction

- For the tart crust
- Combine flour and salt in a mound on a cool, clean surface. Place stick of butter on top of mound. Slice butter into ¼-inch thick pieces. Dip each slice of butter in flour, coating top and bottom.
- Using your thumbs and index fingers, flatten each slice, gently squeezing. As you do this, sections of each slice will fall on to the flour mound. Repeat until you have flattened every slice.
- You should now have a pile of thin, flour coated butter flakes on top of your flour. Slide both hands, palms facing up, under the edges of the flour mound and bring your hands together, raking floury butter flakes and gently combining pieces by pressing your thumbs down against your other fingers. Repeat until you have mostly saw dusty clumps with a few larger flakes.
- Sprinkle 1 T of ice-cold water over pile. Gently work mixture together with your hands to combine dough. If dough gets sticky, dip fingers in flour. Add remaining tablespoon of ice cold water and gather, eventually rolling dough into a smooth ball (be careful not to overwork, or dough will be tough). Wrap ball in a large piece of plastic wrap and flatten into disc (about 1 inch thick and 4 inches across). Fold plastic wrap around edges of disc to seal and refrigerate for at least 30 minutes and up to 1 day.
- When ready to use, remove from refrigerator and allow disc to sit at room temperature for about ten minutes before rolling out. Roll out dough (slightly larger than tart pan) and carefully wind around pin while sliding ceramic tart pan under. Unwind dough from pin into tart pan, carefully pressing into the bottom and up the sides. Trim excess with kitchen shears. Place in the freezer for 10 minutes.
- Preheat oven to 350 degrees F. Line dough with parchment, fill with at least 1 cup of rice or dried beans and bake for 15 minutes. Remove pan from oven, remove parchment and weights, and poke surface of dough all over with a fork. Return to oven for 12 more minutes. Remove and set aside to cool before filling and baking. Do not turn off oven.
- For the filling
- Place bacon slices in a cold pan that is large enough to fit all three slices in a single layer and turn heat to low. Slowly cook bacon, turning up heat if necessary. You want to cook the bacon to the point that the fat just begins to render, without burning. Remove bacon slices

to a paper towel lined plate. Do not turn off burner.
- Pour off all but 1 T of drippings and briefly rest pan on a cool burner. Add cauliflower pieces and return pan to hot burner. Cook cauliflower, constantly turning to prevent burning, about a minute. Add apple cider vinegar and cook for a few seconds, add 1 T of water and continue cooking, stirring. Mix in garlic and cook until cauliflower is tender and golden, about 3 minutes more, adding another tablespoon of water if necessary to prevent burning. Remove pan from heat.
- Cut each bacon slice in half lengthwise and then chop crosswise.
- Assemble tart by sprinkling half of the Emmentaler onto the bottom of the crust. Layer in the bacon, then the cauliflower, and then the diced apple. In a large Pyrex measure, combine the half-and-half with the eggs and the blue cheese. Add fresh ground pepper. Pour egg-cheese mixture over cauliflower filling and top with remaining Emmentaler.
- Transfer to oven and bake for 25-30 minutes, until golden and slightly puffed. Allow quiche to cool for at least 10 minutes before serving. Enjoy!

249. RUGELACH Cookies With Nutella & Chocolate Chips

Serving: Makes about 40 cookies | Prep: | Cook: |Ready in:

Ingredients

- Wondra flour to help keep the dough from sticking
- 2 cups all-purpose flour plus 1/2 teaspoon salt
- 1 cup unsalted butter, 2 sticks, COLD
- 3/4 cup cream cheese, 6 ounces, COLD
- 1/3 cup sour cream, COLD
- 1/4 cup granulated sugar
- 2 teaspoons vanilla bean paste
- FILLING:
- 1 13 ounce jar Nutella spread
- 1 cup mini semi-sweet chocolate chips
- vanilla sugar for rolling

Direction

- MAKE THE PASTRY: To the bowl of a large food processor, add the flour and salt; pulse to aerate. Cut the butter and cream cheese into chunks. Add to the food processor with the sour cream, sugar and vanilla bean paste. Pulse a few times just until crumbly and when pinched the dough stays together. Pieces of butter and cream cheese should still be visible in the dough.
- On a lightly floured surface turn out the dough. Gently knead into a ball and slightly flatten. Roll into a rectangle and fold into 3 like a letter. Repeat 2 more times. Cut the dough into 4 portions. Roll each into a ball and then flatten into a disk. Wrap in plastic and refrigerate until firm; preferably overnight. This dough must be COLD to work with.
- MAKE THE COOKIES: Preheat the oven to 350 degrees. Line four 1/2 sheet pans with parchment paper. Remove 1 piece of dough at a time from the refrigerator. On a lightly floured surface (use Wondra flour), roll the piece of dough into a circle. Flour and turn the dough once or twice as not to stick to the surface. Use an 8" - 9" dessert plate as a guide to cut the circle. Wrap the scraps in plastic and refrigerate. With a small offset spatula, spread Nutella 1" from the edge of the circle in an even layer that is about 1/4" thick. Lightly sprinkle chocolate chips over the Nutella. Use a floured pizza wheel to cut the circle into 8 equal wedges. Roll each wedge beginning with the wide end and ending with the narrow end. Dip the rolled cookie in vanilla sugar. Place 9 to each cookie sheet. Form each cookie into a crescent shape and pinch each tip. The end of the cookie should be on top and should be slightly pressed with your finger as not to separate while baking. Repeat with the

remaining 3 pieces of dough. Roll the refrigerated scraps into a ball, roll into a circle and repeat the process.
- Bake 15 minutes or until golden brown. As the pastry bakes it should have a crunchy crust and a caramelized base. Cool on the pan 15 minutes before removing to cool completely on a tray before storage.

250. Radish Goat Cheese Galette

Serving: Serves 4-6 | Prep: | Cook: | Ready in:

Ingredients

- For The Crust
- 4 ounces unsalted butter
- 2 cups unbleached all purpose flour
- 6 ounces sour cream (not low fat or fat free)
- 2-3 tablespoons ice water
- 1 pinch kosher salt
- Radish and Goat Cheese Galette
- 5 ounces chevre goat cheese
- 1 tablespoon sour cream (optional)
- 1 sour cream pie crust, see above
- 1 tablespoon dijon mustard
- 6 medium size, firm radishes, sliced thin with a mandoline or very sharp knife
- 1/2 tablespoon sherry vinegar
- kosher salt and black pepper to taste
- 1 tablespoon fresh rosemary leaves, or to taste

Direction

- For The Crust
- Combine flour and salt
- Cut butter into flour / salt mixture, mix should be dry and crumble easily
- Slowly add sour cream, while cutting flour / butter mix with a fork
- If dough still looks a bit too dry add a tablespoon of ice water at a time until dough is a fully formed ball, wrap and refrigerate 10 minutes.

- Radish and Goat Cheese Galette
- In a small bowl, combine goat cheese and use sour cream to soften to a spreadable texture, season to taste with kosher salt and pepper
- Roll out chilled pie crust to a roughly round shape and an even thickness.
- Spread the raw crust first with a thin layer of Dijon mustard, the with the goat cheese mixture
- Fold the edges of the galette in, pinching or folding as you go.
- Bake the galette on parchment paper on the middle rack of a 350 degree oven for 20-25 minutes, check frequently for varying oven temps. Crust should be lightly brown and flaky, the goat cheese mix will be lightly cracked. Remove from oven to cool.
- Combine thinly sliced radishes with a scant tablespoon of sherry vinegar, as well as salt and pepper to taste, top the warm - but not hot - galette with radish mixture, and rosemary, slice and serve

251. Radish Salad With Curry Orange Dressing

Serving: Serves 4 | Prep: | Cook: | Ready in:

Ingredients

- 1 cup orange juice
- 1 tablespoon olive oil
- 1/2 teaspoon curry powder
- salt to taste
- 2 cups radishes, washed and roughly chopped
- 1 cup crumbled feta cheese
- 2 tablespoons chopped fresh mint leaves

Direction

- In a small saucepan, bring the orange juice to a boil and cook it until it is reduced to about 1/4 cup (about 20-25 minutes). Take off the heat.

- Whisk the olive oil, and curry powder into the orange juice. Add salt to taste. Toss the chopped radishes with the dressing.
- Divide the radishes between 4 plates. Top with the feta cheese and chopped mint.

252. Raisin, Pecan, And Banana Oatmeal With Flax Seeds

Serving: Serves 1-2 | Prep: | Cook: | Ready in:

Ingredients

- 1/2 cup Old fashioned rolled oats (not instant)
- 1 cup Milk (will be used 1/2 cup at a time)
- 1/2 cup Water
- 1/4 cup Raisins
- 2 tablespoons Coarse ground flax seeds
- 2 tablespoons Pecan pieces
- 1 Banana
- Pinch Salt (optional)

Direction

- Put the oats, flax, raisins, and salt (if using) into a sauce pan and add the water and 1/2 cup of milk. Cook over medium-low until most of the liquid is dissolved.
- While the oats cook, cut the banana into small slices. I just slice it into my bowl.
- Pour the cooked oats over the banana slices, pour the remaining 1/2 cup of milk over the top, and sprinkle on the pecans. From here, I mix everything together and chow down with a mug of green tea.

253. Rapturous Morel Marmalade

Serving: Serves 10-12 | Prep: | Cook: | Ready in:

Ingredients

- Rapturous Morel Marmalade
- 8 ounces Fresh or Rehydrated Morels
- 4   Bacon or Pancetta Slices
- 2 sprigs Fresh Thyme
- 1/2 cup Veal Stock
- Salt & Pepper to Taste
- 1 cup Carrots, Diced
- 1 cup Shallots, Diced
- 1 cup Port Wine
- 1/2 cup Red Wine Vinegar
- 3 tablespoons Brown Sugar
- 1 teaspoon Black Pepper
- Salt to Taste
- Goat Cheese Polenta
- 4 cups Unsalted Chicken Stock
- 1 cup Polenta
- 1/2 cup Goat Cheese
- Salt & Pepper to Taste
- 1 tablespoon Freshy Thyme Leaves

Direction

- Rapturous Morel Marmalade
- In a large sauté pan, cook the bacon till lightly crisp. Remove the bacon and add morels, pinch of salt, and 2 tbs of butter. Cook till the mushrooms develop a nice brown crust. Add veal stock and thyme, simmer rapidly till the stock is more or less evaporated, leaving the mushrooms moist with the tiniest amount of liquid. Set aside.
- In a separate large pan heat 3 tbsps. butter. Saute the shallots and carrots with a pinch of salt till softened, about 10 minutes, stirring frequently. Stir in the sugars, vinegar, port wine, kosher salt and pepper. Cook over medium heat until the liquid has reduced.
- Chop the sautéed mushrooms and bacon bits. Add to the warm sauce and combine gently but thoroughly over low heat till warmed. Check for black pepper, it should be fairly peppery. Serve with goat cheese polenta and crème fraîche. Be warned – highly addictive!!
- Goat Cheese Polenta

- Bring the chicken stock, 2 tbsps. butter, pepper, thyme, and salt to a boil in a heavy-bottomed pot. Sprinkle polenta slowly while constantly stirring the liquid. Reduce the heat to a gentle simmer, and constantly stir the polenta till it pulls away from the sides of the pan. The polenta is cooked when it is creamy and no longer grainy. It should take about 20-25 minutes to get the right consistency. (I cook polenta for at least an hour when I want it extra creamy as I serve it with my short ribs).
- Stir in the goat cheese and taste the seasonings. Pour immediately into a butter glass pan. When cool, cover and refrigerate overnight.
- Cut the polenta into any shape you wish. I usually cut them into bite size since I serve this at my cocktail parties. Heat a big skillet with some olive oil. Pan fry the bites till golden brown on each side. Top it with Morel Marmalade and crème fraîche. Serve warm.

254. Raspberry Dark Chocolate Pavlova Ice Cream

Serving: Serves 3 | Prep: | Cook: | Ready in:

Ingredients

- 200 milliliters whole milk
- 200 milliliters heavy cream
- 80 grams sugar
- 1 pinch salt
- 3 teaspoons cornstarch
- 50 grams cream cheese
- 20 grams dark chocolate
- 2 vanilla meringue shells
- 5 teaspoons deseeded raspberry jam

Direction

- Dissolve the cornstarch in 50ml whole milk, leave to rest.
- For the ice cream base in a small saucepan over medium heat combine the heavy cream, whole milk, sugar, a pinch of salt, stir, being to an almost boil, add the cornstarch milk and cook constantly stirring until thickened. Take off heat, add the cream cheese and mix until smooth. Transfer into the fridge overnight.
- Freeze in your ice cream maker according to the manufacturer's instructions adding shaved dark chocolate and 2 medium size crushed homemade or store-bought vanilla meringue shells. Store in an airtight container swirling in pockets of homemade or store-bought deseeded (!) raspberry jam and freeze for at least 5 hours until set.

255. Red Velvet Cheesecake

Serving: Makes a 10" cheesecake | Prep: | Cook: | Ready in:

Ingredients

- The crust
- 1 cup Honey Graham cracker crumbs
- 1 cup Chocolate Graham cracker crumbs
- 1/2 cup Packed dark brown sugar
- 3/4 cup melted butter
- Cheesecake filling
- 32 ounces Cream cheese, softened (4 of the 8oz packs)
- 1 cup granulated sugar
- 2 Eggs
- 2 Egg whites
- 3 tablespoons Unsweetened cocoa powder
- 1/2 cup Dark chocolate chunks
- 1 cup Sour cream
- 1 cup Pureed canned beets (you can use fresh beets after steaming, but use less, closer to 3/4 c.)
- 2 teaspoons vanilla extract
- 1 handful Pomegranate seeds (for topping)
- 1 dash Powdered sugar (for topping)

Direction

- Preheat oven to 325 degrees.

- Crust: Grind cracker and cookie crumbs together, add brown sugar and mix. Then add melted butter and fold together. Transfer crumb mixture to a 10" springform pan (9" if you want a real-thick cheesecake). Press crumbs onto bottom and up the sides. Set aside.
- Filling: In a large bowl, beat cream cheese, sugar, and vanilla with an electric mixer on medium speed until smooth, add sour cream, continue mixing until silky-smooth. Turn the mixer to low and add eggs, one at a time, mixing after each addition and scraping down the sides, add egg whites, one at a time. Lower the speed to stirring and add in cocoa powder and pureed beets. Finally, add in the chocolate chunks and stir until they're well mixed in. Pour into pan with your crust and smooth the top with a spatula.
- Bake for 45-50 minutes or until edge is set but center still jiggles. Remove from oven; place on cooling rack and immediately run thin knife around inside perimeter of pan to loosen from side. Cool to room temperature; refrigerate for 3 hours. Cover loosely; refrigerate overnight.
- To serve: When you're ready for the grand presentation, sprinkle powdered sugar over the top and then sprinkle your pomegranate seeds on top of that. Voila, beautiful.

256. Red White & Blue Layered Buttermilk Cake

Serving: Serves 4-6 | Prep: | Cook: | Ready in:

Ingredients

- Buttermilk Cake Layers
- 1 cup butter, softened but not melted
- 1 1/2 cup sugar
- 1/2 tsp nutmeg
- 1/2 tsp pure vanilla extract OR orange extract
- 3 cups self-rising flour
- 1 cup buttermilk
- 2 eggs, beaten
- pinch of salt
- Creamy Topping & Berries
- 1 container of Cool whip
- 4 oz soft Neufchatel cheese
- 2 TBSP light corn syrup
- 2 TBSP light sherry or rum
- 1 carton each of fresh strawberries & blueberries

Direction

- Make your Creamy Topping first: Mix all ingredients and blend well with an electric mixer, then cover the bowl and place in the fridge to let it set.
- Butter Cake Layers will require 3 cake pans (8 or 9 in. round). I like to use Baker's Joy to spray them because the cakes will pop out easily. If you don't' have it, then spray the pans with Butter Pam, sprinkle lightly with a little flour until the bottom and sides are covered. Preheat oven to 325.
- Mix the sugar and butter together until creamy. Add the buttermilk, extract, eggs and pinch of salt--blend until smooth. Set aside.
- Mix the self-rising flour, and nutmeg. Make a well in the center and pour in the sugar-egg mix. Use a mixer to blend the batter until smooth, but DO NOT whip. Pour batter into the3 floured-buttered pans and bake about 20 minutes. Ovens are different and you will want to check to see if the cake is done--it should be golden on top and spring back lightly when touched. Do not overbake because it will dry out easily. When done, set the cakes on a rack to cool completely. If the layers are still warm the topping will melt!
- Pick out a nice plate and place the first layer, spoon 13 the topping over it--drips down the side are fine. The topping should be thickened when cool. Layer 1/3 third of the berries and make sure they peek out at the edge, then top with the second and third layers and repeat. I like to gather the blueberries in the middle and surround them with strawberry halves. Be

sure to store in the fridge or cooler until serving.

257. Refried Butternut Squash With Mozzarella And Gremolata

Serving: Serves 4-6 | Prep: | Cook: |Ready in:

Ingredients

- 1 butternut squash
- salt and pepper
- olive oil
- 3 tablespoons sweet cream butter
- 7-10 fresh sage leaves
- 1 ball fresh mozzarella, sliced thin
- 3 cloves garlic, divided and minced
- 3 tablespoons Italian flat-leaf parsley, finely chopped
- 1 teaspoon lemon zest

Direction

- PREP AND ROAST THE SQUASH: Preheat oven to 400. Chop off ends of squash and then cut it in half lengthwise. Scrape out seeds. Cut into half-moons about 1/4-inch thick. Spread evenly on a baking sheet. Drizzle with a little olive oil and season with salt and pepper. Roast in oven until tender and golden brown, about 30 minutes.
- REFRY: Place roasted squash in a mixing bowl and mash with a fork until smooth. Season with salt to taste. Melt butter in a large skillet over MEDIUM HIGH heat. When butter begins to brown, lower heat to MEDIUM LOW and add sage leaves and 1 clove minced garlic. Immediately add squash; smoothing the puree into an even layer in the pan. Let it cook until the underside is browned, about 12-15 minutes. Stir and then spread out the mixture evenly in the pan again and let it cook another 12-15 minutes. The goal is to brown it as much as possible. This releases the sugars. Stir it again and spread it out again evenly.
- TOP WITH CHEESE AND GREMOLATA: Place slices of mozzarella cheese on top of squash and cover skillet. Reduce heat to LOW and let it cook until cheese softens and begins to melt, about 3-5 minutes. Meanwhile, mix the parsley, remaining garlic, and lemon zest in a small prep bowl to make a gremolata. When cheese is melted, sprinkle the gremolata over the squash and serve straight from the pan.

258. Ricotta Crostini With Confited Lemons, Thyme, And Walnuts

Serving: Serves 6-8 | Prep: | Cook: |Ready in:

Ingredients

- Confited Lemons
- 2 lemons
- 1 1/2 teaspoons salt
- 1 cup olive oil
- 4 tsp honey
- For the crostini
- Confited lemons
- 1 fresh baguette
- 2 cups fresh, good quality ricotta
- Bunch fresh thyme, to taste
- toasted walnuts, to taste
- olive oil

Direction

- Make the confit: Preheat the oven to 350F. Scrub the lemons well and cut off both ends. Cut each lemon in half lengthwise, then slice as thinly as possible. Remove and seeds.
- Place lemons in a small baking dish (an 8x8 pan or a loaf pan works well), and add salt, olive oil, and honey. Toss a few times to combine. If lemons are not submerged in olive oil, add a little more to cover.

- Bake lemons for about an hour, until the rind is translucent and meltingly tender. Remove lemons from oil and let cool in a small bowl or other container. NOTE: You may reserve the oil for another use if you like, however, it will be quite bitter from the lemons. I chose to discard mine.
- Assemble the crostini: Slice the baguette on the diagonal, brush the slices with olive oil, arrange on a baking sheet and bake until they begin to toast. When the toast is ready, spread each slice with a little ricotta and drape a few lemon slices on top. Sprinkle each crostini with a pinch of fresh thyme leaves and a scatter some walnuts on top. Finish with a drizzle of olive oil and serve.

259. Ricotta Frittata

Serving: Serves 4-6 | Prep: | Cook: | Ready in:

Ingredients

- 6 large or jumbo eggs
- 3/4 cup fresh ricotta
- 1/2 cup freshly grated parmesan cheese
- 2-3 slices of provolone cheese, or 1/4 cup shredded mozzarella
- 2-3 slices deli ham, optional
- 1/2 tablespoon chopped parsley
- 1/2 teaspoon salt

Direction

- Preheat oven to 375 degrees
- In a large bowl lightly beat your eggs using a whish so you incorporate some air. Once the eggs are whisked, add your ricotta and break it up so that it's well blended with the eggs. Add the Parmigiano cheese and blend well.
- Layer your slices of provolone cheese and ham (if using) and dice them so you end with small squares of each. Add them to the eggs mixture and end with your parsley and salt, which are again whisked together well in the egg mixture.
- Add your frittata mixture to a prepared pie plate that has been sprayed with non-stick cooking spray. Place a cookie sheet underneath, in case of spillage, and bake for 40 to 45 minutes or until firm, being careful not too over bake. The frittata is most delicious straight out of the oven or warm.

260. Roasted Acorn Squash And Goat Cheese Dip

Serving: Serves 2-4 | Prep: | Cook: | Ready in:

Ingredients

- 1 acorn squash
- 1 tablespoon olive oil (plus a little extra for drizzling)
- 1 tablespoon apple cider vinegar
- 3 sprigs thyme
- 1/3 cup goat cheese
- 2 teaspoons maple syrup
- Pinch salt and pepper

Direction

- Preheat the oven to 425F. Half the squash and scoop out the seeds. Place on a roasting pan and rub with olive oil, apple cider vinegar, thyme, and salt & pepper. Roast for 40 mins.
- Remove squash from the oven and let cool. Scoop squash flesh into a food processor. Add goat cheese, maple syrup, and salt & pepper. Blitz together until smooth, drizzling in some extra olive oil if you want. Try it and adjust seasoning to taste.

261. Roasted Butternut Squash Cheesecake

Serving: Serves 12 | Prep: | Cook: |Ready in:

Ingredients

- crust
- 2 cups crushed ginger snaps
- 1 stick of melted butter
- filling
- 2 average sized butternut squash @3 cups
- 24 ounces room temp cream cheese
- 1 cup sugar
- 1/2 cup brown sugar
- 1 tablespoon vanilla
- 3 eggs +1 yolk
- 2 tablespoons flour
- 1/4 cup ricotta cheese
- 1 teaspoon nutmeg
- 1/2 tablespoon salt

Direction

- In a bowl combine the ginger snaps and butter press into a 9" spring form pan. Set aside.
- Preheat oven to 350 degrees. Halve and scoop the seeds from the squash place skin side up and roast for about 30 minutes. Once ready, scoop the squash out of its skin and into a bowl. Set aside to cool @15 minutes. Once cooled squeeze out excess liquid. I put the squash in a colander, let it sit over the same bowl it cooled in, then press with a spoon.
- In another bowl (or kitchen aid) beat the remaining ingredients together. I usually do this in the order they are listed. Then add the squash and continue to mix until everything's incorporated. Pour into the crust and bake for 50-60 minutes. You want it to be a little jiggly so it doesn't overcook and crack. Let it sit for about 15 minutes then cover with plastic and refrigerate for at least 4 hours.

262. Roasted Cauliflower And Barley Salad With Basil Croutons

Serving: Serves 4 | Prep: | Cook: |Ready in:

Ingredients

- Croutons
- 1 cup cup loosely packed basil leaves
- 2 cloves garlic, chopped
- 1/2 cup olive oil
- 4 ounces sourdough or foccacia bread, cut into 1/2-inch cubes
- 1 teaspoon kosher salt
- 2 tablespoons freshly grated Parmigiano
- Salad
- 2 1/2 cups water
- 1 teaspoon kosher salt
- 1 cup barley, rinsed
- 6 tablespoons extra virgin olive oil
- 1 tablespoon butter
- 2 cloves garlic, chopped
- 1/2 teaspoon crushed red pepper
- 1 small head cauliflower, cut into 1-inch florets
- 2 teaspoons balsamic vinegar
- 1 teaspoon Dijon mustard
- 1/2 cup celery leaves, chopped
- 1/4 cup freshly grated Parmigiano
- 2 tablespoons toasted pine nuts

Direction

- Croutons
- Put the basil and garlic in small food processor and pulse until finely chopped. With the machine running, add the oil in a slow stream until completely emulsified. Transfer to an airtight container and store refrigerated until ready to use or freeze for up to one month.
- Put the bread in a large bowl and add 2 tablespoons of the basil purée. Stir in the salt. Spread on a baking sheet. Sprinkle with the Parmigiano and bake until browned and crisp, 8 to 10 minutes. Set aside or store in an airtight container until ready to use.

- Salad
- Preheat the oven to 425°F.
- Put the water and salt in a large saucepan. Bring to a boil over high heat. Add the barley, cover and cook on low heat until tender, about 45 minutes.
- While the barley is cooking, heat 3 tablespoons of the olive oil, the butter, garlic and crushed red pepper in a large, ovenproof skillet over medium-high heat. Add the cauliflower and stir to coat the cauliflower evenly with the olive oil mixture. Cook for 1 to 2 minutes then transfer to the oven. Cook until browned and tender, about 20 minutes.
- Whisk together the balsamic vinegar and mustard in a large bowl. Add the olive oil in a steady stream while continuing to whisk. Stir in the barley, cauliflower (including any bits of garlic or pepper stuck to the skillet), Parmigiano and celery leaves. Season to taste with salt and pepper. Sprinkle the croutons over the top and serve immediately.

263. Roasted Corn And Cojita Quesadillas

Serving: Serves 2 | Prep: | Cook: | Ready in:

Ingredients

- 2 ears fresh corn, or 2 cups frozen corn
- Butter for sauteing corn and frying tortillas
- Pinch cayenne pepper or chili powder
- Splash fresh lime juice
- Sprig cilantro, chopped
- 2 large tortillas
- 1/2 cup queso fresco cheese, grated
- 1/2 cup cojita cheese, grated

Direction

- Cut the corn from the cob using a sharp knife. This will be messy, so be ready for corn to fly in every direction. Sauté the corn with some butter in a pan over medium high heat until it has roasted a bit. Add a pinch of cayenne pepper or chili powder, splash of fresh lime juice, and some chopped cilantro. Stir and then pour into a bowl and set aside.
- Melt some more butter in the same pan. Fill half of a tortilla with the grated cheeses and the corn and then fold it over. Fry in the pan until golden brown on both sides. Garnish with cilantro, salsa, and sour cream and enjoy!

264. Roasted Eggplant And Sautéed Greens Lasagna

Serving: Serves 8 to 12 | Prep: | Cook: | Ready in:

Ingredients

- 2 to 3 small-ish eggplant (about 2 to 3 pounds)
- grapeseed oil
- kosher salt
- 10 to 12 ounces greens, such as Swiss chard, kale, or mustard greens, leaves removed from stems and finely chopped (you should have about 8 oz. greens post trimming)
- 1 quart tomato sauce, homemade is best, see notes above
- 1 box no-boil noodles (about 9 oz, you'll need 12 sheets, see notes above)
- 4 ounces Parmigiano Reggiano, grated (about 1 cup)
- 8 ounces fresh mozzarella (not stored in brine), pulled into small pieces (about 1 cup)

Direction

- Preheat the oven to 450° F. Slice the eggplant into 1/4-inch thick rounds. Spread into single layers on two baking sheets. Drizzle 3 to 4 tablespoons grapeseed oil over top. Toss to coat. Spread back into a single layer and season generously with kosher salt. Roast the eggplant for 20 minutes or so, rotating the pans halfway — the eggplant is done when the undersides are golden brown and release easily from the pan with a metal spatula. This may take longer than 20 minutes and may require more than one rotation of the pans. Be sure to check the eggplant slices periodically — for instance, the slices on the perimeter of my sheet pan always brown/finish cooking first. Transfer eggplant to a plate. Turn the heat down to 350° F.

- Meanwhile, place a large sauté pan over medium-high heat. Add 2 tablespoons grapeseed oil. When the oil shimmers, add the greens, and sauté turning the greens with tongs to help them cook evenly. Season with a good pinch of salt. When the greens have shrunk way down, they're done — this will happen in 2 to 3 minutes. Turn off the heat and transfer the greens to a plate to cool.
- Set up an assembly line with your tomato sauce, no-boil noodles, plate of eggplant and greens, grated parmesan, pulled-apart mozzarella. Spread a 1/2 cup of tomato sauce over the bottom of a 9x13-inch pan. Top with 3 no-boil noodles. Spread another 1/2 cup of sauce over top. Layer eggplant in a single layer over top. Spread a thin layer of greens over top. Spread about 1/4 cup of parmesan over top, then 1/4 cup mozzarella. Repeat this layering until you have four layers of noodles, then top the final layer of noodles with another 1/2 cup tomato sauce (or more) and the remaining cheese. (The idea is to always have about 1/2 cup tomato sauce on either side of the noodles, but you can't go wrong here.)
- Cover pan with foil and refrigerate until ready to bake or transfer to oven and bake 40 minutes covered. Remove foil, and bake for 5 to 10 minutes if desired to lightly brown the top.

265. Roasted Squash Blossoms With Mozzarella And Walnut Oil

Serving: Serves 2 | Prep: | Cook: | Ready in:

Ingredients

- 12 squash blossoms
- 1/2 cup fresh mozzarella, diced
- 2 tablespoons raisins, chopped
- 2 tablespoons oil-packed sundried tomatoes, chopped
- 1/2-1 teaspoons cayenne pepper
- 1 tablespoon olive oil
- 2 teaspoons walnut oil
- salt to taste

Direction

- Mix together the mozzarella, raisins, sundried tomatoes, and cayenne pepper in a bowl. Preheat oven to 350.
- Grease a cookie sheet with a thin film of olive oil.
- Stuff the squash blossoms with the mozzarella - sundried tomato - raisin mixture, twist the ends and tuck them under, placing them on cookie sheet.
- Bake for ten to twelve minutes, then drizzle with walnut oil and salt to taste.

266. Roasted Sungold And Pear Tomatoes With Fontina And Thyme

Serving: Serves 4 | Prep: | Cook: | Ready in:

Ingredients

- 2 heaping cupfuls of little tomatoes (slice before measuring)
- 2 cloves garlic, peeled and chopped
- 1 tablespoon fresh thyme leaves, divided

- 2 tablespoons olive oil
- 2 cups Fontina cheese, cubed (make sure it's Italian Fontina)

Direction

- Preheat oven to 425 degrees F.
- Spread the sliced tomatoes out in a baking dish (I like to use a cast-iron skillet). Add the garlic and 1.5 teaspoons of the thyme leaves to the pan with the tomatoes, and drizzle with the olive oil.
- Place in oven and allow the tomatoes to roast for 20 minutes.
- Remove tomatoes from oven and carefully (because the pan will be very hot) add the cubes of fontina all around the roasted tomatoes. Return the baking pan or skillet to the oven for about 5 minutes, until the cheese is fully melted and bubbly.
- Scatter the rest of the thyme leaves over the cheese, along with a pinch of fine sea salt and a bit of fresh pepper, if you like. Serve hot with your favorite bread or crackers.

267. Roasted Vegetable, Goat Cheese, And Spinach Quesadilla With Spicy Tomato Jam

Serving: Serves 2 | Prep: | Cook: | Ready in:

Ingredients

- 2 large whole wheat tortillas (I used a sprouted whole grain)
- small eggplant, cut in ¼ inch slices
- 1 small patty pan, yellow or zucchini squash, cut in thin slices
- 1 pepper (green, red or Italian frying pepper) cut in big chunks and seeded
- 2 tablespoons olive oil
- 1 clove garlic, minced
- 1 teaspoon sea salt
- 4 leaves fresh basil, torn
- 2 ounces fresh goat cheese (chevre)
- 2 tablespoons grated parmesan or romano cheese
- 2-3 tablespoons spicy tomato jam (or scant 1 Tbsp harissa)

Direction

- Place the vegetables on a flat oiled baking sheet. Brush the veggie slices with a mixture of the olive oil, garlic and salt.
- Roast at 400 until tops are browned, about 30 minutes. Flip, brush again, and roast another 20-30 minutes. Remove from pan and cool slightly.
- Heat a large skillet over medium heat and add one tortilla (no oil needed in the pan) Arrange the vegetables on top in a layer, sprinkle with chopped basil.
- Top with goat cheese, then a layer of the baby spinach, then sprinkle with the parmesan cheese.
- Spread the second tortilla with the tomato jam and then place the second tortilla on top, jam facing down. And cook until bottom tortilla is browning and getting crispy, pressing down with your hand or a spatula to make things stick together.
- Carefully flip the quesadilla to brown the other side. Remove to a plate and cut into four wedges (I use a pizza cutter for this).
- Eat one or two wedges hot today, and eat the rest cold or reheated tomorrow for lunch

268. Rosemary Cherries

Serving: Serves 1 | Prep: | Cook: | Ready in:

Ingredients

- Rosemary Cherry Compote
- 5 cherries, diced
- 1 tablespoon olive oil
- 2 teaspoons rosemary
- Parfait with Granola
- 1 cup (or however much you desire) yogurt

- 1 tablespoon (or however much you desire) your favorite granola

Direction

- Place olive oil and rosemary in a pan on the stove turned on high
- Add diced cherries after a minute or so and immediately turn down the heat
- Let sauté for a minute or two, stirring occasionally, until the fruit is soft and all is very fragrant
- Turn off the heat
- While olive oil still bubbles in the pan, cooling, spoon desired amount of yogurt into a bowl and add rosemary cherries either on top or in between two layers of yogurt
- Sprinkle desired amount of granola over all! Enjoy!

269. Sage + Prosciutto Tartines

Serving: Makes about 2 cups | Prep: | Cook: | Ready in:

Ingredients

- 1 cup packed sage leaves
- 3/4 cup toasted walnuts
- 3-4 ounces prosciutto (I used sliced)
- 1 cup grated parmesan
- 5 cloves of garlic, roughly chopped
- 3/4 cup olive oil
- Juice from half a lemon
- 1 pinch crushed red pepper flakes
- Kosher or sea salt, to taste
- Freshly ground black pepper, to taste
- Baguette or sourdough boule, to serve

Direction

- Add the garlic to a food processor or blender and pulse until it's nicely minced, about 20 seconds.
- Roughly chop the sage, walnuts, and prosciutto. Add them to the food processor with the red pepper flakes and blend until the mixture is coarsely and evenly chopped.
- Add the lemon juice and start the food processor. Add the olive oil in a slow, steady stream.
- Once all of the olive oil is in, add the parmesan and blend until just incorporated.
- To serve, toast or grill sliced of your bread. (If using a pan, brush both sides of the bread with a little oil.) Once they come off the grill or pan, rub the top side with a garlic clove cut in half. Sprinkle with salt and pepper. Spread each slice with pesto and garnish with a light dusting of lemon zest and parmesan. Now tuck in and enjoy.

270. Salad ABC Apples, Bacon, Cumin Cheese

Serving: Serves 4 | Prep: | Cook: | Ready in:

Ingredients

- ABC with lime cream dressing
- 2 apples, golden delicious or Jonagolds, washed & dried
- 12 rashers (smoky) bacon, fried till crisp and then left to cool and then roughly chopped
- 75-100g young (cumin) gouda or edam cheese, cut into small cubes
- 1 teaspoon whole cumin, lightly toasted if you can't find cumin cheese
- 1/3 cup of currants or dried blueberries
- 1/3 cup of pecans, chopped
- To serve, large lettuce leaves for cups
- Lime cream dressing (recipe follows)
- Lime cream dressing
- 2 tablespoons of (Hellmans) mayonnaise
- 1/3 - 1/2 cup of pouring/single cream
- Microplaned zest of 1 lime
- Salt and freshly ground coarse black pepper, to taste

Direction

- ABC with lime cream dressing
- Remove the apple core and chop into small chunks. Place in a bowl. Add the bacon, cumin cheese, currant and pecans and toss till well combined. If you can't find cumin cheese, add the toasted cumin seeds when mixing in the bacon and other ingredients.
- Drizzle with dressing and stir again to combine. Scoop into lettuce cups and enjoy
- Lime cream dressing
- Put the mayonnaise in a small bowl. Whisk in the cream till you get a pouring consistency which should be a bit thicker than the cream.
- Add the lime zest to the cream mixture and stir in. Season to taste with salt and black pepper. Ready for some apples!

271. Salted Pumpkin Caramels

Serving: Makes 64, 1-inch caramels | Prep: | Cook: | Ready in:

Ingredients

- 2/3 cup unsalted pepitas
- 1 1/2 cups heavy cream
- 2/3 cup pumpkin puree
- 1 teaspoon pumpkin pie spice
- 2 cups white sugar
- 1/2 cups light corn syrup
- 1/3 cup good maple syrup
- 1/4 cup of water
- 4 tablespoons unsalted butter, cut in chunks
- 1 teaspoon lemon juice
- 3/4 teaspoon fleur de sel

Direction

- Dry toast the pepitas in a skillet until they start to pop.
- Line the bottom and the sides of an 8-in square glass pan with parchment. Butter the parchment on the sides of the pan. Evenly spread out the toasted pepitos on the bottom of the pan, on top of the parchment.
- In a saucepan, combine heavy cream, pumpkin puree and spices. Get this mixture quite warm, but not boiling. Set aside.
- In a second heavy bottomed pan, with sides at least 4 inches high, combine the sugar, both syrups and water. Stir until the sugars are melted. Then let it boil until it reaches 244 degrees (the soft ball point on a candy thermometer). Then very carefully add the cream and pumpkin mixture, and slowly bring this mixture to 240 degrees as registered on a on a candy thermometer. This can take a while -- like 30 minutes -- but don't leave the kitchen, watch it carefully and stir it more frequently once it hits 230 degrees to keep it from burning at the bottom of the pan.
- As soon as it reaches the 240, pull it off the heat and stir in the butter and lemon juice. Stir vigorously so that butter is fully incorporated.
- Pour the mixture into the prepared pan. Let cool 30 minutes and sprinkle the salt over the top. Let the caramels fully set (at least 2 hours) before using a hot knife to cut them into 1-inch squares and wrapping them individually in waxed paper.

272. Savory Buckwheat Crepes

Serving: Serves 4-6 | Prep: | Cook: | Ready in:

Ingredients

- For the crepe batter
- 1/2 cup buckwheat flour
- 2/3 cup whole milk
- 2 large eggs
- 1 tablespoon butter, melted
- 1/2 teaspoon salt
- For the filling
- 2 tablespoons olive oil, divided
- Kosher salt
- 1 pound chicken thighs

- 1 large red onion, thinly sliced
- 2 garlic cloves, minced
- 1 bunch asparagus, end trimmed, cut on the bias into 1/2 inch pieces
- 2 cups gruyere cheese, shredded
- 1 tablespoon butter, for greasing the pan
- 2 scallions, chopped, as garnish

Direction

- For the crepe batter
- Combine flour, milk, eggs, butter, and salt in a blender. Blend on high for 1 minute.
- For the filling
- Season chicken thighs generously with salt. Heat 1 tablespoon olive oil in a large pan over medium heat. Add chicken and cook until it starts to brown, turning occasionally, until it's cooked through, about 10 minutes. Transfer chicken to a cutting board and let cool slightly. Once cool, shred with forks.
- Add remaining 1 tablespoon olive oil to pan. Turn heat to medium high and add red onion. Cook until it softens, about 5 minutes, then stir in garlic and asparagus, and a pinch of salt. Cook for an additional 5 minutes.
- To assemble the crepes, divide filling evenly among crepes. Fold edges over the center. Place folded crepes back into pan to allow cheese to melt for about 1 minute. Garnish with scallions and serve immediately.

273. Savory Crêpes SuzetteLa

Serving: Serves 4 | Prep: 0hours30mins | Cook: 0hours30mins | Ready in:

Ingredients

- 2 eggs
- 3/4 cup all-purpose flour
- 1/2 cup milk
- 1/8 teaspoon salt
- 1/3 cup cold water
- 1 tablespoon peanut oil or vegetable oil
- 1 1/2 tablespoons melted unsalted butter
- 6 ounces diced ham
- 6 ounces sliced Gruyère cheese
- 1 cup spinach leaves
- 1 ripe tomato, sliced into small pieces
- 3 egg yolks
- 1/2 lemon, juiced
- 1/2 cup soft unsalted butter
- 1 teaspoon cold water
- 1 teaspoon salt
- 1 teaspoon white pepper
- 1/8 teaspoon cayenne pepper
- 1/2 cup chopped chives
- 1/2 cup Parmigiano Reggiano, grated

Direction

- In a medium bowl, whisk together the eggs, flour, milk, and 1/8 t salt until smooth.
- Whisk in the 1/3 c water, oil and 1 T melted butter.
- Heat a pan or a nonstick skillet and rub with a little butter. Tilt the skillet to distribute the butter evenly.
- Add about 2 tbsp. of batter (roughly a ladleful, enough to thinly cover the entire pan). Tilt the skillet to distribute the batter evenly.
- Cook over medium heat until the edges of the crêpe curl up and start to brown, around 45 seconds.
- Flip the crêpe (using either a spatula or your fingers, or just a quick upward flick in the pan) and cook for another 10 seconds, until a few brown spots appear on the bottom.
- Place the crêpe on a baking sheet or plate.
- Repeat with remaining batter to make 6-10 crêpes. You may need to butter the skillet a few times as time progresses. As the pan heats over time, remove it from burner and add/swirl the new batter while the pan is off the heat. Then return it to the burner.
- Hollandaise sauce: Whisk together egg yolks, lemon juice, and 1 t cold water, in a saucepan over low heat.
- Soften 1/2 c butter in another saucepan over low heat, or microwave it.

- By spoonfuls, add the soft butter to the egg mixture, whisking constantly to incorporate each addition. As the emulsion forms, add the butter in slightly larger amounts, always whisking until fully absorbed. Continue adding butter until the sauce has thickened to the desired consistency.
- To keep the eggs from overcooking and separating from the butter, reduce the heat along the way, frequently move the pan off the burner for a few seconds, and then back on. If the butter and egg begin to separate, remove from heat, add a splash of cold water, and whisk briskly.
- Whisk in the salt, cayenne pepper and white pepper. Taste the sauce and adjust the seasoning with lemon juice, salt and pepper. Use immediately or keep warm, to be used within an hour or so.
- Assembling the savory crêpes: Preheat oven to 350F degrees.
- Fold each crêpe in half. Place about 1 ounce each of ham and Gruyere cheese, several spinach leaves, and a few tomato slices onto the bottom half of each folded crêpe. Cover the mixture with the top half of the crêpe.
- Sprinkle grated Parmigiano-Reggiano on top.
- Place the crepes on a baking sheet and warm in the preheated oven for 5 to 10 minutes or until the cheese is melted.
- Serve immediately with a drizzle of Hollandaise sauce, garnished with chopped herbs (chives are great!).

274. Savory Lokshen Kugel (Noodle Pudding)

Serving: Serves 8 | Prep: | Cook: |Ready in:

Ingredients

- • 1 pound wide egg noodles
- • 6 tablespoons unsalted butter, softened
- • 4 large eggs
- • 2 cups whole milk smooth Farmers' or Ricotta cheese
- • 1 cup sour cream
- • 2 teaspoons kosher salt
- • 1/2 teaspoon white pepper
- • 1/4 teaspoon freshly grated nutmeg
- • 1/2 teaspoon cinnamon
- • 1 tablespoon flat leave parsley or basil, coarsely chopped (optional)
- • Zest of 1 large lemon

Direction

- Preheat oven to 350 degrees F. Cook noodles in a large pan of boiling salted water until tender but not mushy. Drain well in a colander and toss with butter in a bowl.
- While noodles are cooking beat eggs, salt, pepper, nutmeg and cinnamon until light and foamy with a mixer in a large mixing bowl.
- Add sour cream, cheese and lemon zest, while continuing beating until the mixture is homogeneous. Fold in noodles and herbs, if using.
- Transfer to a buttered deep baking dish and bake in middle of oven until firm, nicely browned and puffed, 50 minutes to 1 hour.
- Serve hot or at room temperature with sour cream.

275. Savory Mushroom Bread Pudding

Serving: Serves 4 | Prep: 0hours0mins | Cook: 0hours0mins |Ready in:

Ingredients

- 3 cups heaped with 1/2-inch bread cubes (about 6 ounces), I used challah
- 1 tablespoon olive oil
- 1 teaspoon butter, plus more for the baking dish
- 1 cup chopped white or yellow onion
- 1 medium garlic clove, minced

- 8 ounces Baby Bella mushrooms, or brown button mushrooms*, cut into pieces about the same size as the bread cubes
- 1 splash white vermouth, about 2 tablespoons
- 2 teaspoons chopped fresh marjoram leaves
- 2 large eggs
- 3/4 cup heavy cream, half-and-half, or whole milk
- 1/2 cup chicken or turkey stock, preferable homemade
- 3/4 cup shredded, aged, white Cheddar cheese, divided
- Kosher salt
- Freshly ground black pepper

Direction

- Place the cubed bread on a sheet pan and toast in a 350° F oven until somewhat dried, but not brown. Alternately, you can leave the bread out to dry overnight. It will lose some of its volume, but that's okay. Set aside.
- Set a 10-inch skillet over medium-high heat and add the olive oil and butter to the pan. When the butter has melted add the chopped onion and a good pinch of salt. Cook until the onion begins to soften and brown a little at the edges. Add the minced garlic and stir until it is fragrant, then add the chopped mushrooms. Cook and stir until the mushrooms brown and give off some liquid. Add the vermouth and cook until the liquid reduces to a glaze. Stir in the marjoram and check the mixture for seasoning, adding more salt (if necessary) and some pepper. Remove from the heat and set aside.
- Butter a 1 1/2-quart casserole or gratin dish. In a medium bowl, beat the eggs together with the cream and chicken stock. Add 1/2 cup of the shredded cheese and 1/2 teaspoon of salt. Taste the custard mixture and adjust the seasoning to your liking with additional salt and freshly ground black pepper. Fold the dried bread cubes and the mushroom mixture into the custard, pressing the bread down into the liquid. Let stand while you preheat the oven.
- Preheat the oven to 350° F. Place a rack in the lower third of the oven. When the oven is heated, transfer the bread and vegetable mixture to the prepared baking dish. Press the bread down into the custard and smooth the top surface a little; sprinkle on the remaining 1/4 cup shredded cheese.
- Place in the oven and bake for 30 to 45 minutes, or until the top is handsomely golden brown and the custard is set. The baking time will depend on the depth of the baking dish you have chosen. Serve hot and make sure every diner gets a portion of the crusty top. Leftovers can be refrigerated, tightly covered for 2 to 3 days.
- *If you have wild mushrooms available, you can substitute them for part of the total weight of the mushrooms.

276. Savory Baked Breakfast Stack

Serving: Serves 1 | Prep: | Cook: | Ready in:

Ingredients

- For the stack
- 1/2 cup cooked polenta or grits (can be leftover, can be flavored with any savory spice, herb or cheese)
- 2 eggs
- 1 tablespoon rendered bacon fat or melted butter
- 2 ounces cooked meat (diced bacon, crumbled sausage, cubed ham, shredded pork or chicken)
- 1/4 cup white sauce, recipe follows
- 3 tablespoons grated cheese of your choice
- Salt and pepper, to taste
- White sauce
- 1 tablespoon butter
- 1 tablespoon all-purpose flour
- 1/2 cup milk
- salt and pepper to taste

- 1/2 teaspoon paprika
- 4 tablespoons grated cheese, optional

Direction

- Preheat oven to 325. Smooth polenta or grits in the bottom of a 2-cup ramekin or ovenproof bowl. Break two eggs into a separate bowl, and gently slide them atop polenta or grits. Salt and pepper to taste (take into account seasonings in meat). Drizzle eggs with bacon fat or butter, and sprinkle with meat.
- Melt butter in small saucepan; add flour and seasonings and stir until flour begins to turn golden and smell nutty. Add milk and stir until smooth; remove from heat and add cheese, if using.
- Pour white sauce into ramekins, and top with remaining grated cheese. (Note: If you don't want to bother with making white sauce, this is almost as good with just some grated cheese sprinkled over the egg and meat.)
- Bake for approximately 12 minutes, long enough to heat everything through, set the whites and leave the yolk runny, or longer if for some odd reason you like a hard yolk.

277. Savory Buttermilk Brioche With A Pear, Rosemary & Meat Filling

Serving: Makes 1 loaf 25x8 cm | Prep: | Cook: | Ready in:

Ingredients

- for the dough:
- 250 grams AP wheat flour + some for kneading
- 1 teaspoon dry yeast
- 2-3 pinches salt
- 1 teaspoon sugar
- 100 milliliters buttermilk
- 50 grams butter, melted and at room temperature
- 2 eggs
- 1 egg yolk for glaze
- some sea salt / fleur de sel to sprinkle
- 1 handful sesame seeds to cover buttered baking tray (optional)
- for the filling:
- 250 grams meat from raw coarse pork sausage
- 1/2-1 pear (ripe, but firm)
- 1 tablespoon balsamico bianco vinegar
- 1 tablespoon finely chopped fresh rosemary
- 2 spring onions, chopped
- 2 slices bacon or other raw ham, finely chopped
- 10 grams pistaccios, coarsely chopped
- 1 egg

Direction

- In a large bowl, mix flour, yeast, buttermilk and eggs with a fork and let stand for 15 min.
- Melt butter and let cool. Butter baking tray, dust with flour and/or sesame seeds.
- Form dough to a rough rectangle and fold all sides towards the middle, to obtain a smaller rectangle. Folded sides down, place into the bowl again and let prove for another hour.
- Prepare the filling while the dough is rising: marinade diced and peeled pear with rosemary and balsamico bianco vinegar for 15 minutes.
- In a medium pan, fry sliced ham and chopped spring onions in a teaspoon of butter at high heat, for about 3 minutes, until golden and crispy. Remove from heat, add sausage meat (skin removed), and incorporate well with a fork or your hands. Fold in egg, pistachios, and marinated pear.
- Roll the dough in rectangular shape to fit your baking tray. Place filling into the middle and seal with your hands. Let prove again in the baking tray for 45-60 minutes. Glaze with egg yolk, sprinkle with salt.
- Bake in the preheated oven at 175°C for 40 minutes. Best served fresh from the oven, but also lukewarm or cold.

278. Savory Waffles With Goat Cheese And Lardons

Serving: Makes 10 waffles | Prep: | Cook: | Ready in:

Ingredients

- 2.5 tablespoons butter
- 170 milliliters Milk
- 1 cup flour
- 2 teaspoons baking powder
- 2 eggs
- lardon/baking strip
- 1/3 goat cheese log, cut into dices
- 1 handful chives, finely chopped

Direction

- Fry the bacon strips in a pan and strain on paper towel.
- Melt the butter and heat the milk in a saucepan, do not boil.
- In a bowl, combine flour and baking power. Add the egg yolks and stir. Add the butter/milk mixture a little bit at a time, stirring constantly.
- Beat the egg whites until stiff and careful fold into the waffle dough.
- Add the bacon strips, crumbled coat cheese and chives. Do not mix too much. Make the waffles in your waffle maker, you should have about 10.

279. Sexy Spinach Dip

Serving: Makes 16 ounces | Prep: | Cook: | Ready in:

Ingredients

- 8 ounces Cream Cheese (Soft)
- 8 ounces Sour Cream
- 2 ounces Pimentos (Drained)
- 2 Garlic Cloves (Minced)
- 1/2 Medium Onion (Chopped)
- 9 ounces Spinach (Thawed, Drained & Water Squeezed Out)
- 8 or more ounces Mozzarella Cheese (Reserve about ¼ cup for top)
- about 5 ounces Parmesan Cheese (Reserve about ¼ cup for top)
- Salt & Pepper (To Taste)
- Paprika

Direction

- Pre-heat oven to 350 degrees.
- Spray 8 x 8 casserole dish with cooking oil and set aside.
- In a large bowl, beat cream cheese with a hand mixer or mix with a spoon. If it is not soft enough, microwave for 15 seconds.
- Add Spinach and stir. Mix in all other ingredients and pour into the dish.
- Cover with remaining cheese.
- Sprinkle paprika on top.
- Bake 30 minutes or when cheese is melted and golden.
- Serve hot with tortilla chips or bread.

280. Shavuot Ricotta Pastries And Potato Cheese Galette

Serving: Serves makes 18 pastries and 2 gallettes. | Prep: | Cook: | Ready in:

Ingredients

- For Ricotta pastries:
- • 1 1/2 cups fresh homemade ricotta or prepared (drained)
- • 1/2 cup rice cooked in milk
- • 1/2 cup granulated sugar
- • 1 egg yolk plus 1 whole egg for eggwash
- • 3/4 cup raisins
- • Zest of 1 orange
- • 1 package Puff pastry (2 sheets)
- For the Gallette:
- • 2 large russet potatoes (baked) and grated

- • 1 packed cup White Sharp Cheddar (shredded)
- • 1 packed cup Gruyere (shredded)
- • 1/2 cup Parmesan (shredded)
- • 1/4 teaspoon freshly grated nutmeg
- • 1/2 teaspoon freshly minced rosemary
- • 3 tablespoons sour cream
- • 1 egg for the eggwash
- • 1 package Puff pastry (2 sheets)

Direction

- To make Ricotta Pastries: In a mixing bowl stir ricotta with sugar, mix in egg yolk; then add rice and orange zest. On a lightly floured board roll out one sheet of pastry dough to about 12/14 rectangle.
- Spread half of the ricotta mixture all over the sheet, living 1/2- inch border only in the upper side (from you) of the pastry and brush the border with egg wash. Scatter half of the raisins on top of the ricotta mixture and roll it up tightly like a jellyroll (starting with the longer side).
- Reaped the same process with the second sheet of pastry and ricotta filling. Brash egg wash all over the rolls, transfer them to a large, lightly floured, cutting board, seam side down. Place into freezer for 20-25 minutes to tighten up, (it is easier to cut them).
- Preheat the oven to 375 degrees F. Line 2 cookie sheets with parchment paper.
- When ready to bake, get the rolls out and cut them in 1-inch slices. Place each slice (standing up) on the cooking sheets, brash the top and some more the sides with egg wash and transfer to the oven.
- Bake for about 25- 30 minutes or until the tops and the sides of the pastries are golden brown. Rotate the sheets half way of the baking from the lower rack to the upper. Cool for 10 minutes, arrange on a platter and dust with powdered sugar.
- To make the Gallette: Preheat the oven to 375 degrees F. Line 2 cookie sheets with parchment paper.

- Combine all the ingredients in a mixing bowl. On a lightly floured board, roll out one sheet of pastry dough to about 12/14 rectangle.
- Spread half of the mixture all over the sheet, living 1/2- inch borders all around the pastry and brush them with egg wash. Melt 2 tablespoons of butter and mix it with 1/2 a cup of Panko breadcrumbs. Sprinkle half of breadcrumbs on top.
- Reaped the same with the second sheet of pastry, potato-cheese filling and bread crumbs. Bake for about 25- 30 minutes or until the tops and the sides of the pastries are golden brown.
- Rotate the sheets half way of the baking time from the lower rack to the upper. Cool to room temperature, cut into triangle slices. Serve with sour cream mixed with chives, freshly chopped dill, some salt and a pinch or more of cayenne pepper.

281. Sheet Pan Broccoli Cheese Rice Casserole

Serving: Serves 4 to 6 | Prep: 0hours15mins | Cook: 1hours0mins | Ready in:

Ingredients

- 1 stick unsalted butter
- 1 red onion, diced
- 1 teaspoon granulated sugar
- 4 ounces bread, such as brioche, cut into bite-size pieces
- 2 cups cooked, short-grain white rice
- 20 ounces frozen broccoli florets
- 8 ounces shredded sharp cheddar cheese
- 8 ounces sour cream
- 1 cup whole milk
- 2 teaspoons kosher salt, plus more as needed
- Olive oil, for greasing pan
- 1/4 cup panko bread crumbs
- Parmesan, for grating over

Direction

- Preheat oven to 400°F.
- Melt the butter in a large nonstick skillet, then sauté onion with a pinch of salt and teaspoon of sugar for a good 15 to 20 minutes, until caramelized. Add bread to the buttery onions and sauté for another 10 minutes, until slightly toasted. Set aside.
- In a very large bowl, toss together the rice, frozen broccoli, cheese, sour cream, milk, 2 teaspoons salt, and buttery onion-bread mixture until well mixed. Spread into an olive oil-greased half sheet pan, then sprinkle top with panko and a light dusting of Parmesan.
- Bake for 30 minutes, or until bubbly and slightly browned at the edges.
- Do Ahead: You can prep the casserole completely in advance and freeze it or fridge it. Just add a few minutes to the bake time when you're ready to cook it.

282. Shiitake Mushroom Enchiladas

Serving: Makes 8 enchiladas | Prep: | Cook: |Ready in:

Ingredients

- 1 ear of corn, kernels removed and dry roasted
- 8 corn tortillas (6" diameter)
- 1 cup grated pepper jack cheese
- 1 small white onion
- 3 cloves of garlic, minced
- 3 tablespoons chopped cilantro
- 1/2 pound shiitake mushrooms, washed, stemmed, and thinly sliced
- 1 large poblano pepper
- 2 tablespoons butter
- 2 tablespoons flour
- 1 cup milk
- 1/2 teaspoon chili powder
- pinch cayenne pepper
- oil for cooking
- salt and pepper to taste

Direction

- First, dry roast the corn by cooking it in a dry pan over medium high heat until it starts to turn golden on the outside (about 8-10 minutes). No oil is necessary. Set aside. Next, make the mushroom filling. Heat some cooking oil in a large skillet over medium heat, then add 2/3 of the chopped onion. Cook until they are just softened, about three minutes, then add 2 of the garlic cloves and cook another minute. Mix in the mushrooms and cilantro and season with salt and pepper. Cook until all the water has been cooked out of the mushrooms and they have started to brown (about 10 minutes). Remove from heat and set aside.
- To make the sauce, you get to have a little fun with fire. Charring the poblano pepper over (or under) a direct flame makes the skin blister and easy to remove. It is edible, but it's a little bit tough so especially in this application, where the chile is blended into the sauce, it's better to remove it. Turn on the broiler to high and place the poblano pepper as close to the flame as possible (exactly how you do this will depend on your broiler set-up). It's probably a good idea to put the chile either on a baking sheet or a piece of foil so that you can move it in and out easily. Keep an eye on the chile and as soon as the skin starts to blister and bubble, use tongs to turn it over and expose another side to the flame. Keep rotating the pepper until most of the skin is blistered. Transfer it to a plastic or paper bag and close the bag; let it sit for about 10 minutes.
- Remove the pepper from the bag and peel off the skin with your fingers. Roughly chop the chile and set aside.
- To make the sauce, melt the butter in a small saucepan over medium-low heat. Add the remaining 1/3 of the onion and let it cook until softened (3 minutes), then add the remaining 1 clove of garlic and cook one more minute. Mix in the flour and cook until the mixture is bubbling (2 minutes).

- Whisk in the milk and turn up the heat to medium. Continue stirring until the milk has thickened. Pour the mixture into a food processor and add the poblano chile, chile powder, cayenne, and salt and pepper. Blend until smooth.
- Finally, put everything together. Preheat the oven to 375 degrees and get out a baking dish (our 8 inch square was a little too small; we had to put some overflow enchiladas in another little dish so if you have something bigger use that). Spoon some of the poblano sauce into the bottom of the dish (just enough to lightly cover the bottom and keep the enchiladas from sticking).
- Divide the mushrooms into 8 portions and scoop one portion into a tortilla. Add a light sprinkling of cheese (to hold everything together), then roll the tortilla and place it in the baking dish with the seam down. Continue doing this until you've filled all the tortillas, packing them in side by side. Spoon the rest of the sauce over the enchiladas, then sprinkle the corn on top and cover with cheese. Bake until the cheese is bubbling and beginning to brown (about 30 minutes). Serve with refried beans or rice or whatever catches your fancy.

283. Shish Taouk With Toum (Chicken Kebabs With Garlic Sauce)

Serving: Serves 4 | Prep: | Cook: | Ready in:

Ingredients

- For the shish taouk
- 1 cup Greek-style yogurt
- 3 cloves garlic, finely minced
- 1 tablespoon tomato paste
- 3 tablespoons lemon juice
- 1/2 tablespoon za'atar
- 1/2 cup extra-virgin olive oil
- 1/2 teaspoon kosher salt
- 1/4 teaspoon ground coriander
- 1/8 teaspoon pimentón (smoked paprika)
- 1 pound boneless, skinless chicken breasts or thighs
- 12 crimini mushrooms
- 12 peppadew peppers
- 12 cipollini onions
- 2 zucchini, cut into large chunks
- 2 blocks of halloumi cheese, cut into large chunks
- 2 lemons for grilling, cut into rounds or wedges
- 4 rounds of fresh Syrian bread
- 1 bunch fresh thyme, finely chopped
- For the toum (garlic sauce)
- 6 cloves of garlic
- Juice of 1 lemon
- Large pinch of kosher salt
- 1 large egg white
- 2/3 cup canola oil
- Small bowl of ice water
- Up to 1/2 cup of high-quality mayonnaise

Direction

- The night before you want to cook: Mix the first 9 ingredients, from the yogurt to the pimentón, in a large bowl. Cut the chicken into medium-sized chunks, toss in the marinade, cover with plastic wrap, and refrigerate until ready to grill.
- To make the toum (garlic sauce), put the garlic cloves, the salt, and 1/4 of the lemon juice in a blender. Blend on medium speed until the garlic is chopped, scraping down the sides as necessary. With the blender still on medium speed, add the egg white through the feed tube and continue to blend. Add half the oil in a slow, thin stream. At this stage, the emulsification should have taken hold. Switch to a slow blend and slowly add the rest of the lemon juice. Add the rest of the oil in the same fashion.
- Add 1 or 2 tablespoons of ice water while still mixing on low. At this point you should have a sauce with the consistency of a light mayonnaise. Taste for salt and to check the

strength of the garlic flavor. If needed, either to thicken the sauce or to cut the raw garlic punch a bit, whisk in up to 1/2 cup of mayonnaise. Reserve the sauce for dressing your grilled shish taouk.
- When's your ready to make the kebabs, preheat your grill to medium-high heat.
- Place the onions in a pot of water and bring to a boil. Cook for about 5 minutes, to parboil the onions. Remove from the heat and rinse with cold water to cool. Peel and discard the skins and save the onions for grilling.
- Take the chunks of halloumi and zucchini, the onions, mushrooms, peppers, and lemon slices and toss them in a bowl. Drizzle with a little extra-virgin olive oil, and sprinkle with salt and pepper, toss to coat, then place each ingredient on its own metal or pre-soaked wooden skewers for grilling.
- Take the chicken from the fridge and skewer the chunks as you did the veggies. Season lightly with salt and pepper.
- Grill each skewer until it reaches your desired degree of doneness, remove to a platter, and tent with foil to keep warm until all the skewers are complete.
- To serve, place a mix of grilled ingredients on a round of warmed Syrian bread, top with a generous helping of toum, sprinkle with chopped fresh thyme, and squirt with a grilled lemon wedge. Devour at will.

284. Shrimp Cocktail Dip

Serving: Makes 2 cups | Prep: | Cook: |Ready in:

Ingredients

- 1/2 pound large shrimp, peeled and cleaned
- 1 cup cocktail sauce (homemade is better)
- 1/3 cup finely chopped scallions
- 1/2 cup freshly grated Parmesan cheese
- 1/3 cup minced green or red pepper or combination of both
- 1 pound softened cream cheese

Direction

- Add the shrimp into boiling salted water and cook for 1 to 2 minutes until they turn bright pink
- Drain and chop the shrimp
- Combine the cocktail sauce, scallions, grated cheese, peppers and cream cheese
- Fold in the shrimp and refrigerate
- Serve with pita, celery sticks, carrots, or any other vegetable you like.
- Can also be used as a spread for sandwiches

285. Simple Cheese Souffle

Serving: Serves 1 7" souffle | Prep: | Cook: |Ready in:

Ingredients

- parmesan cheese, finely grated
- 4 egg whites
- 3 egg yolks
- 3 tablespoons butter, melted
- 3 tablespoons flour
- 1 cup milk
- 7 tablespoons gruyere, grated

Direction

- Preheat oven to 400. Butter a 7" soufflé dish and then toss finely grated parmesan cheese over the butter.
- Using a whisk, or an electric mixer fitted with the whisk attachment, whip the egg whites until they form stiff peaks. Then, in a separate bowl, beat the yolks until they are smooth.
- Melt the butter over low-heat. Add the flour to melted butter and blend with a whisk. Add the milk and keep stirring the mixture until it is thickened and smooth. Bring to a boil and then remove it from the heat.
- Once the mixture is off the heat add in the cheese and egg yolks. Then, fold the stiff egg whites into the white sauce and pour the

completed mixture into the buttered soufflé dish.
- Bake at 400 for 25-30 minutes, or until the soufflé has risen and set (it is no longer watery looking in the center and the edges are slightly browned). Serve immediately and enjoy.

286. Slow Cooker Cardamom Rice Pudding

Serving: Serves 10 | Prep: | Cook: | Ready in:

Ingredients

- 1/2 gallon half and half
- 3/4 cup short grained rice such as jasmine rice
- 6 green cardamoms, lightly bruised
- 3/4 cup raw turbinado or maple sugar (more to taste)
- 1/2 cup chopped nuts such as pistachios or pecans (optional)

Direction

- Add the half and half, rice and cardamoms and set the slow cooker to a 5 hour high cycle.
- After 2 hours, remove the cover and give the mixture a good stir ensuring that the rice mixes well with the milk and let it cook for another hour and a half.
- Stir the mixture well, at this point the rice should be fair soft and meshing into the milk. Stir in the sugar and let the rice pudding continue cooking until the cycle finishes.
- Stir well, discard the cardamoms if you wish. Let the pudding rest for at least 30 minutes. Garnish with the chopped nuts and serve this hot or cold depending on your preference.

287. Smoked Mackerel Pâté With Horseradish And Dill

Serving: Makes about 1 1/2 cups | Prep: | Cook: | Ready in:

Ingredients

- 8 ounces smoked mackerel (or trout), skin and bones removed
- 4 ounces cream cheese, room temperature
- 2 tablespoons finely grated fresh horseradish, plus extra for garnish
- 2 tablespoons freshly squeezed lemon juice
- 1 teaspoon freshly ground black pepper
- 1/4 cup chopped fresh dill
- Baguette slices
- Dill sprigs for garnish

Direction

- Combine the mackerel, cream cheese, horseradish, lemon juice and black pepper in bowl of food processor. Process until consistency is light and smooth. (If too thick, add additional lemon juice.) Refrigerate until serving. (May be prepared up to 4 hours in advance.) Just before serving, stir in chopped dill.
- To serve, smear on baguette slices. Sprinkle with fresh horseradish and garnish with a dill sprig.

288. Smoked Salmon Red Onion And Feta Cheese Fritatta

Serving: Serves 4 | Prep: | Cook: | Ready in:

Ingredients

- 3 ounces lox or lightly smoked salmon
- 6 eggs (preferably from pasture raised chickens)
- 2 tablespoons extra virgin olive oil
- 3 cloves garlic, chopped small

- 1/3 red onion, chopped small
- 1 green jalapeno pepper, seeded and chopped small
- 2 1/2 tablespoons capers, drained
- Splash of nonfat milk
- 3/4 cup crumbled feta cheese
- 1 red pepper flakes
- Several twists of freshly ground pepper
- 3 tablespoons parsley, chopped
- Some chives

Direction

- In a medium bowl, beat eggs, milk, black pepper and crumbled feta cheese together and set aside.
- Cut the lox into thin strips about 1 inch long.
- Lightly oil a 10" cast iron pan on sides and bottom over medium-low heat. Add onion and jalapeno and sauté for 2 minutes.
- Add the garlic, salmon and capers and cook another 2 minutes or until garlic just starts to get clear.
- Reduce to low heat and add the egg mixture stirring until the eggs cook on the bottom and sides.
- Place in a pre-heated broiler about 4 inches below the element. Cook until eggs are cooked on top, about 3 to 4 minutes.
- Remove hot iron pan from oven and place on hot pad or range until cool enough to eat. Cut frittata into quarters and place on warmed plates. Garnish with chopped parsley, parsley sprigs or chives. Serve with garlic bread, salt, fresh ground pepper and Tabasco sauce.

289. Snickers Protein Smoothie

Serving: Serves 1 | Prep: | Cook: |Ready in:

Ingredients

- 3/4 cup cottage cheese
- 1 scoop chocolate protein powder (** any combination of vanilla, caramel, and chocolate protein powders work well, depending on personal taste)
- 1 tablespoon unsweetened cocoa powder
- 2 tablespoons sugar-free chocolate coffee flavoring syrup
- 2 tablespoons sugar-free caramel coffee flavoring syrup
- 2 tablespoons PB2 (** or natural peanut butter)
- 1/2 teaspoon xanthan gum or 1/4 tsp chia seeds for thickening (optional)
- 1/4-1/2 cups water (** adjust for desired thickness)
- 5-10 ice cubes (** again, adjust for desired thickness .. more ice=thicker)
- Optional toppings: sugar-free chocolate chips, chopped peanuts

Direction

- Toss everything but the ice and thickener into your blender & start it. Add the ice a cube at a time and thicken to taste

290. Soft Scrambled Eggs With Ricotta And Chives

Serving: Serves 1 | Prep: | Cook: |Ready in:

Ingredients

- 1 teaspoon butter
- 2 eggs, lightly beaten
- 2 tablespoons good quality ricotta (homemade or store-bought)
- 2 teaspoons chopped chives, or to taste
- 5 to 6 sprigs pea tendrils (optional)
- 1 thick slice of good bread (such as sourdough)
- Sea salt, to taste

Direction

- Melt the butter in a small saucepan or sauté pan over low heat, or in the top of a double boiler over barely simmering water.
- Add the eggs and a pinch of salt. Stir frequently over very low heat until eggs are just set, yet still very soft. Of course, if you like your eggs scrambled at a different consistency, forge ahead!
- Meanwhile, toast the bread. Once the bread has cooled slightly, spread on a thick layer of ricotta.
- When the eggs are scrambled to your desired level of doneness, take them off the heat and spoon them on top of the ricotta and toast. Sprinkle with sea salt and top with chives. I also added some pea tendrils I had on hand, which added a lovely hint of spring to the dish.

291. Soufflé Omelet With Robiola And Sautéed Ramps

Serving: Serves 4 | Prep: | Cook: | Ready in:

Ingredients

- For the ramps
- 2 tablespoons unsalted butter
- 8 ounces ramps (or scallions) – root ends trimmed, stalks and leaves cut in 1/4" slices (4 cups)
- 1/8 teaspoon sea salt
- freshly ground black pepper to taste
- For the omelet
- 1 tablespoon unsalted butter
- 8 extra large eggs - separated
- 1/4 cup heavy cream
- 1/4 teaspoon sea salt
- freshly ground black pepper to taste
- 4 ounces Robiola (or young Camembert or Goat's Milk Brie) – cut in 1/8" slices

Direction

- Heat a large heavy-bottomed non-stick frying pan over medium-high heat and add the butter. As soon as the butter is melted, add the ramps. Stir well and sauté for 2 to 3 minutes until the ramps are wilted and have turned a shade darker. Add the salt and pepper, stir again and transfer to a bowl. Set pan aside until ready to make the omelet.
- Place the egg yolks, cream, salt and pepper in a large bowl and whisk until well blended. Set aside.
- Place the egg whites in the bowl of an electric mixer and beat at high speed until soft peaks form. Add the egg whites to the egg yolk mixture and carefully fold them in.
- Reheat frying pan over medium-high heat. When the pan is hot, add the butter. When the butter is melted, add the egg mixture. Reduce heat to medium/medium-high and cook the omelet for 2 to 3 minutes, until the eggs begin to set. Place the Robiola slices on top of the omelet and sprinkle the ramps evenly over the whole surface. Cook until the cheese begins to melt and the eggs are cooked to your taste (either runny or firmer), another 2 to 3 minutes. Gently fold the omelet in half and transfer to a serving platter.

292. Southwest Cottage Cheese Muffins

Serving: Makes 12 | Prep: | Cook: | Ready in:

Ingredients

- 4 eggs
- 3/4 cup liquid egg whites
- 1 cup cottage cheese (whole or 2%)
- 1/2 cup oat flour
- 1/2 cup shredded pepper jack cheese
- 1 green onion, chopped
- 1 bell pepper chopped, any color
- 1/2 teaspoon baking powder
- 1/4 teaspoon salt

Direction

- 1. Preheat oven to 375 and grease or line a muffin tin.
- Whisk together eggs and egg whites. Mix in the remaining ingredients.
- Divide mixture evenly among 12 muffin cups.
- Bake for 25-35 minutes, or until golden crust forms on the top and inserted toothpick comes out clean.

293. Southwest Quinoa Salad With Sweet & Spicy Honey Lime Dressing

Serving: Serves 6 | Prep: | Cook: |Ready in:

Ingredients

- 3 cups quinoa, cooked
- 14 ounces black beans, drained and rinsed
- 1 cup frozen corn, thawed
- 1 Jalapeno pepper, seeded and diced
- 1 roma tomato, chopped
- 1/2 small red onion, chopped
- 2 green onions, chopped
- 1 avocado, seeded and chopped
- 1/4 cup cilantro, roughly chopped
- 4 ounces crumbled queso fresco or feta cheese
- Dressing
- 1/2 cup freshly squeezed lime juice
- 1/4 cup extra virgin olive oil
- 2 tablespoons honey
- 1 teaspoon cumin
- 1/2 teaspoon black pepper
- 1/2 tablespoon salt

Direction

- Prepare quinoa according to package instructions. Set aside to cool. Remember to rinse quinoa in cold water prior to cooking.
- While quinoa is cooking, drain and rinse beans and thaw corn. Chop and prepare red pepper, jalapeno, tomato, red onion, green onion, avocado, and cilantro.
- Once quinoa is cool, combine with beans, corn, veggies, and cheese in a large mixing bowl. Toss to combine.
- Prepare dressing by combining lime juice, olive oil, honey, cumin, cayenne pepper, black pepper, and salt in a small bowl. Whisk until well combined.
- Pour dressing over quinoa and veggie mixture and stir to combine.
- Spoon into serving bowl. 1 serving equals roughly 1 cup.

294. Special Cheesy Pasta

Serving: Serves 4 | Prep: | Cook: |Ready in:

Ingredients

- 3 cups pasta
- 8 tablespoons butter
- 1 onion, sliced thin
- 4 pieces bacon
- 1 tablespoon bacon grease
- 1/4 cup all purpose flour
- 2 cups milk
- 1/2 cup cream
- 2 egg yolks
- 1/2 cup gruyere cheese
- 1/2 cup cheddar
- 1/2 cup parmesan cheese

Direction

- Pre-heat oven to 350. Make the white sauce using half of the butter
- Beat the egg yolks in a small bowl and stir in 1/4 cup of the sauce whisking all of the time. Add back into the white sauce.
- Add the cheeses to the sauce and cook until melted.
- Fry the bacon and then remove to a plate and chop.

- Add the remaining butter to the frying pan along with the tablespoon of grease from the fried bacon. Fry the onions in this until soft.
- Add fried onions and bacon to the sauce and season to taste.
- Cook the pasta for half the amount of time it says on the packet then add to the sauce.
- Put in an oven dish and bake for 15-20 mins.

295. Spiced Lamb Salad

Serving: Serves 4 | Prep: | Cook: | Ready in:

Ingredients

- 110 grams fresh hazlenuts
- 80 grams sesame seeds
- 2 tablespoons coriander seeds
- 2 tablespoons cumin seeds
- 2 teaspoons coarsely-ground black epper
- 1 teaspoon sea salt crystals
- zest and juice of 1 lemon
- 2 tablespoons Manuka honey
- 60 milliliters extra virgin olive oil
- sea salt and freshly ground black pepper
- 125 grams couscous
- 150 milliliters boiling water
- 1 tablespoon light olive oil or coconut oil
- 500 grams lean lamb fillet in one piece
- 1/4 watermelon, skinned, de-seeded and sliced or diced
- 150 grams Greek feta cheese, crudely crumbled
- small bag watercress (tough stalks removed)

Direction

- Dry fry the hazelnuts in a shallow sauté pan over a medium heat until they are golden brown and crunchy (watch them, they have a nasty habit of burning when you take your eye off them!)
- Immediately put them between a few sheets of kitchen roll and rub vigorously until most of the outer skins come off then transfer them to a mortar and pestle or grinder and bash/grind until they are coarsely chopped.
- In the same pan, toast the sesame seeds until golden before adding to the hazelnuts.
- In the same pan, toast the coriander and cumin seeds until they start to 'pop' before transferring them to a mortar and pestle or grinder and blitzing until they are finely crushed then add them to the hazelnut/sesame seed mix.
- Add the salt and pepper, mix well and set aside. Whisk the lemon zest, lemon juice, honey and the extra virgin olive oil in a bowl, season to taste and set aside.
- Put the couscous in a medium-sized bowl, gradually pour over the boiling water, mixing with a fork all the time, cover and leave for around 10 minutes.
- Heat the light olive oil or coconut oil in a sauté pan and over a relatively high heat, brown the lamb fillet on all sides before turning down the heat and continuing to cook for a further 5 minutes if you like it pink, 8 minutes if you like it medium and 10 minutes if you like it well-done. Turn the fillet regularly.
- Remove the lamb from the pan, spread the nut, seed and spice mix on a board and roll the lamb in it until it is well-coated before wrapping in foil to keep warm.
- Fork through the couscous to make sure all the grains are separated before adding the lemon/honey/oil mix and stirring to ensure it is well incorporated.
- Place a portion of couscous on each plate, top with the lamb (finely sliced) and arrange the feta, watermelon and watercress around the plate.
- NB: The nut, seed and spice mix will keep in the fridge in a sealed jar for a couple of weeks if you choose to make it beforehand or double the quantities and makes a delicious soup, stew, salad and open sandwich topping.

296. Spiced Plum Cheese Round

Serving: Serves 4 | Prep: | Cook: | Ready in:

Ingredients

- Spiced Plum Cheese Round
- 2 tablespoons maple syrup
- 1 tablespoon ginger wine or 1/2 teaspoon freshly grated ginger
- 1/8 teaspoon cardamom powder
- 1 teaspoon orange zest
- Pinch of cayenne pepper
- 2 plums (I used red plums), stoned and cut into eights
- 1 teaspoon fresh thyme leaves
- 1 portion Labneh (recipe below)
- thyme sprigs, for garnish
- flaked almonds, for garnish
- Labneh - Yogurt Cheese
- 3/4 cup Thick Greek or Turkish yogurt (not Greek-style)
- Pinch of salt

Direction

- Spiced Plum Cheese Round
- Preheat your oven to 250 deg C. Mix the maple syrup, ginger wine or grated ginger, cardamom powder, orange zest and pinch of cayenne pepper. Toss the plum eights in the maple syrup mix and place in a bowl that just contains the mix so they plums 'stew' in the juices while they bake.
- Place the plums in the center of the oven and bake 15 - 20 minutes or until soft.
- Remove from the oven and stir in the fresh thyme leaves, then leave to cool.
- When the plum mixture is cold, spread the Labneh halfway into the base of a 5-6 cm ring or use a ramekin and top the other half with the spiced plums. Return to the refrigerator till ready to serve.
- Serve with toasted flaked almonds and thyme sprigs
- Labneh - Yogurt Cheese
- Stir the yogurt well and season with a pinch of salt. Taste and adjust. You want a hint of the sea and not a gulp. The salt helps draw out the whey (think of cucumbers & aubergines).
- Place the yogurt in the center of a muslin/cheesecloth folded 4 times (or line a sieve with coffee filters). Gather up the ends of the cloth and tie up tight, gently forming a ball. The whey will begin to drip as soon as you begin.
- Pass a skewer through the tie/knot and hang over a deep bowl and refrigerate overnight.
- The next morning, much of the whey will have drained out leaving you creamy yogurt cheese. Keep the whey in the fridge and stir into your breakfast cereal, smoothies or back into yogurt or find out a myriad other ways to use it – it is rich in protein. Remember Little Miss Muffet?

297. Spicy Cheddar Cheese Crackers

Serving: Makes approx. 30 crackers | Prep: | Cook: | Ready in:

Ingredients

- 2 cups shredded sharp cheddar cheese
- 3/4 stick unsalted butter (room temp.)
- 1 tablespoon prepared ranch dressing
- 1/2 cup cream
- 1 1/2 cups all purpose flour
- 1/2 teaspoon cayenne pepper
- 1/2 tablespoon dried dill
- 1/2 tablespoon salt
- 1 teaspoon black pepper

Direction

- Pre-heat oven to 350 degrees.
- Combine dry ingredients in a mixing bowl or standing mixer, and add butter so you have a crumbly dough. Create a well in the middle and add the wet ingredients, including the

cheese. Fold the mixture together until a thick dough has formed.
- Line a baking sheet with parchment paper. With your hands, scoop out small chunks of the dough, roll into a ball, and flatten into a little cracker shape. Place on the parchment paper. Pop the crackers into the oven for about 35 minutes. Keep watching them to make sure they don't burn!

into the panko. Roll that bowl around too and finally remove, with a fork and set on a plate.
- Repeat this till you've used up all the rice. When you're all done, set the plate in the fridge and let it rest for half an hour or longer.
- While it is resting, set up to deep fry. When the oil is hot and a cube of bread browns in 30 seconds, fry the balls till golden brown. Remove with a slotted spoon and serve with a spicy tomato sauce

298. Spinach Arancini

Serving: Serves 4 | Prep: | Cook: | Ready in:

Ingredients

- 1 cup leftover risotto
- 1/3 cup cooked chopped spinach
- 1/2 cup seasoned all-purpose flour, to roll balls
- 1 egg, lightly beaten with 2 tablespoon of milk
- 1 cup Panko/fresh breadcrumbs
- Salt and pepper, to taste
- 25g fresh mozzarella, torn into small balls

Direction

- Mix the risotto rice and spinach together. Season to taste.
- Set up the conveyor belt of crumbing ingredients in individual bowls: seasoned flour in one, the egg and milk mixture in another and the breadcrumbs in a third. A tip for those who hate losing half their breadcrumbs to sticky fingers when dipping, flouring and crumbing stuff, like me - use a spoon, not your hands. You'll also see that you get a more even coating of flour, egg and panko.
- Using a teaspoon or tablespoon, scoop some risotto mix and put it in the flour. At this stage, put a mozzarella piece in the center of the ball.
- Using a spoon, dump it into the egg bowl and use a fork to gently roll around before putting

299. Spinach Balls With Mustard Sauce

Serving: Makes 70 pieces | Prep: | Cook: | Ready in:

Ingredients

- Spinach Balls
- 2 10-ounce packages frozen chopped spinach, thawed & squeezed dry
- 2 cups herb stuffing mix, crushed
- 1/2 cup unsalted butter, melted
- 1 cup firmly packed freshly grated Parmigiano-Reggianocheese
- 2 small green onions, finely chopped
- 3 large eggs
- Dash of freshly ground nutmeg
- Mustard Sauce (see below)
- Mustard Sauce
- 1/3 cup dry mustard (I use Coleman's)
- 1/2 cup white vinegar
- 1/4 cup sugar
- 1 large egg yolk

Direction

- Spinach Balls
- Combine all ingredients except mustard sauce, and mix well.
- Shape into 1-inch balls.
- Bake on ungreased baking sheet in a preheated 375 degree F. oven for 10 to 15 minutes.
- Mustard Sauce

- Combine mustard and vinegar. Cover and let stand at room temperature for 4 hours.
- Mix sugar and egg yolk in a small saucepan. Add mustard-vinegar mixture and cook over low heat, stirring constantly, until slightly thickened. Cover and chill.
- Serve at room temperature.

300. Spinach Gnocchi

Serving: Serves 6 | Prep: | Cook: | Ready in:

Ingredients

- 1 pound fresh spinach
- 2 cups fresh ricotta
- 1 cup grated parmigiano reggiano cheese
- 1/3 cup AP flour + more
- 2 eggs
- nutmeg
- 1/4 cup butter
- Bunch fresh sage
- salt
- pepper
- 1 tablespoon olive oil

Direction

- Bring a big pot of water to boil. Rinse spinach very very well and remove stems. Add 1 tablespoon of salt to the pot and boil spinach for 2 minutes until tender but crisp. Keep the boiling water and rinse them under cool water and drain them. Wring them out to remove all water.
- Chop spinach very thinly and put them in a mixing bowl. Add ricotta, eggs, flour, 2/3 cup Parmigiano reggiano, a pinch of salt, and a little grated nutmeg. Mix well with a fork to combine. Adjust salt to taste.
- Bring a tablespoonful of the mixture and form a ball with your hands. Flour the ball and keep aside. Repeat with all the mixture.
- Add another tablespoon salt and a tablespoon oil to the pot of boiling water (to avoid them to stick). Put the gnocchi into the pot and cook until they rise to the surface.
- In the meanwhile put a sauce pan over medium-low heat and melt the butter and sage be careful not to brown it.
- When gnocchi rise to surface, remove them from the water using a skimmer and put them into a serving dish. Pour melted butter on top and sprinkle the remaining Parmigiano reggiano and a little black pepper. Serve immediately.

301. Spinach And Ricotta Teacakes

Serving: Serves 15 teacakes | Prep: | Cook: | Ready in:

Ingredients

- 2 bags of baby spinach (6 oz each)
- 1 bunch dino kale, ends trimmed, cut in bite size pieces (or substitute with a 3rd bag of spinach)
- 16 ounces part skim ricotta
- 3 ounces spreadable goat cheese (we like Chavrie goat cheese with basil and roasted garlic)
- 2 eggs, lightly beaten
- Freshly ground black pepper
- 1/4 teaspoon crushed red pepper flakes
- 1 pinch salt (we like smoked salt)
- 1 pinch grated nutmeg
- 1 tablespoon each of freshly chopped chervil, dill, parsley
- 1/4 cup toasted pine nuts
- 1/2 cup grated pecorino romano (Parmesan would be great too)

Direction

- Preheat the oven to 325F. Place ricotta and goat cheese in a bowl and mix until smooth and combined. Add the eggs, salt, pepper, red pepper flakes, nutmeg and herbs and mix well.

- Place the spinach in a saucepan of boiling water for 5 to 10 seconds, then drain, squeezing any excess water and chop. If using the kale repeat the previous step with the kale, leaving the kale to blanch for 1 minute before draining.
- Add the spinach, kale, pine nuts & pecorino to the ricotta mixture, mix until well combined. Spoon the mixture into greased muffin tins - if very lazy line with baking cups. Place in the oven for 40-45 minutes or until the teacakes are firm and golden.

302. Spread, Slice, Snip, And Go

Serving: Serves 1 | Prep: | Cook: | Ready in:

Ingredients

- 2 parmesan crisps
- 1/8 ounce fresh ricotta cheese
- 1/8 ounce Bulgarian sheep's feta cheese
- 1 tablespoon snipped fresh basil, dill and flat leaf parsley, snipped
- 2 slices of pickled green tomato
- 2 small heirloom tomatoes, sliced
- dash of kosher salt
- sliced strip of prosciutto or cooked bacon, optional topping
- 2 tablespoons roasted tomato bruschetta, optional topping

Direction

- Mix the ricotta and feta together. Then spread upon the crisps.
- Garnish with the fresh tomatoes and herbs and a dash of salt. Add crumpled bacon or sliced prosciutto and roasted tomato bruschetta for optional toppings, if desired.

303. Spring Onion Bread Soup

Serving: Makes about 4 servings | Prep: | Cook: | Ready in:

Ingredients

- 4 cups very stale bread cubes from a nice rustic bread
- 3 tablespoons butter
- 6 large spring/green onions
- 1 clove garlic, minced
- 6 cups rich chicken broth
- 1/2 teaspoon salt
- 1/2 teaspoon black pepper
- 1 cup light cream or half and half
- 1 tablespoon fresh lemon juice
- 1/2 cup finely grated parmesan cheese

Direction

- Thinly slice the green onions keeping the light green and white slices separate from the dark green slices. Melt the butter in a medium soup pot and add the white and light green onions along with the minced garlic. Sauté until all becomes soft and fragrant.
- Stir in the bread cubes and add the chicken broth, salt and pepper. Bring up to a boil and then down to a simmer. Simmer for about 10 minutes, stirring occasionally.
- Use an immersion blender to puree the soup and then stir in the cream and dark green slices of the onions. Bring up to a simmer and stir in the lemon juice and parmesan.

304. Spring Pea And Ricotta Crostini

Serving: Serves 12 | Prep: | Cook: | Ready in:

Ingredients

- 4 tablespoons olive oil, divided
- 1/4 cup finely chopped shallots

- 1 clove garlic, finely chopped
- 2 cups fresh or frozen spring peas
- 1/2 cup low sodium chicken broth
- 1 tablespoon lemon zest
- 2 tablespoons chopped fresh mint leaves plus extra for garnish
- 1/4 cup grated Parmigiano-Reggiano cheese
- 1 cup good quality, fresh ricotta cheese
- Kosher salt
- Freshly ground black pepper
- 1 baguette, cut into 3/4-inch slices
- Parmigiano-Reggiano cheese shavings for garnish

Direction

- Heat 2 tablespoons oil in a medium saucepan over medium low heat and add the shallots and garlic. Cook until shallots are softened, 3-4 minutes then add the peas and broth. Raise the heat to bring the liquid to a boil, then reduce to a simmer and cover the pan. Cook until the peas are tender, 8-10 minutes for fresh peas and 4-5 minutes for frozen.
- Transfer the contents of the pan to a food processor and add the lemon zest, mint and grated Parmigiano-Reggiano cheese. Puree until smooth. Add the ricotta and pulse until just combined. Season the mixture with salt and pepper to taste.
- Arrange the baguette slices on a baking sheet and brush them on both sides with the remaining olive oil. Place the sheet under the broiler and cook 1-2 minutes until lightly toasted. Flip the bread over and lightly toast on the other side.
- Spread some of the pea and ricotta mixture on each slice of baguette. Top each one with some Parmigiano-Reggiano shavings and mint.

305. Spätzle With Sage Butter, Parmesan, And Toasted Hazelnuts

Serving: Serves 4 to 6 | Prep: | Cook: |Ready in:

Ingredients

- For the spätzle:
- 2 eggs
- 1 cup milk
- 2 cups flour
- 1 pinch salt
- 1 pinch nutmeg
- For assembling spätzle with sage butter, Parmesan, and toasted hazelnuts:
- 1 spätzle (above)
- 3/4 cup skinned hazelnuts
- 1 cup butter or 3/4 cup clarified butter or ghee
- 10 fresh sage leaves, more to taste
- 1 cup grated Parmesan

Direction

- Whisk together the eggs and milk until they are completely combined.
- In a separate bowl, combine the flour, salt, and nutmeg and stir it well, making sure there are no lumps in the dry ingredients.
- Make a well in the center of the dry ingredients and gently pour in half of the egg and milk mixture. Gently stir to mix, and slowly add the remaining egg and milk liquid, incorporating all of the flour and spices. Don't over mix! Cover and refrigerate for an hour.
- While the spätzle batter rests, toast and chop the hazelnuts. Put them aside for later.
- Melt the butter in a large sauté pan. Add the sage leaves. Continue to cook until the butter comes to a boil. Swirling often, continue to cook the butter until you see brown flecks and the butter smells nutty. Remove the pan from the heat immediately. Using tongs, remove the sage leaves and set them on a paper towel-lined plate to cool.

- To cook the spätzle, bring a large pot of salted water to a boil. Do not rest your spätzle press or lid (spätzle-profi) over the boiling water, as it will be hard to use if it heats up. Remove the batter from the fridge.
- If you do not have a spätzle press, you may use a colander to shape your spätzle. Give your press or colander a light coating of nonstick spray or rub it with a paper towel with a few drops of oil on it -- this step is not essential, but I find that it makes the press slightly easier to use.
- Once the water reaches a rolling boil, hold or rest your press or colander over the pot and pour the batter through it. The volume of batter you'll use depends on the size of your press: If you are using a colander, pour about one third of the dough into the colander and use the back of a large spoon to press it through the holes; if you are using a press, follow the manufacturer's directions for use.
- Allow the spätzle to boil 2 to 3 minutes and then remove it from the water using a slotted spoon, a spider, or a mesh strainer. Quickly run the spätzle under cold water and then leave them to dry while you finish cooking the rest. If the spätzle appear to be sticking as they dry, drizzle a tiny bit of oil or melted butter over them. Continue this process until all the batter has been cooked.
- Once the spätzle is cooked, reheat the skillet containing the butter. Once it's hot, add the spätzle to the pan, let them sit for about a minute, and then give them a few gentle tosses. Don't worry if a few pieces get a bit brown or crusty -- those are the best ones!
- Transfer the spätzle to a serving vessel and toss immediately with one cup of grated Parmesan. Sprinkle the chopped hazelnuts over the spätzle and then crumble the fried sage leaves on top. Serve warm.

---

306. Squash And Goat Cheese Lasagna

Serving: Serves 9 small portions, 6 large portions | Prep: | Cook: | Ready in:

Ingredients

- 3 pounds summer squash (any type)
- 1 cup yellow onion - diced
- 2 leeks - sliced
- 8 ounces ricotta cheese
- 8 ounces goat cheese (at room temperature)
- 1 egg
- 2 tablespoons fresh parsley - finely chopped
- 3 cups marinara sauce
- bechamel sauce - see below
- 1/2 cup butter
- 1/3 cup flour
- 1/4 cup cream or half & half
- 8 ounces whole wheat lasagna noodles - cooked

Direction

- To prepare béchamel sauce: melt butter in sauce pan over medium heat, gradually add flour to melted butter, stirring constantly to blend flour into butter. Once all flour has been blended, cook on low for 2-3 minutes. Slowly add cream or half & half to the butter/flour mixture, and cook on low for 3-5 minutes. Remove from heat, blend with marinara.
- To prepare squash: in 1 tablespoon butter, sauté diced onion over medium heat until glistening. Add squash, salt & pepper. Sauté for 3-5 minutes (do not overcook).
- To prepare cheese mixture: blend ricotta and goat cheese together in a large mixing bowl. Add parsley and egg; mix well.
- Layer lasagna: in a 2 quart (8x11") glass baking dish, spread a thin layer of the marinara/béchamel sauce mixture on the bottom of the pan and top with a layer of lasagna noodles. Then layer: sauce, leeks and squash, and cheese mixture. Top with noodles and repeat layering process until you reach the

top of the casserole dish. Top the casserole with cheese sauce. Bake at 350 degrees for 45 minutes to an hour. Let cool for approximately 15 minutes before slicing.

307. Squash N' Spice Milk

Serving: Serves 2 | Prep: | Cook: | Ready in:

Ingredients

- 2 cups cold milk
- 1/4 cup canned or homemade squash purée (unsweetened—pumpkin, butternut, or sweet potato—not a squash, I know—will work well)
- 2 tablespoons light brown sugar
- 1 teaspoon cinnamon

Direction

- Combine all ingredients in a blender, blitz on high to combine thoroughly, and taste for sweetness. Adjust if necessary, then strain into glasses and serve.

308. Stir Fry Pizza

Serving: Serves 4 | Prep: | Cook: | Ready in:

Ingredients

- Basic Pizza Dough (two pizzas)
- 1 packet active dry yeast
- 1 tablespoon brown sugar
- 1&1/2 cups lukewarm water
- 1 tablespoon olive oil
- 1/2 teaspoon salt
- 4 cups flouer
- Stir-Fry Pizza (two pizzas)
- 1 Basic Pizza dough from above
- 3 cups Shredded Mozzarella cheese
- 4 cups favorite stir-fry ingredients (or frozen mix)
- snap peas
- bell pepper
- carrots
- bean sprouts
- water chestnuts
- Broccoli
- brussel sprouts
- shredded ginger
- bock choy
- Soy sauce
- Red pepper flakes

Direction

- Basic Pizza Dough (two pizzas)
- Mix yeast with brown sugar and add lukewarm water. Let stand for 10 minutes.
- Add olive oil, then flour and knead until dough is smooth, elastic and not sticky. Add flour as needed while kneading.
- Rub a large mixing bowl with olive oil. Make dough into ball and lace in bowl. Cover with dish towel and let rise for one hour. Begin preparing toppings while you wait.
- After dough has roughly doubled in size, punch down once with fist and let stand for another 10 minutes.
- Roll out into think round pizza shape, about 16" in diameter
- Stir-Fry Pizza (two pizzas)
- Preheat oven to 450 degrees.
- Dust corn meal on pizza stone or pizza baking sheet.
- Roll pizza dough into thin circular pizza shape, about 16".
- Fold the outer edge back in about ½" with corn meal dusting up.
- Lightly smear sauce around with the back of a large spoon. Not too much.
- Sprinkle with shredded mozzarella. Not too much, sauce should be visible through cheese layer.
- Cut your favorite stir fry mix into 1" sized pieces (some suggestions above). Distribute across pizza, not too thick, cheese should be visible through toppings.
- Drizzle pizza with soy sauce

- Bake for about 20 minutes, season with red pepper flakes as desired, and enjoy with your favorite light beer!

309. Stovetop Mac & Cheese

Serving: Serves 2 to 4 | Prep: 0hours10mins | Cook: 0hours12mins |Ready in:

Ingredients

- 8 ounces elbow pasta
- Kosher salt, for the pasta water, plus more to taste
- 2/3 cup heavy cream
- 6 ounces cheddar, grated (preferably a younger, not super-aged variety)
- 3/8 teaspoon garlic powder
- 1/8 teaspoon white pepper

Direction

- Bring a pot of water to a boil and salt it generously (I estimate 1 tablespoon kosher salt per 1 quart water). Add the pasta and cook until al dente, starting to check the noodles after 4 minutes. Remember, they'll continue to cook in the warm sauce. As soon as the pasta is ready, drain it in a colander.
- Set the empty pot back on the stove over medium heat and add the cream. Bring to a boil and cook for 2 to 3 minutes, until it starts to look slightly thick. Drop the heat to low and add the cheese and spices. Whisk until a smooth cheese sauce forms.
- Stir the pasta into the cheese sauce and give it a taste. More garlic powder, white pepper, or salt? Adjust accordingly, then serve right away.

310. Stuffed Veal Scallops With Chorizo And Manchego

Serving: Serves 4 | Prep: | Cook: |Ready in:

Ingredients

- 8 thin veal scallops
- 24 thin slices of spicy chorizo
- 12 small white onions
- 1 1/4 cups Manchego cheese, grated
- 1-2 handfuls roquette

Direction

- Peel the onions and wash them well.
- Season the scallops with salt and pepper
- Put three slices of chorizo on each scallop then add some cheese and croquette on each. Roll up the scallops and press gently. Tie them up to make sure they remain closed when you cook them.
- Heat some olive oil in a large pan and cook the scallops for 8-10 minutes on medium heat. They should golden on each side. Add the onions and cook until golden as well. Season to taste and serve immediately. I usually eat this with pasta or a salad.

311. Sublime Cheesy Potatoes

Serving: Serves 6 | Prep: | Cook: |Ready in:

Ingredients

- 6 potatoes (red skinned if possible)
- 8 ounces buttermilk
- 8 ounces pouring cream
- 2 tablespoons English mustard (strong)
- 8 ounces cheder cheese (grated)
- 1 ounce parmesan cheese (grated)
- half teaspoon Sea salt
- good pinches black pepper (ground)
- good pinches nutmeg (ground)

Direction

- Preheat oven to 180c. Peel potatoes, cut in half. Gently boil for 10 minutes. Drain & place them flat side down in buttered deep dish - to cover base. In a bowl, mix cream, buttermilk, mustard, salt, pepper and nutmeg, until amalgamated. Pour enough over potatoes to almost cover - leaving top of potatoes peeping out. Sprinkle over grated cheddar cheese and parmesan cheese. You can dot with butter if liked. Bake in oven for 45 mins approx.
- Until cheese is lightly browned and buttermilk cream is almost absorbed. Cover with piece of foil, if cheese browns too much. Leave it sit for 10 - 15 mins - as it is very hot when it comes out of the oven.

312. Sugar Free Tuti Froti Barfi

Serving: Serves 4 | Prep: | Cook: | Ready in:

Ingredients

- 4 cups Milk
- 1 pinch Of saffron
- 1 pinch of citric acid
- 2 teaspoons cornflour
- 2 tablespoons milk
- 1/4 teaspoon green cardamom
- 10 teaspoons artificial sweetener
- 8 pieces chopped amond
- 2 teaspoons tuti froti

Direction

- Bring milk to a boil in a deep pan and simmer till it reduces to half its original quantity. Add saffron and mix well. Mix citric acid in two teaspoon of water and add to the thickened milk. Add dissolved corn flour and stir continuously till the mixture thickness. Add green. Cardamom powder and chopped almond mix well. Take pan off the heat and stir in sugar free natural diet sugar and set aside to cool. Divide the mixture into eight equal portions and shape them into square Barfi. Sprinkle some tuti froti over the Barfi and serve.

313. Sugar Snaps With Bacon, Maple, Feta And Mint

Serving: Serves 2-4 | Prep: | Cook: | Ready in:

Ingredients

- 4 slices bacon
- 3 cups sugar snap peas, washed and trimmed
- 2 tablespoons grade B maple syrup
- 1 large clove garlic, minced
- salt
- freshly ground black pepper
- 15 mint leaves, sliced into ribbons
- 1x1x2" chunk of feta, crumbled

Direction

- Fill a 4 quart pot 1/2 - 3/4 full with water and then add about a tablespoon of salt. Set to boil. In a 10" skillet set over medium-high heat, cook the bacon until crisp. Remove the bacon to a paper-towel lined plate to drain. Pour out from the skillet all but 1 tablespoon of the drippings; set the skillet and drippings aside.
- When the water is boiling, add the sugar snap peas and cook 1-2 minutes until crisp-tender. Drain and run cold water over the peas until they're cool. Set the skillet with the drippings over medium heat, and when warm, add the maple syrup, garlic and 1/2 teaspoon salt. When the syrup has dissolved and the garlic has softened some, add the cool sugar snaps to the skillet, tossing to combine everything and warm through, just about a minute.
- Pour everything from the skillet into a mixing bowl, scraping out any good bits that have stuck to the bottom, and add the mint and crumbled feta. Sprinkle with another 1/4 tsp

of salt and a generous few grinds of black pepper. Crumble the reserved 4 bacon strips over the top and toss to combine. You want the feta to "melt" some; its creaminess plus the maple-bacon pan sauce makes the dressing here. Check the seasoning and add more salt if needed.
- Turn out onto a serving platter and enjoy!

314. Summer Colour Mozzarella

Serving: Serves 1 | Prep: | Cook: | Ready in:

Ingredients

- 1 slice whole grain bread (or your choice)
- 1-2 teaspoons fresh basil
- 2-3 slices fresh mozzarella
- 1 slim slice yellow tomato
- 1 slim slice red tomato
- 1 slim slice orange tomato
- 3 slices of avocado
- 1 large leaf of green basil
- 1 large leaf of purple basil

Direction

- Spread pesto on whole grain bread
- Top pesto bread with ingredients in order listed
- ENJOY!!!

315. Summer Corn Salad With Toasted Grains

Serving: Serves 6 as a side | Prep: | Cook: | Ready in:

Ingredients

- 4 ears corn, shucked
- about 3/4 cups 2% Milk
- 3 strips of bacon, finely chopped
- 1/2 cup sweet onion, finely chopped
- 3 cloves garlic, peeled and smashed with the flat side of a large knife
- 2 tablespoons jalapeño, minced (with seeds and membranes -- you want a little heat)
- Pinch of salt
- 1 teaspoon maple syrup
- 1 cup quinoa, rinsed and drained
- 3/4 cup basmati rice
- 1 3/4 cups plus 2 tablespoons water
- 3 ounces Cotija cheese, crumbled
- 3 tablespoons finely snipped garlic chives
- 1/3 cup snipped cilantro
- Freshly ground black pepper

Direction

- Prep your corn the safe by placing one ear horizontally on a cutting board or the work surface in front of you. Hold one edge of the corn while slicing the kernels off the opposite side with a sharp knife. Rotate cob so that the flat, cut side is now sitting firmly on your work surface and repeat until you have cut around the entire ear. Repeat with remaining ears of corn. You should have between 2 to 3 cups of kernels (depending on the size of your ears). Place in a bowl and set aside.
- Milk your cobs one at a time by standing upright (trimming the end to make it sit flat if necessary) in a pie plate and, carefully work downwards, scraping the cob with the backside of your knife. Continue on all sides of the cob. Repeat with remaining cobs. Transfer mixture to a two cup or quart Pyrex measure -- you should have about 3/4 cup corn milk and pulp. Add enough dairy milk so that entire mixture measures 1 1/2 cups. Set aside.
- In a Dutch oven, cook bacon over medium heat until it's crispy and the fat has rendered. Using a slotted utensil, transfer bacon pieces to a small bowl and set aside.
- Add onion, flattened garlic, corn kernels, and jalapeño to bacon drippings. Add a pinch of salt and maple syrup. Cook for 5 minutes,

stirring to ensure nothing burns. Transfer corn mixture to a bowl and set aside to cool.
- Return Dutch oven to heat and immediately add quinoa and basmati to begin toasting, stirring constantly to prevent burning. Toast until grains are fragrant and golden brown, about 6 minutes. Carefully add water (grains will sizzle and spit) turning heat down if necessary. Add reserved corn milk-dairy milk mixture from Pyrex. Bring mixture to a boil, cover, and reduce heat to low to simmer. Cook for 20 minutes, until liquid is completely absorbed and grains are tender.
- Gently fluff grains with a fork and transfer to a large serving bowl to cool. Help grains cool by pulling from the bottom of the bowl with a spatula, essentially folding from the bottom up.
- Once the grains have cooled a bit, fold in crispy bacon pieces and any oil that accumulated in the bowl. Continue to build the salad by thoroughly folding in the corn-onion-jalapeño mixture, then half of the Cotija cheese, half of the chives, and half of the cilantro. Your ingredients should be evenly distributed.
- Finish salad by topping with remaining cheese, chives, cilantro, and a few grinds of black pepper. Serve immediately or at room temperature. Enjoy!

316. Summer Salad With Fresh Mozzarella & Herbs

Serving: Serves 6-8 | Prep: | Cook: |Ready in:

Ingredients

- 2 cups tomatoes (variety, any type), cubed
- 1 cup green grapes, cut in half
- 1/2 cup red onion, thinly sliced
- 2 cups arugula, washed/dried
- 1 cup fresh mozzarella, cubed
- 1 cup basil leaves, washed/dried
- 2 tablespoons thyme leaves, minced
- 1/2 cup parsley, minced
- 3 tablespoons rice wine vinegar
- 2 tablespoons olive oil
- 1 tablespoon lemon juice
- 1 teaspoon honey
- 1 teaspoon brown mustard

Direction

- In a large salad bowl, add tomatoes, green grapes, red onion, arugula, fresh mozzarella, basil, thyme & parsley.
- In a small bowl, whisk together rice wine vinegar, olive oil, lemon juice, honey & brown mustard.
- Pour over salad, lightly toss & serve.

317. Summer Slab Pie

Serving: Serves 8-10 | Prep: 1hours0mins | Cook: 1hours0mins |Ready in:

Ingredients

- Pie Dough
- 5 cups All purpose flour
- 2 teaspoons Sugar
- 1 tablespoon Kosher salt
- 2 cups Cold butter, (4 sticks) cut into cubes
- 1 cup Ice water
- Pie Filling
- 4 Heirloom tomatoes, sliced 1/2 inch thickness
- 2 cups Heirloom cherry tomatoes, halved
- 1 cup Ricotta
- 1 bunch Scallions, thinly sliced
- 1 cup Basil, torn
- 2 tablespoons Fresh thyme, minced
- 2 Lemons, zested
- 2 tablespoons Heavy cream
- Salt and pepper, to taste

Direction

- To make dough: In a food processor, process dough's dry ingredients. Once incorporated, add in butter cubes and pulse until broken up and flour looks sandy. Now, with the motor on, slowly drizzle in ice water. Stop the second the dough begins to come together. Dump onto clean work surface and knead 3 times until flour is just incorporated. Wrap tightly in plastic wrap, gently smoosh into the rough shape of a rectangle (this will make your life easier later on) and refrigerate for at least an hour and up to 3 days.
- Preheat oven to 375 degrees. Remove dough from fridge about 30 minutes before you're ready to work with it. Slice dough into two pieces, one about two-thirds of the dough, the other about one-third of the dough. The fact that you wrapped this in the shape of a rectangle should help make this and rolling it out as a rectangle a little easier.
- On a floured work surface and with a rolling pin, roll the bigger slab of dough out into a rectangle a little bigger than a 15×10" sheet pan. You want to be able to fold excess dough over to create the outside crust. Don't be scared, it doesn't have to be perfect. Move the dough and add more flour to your work surface as necessary to prevent sticking. Once you're there (or as close to it as you're going to get), transfer the dough to the sheet pan. Roll out the second slab of dough to approximately fit the top of the pie in a similar fashion.
- Lay heirloom tomatoes evenly in one layer on the surface of the dough. Sprinkle with a good amount of salt and pepper. Then dollop ricotta all over and sprinkle the rest of the herbs and lemon zest over top.
- Lay the second sheet of dough over the top. Fold the bottom layer's excess dough over the top and either pinch or crimp the two dough slabs together. Next, brush the top lightly with heavy cream, poke it all over with a fork and sprinkle with salt and pepper. Into the oven is goes for about an hour. Check it after about 50 minutes. If the top is nicely golden, you're good. I like to err on the side of well-browned versus just-bronzed, but that's up to you.

318. Summer Vegetable Galette

Serving: Serves 8 - 10 people | Prep: | Cook: | Ready in:

Ingredients

- Pâte Brisée
- 8 ounces (2 sticks) cold, unsalted butter
- 9.5 ounces unbleached, all-purpose flour
- 2 teaspoons kosher salt
- 1 ½ teaspoons granulated sugar
- 2 - 2 ½ ounces cold water
- Summer Succotash
- 2 ears, sweet corn
- 1 tablespoon unsalted butter (optional)
- extra virgin olive oil
- 3 large leeks, rinsed thoroughly and sliced into ½" half moons
- kosher salt
- freshly cracked black pepper
- 3 tablespoons chopped, fresh dill
- 1 large egg
- 1 tablespoon cream, milk or water
- 4 ounces goat cheese (I prefer something spreadable, but not a "spread", such as a Montrachet)
- 1 - 2 pounds fresh, heirloom tomatoes, sliced into ¼" rounds
- flaked sea salt

Direction

- Take your chilled butter and dice it into ½" cubes. Set them on a small plate or tray and stash, with the water, in the freezer while you prep the rest of your ingredients; for at least 15 minutes.
- Combine the flour, salt and sugar in a large bowl (I'm messy, so I like a lot of space to work with) and toss with your hands to incorporate. Scatter in the chilled butter. Now, everyone has their personal method of blending butter and flour for pie crust, but I

prefer to take large handfuls of the mixture, press them between my hands (as if praying to the pastry gods for a stunning result), and swiftly rub them together, incorporating the butter into the flour as evenly and quickly as possible. In the end, you should have pieces of butter that range in size from a nickel to small peas. Pour in 2 oz. of the cold water and toss with your fingertips to blend. Pick up a handful and give it a feel. If you feel quite a bit of loose flour, and the dough doesn't hold together when you squeeze it, sprinkle in the remaining ½ oz. of cold water. Knead the dough quickly, just until it comes together in a bit of a shaggy mess (I like to err a bit on the dry side).

- Dump the mass onto a lightly floured work surface and form it into a tight mound. Using a bench scraper or a sharp knife, cut the dough in half and stack one on top of the other. Using the palms of your hands, quickly smash the stack down into another tight mound. Repeat this step 3 or 4 times before forming a tight disk with the dough and wrapping it well in plastic wrap. Refrigerate the disk for at least 30 minutes (or in the freezer for 10) in the refrigerator before working with it.
- When you're ready to use the dough, remove the disk from the refrigerator and allow the chill to come off slightly. Scatter a few pinches of flour across a clean work surface, and dust a rolling pin generously. Place the disk on the work surface and dose the top with a pinch of flour. Working from the middle of the disk out, begin rolling away from you, turning the dough a quarter turn after each outward roll, trying your darndest to keep an even "circle" (it will never be perfect). When the disk becomes too large to turn easily, begin rolling from the center, outward, keeping the round stationary. If you feel the dough is beginning to stick to the counter, shimmy it a bit to loosen it, flip it over your rolling pin and give the work surface a few more pinches of flour. Don't worry if small cracks begin to form around the edges, although, if large fissures begin to form, simply pinch them back

together and proceed. Work as quickly as possible, to prevent the dough from becoming too soft on you. If that happens, take a cue from Alton Brown and set a chilled sheet pan on top of the dough for 5 minutes before attempting another go.

- After you have a circle 11 - 12" in diameter, fetch a large sheet pan or sauté pan (I prefer my trusted, 9" cast iron skillet) and transfer the dough to the center of the pan using either deft hands or by draping it over the rolling pin to assist the move. Allow the dough to settle into the pan, but don't press it in. Stash the pan in the fridge while you work on the filling.
- To prepare the filling (this step can be done at least a day in advance), set the cobs of corn, upright in a large bowl and, using a sharp serrated knife, cut the kernels from the cob (being careful not to shave off any of the white pith). Melt the butter with a tablespoon of olive oil in a medium-sized skillet set over medium heat and add the leeks with a generous pinch of salt and a healthy dose of cracked pepper. Lower the heat to medium-low and cook for 3 - 4 minutes, stirring frequently, until the leeks have just softened and sweetened a bit. Add in the corn kernels and 2 tablespoons of dill, and cook for just another minute. Scrape the mixture (and all of its buttery goodness) into a bowl and set aside to cool slightly.
- Preheat the oven to 400 and arrange a rack to the lowest position. Beat together the egg and cream in a bowl with a fork until well mixed.
- Fetch the pie dough from the fridge and, using a pastry brush, paint the entire surface of the dough with the egg wash. Dot or spread the goat cheese in the very center (in an area approximately 6" in diameter, but don't fret about being exact). Pile the leek-corn mixture in the very center of the dough, mounding it up high. Shingle the slices of tomato on top of the veggies in a single layer, overlapping slightly. Fold the edges tightly over the filling, crimping them tightly to keep them in place. Completely egg wash the now exposed pie dough. Drizzle the tomatoes with a tablespoon

or so of olive oil and dose generously with flaked sea salt (I swear by Maldon) and a few grinds of cracked pepper.

- Bake on the bottom rack for 35 - 45 minutes, or until the crust is a rich, golden-brown and the tomatoes are slightly shriveled. If you're feeling particularly dangerous, I like to take a long, offset spatula and lift the galette to make sure the bottom is nice and golden brown as well. Remove from the oven and allow the galette to cool in the pan for an hour before sliding it out onto a cutting board to finish cooling completely. When ready to serve, scatter the remaining tablespoon of fresh dill on the galette, slice it into wedges and serve it with a simple salad of bitter greens.

319. Sunday Sauce With Meatballs & Sausage (LC, GF)

Serving: Makes 16 servings | Prep: 1hours30mins | Cook: 3hours0mins | Ready in:

Ingredients

- Meatballs and Sausage
- 2 pounds sweet Italian sausage (bulk)
- 4 ounces prosciutto (chopped)
- 2 eggs
- 0.75 cups chickpea bread crumbs (or your choice)
- 4 ounces shredded parmesan cheese
- 4 ounces shredded asiago cheese
- 2 tablespoons white pepper
- 1 tablespoon cayenne pepper
- 3 tablespoons fennel seeds
- 2 tablespoons rosemary leaves
- 2 tablespoons basil leaves
- 1 tablespoon Italian seasoning
- 8 Sweet Italian sausages
- Sauce
- 3 28 ounce cans DOP San Marzano tomatoes
- 2 18 ounce tomato sauce
- 4 whole roasted red peppers
- 2 large Vidalia onions, diced
- 4 ounces chopped prosciutto
- 2 tablespoons basil leaves
- 6 tablespoons minced roasted garlic
- 4 tablespoons EVOO
- 2 tablespoons white pepper
- 2 tablespoons rosemary leaves

Direction

- Dice and caramelize the onions in EVOO while you make the meatballs. About half way through with the onions, add the prosciutto and finish them both off.
- Combine all of the ingredients for the meatballs and mix well with your hands; I use a 1/3 –cup scoop to dole out 16 heaping portions onto a large baking pan lined with parchment; then I roll them into balls, spray them with EVOO and bake for 45-60 minutes at 350F under an Al foil tent (depending on their size)
- Set the onions and prosciutto aside. While the meatballs are cooking, make the sauce. If you have a countertop convection oven, roast the sausages (425F for 45 min, turning intermittently, then broiling at 500F for 10 minutes on each side), otherwise, wait until the oven is free.
- I make the sauce in two portions in a food processor (sue to space). Into the processor put half of each of the tomatoes, peppers, onion/prosciutto, paste, garlic, and seasonings. Process for about 30-45 seconds; transfer to a large saucepot. Repeat.
- Heat the sauce to simmer (less than medium-low heat). Add the meatballs. Cut the cooked sausages in half and add them. Simmer for 2-3 hours.
- Serve over a portion of pasta, or alone, topped with cheese.

320. Sweet Corn Arepa Pancakes

Serving: Serves 8-10 pancakes | Prep: | Cook: | Ready in:

Ingredients

- 3/4 cup freshly squeezed orange juice
- 2 tablespoons butter
- 2 ears of corn, cut from cob (puree one ear and reserve the other ear or corn)
- 1/3 cup farmers cheese
- 1 egg
- 1 cup cornmeal
- 1/4 cup sugar
- 1/4 teaspoon salt

Direction

- Bring orange juice to a boil and add the butter. Take off the heat and let sit until butter melts. Let cool.
- In a large mixing bowl, combine the cornmeal, sugar, and salt. Stir in the orange juice and butter mixture, pureed and whole corn kernels, egg, and farmer's cheese, and mix to combine. Let sit for a few minutes to let flavors marry.
- Melt a tablespoon of butter in a large skillet or griddle over medium heat and pour 1/4 c. of batter into the skillet. Fit as many pancakes as you can without overcrowding. Cook for about 5-7 minutes and flip when browned on the bottom...some dark brown spots are good. Flip them and cook the other side for about another 5 minutes.
- Serve with berries/syrup, with ice cream, with more crumbled farmer's cheese on top, or my favorite...cold out the refrigerator.

321. Sweet Potato Shrimp & "Grits"

Serving: Serves 6 | Prep: | Cook: | Ready in:

Ingredients

- 2 cups almond milk or 1 cup almond milk and 1 cup water (using milk only will make it creamier)
- 1 cup Purely Elizabeth Organic 6-Grain Oatmeal
- 1/2 cup Water as needed to thin out grits
- 1 tablespoon creole seasoning
- 1.5 teaspoons smoked paprika
- Pinch cayenne pepper
- 1 teaspoon agave nectar
- 2 pounds shrimp
- 3 smoked turkey sausage links or 1/2 package of diced uncooked bacon
- 3 cloves of garlic minced
- 1-2 tablespoons olive oil
- 3/4 cup chopped sweet onion
- 2 teaspoons agave nectar
- Pinch salt
- 1 cup cooked and mashed sweet potatoes
- 4 ounces smoked gouda cheese
- Pinch ground black pepper
- cilantro for garnish

Direction

- Combine the oats and milk in a saucepan and cook over medium heat until liquid has been absorbed (cook just as you would your normal oatmeal). While still hot add the sweet potatoes, gouda cheese and pinch of black pepper. Stir to mix well. If the mixture becomes too thick add water.
- Meanwhile heat olive oil in a saucepan over medium and add onions with a pinch of salt and 2 tsp of agave. Sauté until soft and caramelizing slightly. Now add the garlic and sauté a few more minutes, careful to prevent burning. If using bacon add it now and let it cook through.
- Add the shrimp and turkey sausage (if not using bacon) to the saucepan and begin adding the creole, paprika & cayenne pepper. Turn the heat down to medium/low and add a couple of tbsp. of water to the pan. Mix the

ingredients around and let sauté about 5 minutes. Add the last 1 tsp of agave.
- To serve place oat-sweet potato-gouda mixture in a bowl and top with the shrimp mixture (the shrimp mixture should have somewhat of a thin sauce from the water that was added, this is what you want!) Top with fresh cilantro and enjoy!

- Pour egg mixture into pan with sweet potatoes, add shallots next, spinach and finally chunks of goat cheese evenly distributed. Cook for two minutes on the stove-top on medium heat.
- Transfer to broiler and cook for another 2 - 2 1/2 minutes or until eggs puff. Remove from oven, let cool 5 minutes and serve.

322. Sweet Potato, Spinach & Goat Cheese Frittata

Serving: Serves 4-6 | Prep: | Cook: |Ready in:

Ingredients

- 12 eggs
- 1/2 - 1 cups milk or half n' half
- 4-6 ounces goat cheese
- 1 shallot finely chopped
- 1 large sweet potato or yam
- 4 tablespoons butter or olive oil
- 1 bunch spinach - washed & destemmed
- 1 teaspoon salt (or less depending on taste)
- 1 dash black pepper

Direction

- Peel sweet potato and slice into quarter inch thick rounds.
- Melt 2 tablespoons of butter or olive oil in the bottom of a large cast iron skillet. Once oil/butter is warm cover bottom of skillet with one layer of sweet potato rounds. Let cook for 4-5 min.
- Meanwhile chop shallot and sauté in remaining 2 tablespoons of butter/olive oil in separate pan.
- Turn off sweet potatoes (no need to turn - they cook fast).
- Whisk eggs together and then whisk in milk or half n' half, salt and pepper. Set aside.
- Wash and de-stem one bunch of spinach or one package of baby spinach. Make sure to remove the stems to avoid stringiness.

323. Sweet Savory Apricot Curry Cheesecake

Serving: Serves 2 | Prep: | Cook: |Ready in:

Ingredients

- Cracker base
- 60g crackers, crumbled
- 30g butter
- 1/2 teaspoon curcuma powder
- Apricot jam and cheese topping
- 4 dried apricots
- 4 fresh apricots
- 1 teaspoon curry
- 50 milliliters tea
- 1/2 tablespoon sugar
- 50g creamy ewe's milk, almost brie style
- 100g quark
- 30 milliliters soy cream
- 75g cream cheese
- 2 eggs
- 1 apricot

Direction

- Cracker base
- Preheat the oven on 350FMelt the butter and mix together with crackers and curcuma.
- Press the cracker mixture on the bottom of two small springform pans and bake for about 10 minutes
- Apricot jam and cheese topping
- Cut the apricots into dices. Cook them in a saucepan on medium heat with the tea, sugar and curry powder for 15 minutes.

- In a another sauce pan, melt the goat cheese with the soy cream on low heat
- In a bowl, combine this mixture with the cream cheese and quark. Beat the eggs and add to the cheese mixture. Season with pepper.
- Take the base of the cheesecake out of the oven. Spread apricot jam on the cracker-base then pour the cheese mixture on top.
- Cut the remaining apricot into slices and arrange on top of the cheesecake.
- Bake for 25-30 on 320F

324. Swiss Cheese And Chocolate Sandwich

Serving: Serves 2-3 | Prep: | Cook: |Ready in:

Ingredients

- 1 French Baguet
- 1/2 pound Sliced Swiss Cheese
- 1 piece Good quality Milk Chocolate Bar
- Butter

Direction

- Preheat your oven to 350 degrees. Cut a sandwich-length piece of baguette and slice it open like you would to make a hero. Apply a thin layer of butter inside and put a few slices of Swiss cheese on both sides of the bread. Leaving it open, place the sandwich in the oven for about 10 minutes, or until the cheese is melted and gooey. Remove it from the oven and add a couple pieces of milk chocolate, then close the sandwich and let it rest for a minute

325. Tender Cherry Cheesecake

Serving: Serves 8-10 | Prep: | Cook: |Ready in:

Ingredients

- Graham cracker crust & Cherry Topping
- 2 1/4 cups Graham cracker crumbs
- 10 tablespoons melted butter
- 1 tablespoon granulated sugar
- 20 ounces Frozen tart cherries
- 1/3 cup granulated sugar
- 1 tablespoon lemon juice
- 1 tablespoon cornstarch
- Cheesecake filling
- 2 pounds Full fat cream cheese
- 5 Whole large eggs
- 2 Egg yolks
- 1 cup Greek yogurt
- 1 cup Granulated sugar
- 1 teaspoon vanilla extract
- 1/4 teaspoon salt
- 1 tablespoon cornstarch
- 1 tablespoon lemon juice

Direction

- Graham cracker crust & Cherry Topping
- Preheat the oven to 350°F with a rack in the lower-middle position. Take the blocks of cream cheese out of their boxes and let them warm on the counter while you prepare the crust, about 30 minutes.
- Grease the springform with butter or cooking spray.
- Set the springform in a slow cooker liner to prevent water leakage. Alternatively, you can prepare the traditional way and wrap it in two pieces of aluminum foil.
- Mix melted butter this into the graham cracker crumbs. The mixture should look like wet sand and hold together in a clump when you press it in your fist. Use a glass to press the crumbs evenly on the bottom of the pan and up the sides.

- Place the crust in the oven (be careful not to tear the foil if using). Bake for 8 to 10 minutes until the crust is fragrant and just starting to brown around the edges. Let the crust cool on a cooling rack while you prepare the filling.
- Combine frozen unsweetened cherries, sugar and 1/4 cup water in a medium saucepan and bring to a boil over medium heat until defrosted and sugar melts. Stir often to prevent burning.
- Combine 1 tsp of zest from the lemon, lemon juice, and the cornstarch in a small bowl. Add the slurry to the cherries and bring to a boil. Cook this until it is thickened to your liking. Remove it from heat and allow to come to room temperature before putting it on your cheesecake
- Cheesecake filling
- Combine the warmed cream cheese, sugar, cornstarch, and salt in the bowl of a stand mixer fitted with a paddle attachment (or use a handheld mixer). Mix on medium-low speed until the mixture is creamy, like thick frosting, and no lumps of cream cheese remain. Scrape down the beater and the sides of the bowl with a spatula.
- Add the yogurt, lemon juice, and vanilla to the bowl and beat on medium-low speed until combined and creamy. Scrape down the beater and sides of the bowl with a spatula.
- Mix in the eggs and yolk one at a time. Wait until the previous egg is completely mixed into the batter before adding the next one. Scrape the sides and make sure there are no clumps.
- Pour the batter over the cooled crust and spread it into an even layer against the sides of the pan.
- Transfer the pan to a roasting pan or other baking dish big enough to hold it. Bring a few cups of water to a boil and pour the water into the roasting pan, being careful not to splash any water onto the cheesecake. Fill the pan to about an inch, or just below the lowest edge of foil.
- Bake the cheesecake: Bake the cheesecake at 350°F for 50 to 60 minutes. This is usually closer to 50 minutes, and the temperature should be about 150 degrees F. The inner center should still look jiggly. Some spots of toasted golden color are fine, but if you see any cracks starting to form, move on to the next step right away.
- Turn off the oven and crack the door open. Let the cheesecake cool slowly for one hour.
- After an hour, remove the cheesecake from the oven and from the water bath, unwrap the foil, and transfer it to a cooling rack. Run a thin-bladed knife around the edge of the cake to make sure it's not sticking to the sides (which can cause cracks as it cools). Let the cheesecake cool completely on the rack.
- Chill the cheesecake for four hours in the refrigerator: Chill the cheesecake, uncovered, for at least four hours or up to three days in the refrigerator.
- Take the cheesecake out of the fridge about 30 minutes before you plan to serve. Unmold the cake and top the cheesecake just before serving. You can serve the cake right from the bottom of the springform pan, or use a large off-set spatula to gently unstick the crust from the pan and transfer it to a serving platter. Leftovers will keep, uncovered and refrigerated, for several days.

326. The Incredible Bacon Tamale

Serving: Makes 3 dozen | Prep: | Cook: | Ready in:

Ingredients

- 1 1/2 pounds bacon, or up to 2 pounds if you really like bacon
- 1 cup butter, softened
- 16 ounces cottage cheese
- 5 pounds masa
- 1 1/2 cups pureed roasted green chiles
- salt

- 1 27-ounce can of green chiles, or the equivalent of fresh roasted green chiles, cut or torn into strips
- 1 1/2 pounds cheese, cut into 1/2" sticks
- husks

Direction

- Cut the bacon into ½" pieces and cook until crispy.
- Drain the fat into a very large bowl and set the bacon aside.
- Soak the husks in hot or boiling water.
- To the bowl, add the butter, cottage cheese, masa and green chiles. Mix until well-combined, seasoning with salt as you go to taste. Add a little water if it seems too dry — I ended up adding about ¼ cup.
- Assemble the tamales. Spread masa on a husk. Place a stick of cheese, some green chile strips, and some bacon pieces on the masa, roll it up and fold the end over. Repeat until you run out of something. I ran out of bacon, so I ended up with a few green chile and cheese tamales.
- Steam for about 45-60 minutes, or until the masa is firm.

327. The Perfect Summer Salad (Watermelon, Feta, Avocado, And Mint Salad)

Serving: Serves 2 | Prep: | Cook: |Ready in:

Ingredients

- Watermelon, feta, avocado, mint (optional: radish)
- 1 cup Cubed Watermlon
- 1/2 cup Feta
- 1/2 Diced Avocado
- 2-4 Radish
- 1 sprig Mint
- EVOO, sea salt, and freshly ground pepper
- 1 splash EVOO
- 1 dash Sea Salt
- 1 dash Freshly Ground Pepper

Direction

- Watermelon, feta, avocado, mint (optional: radish)
- Dice up all salad ingredients into cubes, to the same size.
- Add radishes, if desired.
- Arrange salad ingredients as desired. Possible options: checkerboard, cube, pyramid, or simple tossed together.
- Chiffonade mint leaves.
- EVOO, sea salt, and freshly ground pepper
- Splash EVOO. Season with sea salt and freshly ground pepper as desired (to taste).

328. The Saints Grits N Eggs

Serving: Serves 1 | Prep: | Cook: |Ready in:

Ingredients

- 1 egg
- 1 teaspoon butter
- a pinch of granulated garlic
- 1 cup water
- 1/4 cup quick grits
- 1/4 cup shredded sharp cheddar cheese
- cracked black pepper
- a lot of Louisiana Hot Sauce

Direction

- Crack the egg into a dish (makes it easier at poaching time) and bring a pot of salted water to a simmer.
- In a small saucepan, bring the butter, cup of water and pinch of garlic to a boil. Once it's boiling, stir in the grits.
- After the grits have been cooking a couple minutes, slide the egg into the poaching water.

- Once the grits are cooked (5 minutes) stir in the cheese and pour into your bowl. Get that egg and drain off all excess water, and plop it into the grits.
- Grind some pepper over top and then add a LOT of Louisiana Hot Sauce - it'll start your day right I GUA-RAN-TEE!!!!!!

329. The Zuppa

Serving: Makes 1 large stockpot of soup | Prep: | Cook: | Ready in:

Ingredients

- 1 small yellow onion
- 1 1/2 pounds pork sausage
- 6-8 russet potatoes
- 32 ounces chicken broth
- 4 cups water
- 10.5 ounces cream of chicken soup (1 can)
- 1 1/2 tablespoons Italian seasoning
- 1/2 teaspoon crushed red pepper flakes
- 1 1/2 tablespoons minced garlic (jar)
- 2 bay leaves
- Salt and pepper to taste
- 1/2 pint heavy whipping cream
- 3 cups fresh kale
- crumbled bacon
- shaved parmesan

Direction

- Slice onion into smaller pieces and place in skillet on stove with two tablespoons of salted butter. Cook on medium until onions start to soften. Set aside.
- Brown the sausage. We sprinkle some crushed red pepper flakes in with the sausage!
- Slice the potatoes with the skin on. Do not cut into too small slices because as they cook down they shrink!
- Place sliced onions, sausage, sliced potatoes, chicken broth, water, cream of chicken, Italian seasoning, minced garlic, bay leaves, and salt and pepper in a stock pot. Cook on medium to high until potatoes are soft. After potatoes are soft taste the base of your soup and add more salt and pepper to your liking!
- Time for garnishes! Frozen bacon is so much easier to work with. It slices pretty nice when it's froze! Slice bacon with kitchen scissors into 1 inch pieces and cook until crispy!
- Add the heavy whipping cream and chopped kale into the soup and heat until heated through. Serve immediately.
- Garnish soup with crumbled bacon, shaved parmesan cheese and crushed red pepper flakes!

330. Tomato Soup (Ree Drummond)

Serving: Serves 8 | Prep: | Cook: | Ready in:

Ingredients

- 1 medium white or yellow onion, sliced
- 6 tablespoons butter (3/4 stick)
- 2 cans diced tomatoes (14.5 each)
- 3-6 tablespoons sugar (to neutralize tomato acidity)
- 3 chicken bouillon cubes
- black pepper, freshly ground
- 1 cup sherry (optional, but essential to me!)
- 1 1/2 cups heavy cream
- 1/4 cup basil, chopped
- 1/4 cup flat-leaf parsley, chopped

Direction

- Sauté onion in butter until translucent. Add tomatoes, tomato juice, sugar, bouillon, (lots of) ground pepper.
- Heat almost to a boil. Turn heat off. (Can be cooled and kept in refrigerator up to this step.) Add sherry, cream, basil and parsley. Serve hot, warm or cold.

331. Tomato Tarte Tatin Starring Triple Cheese

Serving: Serves 4-6 | Prep: | Cook: | Ready in:

Ingredients

- For the Pastry
- 175 grams Self-raising flour
- 85 grams butter
- 50 grams Parmesan, finely grated
- 1 large, free-range egg yolk
- 1 handful fresh thyme leaves
- For the Tomatoes & Filling
- 25 grams butter
- 2 tablespoons olive oil
- 2 teaspoons sugar
- 1 fat garlic clove, thinly sliced
- 5 Plum tomatoes, halved length-ways and woody stem removed (with a 'V' cut)
- 1 handful fresh thyme leaves
- 50 grams Feta cheese, crumbled
- 50 grams Mature Cheddar Cheese, grated
- Black pepper and sea salt to taste

Direction

- 1. For the pastry, rub the butter into the flour to make fine crumbs. Stir in the parmesan, thyme and a pinch of salt. Add the egg yolk and 2 tbsp. cold water, and then mix to make a dough (Don't over handled the dough). Wrap in cling film and refrigerate.
- 2. Preheat the oven to 200C/gas 6/fan 180C.
- 3. For the tomatoes, first lightly salt the tomatoes on their cut side. Heat the butter and oil in a 20cm tart tatin tin on the hob until quite hot. Stir in the sugar and garlic, then put in the plum tomatoes cut-side down, and sizzle for no more than 1 minute. Take off the heat.
- 4. Mix the crumbled Feta with the grated Cheddar well and add thyme leaves and black pepper to taste. Dot the mixture into the spaces between the tomatoes.
- 5. Roll out the pastry until it's slightly bigger than the top of the tin. Lay it over the tomatoes and cheese mixture and tuck any excess down the sides (creating an upside down bowl shape).
- 6. Bake on a baking sheet for 25 minutes until golden. Cool for 5 minutes, invert a plate over the top and upturn the tart onto it. Scatter with more thyme and black pepper.

332. Traditional Fondue Fribourgeois Legendary And Original

Serving: Serves 4 | Prep: | Cook: | Ready in:

Ingredients

- Ingredients
- 1 garlic clove, peeled and smashed
- 400 milliliters dry white wine (Fendant du Valais, Languedoc, Rhone,etc...)
- 14 ounces Gruyere cheese (preferably aged), cubed or shredded
- 14 ounces Vacherin Fribourgeois, cubed
- 1 pinch freshly grated nutmeg
- 2 pinches freshly ground black pepper
- 1 teaspoon lemon juice
- 1 shot Kirsch (cherry brandy)
- 1 tablespoon corn starch
- Bread for dipping
- Procedure

Direction

- Rub the garlic around the inside of a ceramic or heavy saucepan, then remove the pieces, just leaving the "taste" of it.
- Add the wine and warm it over low heat.
- Start by SLOWLY adding the cheese....and stir vigorously, but slowly, IN ONE DIRECTION only. The cheese will start to melt.

- When the molten cheese starts becomes uniform in consistency, add the nutmeg, pepper, and lemon juice.
- Stir together the corn starch and the Kirsch (IMPORTANT!!). Add to the fondue, to give it viscosity. This is an important step. The secret is: if the corn starch is not diluted in the Kirsch, as it hits the cheese it will coagulate and create little "balls" in the cheese. Then you might as well try to cook something else!
- You are done. If the fondue is too liquid, add more corn starch, mixed with a few drops of water. If too thick, add more wine.
- Cut the bread in pieces (French baguette or whole wheat bread, or both) and enjoy it! Remember not to drink water with the fondue. Only wine or hot tea. Fondue experts say that water will make the cheese lump up into a ball in the stomach. Recent critics have discovered that this is a myth, but I have chosen to ignore them and enjoy my wine with the fondue.

333. Tri Colored Caprese Salad On Toast With Peach Balsamic Vinegar

Serving: Serves 12 | Prep: | Cook: | Ready in:

Ingredients

- 1 red vine-ripe tomato
- 1 yellow vine-ripe tomato
- 1 orange vine-ripe tomato
- 1 large ball of fresh mozzarella
- 12 large fresh basil leaves
- 12 splashes peach-balsamic vinegar
- 1 baguette

Direction

- Preheat oven to 400 degrees.
- Wash tomatoes and basil leaves, and pat dry.
- Cut each tomato into 4 equal slices.
- Cut the ball of mozzarella into 12 equal slices.
- Cut 12 medallion slices off the baguette so that each slice is about 1/2" thick and about 3 inches wide.
- Toast baguette slices in the hot oven for about 5 minutes or until slightly browned.
- Top each baguette slice with a slice of tomato, a basil leaf and a slice of mozzarella, in that order so that the mozzarella is on top.
- Arrange the adorned baguette slices into rows of each color, and drizzle peach-balsamic vinegar on top of each.
- Serve immediately.

334. Tropical Dessert Smoothie

Serving: Serves 2 to 4 | Prep: | Cook: | Ready in:

Ingredients

- 4 bananas
- 2 medjool dates
- 3 tablespoons Brooklyn Seasame Halva Spread with Toasted Coconut
- 2 cups 2% organic milk (or almond or soy milk)
- 1/4 teaspoon cardamom (optional)

Direction

- Slice bananas and freeze them overnight.
- Cut the dates into smaller pieces, then, in a blender, combine the dates with the rest of the ingredients and blend until smooth -- about 30 seconds. Serve in a tall glass with a straw, top with a pinch of cardamom, and serve immediately. Enjoy!

335. Turkey Lasagna

Serving: Serves 12 | Prep: 0hours20mins | Cook: 2hours0mins | Ready in:

Ingredients

- For the sauce:
- 1/2 tablespoon olive oil, plus 1/2 tablespoon, divided
- 1 tablespoon olive oil
- 1 small sweet onion, diced
- 1/2 green bell pepper, diced
- 1-2 teaspoons garlic
- 2 small carrots, grated
- 1 can (28 ounces) of Muir Glen crushed tomatoes
- 1 can (14 1/2 ounces) of Muir Glen diced tomatoes
- 1/2 teaspoon salt
- 1/2 teaspoon freshly ground black pepper
- 1/2 teaspoon dried basil
- 1 1/2 teaspoons Italian seasoning
- For the lasagna:
- 1 pound ground turkey
- 1-2 teaspoons garlic
- 1/2 teaspoon fennel seed
- 1/4 teaspoon crushed anise
- 1/2 cup shredded, part-skim mozzarella
- 15 ounces fat-free ricotta cheese
- 1/4 cup grated parmesan
- 2-3 sprigs fresh parsley, finely chopped
- 1 egg, beated
- 1 box no-boil-necessary lasagna noodles

Direction

- To make the sauce: Warm 1/2 tablespoon olive oil in a nonstick saucepan to medium heat. Add onion and bell pepper and cook, stirring often, for 5 to 8 minutes, or until softened and slightly cooked down. Add garlic and carrot; sauté for another 1 to 2 minutes. Add both cans of tomato, salt, pepper, basil, and Italian seasoning. Simmer for 1 hour.
- To make the lasagna: Heat a nonstick frying pan to medium heat and add 1/2 tablespoon olive oil. Add the turkey; sprinkle on the fennel, anise, salt, and pepper. Cook until the turkey is fully done (no longer pink). Turn the heat off and stir in one cup of sauce.
- In a large bowl, mix the ricotta, parmesan, egg, and parsley. Add salt & pepper to taste if desired.
- Preheat the oven to 375° F. Take a large lasagna pan. Spoon 3/4 cup of the tomato sauce onto the bottom of the pan. Next, put down one layer of noodles, followed by another 1/2 cup of sauce, evenly distributed. Add a layer of half the turkey, followed by half of the ricotta mixture. Then spoon over 1/2 cup of sauce; add another layer of noodles. Again, place down 1/2 cup of sauce followed by the rest of the turkey and the rest of the ricotta mixture. Finish with a layer of noodles and then the rest of the sauce. You may not use all of the noodles; this is ok!
- Sprinkle on the mozzarella cheese. Cover with foil; let the lasagna sit for 10 minutes. Bake for 45 minutes, then remove the foil. Increase the heat to 450° F and cook for another 10 minutes or until the cheese is melted. Let sit 5 minutes before cutting into it to serve.

336. Turkey Tetrazzini

Serving: Serves 6-8 | Prep: | Cook: | Ready in:

Ingredients

- Dark meat from one leftover turkey thigh and drumstick, pulled or shredded
- 4 tablespoons butter, divided, plus more for preparing the baking dish and finishing
- 1 tablespoon olive oil
- 1 large yellow onion, small dice
- Salt and freshly ground black pepper
- 5 garlic cloves, minced
- 1 tablespoon fresh thyme leaves
- 1/2 cup dry white wine
- 3 tablespoons flour
- 4 cups milk, at room temperature
- 1 cup heavy cream, at room temperature
- 1/2 cup turkey stock (chicken is fine)
- 1/2 cup leftover turkey gravy

- 1/8 - 1/4 teaspoons freshly grated nutmeg
- 1 cup frozen green peas, thawed
- 1 cup fresh breadcrumbs
- 1 cup grated Parmesan cheese
- 1 pound fusilli
- Chopped fresh parsley, for garnish (optional)

Direction

- Place the turkey in a large mixing bowl. Preheat the oven to 450° F. Prepare a 13"x9"x2" baking dish by lightly greasing it with butter.
- In a large sauté pan with high sides, melt 1 tablespoon of butter with 1 tablespoon of olive oil and cook the diced onion and thyme with a pinch of salt and pepper over medium heat until translucent, about 7 minutes. Add the minced garlic and cook for an additional minute, stirring frequently. Add the wine and deglaze the brown bits from the bottom of the pan. Bring to a simmer and cook until the wine is mostly evaporated, about 3 minutes. Transfer the mixture to the bowl with the turkey.
- In the same pan, melt the remaining 3 tablespoons of butter over medium heat. Whisk in the flour and cook about 1 minute. Whisking constantly, add the milk, cream, stock, and gravy. Season with the 1 3/4 teaspoons salt, 3/4 teaspoon black pepper, and the nutmeg. Bring to a simmer and cook, stirring frequently, for about 10 minutes until the mixture is thick and coats the back of a spoon. Taste for seasoning.
- While the white sauce is simmering, bring a large pot of salted water to boil and cook the fusilli until al dente, about 8-9 minutes or one minute less than the package's directions. Drain and add to the turkey and onion bowl.
- Add the peas to the turkey mixture then pour in the white sauce, stirring to combine. Pour into your prepared baking dish.
- In a small bowl, combine the breadcrumbs and Parmesan cheese with a few grinds of black pepper and distribute evenly over the top of the casserole. Place a few dots of butter across the top of the breadcrumbs, if desired.
- Bake for 20 minutes, until the breadcrumbs are brown and the mixture is bubbly. Remove and let rest 10 minutes before serving. Sprinkle individual servings with fresh parsley, if desired.

337. Tuscan Roasted Chicken Stuffed Wtih Swiss Chard Couscous And Cheese

Serving: Makes 4lb chicken | Prep: | Cook: | Ready in:

Ingredients

- Swiss Chard Stuffing
- 2 bunches of green swiss chard
- 1/2 cup cooked couscous (see note below on how I cooked it)
- 1 onion, finely diced
- 2 tablespoons butter
- 5 cloves of garlic, peeled and minced
- 6 tablespoons ricotta cheese, drained
- 3 tablespoons parmesan cheese, grated or shaved
- 1/2 teaspoon kosher salt
- 1/2 teaspoon ground pepper
- 1 tablespoon capers
- 1 1/2 tablespoons sun dried tomatoes, julienned
- juice from 1/2 lemon
- 1 1/2 tablespoons toasted pine nuts
- 1 tablespoon butter, very warm or slightly melted
- 1 large egg
- Prepping and Roasting the Chicken
- 4 lb chicken, cleaned
- 2-3 teaspoons salt (divided)
- 1/2 teaspoon pepper
- 1 tablespoon olive oil
- 1 large lemon

Direction

- Swiss Chard Stuffing

- Tear the leaves of the Swiss chard into large pieces, discarding the central stalk/rib. Place in a large pot of boiling salted water and cook until tender, about 10 minutes. Drain well. When cool enough to handle, roll tightly into a towel to soak out as much moisture as possible. Coarsely chop and set aside.
- To make the couscous, bring 1 1/2 cups of chicken broth to boil with 1 smashed, peeled garlic clove, lemon zest from 1/2 lemon, 1 Tablespoon of olive oil and 1 teaspoon of salt. When it's all boiling, add 1 cup of dry couscous, remove from the heat, cover and wait 10 minutes. Fluff and measure out 1 cup and place in a large bowl you will use for the stuffing.
- Sauté the onion in the butter until tender. Add to the bowl with the couscous and add the Swiss chard. Add the cheeses, and everything else except the egg. Mix well with a large spoon. Lightly whisk the egg and add to the stuffing and mix well again. Adjust for salt and pepper. Set aside while prepping the chicken.
- Prepping and Roasting the Chicken
- Chickens can contain a lot of water from the process used to pluck them, so I always salt the chicken the night before I'm going to roast it and lightly wrap it in the refrigerator. If you don't do this the night before, do it anyway as much before roasting time as possible. It results in a more tender chicken with a crispier skin every time.
- Preheat the oven to 400F. You can either flatten the chicken for roasting by cutting out the backbone and then forcibly flattening the chicken or roast it as is. I find the stuffing will stay under the skin better if I flatten it, I'll get a more even crispy skin, and can to shorten the roasting time, and the overall flavor doesn't seem to be affected.
- Loosen the skin in the area of the breasts, legs and thighs for inserting the stuffing. Gently push the stuffing under the skin, moving it gently around by massaging the skin. If you don't use all the stuffing, you can cook it separately in a small pan in the oven and add it to the chicken later in serving.
- Once the chicken is stuffed, spread olive oil on the skin and salt and pepper. Squeeze lemon juice at the end, and assuming you didn't flatten the chicken, place the squeezed lemon inside the cavity of the chicken along with the used lemon slices you used for making the stuffing.
- Roast for about 1 hour 15 minutes, or until the meat thermometer reads about 165-170F in the breast. If you cook it any longer than that, the moistness of the stuffing will prevent it from tasting too dry, but the texture will not be as appealing. If the skin gets too dark and crispy, just place some foil over the top. We like our skin pretty crispy, but that's a personal preference.
- Let sit for 10 minutes to collect and distribute the juices before carving.
- Thanks to the stuffing, you need only serve a salad or some asparagus on the side to complete the meal. Enjoy!!!

338. Twice Baked Potato Stuffed With Shrimp And Blue Cheese

Serving: Serves 2 | Prep: | Cook: | Ready in:

Ingredients

- 1.6 pounds baking potato
- 9 ounces pre-cooked shrimp, 31-40 size that is frozen, thawed, cleaned, and roughly chopped (set aside 6 whole shrimps for garnish)
- 1/2 stick of butter
- 1/4 cup blue cheese
- 1/2 cup sour cream
- 1/4 teaspoon garlic infused olive oil
- optional: chopped chives

Direction

- Wash and carefully scrub the potato skin. Prick the potato with a fork in several places. This will release steam during baking. Place potato on a cookie sheet and bake 1 to 1-1/2 hours. Turn the potato over about mid-way during baking. To test for doneness, gently squeeze the sides and press down on the top. There should be about 1/8 inch of give.
- Cut the potato lengthwise into two halves. With a small spoon, scoop out and place the flesh of the potato in a medium size bowl. (When you scoop, leave about 1/8" flesh attached to the skin.) Smash 1/4 of a stick of butter into the potato filling and mix well. Add 1/2 cup of sour cream. Stir until smooth. (If you like your mashed potatoes light and fluffy, you may want to use a food processor or just use a hand mixer.)
- Gently fold in the blue cheese. Then gently fold in the chopped shrimp. Divide mixture evenly into two parts. Scoop one part into one half of the potato. Be careful not to press too hard on the mixture to avoid breaking the skin. Repeat this step for the second half potato.
- Return stuffed potato halves to the baking sheet and bake for 15-20 minutes. For nice brown peaks on your potato halves, change the oven setting from baking to broiling. Broil the potato halves for approximately 3 minutes. On this step, watch very carefully not to burn the stuffing. Remove from oven and set aside.
- Garnish with Additional Shrimps and Blue Cheese: On the stove top, turn the burner to a medium high heat. In a skillet, melt the remaining butter and add the garlic infused olive oil. When this is very hot, add remaining whole shrimps. Brown on one side, turn over and brown the other side. (Remember, these are pre-cooked shrimp, so don't overdue the cooking.) Casually place 3 shrimps over each of the two stuffed potato halves. Pour any remaining oil and butter over the shrimps and potato halves. Sprinkle additional blue cheese on top of the potatoes
- Optional: For a little more color, sprinkle chopped chives on top of the stuffed potatoes.
- Cooking Notes: For this recipe, the potato is 1.6 pounds because it is intended to be the main course. If you want to make it as a side dish, try a 9 oz. baking potato. Just be sure to adjust the ingredient quantities for a smaller baking potato. You can also freeze the stuffed potato halves.

339. Variation On Ronald Reagan's Mac And Cheese

Serving: Serves 4 | Prep: | Cook: | Ready in:

Ingredients

- 1/2 pound Tortiglioni(my favorite) or elbows
- 1 egg, beaten
- 1.5 tablespoons butter
- 3 cups grated sharp cheddar
- 1 cup half and half - room temperature
- 1 teaspoon salt
- 1 teaspoon pepper
- 1.5 teaspoons of mustard
- 0.5 teaspoons Worcestershire sauce
- 1 teaspoon paprika for sprinkling on top

Direction

- Heat your oven to 350° F. Butter a 2 qt. Pyrex/casserole dish and set aside
- Boil pasta according to instructions in salted water. Drain and transfer to mixing bowl.
- Mix pasta with butter, add beaten egg (make sure the pasta isn't too hot otherwise the egg will cook too soon), add 2.5 cups of cheese. Mix until evenly combined. Pour into your buttered casserole dish.
- In another bowl mix together half and half, salt, pepper, mustard, and Worcestershire sauce. Then pour this mixture over the pasta.
- Sprinkle the remaining half cup of cheese over the pasta. Sprinkle on the paprika.
- Bake for 35 minutes. I like to serve this with a garlic and shallot spinach sauté, but any side of greens will work great.

340. Waiting For Bonaparte Muffaletta (The Remix Edition)

Serving: Serves an army | Prep: | Cook: | Ready in:

Ingredients

- For the olive salad:
- 1/2 cup Spanish pimento olives
- 1/2 cup pitted black olives (Kalamatas work fine)
- 4 to 6 cornichons
- 2 cloves garlic (see note below)
- 2 teaspoons dried Italian oregano
- 1/2 cup extra-virgin olive oil
- 2 tablespoons red wine vinegar
- 1/4 teaspoon ground black pepper
- For the sandwich components:
- one 6-ounce crusty Italian roll
- A little creole mustard
- 1/4 pound thinly sliced premium cooked or cured ham (even prosciutto or jamon Serrano)
- 1/4 pound thinly sliced capicola (as the name suggests, this is most often made from pig neck)
- 1/4 pound sliced provolone cheese

Direction

- It's easy to make the olive salad in the bowl of a food processor using the olives, cornichons, garlic, oregano, olive oil, vinegar, and black pepper. Give everything a few quick pulses. It should remain a bit chunky -- somewhat coarser than a tapenade.
- Spoon the olive salad into a non-reactive bowl and cover it with cling wrap. It should then go into the refrigerator to rest for at least 5 to 8 hours, and it will keep overnight.
- To assemble, use a sharp bread knife to divide the loaf into two halves horizontally like a giant hamburger bun. Smear some mustard on the bottom half and top with ham, capicola, provolone, and a generous amount of olive salad. Cover with the top portion of the roll and divide into halves or quarters. Bring napkins.
- Notes to the cook: For the garlic, I use a "garlic confit". What that consists of is about 40 peeled cloves of garlic covered in canola oil and poached for about forty minutes -- a flame tamer is advised. Store the garlic and oil in a sealed container in the refrigerator. After a few days the oil will be highly perfumed. I think the little Corsican would like that touch. It's handy to have on hand and you can add a little of the oil to the salad. Otherwise, use fresh garlic cloves.
- The cornichon included in the olive salad is untraditional but one of my New Orleans friends really liked it, so I think it really works. Don't be stingy with the olive salad.

341. Warm Lentil Salad With Swiss Chard, Feta And Red Wine Black Pepper Vinaigrette

Serving: Serves 2-4 as a light meal | Prep: | Cook: | Ready in:

Ingredients

- For the Red Wine-Black Pepper Viniagrette:
- 1 tablespoon extra virgin olive oil
- 1/2 cup sliced sweet onion (trimmed, thin wedges)
- 1 large garlic clove, peeled, smashed with flat side of a knife
- 2 tablespoons good quality red wine vinegar
- 3 fresh sweet basil leaves
- 1/2 teaspoon Dijon mustard
- 1 shallot, peeled, rough chopped
- 1 teaspoon freshly ground black pepper
- 1/2 teaspoon dried thyme
- 6 tablespoons extra virgin olive oil
- Pinch of sea salt
- For the Lentil Salad:

- 1 cup black Beluga lentils (or Du Puy lentils - you want one that will hold its shape after cooking), rinsed, picked over
- 2 1/2 cups water
- 6 large rainbow Swiss chard leaves, with stems (ends trimmed)
- 1 link Italian sausage (optional)
- 2-3 tablespoons feta cheese
- 2-3 tablespoons Red Wine-Black Pepper vinaigrette
- plus 1/2 T olive oil if not using sausage

Direction

- In a 10-inch skillet, start to make the vinaigrette by heating 1 tablespoon of olive oil over medium heat. Add sliced onion wedges, garlic clove, and slowly caramelize, turning down heat if necessary to prevent burning. Cook for about 10 minutes, until onion is fragrant, golden brown and slightly stringy. Remove skillet from heat.
- While onion and garlic are caramelizing, start your lentils. In a large saucepan bring lentils and water to a boil. Cover pot, reduce heat and slowly simmer for 15 minutes. After 15 minutes, turn off the heat and leave lentils covered for 5 minutes more. At this point, I removed the lid and left the lentils in the warm cooking water (pot on the burner) until I was ready to put the salad together, and they were perfectly cooked. If you are wary, you can drain them, but lentils may not be as warm when you put the salad together.
- While the lentils are cooking, finish the vinaigrette. Transfer caramelized onion and garlic to a blender (set skillet aside - you will use it again in step 5). Add the vinegar, basil, Dijon mustard, shallot, ground black pepper, dried thyme and puree until combined. Carefully drizzle oil in through the lid, while blender is on (with one hand drizzling the oil in, I used my other hand to shield the top of the blender, preventing dressing splatter), pureeing vinaigrette. Scrape dressing with a spatula in to a container with a lid. Add a pinch of sea salt. Shake and set aside.
- Separate chard stems from leaves. Chop stems and set aside. Chop leaves crosswise, into thin ribbons. If you are including sausage in your salad, continue with step 5. If you are not including sausage, skip 5 and proceed with step 6.
- Heat skillet over medium heat. Remove sausage from casing and cook, crumbling meat with a wooden spoon. Cook until no longer pink. Transfer to a bowl lined with a paper towel. Add chard stems and cook in sausage grease for a minute, stirring. Add chopped leaves and cook for a minute more, until bright green and beginning to wilt. Remove skillet from heat. Skip to step 7.
- Heat 1/2 tablespoon of olive oil in skillet over medium heat. Add chard stems and cook for a minute, stirring. Add chopped leaves and cook for a minute more, until bright green and beginning to wilt. Remove skillet from heat.
- Drain lentils and transfer to a large serving bowl. Carefully fold in chard (and sausage, if using). Fold in the feta to taste (I used 2 1/2 tablespoons). Top with dressing to taste (I used 2 tablespoons) and fold to combine evenly. Serve immediately and enjoy.

342. Waste Not Pasta

Serving: Serves 4 | Prep: | Cook: | Ready in:

Ingredients

- 1 pound whole wheat spaghetti
- Kosher salt
- 2 to 3 bunches radish or baby turnip greens (or really whatever tender greens you've got)
- 2 ounces Pecorino Romano (plus additional for serving)
- 2 ounces Grana Padano (or substitute Parmesan)
- 2 to 3 teaspoons freshly ground black pepper (plus additional for serving)
- 1/4 cup extra-virgin olive oil

- 2 to 3 generous handfuls baby arugula or baby spinach, rinsed if needed
- 1 tablespoon unsalted butter

Direction

- Bring a large pot of water to a boil. While the water is coming to a boil, and while the pasta is cooking, the prep for the rest of the dish can be done.
- Clean the radish greens (or other greens). If there are any tough stems, cut them away. Very roughly chop the greens, then place them in a large strainer. Set the strainer in the sink in preparation for draining the pasta.
- Grate both cheeses on the fine holes of a box grater. If you haven't already done so, grind 3 teaspoons of black pepper, semi-coarse in texture. Set aside.
- Add a palmful of kosher salt and the spaghetti noodles to the boiling water. Cook as directed on the package, checking for doneness 4 minutes early. You want the noodles to be slightly firmer than "al dente." When done, ladle out 1 1/2 cups of the pasta water into a glass measure. (I set my glass measure in the strainer, so I don't forget this critical step.) Drain the noodles through the prepared strainer.
- Replace the pot on the burner over medium-high heat, and once any residual water has evaporated, add the olive oil. Give the noodles and greens a good shake, then transfer them back into the pot. (The greens will likely stick in the strainer, just use a fork or spoon to scrape them into the pot.) Add about 1/2 cup of the reserved pasta water to the pot. Stir the pasta and greens continuously for 3 to 4 minutes with a wooden spoon to scrape up any sticky bits and break up large clumps of greens. Add more pasta water as needed to prevent excessive sticking. The noodles will start to break up a bit when they are ready. At this point, stir in the arugula or spinach, just until it's wilted.
- Remove from heat and add the cheeses, butter, and 2 teaspoons black pepper. Stir to combine thoroughly, adding pasta water as needed to loosen the mixture. Taste and add more black pepper if desired.
- Divide amongst plates. Garnish each serving with more Pecorino and a few grinds of black pepper. Serve immediately.

343. Welsh Rarebit Yorkshire Pudding For One

Serving: Serves 1 | Prep: 0hours5mins | Cook: 0hours20mins | Ready in:

Ingredients

- 1 teaspoon olive oil (or beef drippings, if you've got it)
- 1 large egg
- 1/4 cup flour
- 1/4 cup milk
- 1/2 teaspoon English mustard powder
- 1/2 teaspoon Worcestershire sauce
- 1 pinch salt
- Freshly ground black pepper
- 1 tablespoon grated sharp cheddar

Direction

- Brush a single 6 to 8-ounce ramekin with the teaspoon of oil or fat (being unafraid to leave behind grease, at the bottom especially). Place on a baking sheet and transfer to the oven, which should then be set to 450°F. (As the oven preheats, the fat will get necessarily hot.)
- In a small bowl, whisk together the egg, flour, milk, mustard powder, Worcestershire sauce, salt, pepper, and cheddar. Let this mixture rest for 10 minutes (because for some reason you're supposed to), or until the oven is nice and hot. Carefully pour the batter straight into the super-hot ramekin and bake for 20 minutes—do NOT peek.
- Eat on its own or, as I like to do, with a simple side salad and glass of wine.

344. Whipped Feta Dip With Spiced Pita Chips

Serving: Makes 1 appetizer | Prep: | Cook: | Ready in:

Ingredients

- Whipped Feta Dip
- 8 ounces block feta cheese, crumbled
- 1/2 cup greek yogurt
- 3 tablespoons olive oil, divided
- 1 tablespoon fresh lemon juice
- 1 tablespoon chopped fresh chives + more for serving
- 1/2 teaspoon freshly ground black pepper
- 1-2 tablespoons pine nuts
- 1/4 teaspoon crushed red pepper flakes
- Spiced Pita Chips
- 2 pita pocket breads
- 1 tablespoon olive oil
- 1 teaspoon za'atar
- 1/2 teaspoon smoked paprika

Direction

- Whipped Feta Dip
- Combine feta, Greek yogurt, 2 Tbsp. olive oil, lemon juice, chives, and black pepper in a food processor. Process until a smooth consistency is achieved. Transfer dip to a serving bowl.
- Heat the remaining 1 Tbsp. olive oil and crushed red pepper flakes in a pan over medium high heat. Stirring constantly to prevent chile flakes from burning, cook until oil is very hot and infused with the chile, about 2 minutes. Add the pine nuts, and continue to cook, stirring constantly, until pine nuts are a deep golden brown. Immediately pour toasted pine nuts and chile oil atop feta dip. Top with additional chopped chives and serve with spiced pita chips for dipping.
- Spiced Pita Chips
- Preheat oven to 350 degrees.
- Cut the pita breads into eighths. Separate each pita triangle into two pieces (the top and bottom of the pocket) by tearing along the top edge.
- Spread pita triangles on a baking sheet and toss evenly with the olive oil, za'atar, and smoked paprika.
- Bake at 350 for 15-20 minutes or until pita chips are golden brown and toasty.

345. White Cheddar Fig Grilled Cheese

Serving: Makes 2 sandwiches | Prep: | Cook: | Ready in:

Ingredients

- 2 pieces eveything bagel thins
- 1 tablespoon butter
- 2 tablespoons fig preserves
- 4 slices white cheddar cheese
- 6 slices brie (from a brie cheese wheel)
- 1/2 cup arugula

Direction

- Preheat George Foreman grill.
- Separate bagels and add butter to one side. Set aside.
- Slice brie cheese. I lay the wheel down so it is flat and cut 6 pieces. The pieces should be about an inch wide. Trim off the rind.
- If using a skillet, set heat to medium high. Lay one side of bagel thin on grill/skillet. Add one slice of white cheddar cheese, a thin layer of fig preserves (so it is coated, but not overflowing), three pieces of brie and the second slice of white cheddar. Top with bagel thin top. Repeat with other sandwich.
- Close George Foreman grill and cook for 4-5 minutes. Sandwich is done when cheese is melted. If using a skillet, heat 4-5 minutes on one side and flip. Cook for 4-5 more minutes.
- Lift one bagel thin top and had a small handful of arugula; repeat on other side.
- Serve immediately.

346. White Cheddar And Rosemary Mac And Cheese

Serving: Serves 2-3 | Prep: | Cook: |Ready in:

Ingredients

- 1/2 pound large elbow macaroni
- 1 + 1/2 tablespoons butter, divided
- 3 tablespoons very finely minced fresh rosemary
- 1 clove of garlic, minced
- 1 cup cream
- 1/4 pound sharp white cheddar, grated
- freshly cracked black pepper
- 1/3 cup panko breadcrumbs

Direction

- In a large pan, bring enough slightly salted water to cover the noodles to a boil. Add the noodles and cook until just under al dente, about 10 minutes.
- While the macaroni is cooking, prepare the sauce. In a larger sauce pan, melt 1 tbs. of butter on medium high heat until it starts to brown. Add the rosemary and the garlic and cook until the aroma in them just starts to release. This only takes seconds.
- Add the cream, allow it to bubble and reduce a little on medium high heat, then turn the heat down to low.
- Add the cheese and whisk it in, stirring occasionally until all the cheese is melted. Feel free to add a generous amount of black pepper.
- Let the sauce reduce slightly until it thickly coats the back of a spoon, then turn off the heat.
- When the noodles are done, strain them in a colander then stir them into the sauce. As the sauce cools with the noodles in it, it will thicken up. Stir occasionally to help the mac and cheese thicken evenly. When the mac and cheese has cooled, it can be plated up.
- Make the breadcrumbs by melting ½ tablespoon of butter in a small pan on medium high heat, then add the panko crumbs. Stir constantly until the breadcrumbs become even crispier and a beautiful golden brown. Sprinkle the breadcrumbs on top.

347. White Chocolate & Poppy Seed Cake With Lemon Syrup

Serving: Serves 24 | Prep: | Cook: |Ready in:

Ingredients

- Poppy Seed Cake
- 540 grams Self raising flour
- 300 grams Caster sugar
- 1 teaspoon Sea Salt
- 5 tablespoons Poppy Seeds
- 300 grams Butter
- Zest of 2 large lemons
- 420 Buttermilk
- 5 Egg whites
- 1 teaspoon Almond Extract
- Lemon Syrup & White Chocolate Icing
- 100 grams Sugar
- 20 milliliters Water
- Juice of 2 lemones
- 200 grams White chocolate
- 400 grams Light Cream Cheese
- 400 milliliters Cream to whip
- 1 teaspoon Potato starch
- Rose petals and white chocolate, chopped

Direction

- Poppy Seed Cake
- Mix all the dry ingredients.
- Melt butter, beat the egg whites till firm and join together. Stir well.
- Divide the batter between 3 or 4 parts. Bake every each of them for 20 min @ 180°.
- Lemon Syrup & White Chocolate Icing

- For the lemon syrup mix sugar, water and lemon juice, bring to boil, let thicken for some minutes. Brush generously the cake layers while warm. Leave to cool down completely before icing.
- For the icing melt white chocolate, just don't heat up too much. Mix well with the cream cheese. Separately whip the cream with 1 tsp of starch till firm. And gently add to the cream cheese and chocolate paste stirring in slowly.
- Spread the icing on the cake layers building up the cake, giving a nice finish. Decorate with some chopped white chocolate and edible rose petals.

348. White Chocolate Cheesecake With Raspberry Sauce, Fresh Raspberries And White Chocolate Glaze

Serving: Serves 12 | Prep: | Cook: | Ready in:

Ingredients

- Crust
- 1 1/4 cups shortbread cookie crumbs
- 1/4 cup almonds
- 2 teaspoons sugar
- 1/2 teaspoon almond extract
- 3 teaspoons butter
- Filling and Topping
- 6 ounces White chocolate (chips or chopped)
- 32 ounces cream cheese softened
- 5 eggs at room temperature
- 3/4 cup sugar
- 3 tablespoons flour
- 1 1/2 teaspoons almond extract
- 1 cup raspberry jam
- 12 ounces white chocolate
- 1 cup heavy cream
- 2 pints fresh raspberries

Direction

- Crust
- In the bowl of a food processor, finely grind the almonds, then add the shortbread cookies pulsing until crumbs. Add the sugar and melted butter pulsing until mixed.
- Place the mixture in the bottom of a 9 inch spring form pan, using a small cup to press them flatly to the bottom.
- Bake at 400 degrees for 5-6 minutes. Remove from the oven and grease the sides of the pan lightly or spray with vegetable spray.
- Filling and Topping
- Melt and cool 6 ounces of the white chocolate. Mix together the cream cheese and add eggs one at a time. Add the sugar, flour and almond extract.
- With mixer on low, slowly add the white chocolate and mix well.
- Pour into the pan and bake at 325 degrees for forty minutes or until the edges are firm but the center is still a little soft. Allow the cheesecake to cool in the oven with the door open for 15 minutes, then at room temperature for at least one hour. A sudden temperature change will cause cracking so cool it gradually.
- Microwave the whipping cream to just under a boil, about 1 minute, then pour over the remaining 12 ounces of white chocolate, stirring until it forms a smooth sauce. Set aside, it will thicken as it cools.
- Microwave the jam for about 1 minute, just until it warms enough to pour. Pour the jam over the cheesecake in an even layer.
- Pour or drizzle the white chocolate glaze over the top of the jam. There will be plenty left to put on the serving plate. Arrange the fresh raspberries on top of the glaze in whatever design you like.

349. White Chocolate Whipped Cream

Serving: Makes about 2 cups | Prep: | Cook: | Ready in:

Ingredients

- 4 ounces white chocolate, finely chopped
- 3/4 cup heavy cream
- 3 tablespoons water
- A pinch or two of salt (optional)

Direction

- Put the chocolate in a medium bowl.
- Bring the cream and water to a simmer in a saucepan and pour over the chocolate. Let stand for 30 seconds, then stir well.
- Let stand for 15 minutes or so to finish melting the chocolate, then stir again until every last bit of chocolate is melted into the cream. Let cool.
- Taste and add salt, if desired. Cover and refrigerate for at least several hours, or until completely chilled (I like to leave it overnight, and it can be prepared to this point up to 4 days ahead).
- To serve, whip the cream with an electric mixer until it holds a shape (it won't be smooth if you over whip it). Use immediately or refrigerate until needed.

350. White Chocolate Cake With Dried Strawberries

Serving: Serves 4 | Prep: | Cook: | Ready in:

Ingredients

- 75g white chocolate
- 75g sugar
- 125 milliliters milk
- 125g ricotta
- 125g flour
- 1/2 packet yeast
- 1/2 packet vanilla sugar
- 1 egg
- 25g pistachios
- 25g walnuts
- 50g dried strawberries

Direction

- Preheat oven on 300F
- Ground pistachios and walnuts. Beat the egg
- Heat the milk with the vanilla sugar. Bring almost to a boil, then remove from heat and add chocolate and sugar. Stir until chocolate has melted and mixture is smooth. Let cool for a few minutes then the ricotta, flour, yeast and egg. Combine well
- Add dried strawberries, pistachios and walnuts
- Pour into a cake pan and bake for about an hour. Cover with aluminum sheet if the top of the cake starts to brown too quickly.

351. Winter Panzanella

Serving: Serves around 4-6 | Prep: | Cook: | Ready in:

Ingredients

- Salad ingredients
- 6 cups 1-inch cubes of good, crusty sourdough, a day old
- 2 1/2 cups butternut squash, peeled and cut in 1 inch cubes (about 1/2 squash)
- 1 large purple beet, peeled and cut into 1 inch cubes
- 2 cups very thinly sliced cavolo nero (Tuscan kale)
- 1/2 cup finely diced, red onion
- 1 crisp, tart apple (Granny Smith or Braeburn, or your preference), cored and cut into cubes
- 10 ounces smoked mozarella, cut into 1/2 inch cubes (the salad is also quite tasty, not surprisingly, with crumbled blue cheese, if you prefer that.)
- olive oil
- salt and freshly ground black pepper
- Maple-mustard balsamic vinaigrette
- 2 tablespoons balsamic vinegar
- 1/4 teaspoon salt
- 1 teaspoon maple syrup

- 1 teaspoon grainy mustard
- 1/8 teaspoon crushed garlic (I know that seems like a weird amount, but I just don't like my salad dressings very garlicky. You can add more if you like more.)
- 1/4 cup olive oil

Direction

- Preheat your oven to 425F. Toss the beet cubes with a small amount of olive oil and a sprinkling of salt and pepper. Spread them in a baking pan and pop them into the oven. Roast until just for tender, about 40 minutes.
- In the meantime, toss the butternut cubes with a bit of olive oil, salt and pepper, spread them in another baking pan and roast alongside the beets until tender, but not about to fall apart. About 20-25 minutes.
- Take the butternut squash and the beets out of the oven as they are finished and set aside to allow them to cool for a while.
- In a very large sautee pan, heat about 2 Tbs. olive oil over high heat until shimmering. Toss in the bread cubes and toss them around. Cook, tossing frequently, until they become golden browned, 10ish minutes. Take off the heat and set aside.
- At this point, slice the kale and the red onion and put them in a large salad bowl. In a small bowl, whisk together all of the dressing ingredients except the olive oil. Then, gradually whisk in the olive oil to emulsify. Pour about half of the dressing in with the kale and onion and toss to coat.
- Once the bread, butternut squash, and beets are lightly warm, but not hot toss them with the kale and onion in the bowl. Add the rest of the dressing and toss more. Finally, add the cheese and apple pieces (and a few sliced sage leaves, if you wish) and toss thoroughly until everything is well combined. If you like your salad with more dressing, feel free to double the dressing amount. I've always preferred 'scantily clad' salads, but this has been a bone of contention at times in my family since others prefer thoroughly drenched salads.
- Serve immediately, or allow to sit for about a half hour at room temperature before serving to allow the bread to soften and the flavors to mingle.

352. Yogurt With Marzipan, Poppy Seeds & Walnuts

Serving: Makes 2 servings | Prep: | Cook: | Ready in:

Ingredients

- 500 grams greek yogurt
- 1 tablespoon marzipan paste
- 1 tablespoon poppy seeds
- 1 handful of walnuts

Direction

- Add about 2 tablespoons of yogurt and the marzipan paste in a small saucepan. On low heat (don't the yogurt overheat or boil) dissolve the paste really well.
- Then add the rest of the yogurt and the poppy seeds. Last but not least, sprinkle with walnuts.
- It can be eaten warm or cold, with oatmeal or not. Whatever you want. Bon appetite!

353. Yogurt Tahini Sauce

Serving: Makes 1/2 cup | Prep: | Cook: | Ready in:

Ingredients

- 1/4 cup Greek yogurt
- 1/4 cup well-stirred tahini paste
- 1 tablespoon apple cider (or other) vinegar
- 1/2 teaspoon kosher salt
- 1 teaspoon honey
- 1 tablespoon water, plus more as needed
- Sriracha, to taste, optional

Direction

- Stir together the yogurt, tahini, vinegar, salt, honey, and water in a small bowl. Add more water by the teaspoon to achieve the right consistency — mixture should be spreadable but not pourable. Taste. Add salt or vinegar to taste.

354. Zucchini "Brake"

Serving: Serves 8 | Prep: | Cook: |Ready in:

Ingredients

- 1 1/4 cups zucchini, grated
- 1 1/3 cups unsalted butter, at room temperature
- 2 eggs
- 3 tablespoons milk
- 1 cup light brown sugar
- 1 teaspoon real vanilla extract
- 1 3/4 cups all-purpose flour
- 1 teaspoon baking powder
- 1/2 teaspoon salt
- 1/2 teaspoon baking soda

Direction

- Preheat the oven to 350 degrees F.
- Grate the zucchini into a colander and let drain briefly.
- Then, stir together zucchini, butter, eggs, milk, and brown sugar in a bowl. Add flour, baking powder, salt and baking soda and mix together until combined.
- Pour mixture into an 8" or 9" cooking spray sprayed pan. Bake for 60 minutes or until a toothpick inserted in the center comes out clean.
- Remove from oven and let cool in pan for 10 minutes, then gently turn out onto a wire rack to cool completely.

355. Zucchini Lasagna

Serving: Serves 6-8 | Prep: | Cook: |Ready in:

Ingredients

- 5 Zucchini peeled with ends trimmed
- 8 Tomatoes diced
- 1 cup Parm/romano cheese
- 1 pound Ground meat of choice
- 1/2 cup Fresh basil
- 2 Cloves of garlic
- 1 sprig Oregano
- 8 ounces Ricotta cheese
- 2 Eggs
- 1 Non-stick spray
- 1 teaspoon Salt
- 1 tablespoon Sugar
- 1 cup Water
- 1 cup Red wine (your preferred choice)
- 1 pound Mozzarella cheese

Direction

- Brown ground meat with a pinch of salt, basil, garlic, and some of the oregano and drain oil and place back on heat.
- Let sizzle then Add 1 cup red wine, wait a minute and add 1 cup of water, sugar, and diced tomatoes. In that order. Let it simmer.
- Mix ricotta cheese, eggs, oregano, and half the parmesan/romano cheeses.
- Spray pan and put in some sauce to cover bottom. Then make a layer of zucchini. Sprinkle mozzarella cheese in between each layer along with zucchini, sauce, and ricotta chesses. Put remaining cheeses on top. Bake for 1 hour on 300 and keep checking. Should be golden brown and bubbling when finished. Sprinkle more parmesan and eat. Yummy!!!

356. Caprese Dog

Serving: Serves 1-2 | Prep: | Cook: | Ready in:

Ingredients

- buns
- hot dogs (regular or vegetarian)
- mini mozzarella balls
- basil leaves
- grape tomatoes, sliced
- olive oil, just a drizzle

Direction

- Grill your hot dogs.
- Warm the buns.
- Put the dogs in the buns and top with basil, mozzarella, and tomatoes.
- Drizzle with olive oil and enjoy!

357. Caramelised Onion, Goats Cheese & Cauliflower Quiche

Serving: Serves 6 | Prep: | Cook: | Ready in:

Ingredients

- 2 eggs
- 1/3 cup rice bran oil
- 3 teaspoons guar gum
- 1/2 cup cauliflower florets
- 3 medium sized onions, finely sliced
- 8-10 brown swiss or button mushrooms
- 150gm goats feta or goats curd
- 1/3 cup rice, goat or soy milk
- 6 eggs

Direction

- Heat a frying pan on low heat and add the onions. Cook slowly to caramelized, which shall take around 20 minutes.
- In the meantime, make pastry by combining millet flour, salt and guar gum. Make a well in the center and add 2 eggs, oil and water. Combine well with a wooden spoon, then knead mixture for a minute or two. Place in the fridge wrapped in cling wrap for around 30 minutes. Whilst the pastry is in the fridge, steam cauliflower until just tender.
- Heat oven to 180c fan forced, or 200c gas. Take out the pastry and roll out with a rolling pin until about 3 mill thick. Place in a baking or pie dish and then blind bake for 5-6 minutes. Remove from oven and scatter in pastry shell mushrooms, caramelized onions, steamed cauliflower and feta or goat's curd.
- In a separate bowl beat remaining 6 eggs and stir in milk of choice. Pour mixture into tart shell over vegetables. Bake in the oven for 40-45 minutes or until golden brown and set into the middle. The tart will have a slight wobble yet should not be runny when cut.
- Serve with a crispy green side salad whilst still warm.

358. Crisped Spanish Chorizo & Two Cheese Mashed Potatoes

Serving: Serves 4-5 | Prep: | Cook: | Ready in:

Ingredients

- 10 to 12 small to medium white potatoes (thin skin), boiled until fork tender; drain (keep warm)
- 1 small to medium (mild or spicy to your personal taste) spanish chorizo sausage; cut into small dice
- 1 cup or so of grated pecorino crotonese sheep's milk cheese (use the large holes to grate this cheese)
- 1/2 cup or so grated parmigiano-reggiano cheese
- 1-2 cups organic chicken or vegetable stock; preferably homemade (use as needed)

- splash or two of lactose-free or whole milk
- fresh italian flat leaf parsley (chopped finely)
- sea salt and fresh ground cracked black pepper to taste
- equipment needed: large potato ricer

Direction

- In a large skillet on high heat; sauté the diced chorizo turning often until it crisps up and gets crunchy and the fats render out a bit. Remove from heat and set aside.
- In a large stockpot filled with water; add the cleaned and scrubbed potatoes (skin on) and boil until cooked through and fork tender. Drain and keep warm.
- While the potatoes are hot to warm, you need to "rice" them using your ricer until they are all shredded nice and thinly.
- Note: Leave the skins on as they are thin and the ricer will push the potato right through leaving the skins behind.
- I use my potato ricer for making delicious gnocchi pasta. I always rice my potatoes for mashed potato recipes; this creates the best texture, both smooth and creamy with no lumps!
- Once the potatoes are all riced and in the pot; add a good amount of the stock and a splash or two of the milk and place on medium heat and stir this with a wooden spoon until well blended and the liquid dissolves a bit.
- Add in the crisped chorizo and any rendered fat into the potato mixture and mix in well.
- While still on the heat add in the grated crotonese cheese and mix well and taste for flavor, etc.
- Season at this point with a bit of salt (if needed, both cheese have a good amount of salt flavor built in) and a healthy amount of black pepper to taste.
- Add in a small amount of the Parmigiano-Reggiano cheese to taste and drizzle a good dose of olive oil at this point and continue blending.
- Remove from the heat and add in the chopped parsley and blend well.
- Plate and serve immediately while steaming hot; drizzle with olive oil and add more Parmigiano-Reggiano cheese per serving if desired.

359. Crustless Blender Cheesecake With Quick Raspberry Sauce

Serving: Serves 8 | Prep: 0hours10mins | Cook: 1hours0mins | Ready in:

Ingredients

- for the cheesecake:
- 200 grams cottage cheese
- 200 grams low-fat cottage cheese
- 100 grams non-fat greek yogurt
- 50 milliliters milk (I used a cashew-coconut blend)
- 1 tablespoon maple syrup
- one ripe banana
- 2 eggs
- 3 spoonfuls cornstarch
- a pinch salt
- for the quick raspberry topping:
- 50 grams raspberry jam (no sugar added)
- a splash orange juice

Direction

- For the cheesecake:
- Blend the cheesecake mixture. Preheat oven to 160 C. Grease a 20cm springform pan with coconut oil, then line the inside with parchment paper. If you're going for the sleek, bakery style look, cut a circle of parchment that's the same size of the inside of the pan. Cut another piece of parchment long enough to line the sides of the pan. Make sure all the pieces stick to the sides and bottom thanks to the coconut oil.
- To a high speed blender, add cottage cheese, Greek yogurt, milk and maple syrup and blend until smooth. Scrape the sides of the

machine as needed. Blend in the banana, chopped into large pieces. Crack in the eggs and run the blender on high for about one minute, then sift in cornstarch, add salt and whizz one more time to combine.
- Bake the cheesecake and allow it to cool. Pour the cheesecake mixture into prepared pan and bake for one hour. When it's done allow the cake to cool down into the oven for about 20 minutes. This should prevent the top from cracking. Take it out and let cool completely before transferring the cake to the fridge for at least 4 hours, ideally overnight.
- For the quick raspberry topping:
- Prepare the quick raspberry sauce.in a small bowl combine raspberry jam with enough orange juice to achieve a smooth and slightly runny but not liquid consistency.
- Serve the cake. Top the cheesecake with the raspberry mixture and enjoy!

360. Green Chile And Cheese Pancakes

Serving: Makes maybe 4 people | Prep: | Cook: | Ready in:

Ingredients

- 1/2 cup roasted, peeled and chopped green chiles, or 1/2 c. canned
- 1 egg, separated
- 1 1/2 teaspoons flour
- 1 teaspoon fresh oregano (or 1/2 t. dry)
- 1 pinch kosher salt (optional)
- 1/2 cup cheddar or colby cheese, grated
- 1 teaspoon parsley, chopped (or cilantro)
- 1/4 cup celery, chopped small
- 1/3 cup onion, chopped small
- 1/2 teaspoon worchestershire sauce

Direction

- Separate egg-beat white till stiff in bowl big enough to hold everything eventually in-set aside. Beat yolk in separate bowl.

- Beat flour, salt and oregano into yolks, then the rest of ingredients
- Fold all into the stiff egg whites
- Heat skillet fairly hot, oil lightly and drop 1-2 T per pancake into pan. Reduce heat to finish cooking, turning once. (These look weird before cooking-not to worry)

361. Harvest Cake

Serving: Serves 8 | Prep: | Cook: | Ready in:

Ingredients

- 1 cup buttermilk
- 1/2 cup applesauce
- 1 egg
- 2 tablespoons dark rum
- 1 teaspoon vanilla extract
- 1 1/2 cups all purpose flour
- 1 cup light brown sugar
- 1 teaspoon baking soda
- 1/2 teaspoon baking powder
- 1 teaspoon cinnamon
- 1/8 teaspoon cloves
- 1/2 teaspoon nutmeg
- 1/8 teaspoon allspice
- 1/2 cup salt
- 3/4 cup chopped walnuts
- 1 apple, peeled, cored, shredded
- 1/2 cup golden raisins
- powdered sugar, optional

Direction

- Preheat oven to 350 degrees. Cut a piece of parchment paper to fit the bottom of a 9-inch cake pan or 8x8 inch square baking pan. Spray pan liberally (bottom and sides) with vegetable spray. Place the parchment in the bottom of the pan and spray the parchment with vegetable spray. Set aside.
- In a 2 cup glass measuring cup add the buttermilk, applesauce, egg, rum and vanilla. Whisk to combine. Set aside.

- In a large mixing bowl combine the flour, brown sugar, baking soda, baking powder, cinnamon, cloves, nutmeg, allspice and salt. Whisk until well combined then stir in the liquid ingredients, shredded apple, walnuts and raisins. Stir several times to assure that dry ingredients are blended into the wet and that the solids are evenly distributed throughout the batter.
- Pour the batter into the pan and bake for 40-45 minutes or until a cake tester comes out clean.
- Cool on a wire rack to room temperature and dust with powdered sugar if desired.

362. Loaded Baked Potato Quiche

Serving: Serves 6 | Prep: | Cook: | Ready in:

Ingredients

- 1 9-inch pie crust
- 1/4 pound bacon, cooked to crisp and chopped or crumbled
- 1/2 pound red potatoes, cut into 1/4"-1/2" dice
- 3   scallions, thinly sliced
- 1 1/2 teaspoons fresh rosemary, finely minced
- 1 1/2 teaspoons chives, minced
- 4   eggs
- 1/2 teaspoon kosher salt
- 1/4 teaspoon freshly ground black pepper
- 1/2 cup milk
- 1/2 cup cream
- 1 cup grated cheddar cheese, 1 tablespoon reserved
- 1 cup grated monterey jack cheese, 1 tablespoon reserved
- fresh snipped chives for garnish (optional)

Direction

- Preheat the oven to 450 degrees.
- Arrange the pie crust in your pie plate. Fold the overhanging edges under on itself and either use the tines of a fork to press the edges onto the rim of the pie plate, or create an edge by pinching the thumb and forefinger together and pressing the dough into the crease using the forefinger of your other hand - follow the rim of the crust until completely crimped. Bake for 8-9 minutes until lightly browned. Set aside.
- Reduce oven temperature to 350 degrees.
- Add the potatoes to a small pan of water and bring to a boil. Reduce heat to simmer and cook until potatoes are tender, about 7-10 minutes. Drain potatoes and set aside to cool.
- Meanwhile crack the eggs into a large bowl. Add the salt and pepper and whisk until combined. Add the milk and cream and whisk again. Add the bacon, potatoes, scallions, rosemary, chives, and cheeses and stir together until well combined.
- Pour the egg mixture into the prepared pie shell. Smooth the ingredients evenly into the crust and sprinkle with remaining cheeses. Bake for 45 minutes to 1 hour until custard is set. Let rest for 20-30 minutes before cutting.
- Can be made a day ahead and rewarmed the next day at 300 degrees for 20 minutes.

363. Oreo Orange Cheesecake

Serving: Serves 2 | Prep: | Cook: | Ready in:

Ingredients

- 3 tablespoons Orange juice
- 1 tablespoon Marmalade
- 1 teaspoon gelatin
- 2 tablespoons cream
- 4 tablespoons mishti doi (sweet yogurt)
- 5 pieces oreo biscuits
- 1 teaspoon butter

Direction

- Crush Oreo biscuits and mix well with butter, place at bottom of glass refrigerate for 5 minutes
- Mix misthi doi and cream, make second layer, refrigerate for 15 minutes
- Cook orange juice, marmalade and gelatin for 2 minutes let it cool.
- Make top layer with this orange jelly and set in refrigerator for 15 to 20 minutes
- Serve chilled

364. Ravioli Di Fonduta With Truffle

Serving: Serves 4 | Prep: | Cook: | Ready in:

Ingredients

- for filling
- 300 milliliters whole milk
- 2 egg yolks
- 300 grams fontina cheese or similar
- for pasta and seasoning
- 2 eggs
- 200 grams all-pourpose flour
- 80 grams butter
- truffle to taste

Direction

- For pasta: prepare the pasta by kneading the flour and whole eggs for at least 10 min. If the dough still crumbles, just wet your hands and continue kneading to obtain a soft dough. If the dough is too sticky, add more flour. Cover the dough with a damp cloth.
- For filling: cut the fontina in small pieces, put it in a pan together with the milk and cook at low heat. Stir until the cheese is completely melted. The fondue should never get to boiling temperature. Once the cheese is melted and smooth, remove the pot from the heat and add one egg yolk at a time, keep stirring. Let the mixture cool to make it harder.
- Cut a piece of dough (work with small portions at a time and leave the rest covered) and roll out into a thin sheet (-0.5 mm), and put dollops of fonduta filling on it. Cover with another sheet of pasta and cut into rectangles, or use a round pastry cutter, taking care to seal the edges of the pasta firmly (lightly brush a little water around the filling, before folding the pasta) and making sure to press out all of the air. Dust the ravioli with some flour to keep them from sticking together.
- In a fry pan over medium heat, melt the butter. Cook, swirling the pan, until the butter foams and begins to brown, about 3 minutes. Be careful not to burn the butter, remove from the heat and cover to keep warm. Fill a large pot three-fourths full of water and bring to boil. Add the salt and then the ravioli. Cook, stirring occasionally, until the ravioli rise to the surface and are al dente, 3 to 4 minutes. Drain the ravioli mix with the melted butter; finish with the grated or sliced truffle, to taste.

365. The Best Mac & Cheese, Ever.

Serving: Serves 6-8 adults | Prep: | Cook: | Ready in:

Ingredients

- 1 pound elbow macaroni
- 8 tablespoons butter, unsalted
- 6 tablespoons flour
- 4 cups milk, whole
- 1 pound sharp cheddar, or 1lb mix of cheddar, gouda & parm
- 2 cups cottage cheese, 4%
- 2 teaspoons salt
- 1/2 teaspoon pepper
- 1/2 teaspoon smoked paprika
- 1 1/2 tablespoons mustard powder
- 1/2 cup parmigiano, grated

Direction

- Preheat oven to 375, grease a 9 X 11" glass pan with butter or grape seed oil spray.
- Start by grating all your cheese. You may use sharp cheddar solely but gouda, sharp cheddar & parmesan make a fine mix. Keep the 1/2C parmigiano separated for topping.
- Follow the directions on the package for 1lb macaroni. Salting the water, heavily. Drain but don't rinse pasta.
- in a Dutch oven melt your butter, when bubbles subside add the flour & stir to form a paste, let cook 2-3 minutes until it darkens slightly.
- In 1C increments add your milk, stirring to incorporate with each addition.
- Turn the heat off & add salt, pepper, paprika & mustard.
- While whipping the béchamel sauce with your right hand, dump in the grated cheddar cheese with your left. Whip the sauce to melt the cheese. if it doesn't all melt, turn the pan back on medium low and whisk vigorously to melt, making sure not to burn the bottom.
- Add the cottage cheese. Stir to incorporate. Stir in pasta, taste for paprika, mustard, salt & pepper.
- Pour macaroni into prepared pan. Top with remaining parmigiano. Bake for 20 minutes or until it bubbles.
- Once ready, let cool for 5 minutes, until bubbles subside. Serve warm with your favorite greens & a crisp beer. Enjoy.

Index

A

Ale 3,11

Almond 3,4,5,13,14,15,21,56,103,112,212

Apple 3,4,5,7,11,18,19,40,43,66,92,166

Apricot 7,197

Arborio rice 106

Artichoke 4,52,62,73

Asparagus 3,6,20,151

Avocado 3,5,6,7,22,32,96,136,200

B

Bacon 3,4,5,6,7,23,43,47,50,58,76,99,125,157,166,190,199

Baguette 4,5,82,83,166,177

Baking 18,25,68,151

Banana 3,6,13,14,25,26,157

Barley 7,162

Basil 3,6,7,22,26,27,29,32,129,143,162,192

Bay leaf 95

Beer 3,36,85

Beetroot 3,30

Biscuits 3,4,41,50,67,68

Black pepper 202

Blood orange 126

Blueberry 3,34,35

Bran 3,11

Bread 3,4,5,6,7,13,22,25,49,63,69,73,87,101,102,116,117,120,138,148,152,169,185,202

Bresaola 3,38

Brie 3,6,39,65,69,76,135,152,179

Brioche 7,171

Broccoli 3,4,7,17,39,40,74,143,173,188

Brussels sprouts 61,66

Buckwheat 7,29,167

Butter 3,4,5,6,7,16,17,18,19,21,23,24,25,36,38,39,40,43,49,68,76,90,99,104,112,117,118,119,120,123,124,128,138,141,142,143,144,154,159,160,162,163,167,170,171,176,186,198,207,212

C

Cake 3,4,6,8,13,14,33,34,35,56,73,159,212,214,219

Camembert 3,43,179

Capers 3,24

Caramel 3,4,5,7,8,16,40,44,45,85,99,104,167,217

Cardamom 4,7,60,66,177,190

Carrot 3,4,32,44,46,95,157

Caster sugar 212

Cauliflower 7,8,162,217

Cava 4,47

Cayenne pepper 126

Celery 95

Champ 20

Chard 4,8,48,57,205,208

Cheddar 3,4,6,7,8,17,19,23,45,49,50,51,52,75,113,125,170,173,182,202,211,212

Cheese 1,3,4,5,6,7,8,9,15,16,18,19,22,23,24,26,27,29,35,39,41,44,46,50,51,52,53,56,58,60,65,66,69,70,71,74,75,83,84,86,88,89,90,94,95,97,99,104,108,110,113,116,118,119,120,122,123,124,126,128,129,130,135,140,141,142,143,148,149,153,154,156,157,158,161,162,165,166,172,173,176,177,179,182,187,189,197,198,199,202,205,206,207,211,212,213,217,218,219,220,221

Cherry 4,7,38,52,53,56,86,146,165,198

Cheshire 19

Chicken 3,4,5,7,8,17,24,53,54,65,93,95,151,157,175,205,206

Chipotle 79

Chips 6,8,155,211

Chives 6,7,91,131,140,178

Chocolate 3,4,6,7,8,33,37,56,57,155,158,198,212,213,214

Chorizo 4,7,8,57,61,189,217

Ciabatta 65,117

Cider 3,4,40,58

Cinnamon 3,9

Clams 5,87

Clementine 127

Cloves 128,172,216

Cocktail 4,7,59,86,176

Coconut 6,124,203

Cognac 11

Coriander 5,59,103

Cornflour 112

Cottage cheese 112

Couscous 5,8,117,205

Crab 4,72,73

Crackers 5,7,35,36,89,182

Cranberry 5,99

Cream 3,4,5,6,8,10,13,14,15,17,22,26,30,36,37,39,46,56,60,61,62, 63,84,87,90,108,112,122,124,136,138,142,144,146,158,159,172,212,213

Crisps 42,43

Croissant 5,115,116

Crostini 4,6,7,64,65,147,160,185

Crumble 32,38,60,65,74,191

Cucumber 4,32,67,143

Cumin 7,166

Curd 4,67,68

Curry 4,6,7,69,156,197

Custard 139

D

Dark chocolate 158

Dijon mustard 16,42,57,64,71,98,107,127,156,162,208,209

Dill 3,6,7,20,29,131,177

Double cream 119

E

Edam 138

Egg 3,4,5,6,7,13,15,17,20,21,22,25,65,72,75,87,91,99,116,124,125,128,134,144,150,158,163,178,198,200,212,216

Emmental 138,154,155

English mustard 189,210

F

Fat 52

Fennel 3,4,43,44,80

Feta 3,5,6,7,8,23,24,52,86,117,126,177,190,200,202,208,211

Fettuccine 4,78

Fig 3,4,5,6,8,39,79,83,84,151,211

Flatbread 3,5,29,93

Flour 13,18,21,25,29,90,128,147,155,184

Fontina cheese 80,81,165

French bread 22,81,82

Fruit 20,100

G

Garam masala 60

Garlic 5,7,52,85,87,95,109,128,172,175

Ghee 5,105

Gin 3,5,25,87

Gnocchi 3,5,7,11,103,184

Gorgonzola 5,20,38,90,91

Grain 3,7,29,63,142,191,196

Grapefruit 144

Grapes 5,12,90,116

Gratin 3,4,5,11,82,90

Green cabbage 138

H

Halloumi 5,99

Ham 3,5,40,91,99,116

Harissa 4,67

Hazelnut 7,186

Heart 52

Herbs 7,192

Hollandaise sauce 168,169

Honey 3,4,5,7,36,65,67,68,69,71,84,91,97,111,112,119,158,180

Horseradish 7,177

I

Icing 119,122,212

J

Jam 4,7,50,79,165

Japanese pumpkin 111

Jus 33,59,86,89,143,150,153,174,177,207

K

Kale 4,6,73,77,125,153

Kirsch 202,203

L

Lamb 5,7,84,85,181

Lard 7,172

Lasagne 5,115

Leek 3,5,39,44,86

Lemon 3,5,6,8,21,32,34,52,81,91,95,103,112,118,119,120,127,143,160,192,212

Lime 3,6,7,22,25,59,121,166,167,180

Lobster 4,51

M

Macaroni 62,142

Mace 139

Mackerel 7,177

Manchego 7,189

Mango 5,6,112,124

Marmalade 6,157,158,220

Marzipan 8,215

Mascarpone 6,40,41,127,131

Meat 4,6,7,53,70,72,121,171,195

Milk 5,6,7,13,21,23,27,52,102,111,116,128,130,144,157,172,179,188,190,191,198

Millet 29

Mince 52,94,172

Mint 5,6,7,117,120,131,190,200

Morel 6,157,158

Mozzarella 3,4,5,6,7,26,48,52,53,85,93,96,101,128,133,147,151,152,160,164,172,188,191,192,216

Muffins 7,179

Mushroom 4,6,7,47,133,134,138,169,174

Mustard 5,7,22,32,85,92,116,142,183

N

Nachos 5,93

Nectarine 6,136

Noodles 4,62

Nut 3,5,6,20,36,102,103,141,144,155

O

Oatmeal 6,157,196

Oil 4,7,20,22,27,29,32,38,40,43,45,52,56,60,73,84,86,91,103,117,128,129,147,164

Olive 4,6,14,20,22,27,29,32,38,40,41,45,48,54,56,73,84,86,91,95,

98,103,113,128,129,140,173

Onion 3,4,5,7,8,16,23,40,45,52,56,81,82,85,90,95,99,104,116,128,172,177,185,217

Orange 3,4,6,8,30,44,56,60,156,220

Oregano 6,141,146,147,216

P

Pancakes 5,7,8,119,120,196,219

Pancetta 157

Paneer 4,5,59,60,63,103,112

Paprika 172

Parfait 6,152,165

Parmesan 3,4,6,7,15,19,22,28,32,33,42,47,51,55,56,64,75,79,85,100,103,104,113,115,116,117,123,128,134,140,141,148,172,173,174,176,184,186,187,202,205,209

Parsley 52,128,138,151

Pasta 6,7,8,123,142,143,150,180,209

Pastrami 6,142

Pastry 45,81,125,202

Peach 5,6,8,84,93,96,143,144,146,203

Pear 3,4,5,6,7,11,13,20,36,45,65,79,91,148,164,171

Peas 5,120

Pecan 3,4,5,6,40,58,85,148,157

Pecorino 41,142,209,210

Peel 18,19,20,30,38,41,55,58,81,91,96,104,137,146,150,176,189,190,197

Pepper 3,4,8,12,20,22,27,28,31,32,36,38,52,54,61,79,82,84,86,90,107,116,128,134,138,140,146,147,157,172,200,208,209

Pesto 3,5,29,103,128

Pie 3,4,5,6,7,11,18,57,88,106,123,132,139,155,192

Pine nut 16,32

Pistachio 3,4,5,18,60,104,112,144

Pizza 3,4,5,6,7,14,18,44,66,79,84,88,109,117,125,126,146,147,188

Plum 3,6,7,40,147,182,202

Polenta 3,6,42,130,148,157

Pomegranate 158

Popcorn 6,140

Pork 6,148

Port 157

Potato 3,4,5,6,7,8,23,58,59,60,90,131,149,172,189,196,197,206,212,217,220

Prosciutto 5,6,7,93,148,151,166

Puff pastry 172,173

Pulse 10,37,43,60,68,69,92,106,118,142,155

Pumpkin 5,6,7,111,152,153,167

Puy lentils 209

Q

Quinoa 4,7,52,180

R

Radicchio 5,91

Radish 4,6,16,67,156,200

Raisins 157

Raspberry 4,5,6,8,56,84,85,101,109,119,158,213,218

Red wine 216

Rice 5,7,31,63,106,173,177

Ricotta 3,4,5,6,7,15,17,18,27,35,40,44,65,67,68,69,76,79,84,100,101,114,128,147,150,160,161,169,172,173,178,184,185,192,216

Rocket 86

Rosemary 3,7,8,27,67,151,165,171,212

Rosewater 144

S

Saffron 144

Sage 4,5,7,77,88,151,166,186

Salad
3,4,5,6,7,8,9,20,22,32,38,42,63,67,74,75,84,92,143,156,162,163,166,180,181,191,192,200,203,208,214

Salami 5,97

Salmon 7,177

Salsa 3,30,31

Salt
4,7,11,13,19,20,22,23,25,27,29,32,38,40,43,45,52,54,55,59,60,65,67,79,82,84,90,98,99,103,104,107,117,120,128,132,135,138,140,147,157,166,167,170,171,172,183,192,200,201,204,212,216,222

Sausage 5,7,107,108,195

Savory 3,5,7,13,101,167,168,169,170,171,172,197

Scallop 7,189

Sea salt 12,25,61,75,178,189

Seafood 4,80

Seeds 6,8,157,212,215

Self-raising flour 202

Serrano ham 40

Shallot 5,88,157

Sherry 82

Shin 194

Shortbread 119

Soup 3,4,5,6,7,8,27,81,82,87,130,131,185,201

Soy sauce 188

Spinach
3,4,6,7,20,32,52,62,63,80,128,165,172,183,184,197

Squash
3,4,5,6,7,40,77,104,111,117,141,160,161,162,164,187,188

Stew 35

Stock 157

Strawberry 4,6,71,79,138,139

Stuffing 5,6,99,151,205

Sugar
6,7,13,21,25,85,112,124,144,148,157,190,192,212,216

Sumac 113

Swiss chard 163,206,209

Syrup 5,8,85,101,109,112,119,212

T

Tabasco 178

Tahini 8,215

Taleggio 5,97

Tea 7,68,94,136,184,206

Tequila 5,98

Thyme 6,7,45,90,95,151,157,160,164

Tomatillo 3,30,31

Tomato
3,4,5,6,7,8,14,20,24,26,27,52,53,56,63,76,85,86,113,129,135,147,164,165,201,202,216

Truffle 4,5,6,8,65,80,91,97,140,221

Turkey 3,4,8,30,70,203,204

V

Vacherin 202

Vanilla extract 124

Veal 7,157,189

Vegetarian 28

Vinegar 8,157,203

W

Waffles 7,172

Walnut 3,5,6,7,8,9,20,85,88,91,160,164,215

Watermelon 5,7,98,200

White chocolate 212,213

Wine 4,8,19,65,157,208,209

Worcestershire sauce 42,74,207,210

Y

Yeast 21

Z

Zest 17,21,25,36,45,88,98,113,126,127,144,169,172,212

L

lasagna 15,114,187,204

Conclusion

Thank you again for downloading this book!

I hope you enjoyed reading about my book!

If you enjoyed this book, please take the time to share your thoughts and post a review on Amazon. It'd be greatly appreciated!

Write me an honest review about the book – I truly value your opinion and thoughts and I will incorporate them into my next book, which is already underway.

Thank you!

If you have any questions, **feel free to contact at:** author@shellfishrecipes.com

Ebony Garcia

shellfishrecipes.com

Printed in Great Britain
by Amazon